Study Guide

for

Physiology of Behavior

Study Guide

for

Physiology of Behavior
Seventh Edition

Prepared by

Mary Carlson

Neil R. Carlson
University of Massachusetts at Amherst

Allyn and Bacon
Boston   London   Toronto   Sydney   Tokyo   Singapore

Copyright © 2001 by Allyn & Bacon
A Pearson Education Company
160 Gould Street
Needham Heights, MA 02494

Internet: www.abacon.com

ISBN 0-205-32588-2

Printed in the United States of America

10 9 8 7 6 5 4 3 2 1   05 04 03 02 01 00

Table of Contents

Preface

Welcome to your textbook and to your study guide. We remember what it was like to be students, and we have tried to write something that will help you learn the information in the text in a way that it will stay with you. Your goal is to learn something interesting and useful, and our goal is to help you accomplish that.

The purpose of a study guide is, as its name suggests, to guide you through the text and make sure you see the important points, think about them, write about them, and, most important, *remember* them. We hope that you will remember what you learn even after the semester is over.

Learning is an active process, not a passive one. It is easy to read a chapter and say to yourself, "Yes, I understand that," but still learn and remember very little. If you do not put some effort into your studying, you are not spending your time very effectively.

Although you already have some well established study habits, we urge you to think about trying something different this semester. Begin by leafing through the chapter so that you can see what it is about. Look at the outline at the beginning of the chapter, then read the chapter. Don't take notes or worry about remembering too many details—you only want to see what the chapter is all about. Do all of this *before your professor lectures about the material.* If you are familiar with the chapter, you will understand the lecture much better, and you will remember much more of what you hear. Your lecture notes will also be much clearer.

Now you are ready to work with the study guide. With the exception of Chapter 1 (which is short) we have divided each chapter into two lessons. Finish the first lesson and take a break. You will find it easier to work if you have a break to look forward to. Take some time off, even if you feel that you could finish the chapter in one sitting. As the semester goes on, you will find it easier to begin studying if the habit of taking a break is well established.

Each lesson in the study guide is broken into learning objectives, which are enclosed in a box. The objective states what you should learn to do. Before the first objective, you will see the following statement: "Read the interim summary on page 000 of your text to re-acquaint yourself with the material in this section." Do just that. The interim summaries will remind you about what you read previously. Then, after the objective, you will find the following statement: "Read pages 000-000 and answer the following questions." Do that, too. Then, begin answering the questions. *Try to answer each question without looking at the book.* If all you do is to copy the answer from the book into the study guide, you will learn very little. If the purpose of having a study guide were simply to have a list of answers to a list of questions, we could have written the answers, too. Don't be a scribe, copying from the book to the study guide. That's boring and pointless. If you can't answer a particular question, read the appropriate section in the text again, close the book (or at least push it away so that you can't see it), and then write the answer from memory. *If you cannot remember an answer a short time after reading the information in the book, how can you expect to remember it when you take the exam?* The delay between reading the information and writing it in your own words is crucial to your remembering what you have read.

The study guide contains some features that will help you to study your text. It lists the pages that you should read, and many questions refer to specific figures that contain information that you will need to answer a question. We have also included a set of concept cards. These cards contain most of the terms that are listed in the margins of each chapter. Learning these terms will help you acquire the vocabulary of physiological psychology. To use the concept cards effectively, cut them apart, put them in a stack, and test yourself. Obviously, you do not need to learn the definitions word-for-word, because there is more than one way to explain a term. But if you forget something important about a term, put the card into a stack that you will go through again until you are satisfied with your performance.

We have tried to supply you with the tools to change some neural circuits in your brain—after all, that is what learning is all about. Let us know how the study guide works for you. If you have some suggestions for the next edition, please write to us at the address listed in the preface of the textbook.

Good luck!

Mary Carlson
Neil Carlson

Chapter 1
Introduction

Read the interim summary on page 6 of your text to re-acquaint yourself with the material in this section.

> *Learning Objective 1-1*   Describe blindsight and the behavior of people with split brains, and explain the contribution of these phenomena to our understanding of self-awareness.

Read pages 2-6 and answer the following questions.

1. How did animists explain the behavior of both living and nonliving objects?

2. Briefly describe the mind-body question.

3. _____ and _____ are two different explanations of the relationship between the mind and body.

4. Dualism is the belief that mind and body are _____ and only the _____ is ordinary matter.

5. Monism, on the other hand, is the belief the mind and body are not _____ entities and that the _____ is a phenomenon of the nervous system.

6. Which approach is favored by modern physiological psychologists?

7. a. What evidence suggests that consciousness is a physiological function?

    b. How might verbal communication be related to consciousness?

8. Study Figure 1.2 in your text. List the two visual systems of the brain (noting which is older), and indicate the behavioral mechanisms controlled by each system.

9. a. If the mammalian visual system on the left side of the brain is damaged, what does the person report seeing in the right half of his or her visual field?

    b. If the person is asked to reach for an object that has been placed in the blind field, will he or she be able to do so?

c. What is this phenomenon called? (Weiskrantz et al., 1974)

d. What does this phenomenon suggest about the nature of consciousness?

10. Very severe epilepsy that does not respond to medication may be controlled by a split-brain operation. Study Figure 1.3 in your text and explain how the cerebral hemispheres are split. Be sure to refer to the corpus callosum in your answer.

11. Explain why patients recovering from split-brain surgery are surprised to find their left hand putting down a book they were reading with interest.

12. Study Figure 1.4 in your text and describe the responses of a person with a split brain.

a. Will the patient say "I smell a rose" after sniffing a rose through the left nostril? the right nostril?

b. The patient sniffs a rose through the right nostril. Will the patient then correctly select the flower from among other objects with the left hand or the right hand?

c. Explain why the aroma must enter the left nostril in order for the patient to become conscious of the sensation of odor.

13. What does work with patients who have undergone a split-brain operation contribute to an understanding of consciousness?

Read the interim summary on page 11 of your text to re-acquaint yourself with the material in this section.

Learning Objective 1-2   Describe the nature of physiological psychology and the goals of research.

Read pages 6-8 and answer the following questions.

1. _____ _____ wrote the first textbook of psychology, which was called _____ of _____ _____.

2. a. What is the ultimate function of the brain?

b. How do behaviors such as perception and thinking support it?

c. Why then did the abilities to learn and remember evolve?

3. The two forms of scientific explanation are _____ and _____.

4. Decide whether the examples below illustrate generalization (G) or reduction (R). You will find answers at the end of this chapter.

_____   When an acid is poured over a carbonate, a gas is formed.

_____ When some people have coffee after dinner they have trouble falling asleep.

_____ The sky looks blue because particles in the atmosphere scatter light of short-wavelengths.

_____ Because she was stung several times by bees when she was young, Jessica is now afraid of them.

_____ $E=MC^2$.

_____ Lemon juice tastes sour because the hydrogen ions present in citric acid stimulate special receptors in the tongue.

5. State the goal of psychological research.

Learning Objective 1-3   Describe the biological roots of physiological psychology.

Read pages 8-11 and answer the following questions.

1. a. According to many ancient cultures, which organ was responsible for thought and emotions?

    b. Both _____ and _____ disagreed believing instead that thought and emotions

    originated in the _____.

2. a. How did Descartes explain the automatic responses of humans, which he named reflexes? (See Figure 1.5 in your text.)

    b. Describe the relationship between the mind and the body hypothesized by Descartes and illustrated in Figure 1.6 in your text. Be sure to explain the role of the pineal body in your answer.

3. a. Descartes's early visits to the Royal Gardens suggested a _____ to explain how the human body worked.

    b. Define _model_ in your own words.

    c. What is an important advantage of using a model?

4. Why did Galvani's experiment with muscular contraction stimulate further research?

5. When Müller first began his career, what two techniques were widely used by natural scientists?

    1.   2.

6. What kind of new research techniques did he propose using?

7. Explain the doctrine of specific nerve energies.

8. How did Flourens extend Müller's advocacy of experimentation? (Be sure to mention experimental ablation in your answer.)

9. How did Broca modify the principle of experimental ablation for work with humans? (See Figure 1.8 in your text.)

10. Describe early studies by Fritsch and Hitzig using electrical stimulation of the brain.

11. a. List several important contributions to 19th century science by von Helmholtz.

    b. How did von Helmholtz's views differ from those of his teacher, Müller?

Read the interim summary on pages 19-20 of your text to reacquaint yourself with the material in this section.

Learning Objective 1-4   Describe the role of natural selection in the evolution of behavioral traits.

Read pages 11-14 and answer the following questions.

1. Who proposed the principles of natural selection and evolution?

2. a. Define *functionalism* in your own words and explain its importance in understanding behavior.

    b. Explain the difference between function and purpose. (See Figure 1.10 in your text.)

3. How did Blest (1957) confirm a useful function of eyespots on the wings of certain species of moths and butterflies? (See Figure 1.11 in your text.)

4. Summarize these principles incorporated in Darwin's theory of evolution.
    a. natural selection

    b. mutation

c. selective advantage

5. a. What is the effect of most mutations? (See Figure 1.12 in your text.)

b. What kind of effect does a small percentage of mutations have?

c. Explain how the selective advantage conferred by beneficial mutations can indirectly affect the behavior of the next generation or of subsequent ones.

d. Explain how mutations that are not immediately beneficial may eventually benefit the species.

6. Match these scientists with their contributions.

___ Wilhelm Wundt   a. Doctrine of specific nerve energies

___ René Descartes   b. Method of experimental ablation

___ Johannes Müller   c. *Principles of Physiological Psychology*

___ Pierre Flourens   d. Principle of natural selection

___ Fritsch and Hitzig   e. Modified method of experimental ablation to work with humans

___ Paul Broca   f. Used electrical stimulation to study brain

___ H. von Helmholtz   g. Electrical stimulation, not pressurized fluid, caused muscular contraction

___ Charles Darwin   h. Early use of a model

___ Luigi Galvani   i. Measured speed of conduction through nerves

Learning Objective 1-5   Discuss the evolution of the human species and a large brain.

Read pages 14-19 and answer the following questions.

1. Explain the process of evolution in your own words.

2. a. Which species of vertebrates was the first to emerge from the sea, and how does the sea continue to play an integral part in their life cycle?

b. Approximately how many million years ago did the first reptiles appear?

c. What advantage did reptiles have over amphibians and how did this advantage contribute to their survival?

3. Reptiles soon divided into three lines. List them and some of the animals which evolved from each division. (The evolution of the vertebrates is illustrated in Figure 1.13 in your text.)

4.   a. What event triggered a mass extinction at the end of the Permian period?

       b. Among the survivors was the _____, a small _____, the direct ancestor of the _____.

5.   Briefly explain why the earliest mammals had better hearing than the cynodonts and describe the advantage of this ability. (Study Figure 1.14 in your text.)

6.   a. What animal dominated the world for millions of years, forcing mammals to remain inconspicuous?

       b. What led to their extinction, permitting mammals to evolve and become more numerous?

       c. What are our most direct ancestors? Where did they first evolve?

       d. Describe these early primates.

       e. How did the appearance of fruit-bearing trees benefit the evolving primates?

7.   a. On which continent and in what kind of environment did the first hominids appear?

       b. What kind of skills did they develop?

       c. List the four major species of hominids and compare the percentage differences in their DNA. (Study Figures 1.15 and 1.16 in your text.)

8.   a. Which species of hominids was the first to leave Africa?

       b. To what regions did they migrate?

       c. Name the human-like species that appears to have evolved from *Homo erectus* and settled in Western Europe.

       d. Where did our own species *Homo sapiens* evolve?

       e. Study the migration routes of *Homo sapiens* shown in Figure 1.17 in your text.

       f. Offer two reasons why *Homo sapiens* replaced the Neanderthals after coexisting for about 10,000 years.

9.   List at least four characteristics that enabled mature humans to become the dominant species.

     1.   3.

     2.   4.

10.   a. How did an upright posture affect the evolution of the size of a newborn baby's head and brain?

        b. How did the restricted size of the baby's head affect the level of complexity of the brain at birth?

c. And how did, (and still does), an immature infant brain affect the nature and length of parental care?

11. a. If we calculate and compare the percentage of brain weight to body weight for humans and other animals, the comparison will not yield meaningful results. Why?

    b. Study Figure 1.18 in your text and explain a more useful comparison.

12. Define *neoteny* in your own words and explain how this phenomenon contributes to the larger brain size of humans.

Read the interim summary on pages 22-23 to reacquaint yourself with the material in this section.

Learning Objective 1-6   Discuss the value of research with animals and ethical issues concerning their care.

Read pages 20-21 and answer the following questions.

1. List several ways in which the humane care of animals used in scientific research is assured.

2. According to Miller (1983), what are some of the animal care regulations that scientific researchers are required to follow, but pet owners are not?

3. Describe the statistics that indicate that the use of animals in research and teaching is a special target of animal rights activists. (Nicholl and Russell, 1990)

4. Explain the statement that the use of animals in research and education is the only indispensable use of animals.

5. Describe some actual and potential benefits of research with animals.

Learning Objective 1-7   Describe career opportunities in neuroscience.

Read page 22 and answer the following questions.

1. a. In general, what do physiological psychologists study? neuroscientists?

   b. More specifically, what are some of the research topics in these fields?

2. a. What kind of academic degree do most physiological psychologists and neuroscientists obtain?
   b. What kind of subsequent training do they receive?
   c. Where do most professional physiological psychologists and neuroscientists work?

3. a. What do neurologists and experimental neuropsychologists study?

   b. What kind of degree is appropriate for each of these professions?

4. What kind of careers in neuroscience are open to those without a Ph.D.?

Self Test

1. A person who argues that the body and mind consist of physical matter and energy believes in

   a. animism.
   b. dualism.
   c. monism.
   d. ethnocentrism.

2. The phenomenon of blindsight confirms that

   a. visual information must enter our consciousness for us to respond appropriately.
   b. consciousness is not a general property of all parts of the brain.
   c. there is no evolutionary advantage to possessing two visual systems.
   d. the mammalian visual system is responsible for consciousness.

3. The right hemisphere of a person who has had a split-brain operation can no longer

   a. perceive sensory information.
   b. understand verbal instructions.
   c. produce speech.
   d. control movements of the right hand.

4. The effects of the split-brain operation suggest that

   a. consciousness developed in the right hemisphere.
   b. the left hemisphere is more adept at analyzing sensory information than the right hemisphere.
   c. all cognitive processes are located in the left hemisphere.
   d. information does not reach consciousness unless it reaches those parts of the brain responsible for verbal communication.

5. A researcher concluded that a drug made animals eat because it altered the insulin level in their blood. What kind of explanation did the researcher provide?

   a. generalization
   b. reduction
   c. rationalization
   d. deduction

6. Models, first used by Descartes to study how the body worked,

   a. were the forerunners of the scientific method.
   b. were useful because they could be tested experimentally.
   c. challenged the usefulness of philosophical speculation.

d. negated the distinction between function and purpose.

7. The work of Müller and many physiologists who followed him is characterized by

    a. experimentation and logical deduction.
    b. observation and classification.
    c. self-report and introspective evidence.
    d. philosophical speculation.

8. Darwin's theory of evolution suggests that all of an organism's characteristics

    a. are given to it by its creator.
    b. confer a selective advantage on the species.
    c. have been naturally selected by its ancestors.
    d. have functional significance.

9. A small _____ survived a mass extinction to become the direct ancestors of the _____.

    a. anapsid; amphibian
    b. diapsid; vertebrate
    c. cynodont; mammal
    d. therapid; hominid

10. The human brain

    a. at birth is comparable to that of other mammals relative to body weight.

b. at birth contains an abundance of circuits that can be modified through experience.
c. and skull change much less from birth to adulthood than do those of other mammals.
d. following birth grows at a rate proportional to the growth of the body.

11. Which is the only true statement about animal research?

    a. Behavior cannot be studied using tissue cultures or computers.
    b. The characteristics of tissue cultures are similar enough to living organisms to replace them in research.
    c. Computer research can replace animal research if the results are interpreted cautiously.
    d. The results of research using tissue cultures can be more reliably replicated that the results of research using animals.

12. Most professional physiological psychologists work in

    a. industry.
    b. hospitals.
    c. colleges and universities.
    d. government.

Answers for Self Test

1. c Obj. 1-1
2. b Obj. 1-1
3. c Obj. 1-1
4. d Obj. 1-1
5. b Obj. 1-2
6. b Obj. 1-3
7. a Obj. 1-3
8. d Obj. 1-4
9. c Obj. 1-5
10. b Obj. 1-5
11. a Obj. 1-5
12. c Obj. 1-6

Answers to Learning Objective 1-2, question 4.

G   This one is tricky. Even though the statement contains chemical terms, it only describes what happens; it does not explain *why* a gas is formed.

G   If the statement had talked about the physiological effects of caffeine, it would have been an example of reduction.

R   The perceptual phenomena are explained in terms of physical events.

G   A behavioral phenomenon is being explained in terms of environmental events. If the statement had talked about changes that had taken place in her brain, it would have been an example of reduction.

G   This one is tricky, too. Even though it is a formula, it relates physical observations (energy = mass multiplied by the speed of light, squared). To be an example of reduction, the statement would have had to talk about the characteristics of electromagnetic radiation, the attraction between particles, or other events on a molecular level.

R   Because this example describes a psychological event in physiological terms, it clearly qualifies as an example of reduction

CHAPTER 2
Structure and Functions of Cells of the Nervous System

Lesson I: Cells of the Nervous System and Communication Within a Neuron

Read the interim summary on pages 38-39 of your text to reacquaint yourself with the material in this section.

Learning Objective 2-1   Name and describe the parts of a neuron and explain their functions.

Read pages 27-34 and answer the following questions.

1. List the three types of neurons that respond to the environment or control the muscles.

    1.   2.

    3.

2. List the two divisions of the nervous system and their principal parts.

    1.   2.

3. Label the four principal structures of the neuron shown in Figure 1, below. (See Figure 2.1 in your text.)

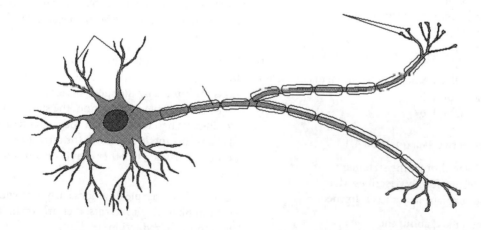

Figure 1

4. Where is the cell nucleus located?

5. a. Communication between neurons occurs across the _____, which is a junction between the

_____ _____ of the sending cell and a portion of the _____ or

_____ _____ of the receiving cell. In general, communication proceeds in

_____ direction; from the _____ _____ to the _____ of the

other cell.

b. Briefly describe the appearance and explain the role of these structures of the neuron in communication.

1. axon (Be sure to refer to the action potential.)

2. terminal buttons

3. dendrites

6. Study Figures 2.1 and 2.2 in your text and describe the difference between unipolar, bipolar, and multipolar neurons.

7. Study Figure 2.3 in your text and describe the appearance of the nerves.

8. Name the type of chemical secreted by terminal buttons and identify the effects it can have on the receiving cell.

9. Study Figure 2.4 in your text and describe the nature of synaptic connections in your own words.

10. Let's look at the internal structure of a typical multipolar neuron shown in Figure 2.5 in your text.

a. Describe the composition of the cell membrane.

b. List some of the functions of the protein molecules that are embedded in the cell membrane.

11. Name the material that covers the nucleus of a cell.

12. Describe the function of the following components of the nucleus.

a. nucleolus and ribosomes

b. chromosomes and messenger ribonucleic acid (mRNA). (Study Figure 2.6 in your text.)

13. Briefly describe the role of proteins, including serving as enzymes.

14. What substance fills the cell?

15. Briefly discuss these aspects of mitochondria.

   a. appearance

   b. function (Be sure to mention ATP.)

   c. presumed origin

   d. reproduction

16. a. List the two forms of endoplasmic reticulum and describe their appearance.

   1.   2.

   b. Explain their functions.

17. a. Name a special form of smooth endoplasmic reticulum, and explain its functions.

   b. Briefly summarize the process of exocytosis.

   c. What is the function of the lysosomes?

18. a. What is the name of the matrix that gives the cell its shape?

   b. Describe its composition.

19. a. Why is axoplasmic transport required by the cell?

   b. Movement from the soma to the terminal buttons is called _____ axoplasmic transport and is accomplished by the protein _____.

   c. Explain how this protein transports its cargo. (Study Figure 2.7 in your text.)

   d. Movement from the terminal buttons to the soma is known as _____ axoplasmic transport and is accomplished by the protein _____.

To review: The principal internal structures of a multipolar neuron are shown in Figure 2.5 in your text.

Learning Objective 2-2   Briefly describe the role of neural communication in a simple reflex and its inhibition by brain mechanisms.

Read pages 34-35 and answer the following questions.

1. In your own words, describe the path of neural communication involved in the withdrawal reflex and shown in Figure 2.8 in your text.

2. What is the function of the

    a. sensory neuron?

    b. interneuron?

    c. motor neuron?

3. Now explain how neural circuits in the brain can inhibit the withdrawal reflex shown in Figure 2.9 in your text.

4. Thus, communication received from terminal buttons produces one of two possible effects on the rate of firing of the receiving neurons. Name them.

    1.   2.

Learning Objective 2-3   Describe the supporting cells of the central and peripheral nervous systems and explain the blood-brain barrier.

Read pages 35-38 and answer the following questions.

1. Why are the supporting cells essential?

2. _____ are the most important supporting cells in the central nervous system (CNS).

3. List four functions performed by these cells.

    1.   3.

    2.   4.

4. List the three most important types of glial cells.

    1.   3.

    2.

5. a. Describe five general functions of astrocytes.

    1.   4.

    2.   5.

    3.

    b. What did the arrangement of the processes of astrocytes suggest to Golgi (1903)?

    c. What do recent literature reviews suggest about Golgi's hypothesis? (Study to Figure 2.10 in your text. Tsacopoulos and Magistretti, 1996; Magistretti et al., 1999)

6. Describe how certain kinds of astrocytes clean up the debris from dead neurons through phagocytosis. Be sure to describe how they provide physical support once the dead tissue has been removed.

7. Which supporting cells in the CNS produce myelin?

8. a. Study Figure 2.11 in your text and describe how the oligodendroglia form the myelin sheath around an axon. Be sure to mention the nodes of Ranvier in your answer.

   b. Go back to Figure 1 in this study guide and add labels for the myelin sheath and nodes of Ranvier.

9. Summarize the functions of microglia.

10. The _____ _____ in the PNS perform the same functions as the _____ in the CNS.

11. How do the segments of myelin surrounding axons in the PNS differ from those in the CNS? (Study Figure 2.12 in your text.)

12. Contrast the restorative roles of astrocytes in the CNS and Schwann cells in the PNS if axons are damaged.

13. a. What tissue is tinted when dye is injected into an animal's bloodstream? an animal's brain ventricles? (Bradbury, 1979)

   b. What does this experiment demonstrate about the relationship between the blood and the fluid that surrounds the brain?

14. Look at Figure 2.13 in your text and explain why some substances pass easily through the blood-brain barrier and others do not.

15. Discuss the uniformity of the blood-brain barrier throughout the nervous system and its relationship to the control of vomiting. Be sure to use the term *area postrema* in your answer.

Read the interim summary on pages 48-49 your text to re-acquaint yourself with the material in this section.

Learning Objective 2-4   Describe the measurement of the action potential and explain the dynamic equilibrium that is responsible for the membrane potential.

Read pages 39-44 and answer the following questions.

1. What kind of axon do neuroscientists find useful for studying the electrical potentials of axons? Why?

2. Define *electrode* and *microelectrode* in your own words.

3. a. Now describe how we can use them to measure the membrane potential of an axon shown in Figure 2.14 in your text.

    b. Is the inside of the membrane positively or negatively charged with respect to the outside?

    c. What is the approximate value of the electrical charge across the membrane of the axon?

    d. What is this electrical charge called?

4. a. If we wish to study changes in the membrane potential that occur when a message is conducted down an axon, we will need some equipment more complicated than a voltmeter. Why?

    b. What does an oscilloscope do and what kind of record does it produce?

5. Now define *resting potential* in your own words.

6. If we wish to alter the resting potential, what device is necessary? (See Figure 2.15 in your text.)

7. If a positive electrical stimulus is applied to the inside of the membrane, what will be the effect on the membrane potential? What term is used to describe this change?

8. a. Study Figure 2.16 in your text. What happens to the membrane potential when the membrane receives a very weak depolarizing stimulus?

    b. Describe what happens to the electrical charge across the membrane after it receives a sufficiently large stimulus (number 4 on Figure 2.16).

    c. As the membrane returns to a normal, it overshoots the resting potential. Name this phenomenon.

    d. About how long does the entire process–from the electrical stimulus to the return to a normal resting potential–take?

    e. What do we call this phenomenon and the voltage level at which it is triggered?

9. A spoonful of sugar has been poured into a container of water. What eventually happens to the sugar?

10. a. Name the process that you just described.

    b. State the rule that describes how molecules will diffuse.

11. _____ are substances that split into two parts when dissolved in water. The charged particles into which they decompose are called _____. _____ have a positive charge and _____ have a negative charge. The force of attraction or repulsion between these particles is called _____ _____.

12. Read the explanation of ionic movements between the intracellular and extracellular fluid and study Figure 2.17 in your text. Now, without looking back, make the following additions to Figure 2:

    a. Minus signs are located both above and below the membrane. Change the appropriate ones to plus signs.

    b. Write the names of the four ions in the 7 boxes.

    c. Add two arrows, oriented appropriately, to each of the large boxes, indicating the direction of the force of diffusion and electrostatic pressure operating on each ion. (Add just one arrow to the box representing the ion that cannot leave the cell.)

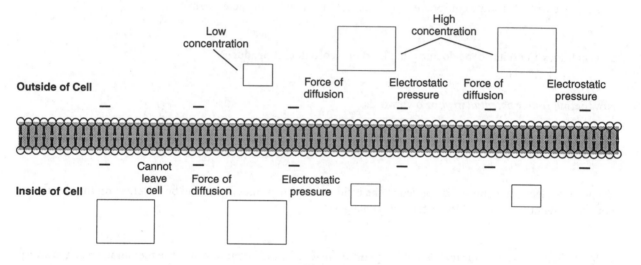

Figure 2

13. a. Explain why sodium stays where it is.

    b. Study Figure 2.18 in your text and describe the action of the sodium-potassium transporters that compose the sodium-potassium pump including the

       1. source of energy.

       2. exchange ratio between sodium and potassium and direction of movement of these ions.

14. What is the relative permeability of the membrane to sodium and potassium?

Learning Objective 2-5   Describe the role of ion channels in action potentials and explain the all-or-none law and the rate law.

Read pages 44-48 and answer the following questions.

1. Describe what would happen if the membrane suddenly became very permeable to sodium ions.

2. What pathways do ions use to enter and leave a cell? (Study Figure 2.19 in your text.)

3. Read the description and carefully study Figure 2.20 in your text. Then add numbers to Figure 3, below, that indicate the following:

   1. threshold of excitation reached
   2. opening of voltage-dependent sodium channels and entry of sodium
   3. opening of voltage-dependent potassium channels and outflow of potassium
   4. closing of sodium channels
   5. peak of action potential

   6. closing of potassium channels
   7. point when membrane overshoots resting potential
   8. diffusion of potassium outside cell
   9. return to normal value of resting potential and voltage level

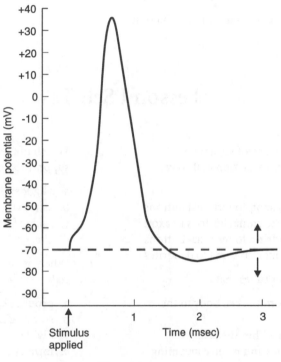

Figure 3

4. During an action potential there is only a slight increase in the concentration of sodium ions in the axoplasm. (Study Figure 2.21 in your text.) Why, then, are sodium-potassium transporters important?

5. Study Figure 2.22 in your text and state the all-or-none law in your own words.

6. Explain how action potentials, which are transmitted according to the all-or-none law, are able to transmit information of varying strength (for example, sensory stimuli of differing intensities). Be sure to use the term *rate law* in your answer. (See Figure 2.23 in your text.)

7. Compare the conduction of an electrical signal along an axon and an underwater cable. Be sure to use the terms *decremental conduction* (illustrated in Figure 2.24 in your text) and *cable properties* in your answer.

8. Study Figure 2.25 in your text and describe the step-by-step conduction of the action potential along a myelinated axon using these terms in this order.

    a. Schwann cells or oligodendroglia
    b. nodes of Ranvier
    c. inward flow of sodium
    d. extracellular sodium

    e. cable properties
    f. decremental conduction
    g. renewed signal strength
    h. saltatory conduction

9. Identify the two advantages of saltatory conduction.

Lesson I Self Test

1. What is the correct sequence of structures encountered by neural information as it travels along a neuron?

    a. dendrites to soma to axon to terminal buttons
    b. dendrites to soma to terminal buttons to axon
    c. soma to axon to dendrites to terminal buttons
    d. terminal buttons to axon to soma to dendrites

2. Microtubules are slender tubes that

    a. carry information from the cell body to the terminal button.
    b. transport substances within the cell.
    c. resemble tree branches and receive incoming messages.
    d. wrap around portions of the axon.

3. Which of the following are the *least* similar in their functions?

    a. lysosomes and mitochondria
    b. axons and dendrites
    c. chromosomes and genes
    d. nucleolus and ribosomes

4. What role does the inhibitory interneuron play in preventing a withdrawal reflex that would make you drop a hot casserole on the floor?

    a. It signals the neural circuits in the brain of the consequences of the action potential.
    b. It inhibits a sensory neuron.
    c. It inhibits a motor neuron.
    d. It prevents pain signals from entering the spinal cord.

5. Which of these alternatives does *not* provide support to neurons?

    a. oligodendrocyte
    b. astrocyte
    c. node of Ranvier
    d. glia

6. When nerves in the PNS are damaged, Schwann cells

    a. produce scar tissue.
    b. secrete enzymes that stimulate neurons to divide.
    c. form cylinders to guide the new axon sprouts.
    d. manufacture extra myelin.

7. Fewer substances enter or leave the brain across the blood-brain barrier in the _____ because the walls of the capillaries _____.

    a. PNS; have gaps
    b. PNS; do not have gaps
    c. CNS; have gaps
    d. CNS; do not have gaps

8. If the membrane of an axon receives a sufficiently large depolarization, the resulting rapid reversal of charge is called a(n)

    a. threshold of excitation.
    b. membrane potential.
    c. action potential.
    d. resting potential shift.

9. The membrane potential is the result of two forces:

a. diffusion and electrostatic pressure.
b. hyperpolarization and depolarization.
c. equilibrium and inertia.
d. the resting potential and the threshold of excitation.

10. Sodium-potassium transporters keep the intracellular concentration of

a. Na^+ low.
b. K^+ low.
c. Na^+ high.
d. Cl^- high.

11. All of the following are true about conduction of an action potential in a myelinated axon *except:*

a. Saltatory transmission is more energy efficient than transmission in unmyelinated axons.

b. Conduction of the message under the myelin segment is via passive cable properties.
c. Saltatory transmission is slower than transmission in unmyelinated axons.
d. Action potentials occur only at the nodes of Ranvier.

12. Saltatory conduction is advantageous because

a. it is unaffected by diseases that damage myelin.
b. it permits myelinated axons to transmit action potentials almost as fast as unmyelinated axons.
c. nodes of Ranvier are bypassed.
d. less energy is required to operate the sodium-potassium transporters.

Lesson II: Communication Between Neurons

Read the interim summary on pages 61-62 of your text to re-acquaint yourself with the material in this section.

Learning Objective 2-6   Describe the structure of synapses, the release of transmitter substance, and the activation of postsynaptic receptors.

Read pages 49-56 and answer the following questions.

1. What event produces a postsynaptic potential and what are its two possible effects on an axon?

2. Explain the differences between neurotransmitters and neuromodulators, both of which are released by terminal buttons.

3. Name a third type of chemical that is involved in neural communication and where it is produced. What is the general name for the cells that respond to these chemicals?

4. What is the relationship between a binding site and a ligand?

5. Name the three types of synapses illustrated in Figure 2.26 in your text.

6. A synapse is a(n) _____ between the _____ _____ at the ends of axons of one neuron with the _____ of another neuron. The membrane of the transmitting neuron is called the _____ membrane, and the message is received by the _____ membrane. These two membranes are separated by a small gap called the _____ _____.

7. On Figure 4 on the next page, label all the parts listed in question 6. (See Figure 2.27 in your text.)

8. List and describe the functions of the three structures found in the cytoplasm of the terminal button.

    1.

    2.

    3.

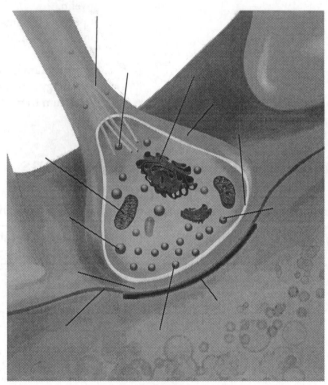

Figure 4

9. Where are large and small synaptic vesicles produced and how are they transported to the terminal buttons?

10. What constitutes the postsynaptic density?

11. Go back to Figure 4 and label these features: microtubule, synaptic vesicles, postsynaptic density. (Look at Figure 2.27 again.)

12. Figure 2.28 in your text is a photomicrograph of the release of transmitter substance by the synaptic vesicles of a terminal button into the synaptic cleft. Describe the experimental procedure used by Heuser (1977) and Heuser et al. (1979) that confirmed this process.

13. Study Figure 2.29 in your text and describe the process by which action potentials arriving at the terminal button cause the release of transmitters from vesicles. Include the roles of "docking" and calcium in your answer. (Almers, 1990)

14. When synaptic vesicles fuse with the membrane of the terminal button it becomes slightly larger. Describe the process that keeps the terminal buttons from becoming enormous. (Study Figures 2.30 and 2.31 in your text. Heuser and Reese, 1973; Betz and Berwick, 1992)

15. When molecules of the neurotransmitter diffuse across the synaptic cleft to the postsynaptic membrane, what structures do they bind with? Once binding occurs, what happens next?

16. a. Neurotransmitters open ion channels in at least two different ways. First explain the direct method involving ionotropic receptors illustrated in Figure 2.32 in your text.

    b. Now explain the indirect method involving metabotropic receptors and the G protein illustrated in Figure 2.33 in your text.

    c. What are chemicals that open metabotropic receptors called?

    d. What are some of their other functions?

Learning Objective 2-7   Describe postsynaptic potentials: the ionic movements that cause them, the processes that terminate them, and their integration.

Read pages 56-61 and answer the following questions.

1. a. To review: What are the two possible effects of postsynaptic potentials?

   b. What determines which effect will occur?

2. List the four major types of neurotransmitter-dependent ion channels in the postsynaptic membrane.

   1.   3.

   2.   4.

3. Describe the movements of sodium and potassium ions during an

   a. EPSP. (See Figure 2.34a in your text.)

   b. IPSP. (See Figure 2.34b.)

Now describe the movement of

c. chloride, which neutralizes an EPSP. (See Figure 2.34c.)

d. calcium, which produces special effects as well as an EPSP. (See Figure 2.34d.)

4. Define *postsynaptic potential* in your own words.

5. Name and describe the mechanism that terminates almost all postsynaptic potentials. (See Figure 2.35 in your text.)

6. And now for the alternative mechanism. Name and describe the mechanism that deactivates the neurotransmitter acetylcholine. Be sure to use the term *acetylcholinesterase (AChE)* in your answer.

7. a. Define *neural integration* in your own words.

   b. Explain what happens to the axon of a neuron when several excitatory synapses or several inhibitory synapses become active at the same time. (Study Figure 2.36 in your text.)

      1. excitatory synapses

      2. inhibitory synapses

   c. What controls the rate at which a neuron fires?

8. Explain why neural inhibition or excitation does not always result in behavioral inhibition or excitation.

9. Many neurons contain _____, which respond to the neurotransmitter they themselves produce.

   a. Where are they found and what seems to be their function?

   b. What is the usual effect of their activation?

10. Axoaxonic synapses alter the amount of _____ released by the terminal buttons of the

    _____ _____ to produce _____ _____. If the activity of these synapses decreases the amount of _____ the effect is called _____ _____, but if their activity increases the amount of _____ the effect is called _____ _____. (See Figure 2.37 in your text.)

11. a. What may be the function of dendrodendritic synapses formed by small neurons with short processes?

b. At electrical synapses the membranes of two neurons meet and almost touch. What do we call the gap between them? (See Figure 2.38 in your text.)

c. Explain how these adjacent neurons influence the activity of each other across this gap.

12. a. List two kinds of receptors found in neurons that play a role in neural communication.

1.   2.

b. Now list two classes of hormones that stimulate these receptors to influence the activity of their target cells. (See Figure 2.39 in your text.)

1.   2.

Lesson II Self Test

1. Which statement about the chemicals involved in neural communication is not true?

a. Most neuromodulators are composed of peptides.
b. Hormones travel in the bloodstream and affect distant receptors.
c. Neurotransmitters are secreted in larger amounts and travel longer distances than neuromodulators.
d. Ligands that activate receptors can be found in the body, in nature, and in the laboratory.

2. Which statement about the synapse is true?

a. Cisternae are involved in production of large synaptic vesicles.
b. Small vesicles typically contain neuropeptides.
c. Mitochondria play a role in the repackaging of neurotransmitters into vesicles.
d. Most synaptic vesicles congregate near the part of the presynaptic membrane called the release zone.

3. Large synaptic vesicles are produced in the _____ and are transported to the _____.

a. cytoplasm; dendrites
b. soma; terminal buttons

c. dendrites; release zone
d. synapse; extracellular fluid

4. What ion plays a crucial role in propelling synaptic vesicles toward the presynaptic membrane?

a. Na^+
b. Cl^-
c. Ca^{2+}
d. K^-

5. The membrane of synaptic vesicles is recycled by

a. being incorporated into the membrane of the terminal button, after which small buds pinch off into the cytoplasm.
b. being incorporated into the membrane of the terminal button, after which it subdivides into replicas of itself.
c. resealing their membranes and filling them with neurotransmitter.
d. fusing with mitochondria, which provide energy to regenerate.

6. Postsynaptic receptors bind with molecules of neurotransmitter and

a. transport them to synaptic vesicles.
b. open neurotransmitter-dependent ion channels.

c. release them during an EPSP or IPSP.

d. deactivate them through reuptake.

7. The acetylcholine receptor studied in the electric ray

a. is a metabotropic receptor.

b. opens potassium channels when stimulated.

c. is linked to a G protein that activates an enzyme in the membrane.

d. opens ion channels directly when stimulated.

8. Which statement about metabotropic receptors is not true?

a. When stimulated, they require the cell to expend energy.

b. They are found on the postsynaptic membrane but not the presynaptic membrane.

c. They open ion channels indirectly via activation of second messengers.

d. They are located in close proximity to G proteins.

9. During an EPSP

a. Na^+ enters the cell.

b. K^+ enters the cell.

c. Na^+ leaves the cell.

d. Cl^- leaves the cell.

10. At most synapses, postsynaptic potentials are terminated by

a. reuptake.

b. enzymatic deactivation.

c. ionic flow.

d. phagocytosis.

11. A neuron's own neurotransmitter, detected by its autoreceptors,

a. initiates changes in the local membrane potential.

b. opens the gates of neurotransmitter-dependent ion channels.

c. facilitates the synthesis of other neurotransmitters.

d. inhibits the synthesis of that neurotransmitter.

12. Peptides

a. stimulate metabotropic receptors that alter the activity of the cell's nucleus.

b. are small fat-soluble molecules.

c. are hormones secreted by the sex glands and the adrenal glands.

d. are synthesized from cholesterol.

Answers for Self Tests

Lesson I

1.	a	Obj. 2-1
2.	b	Obj. 2-1
3.	a	Obj. 2-1
4.	c	Obj. 2-2
5.	c	Obj. 2-3
6.	c	Obj. 2-3
7.	d	Obj. 2-3
8.	c	Obj. 2-4
9.	a	Obj. 2-4
10.	a	Obj. 2-4
11.	c	Obj. 2-5
12.	d	Obj. 2-5

Lesson II

1.	c	Obj. 2-6
2.	d	Obj. 2-6
3.	b	Obj. 2-6
4.	c	Obj. 2-6
5.	a	Obj. 2-6
6.	b	Obj. 2-6
7.	d	Obj. 2-6
8.	b	Obj. 2-6
9.	a	Obj. 2-7
10.	a	Obj. 2-7
11.	d	Obj. 2-7
12.	a	Obj. 2-7

CHAPTER 3
Structure of The Nervous System

Lesson I: Basic Features of the Nervous System and Some Structures of the Central Nervous System

Read the interim summary on pages 71-72 in your text to re-acquaint yourself with the material in this section.

> **Learning Objective 3-1**   Describe the appearance of the brain and the terms used to indicate directions and planes of section.

Read pages 64-66 and answer the following questions.

1. Draw two pictures of a snake. Make the first a side view and the second a front view. Label your drawings with these terms of anatomical direction: neuraxis, anterior, posterior, rostral, caudal, dorsal, ventral, lateral, and medial. (Study Figure 3.1 in your text.)

2. Now repeat this exercise by labeling two stick figure drawings of a human.

3. Define these frequently used terms in your own words.

    a. ipsilateral

    b. contralateral

4. To confirm your understanding of the nomenclature for planes of section, try using these terms to describe these pieces of food: *cross* or *frontal, horizontal,* and *sagittal.* You will have to imagine the neuraxis. (Study Figure 3.2 in your text.)

_____ cutting a hamburger bun into top and bottom halves

_____ a slice of bread

_____ slicing a fish into two symmetrical halves

Learning Objective 3-2   Describe the blood supply to the brain, the meninges, the ventricular system, and flow of cerebrospinal fluid through the brain and its production.

Read pages 66-71 and answer the following questions.

1. Name the two major divisions of the nervous system and then list their parts. (See Table 3.1 and Figure 3.3 in your text.)

    1.

    2.

2. a. Approximately how much of the blood flow from the heart does the brain receive?

   b. Why is an uninterrupted blood supply essential?

   c. What are the consequences if blood supply is interrupted for 1-second? 6-seconds? a few minutes?

3. a. Name and describe the blood vessels through which blood flows after it leaves the heart.

   b. List the major sets of arteries in the brain and identify the areas they serve. (See Figure 3.4 in your text.)

      1.   2.

   c. How is the normal flow of blood affected if a blood vessel becomes blocked?

4. The entire nervous system is covered with two or three layers of connective tissue called _____.

5. a. Return to Figure 3.3 in your text and then list and describe the three layers of the meninges beginning with the outer layer.
      1.
      2.
      3.

   b. What area lies between the arachnoid membrane and the pia mater?

   c. What liquid fills this space?

   d. Which two layers of the meninges fuse outside the CNS? What does this sheath cover?

6. Describe how CSF protects the brain.

7. Define *ventricles* in your own words.

8. Study Figure 3.5 in your text and describe the major components of the ventricular system.

   a. Name the two largest chambers in the brain.

   b. What structure

      1. crosses the middle of the third ventricle?

      2. connects the third and fourth ventricles?

9. Where is CSF produced and how is it reabsorbed?

10. Write a sentence describing the flow of CSF, using all of the following terms: lateral ventricles, third ventricle, fourth ventricle, blood supply, choroid plexus, arachnoid granulations, small openings, subarachnoid space, cerebral aqueduct, superior sagittal sinus

11. What is the cause and treatment of obstructive hydrocephalus? (See Figure 3.6 in your text.)

12. To review: The interim summary presents important anatomical nomenclature, the divisions of the central and peripheral nervous system, and an overview of the ventricular system and cerebrospinal fluid.

Read the interim summary on pages 89-90 of your text to re-acquaint yourself with the material in this section.

Learning Objective 3-3   Outline the development of the central nervous system and the evolution of the human brain.

Read pages 72-77 and answer the following questions.

1. a. Describe how, between about the eighteenth and twenty-first days after conception, the ectoderm of the back of the embryo develops into the neural tube. (Study Figure 3.7 in your text.)

   b. What structures develop from the neural tube? the ridges which break away?

2. Let's look more closely at the early development of the neural tube illustrated in Figure 3.8 in your text.

   a. What change occurs to the rostral end of the neural tube by the twenty-eighth day of development?

   b. What structures develop from these chambers? the surrounding tissue?

    c. What change now occurs to the rostral one of these chambers?

    d. And what structures will develop around the lateral ventricles? the third ventricle?

    e. How does the chamber inside the midbrain continue to develop? the hindbrain?

3. With the help of Figure 3.8, label the portions of the neural tube shown in Figure 1a that become the forebrain, the midbrain, and the hindbrain.

4. On Figure 1b, indicate how the forebrain continues to develop by labeling the telencephalon, the diencephalon, the mesencephalon, and the two parts of the hindbrain—the metencephalon and the myelencephalon.

5. On Figure 1c, indicate the location of the cerebral hemisphere, cerebellum, thalamus, hypothalamus, pituitary gland, midbrain, pons, medulla, brain stem and spinal cord.

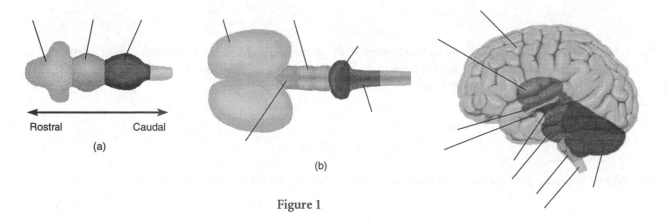

Rostral   Caudal

(a)

(b)

Figure 1

(c)

6. Immediately review what you have just learned by studying Table 3.2 in your text. Now complete the blank version of that table below.

Anatomical Subdivisions of the Brain			
Major Division	*Ventricle*	*Subdivision*	*Principal Structures*

7. Where are the cells that give rise to the cells of the central nervous system found?

8. a. What tissue surrounds the cerebral hemispheres and what are some of its functions?

    b. Compare its size with that of other species.

9. a. Explain how researchers use radioactive labeling to study brain development.

    b. What do studies using this technique indicate about the development of the cerebral cortex?

10. By what means do newly formed neurons reach their final destination? (Rakic, 1972, 1988)

11. a. What is the name of the cells in the ventricular zone that give rise to neurons?

    b. Study Figure 3.9 in your text and complete this table summarizing the two periods of division these cells undergo.

Name of Division	Begins	Ends	Neural Development

    c. Approximately how long does it take the first neurons to reach their final destination? the last neurons?

    d. Name and describe the event that stops cortical development?

12. a. Describe how neurons continue to develop and form synaptic connections with postsynaptic cells after they reach their final locations. Be sure to mention the role of the postsynaptic cell.

    b. What happens to about half of the neurons produced in the neural tube which fail to form synaptic connections?

    c. Outline a possible explanation for this phenomenon.

13. What role may the founder cells play in the specialization of a particular region of cerebral cortex?

14. a. Why did Krubitzer and her colleagues use opossums to study the role of axons in specialization? (Krubitzer, 1998. Study Figure 3.10 in your text.)

    b. They removed a portion of the cerebral cortex of an opossum before what kind of brain connections developed?

c. When brain development ended, they examined various regions of cortex. What did their examination reveal and what does it suggest about the role of axons in specialization?

15. What additional influence on brain development was suggested by research on stereoscopic vision by Poggio and Poggio (1984)?

16. How was the adult brain affected by

    a. amputation of a person's arm? (Elbert et al., 1994; Kew et al., 1994; Yang et al., 1994)

    b. playing a stringed instrument?

    c. reading Braille? (Elbert et al., 1995; Sadato et al., 1996)

17. a. Explain genetic duplication in your own words, noting what it contributes to the evolution of a complex brain. (Allman, 1998; Lewis, 1992)

    b. How did duplication influence the development of the vertebrate rhombomeres? (Be sure to refer to master genes in your answer. Study Figure 3.11 in your text.)

18. Summarize Rakic's explanation of how the length of the periods of symmetrical and asymmetrical division be responsible for the ultimate development of the brain.

Learning Objective 3-4   Describe the telencephalon, one of the two of the two major structures of the forebrain.

Read pages 77-82 and answer the following questions.

1. List the two major components of the forebrain.

    1.   2.

2. The telencephalon includes most of the two _____ _____, which are covered by the

    _____ _____.

3. List two subcortical structures of the telencephalon that are found deep within the cerebral hemispheres.

    1.   2.

4. a. Large grooves in the cerebral cortex are called _____ and small ones are called

        _____. The bulges between grooves are called _____. (See Figure 3.12 in your text.)

    b. To what extent do the convolutions affect the total surface area of the cortex?

c. What do the following terms apply to, and what is responsible for the colors?

    1. gray matter

    2. white matter

5. Study Figure 3.13 in your text and describe the location of these three areas of cerebral cortex noting nearby fissures or sulci.

    1. primary visual cortex

    2. primary auditory cortex

    3. primary somatosensory cortex

6. What kind of sensory information is not sent to the contralateral side of the brain?

7. In general, what kinds of functions are mediated by the anterior and posterior regions of the cerebral cortex?

8. Label the following regions on Figure 2 below: the four lobes; the primary visual, somatosensory, auditory, and motor cortex; and the central sulcus. Indicate rostral, caudal, dorsal, and ventral, making a total of 13 items to label. Study Figures 3.13 and 3.14 in your text.

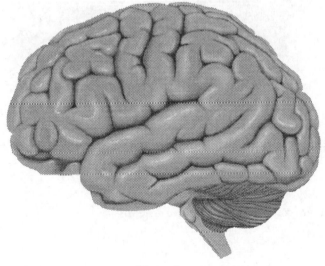

Figure 2

9. Compare the functions of sensory association cortex located close to and farther away from primary cortex.

10. What are the general functions of the motor association cortex? the prefrontal cortex?

11. The functions of the cerebral hemispheres are _____. The right hemisphere is involved in the _____ of information and the left is involved in the _____ of information.

12. a. Name and describe the function of the largest commissure in the brain.

    b. Name the portion of cerebral cortex that covers most of the surface of the cerebral hemispheres. (See Figures 3.14 and 3.15 in your text.)

    c. Now name the portion of cerebral cortex located around the medial edge of the cerebral hemispheres and an important region found there.

13. Label the regions indicated by the lines on Figure 3.

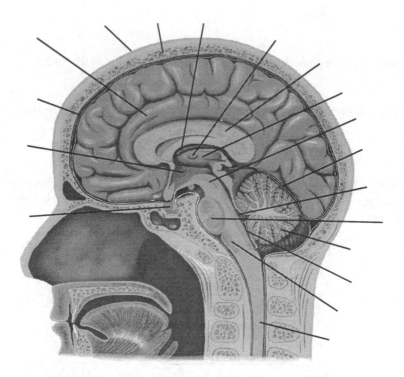

Figure 3

14. Study Figure 3.16 in your text and list the three most important structures that are a part of the limbic system.

    1.   3.

    2.

15. What kinds of functions are controlled by the limbic system?

16. What structure connects the hippocampus with other parts of the brain?

17. a. List the major parts of the basal ganglia. (Figure 3.17 in your text shows their location.)

    1.   3.

    2.

b. What is the general function of the basal ganglia?

c. Describe the cause and some of the symptoms of Parkinson's disease.

Lesson I Self Test

1. As you look down on the snake, you see its _____ surface, and it slithers along the ground on its _____ surface.

    a. lateral; ventral
    b. ventral; medial
    c. dorsal; ventral
    d. dorsal; lateral

2. Which of the following would not be visible in a midsagittal view of the brain?

    a. the lateral fissure
    b. the cerebral aqueduct
    c. the corpus callosum
    d. the cingulate gyrus

3. The meninges and subarachnoid space surround the brain in the following order, beginning with the outer layer:

    a. dura mater, pia mater, arachnoid membrane, subarachnoid space.
    b. dura mater, arachnoid membrane, subarachnoid space, pia mater.
    c. pia mater, dura mater, subarachnoid space, arachnoid membrane.
    d. pia mater, arachnoid membrane, subarachnoid space, dura mater.

4. Cerebrospinal fluid is produced by the

    a. meninges.
    b. subarachnoid space.
    c. choroid plexus.
    d. ventricles.

5. After cerebrospinal fluid has circulated through the brain and subarachnoid space it is

    a. excreted by the kidneys.
    b. recirculated for the next three hours.
    c. reabsorbed into the blood supply.
    d. transported through the central canal to the abdomen.

6. In the central nervous system neurons develop in the

    a. ventricular zone of the neural tube.
    b. radial glial cells.
    c. in the chambers which become the ventricles of the brain.
    d. growth cones.

7. The three major parts of the brain are the

    a. telencephalon, the diencephalon, and the metencephalon.
    b. cerebral cortex, the association cortex, and the brain stem.
    c. frontal lobe, the parietal lobe, and the temporal lobe.
    d. forebrain, the midbrain, and the hindbrain.

8. Neurons that do not establish synaptic connections with a postsynaptic cell

    a. migrate to the bone marrow.
    b. are destroyed through apoptosis.
    c. may later become malignant.
    d. attract synaptic connections from presynaptic cells.

9. Genetic duplication

    a. increases the size of the ventricular zone.
    b. preserves important functions even if mutation occurs.
    c. ceases when the neural tube closes.
    d. is limited to approximately three or four symmetrical divisions.

10. The corpus callosum connects the

    a. two hemispheres of the brain.
    b. structures of the limbic system.
    c. pituitary gland and the hypothalamus.
    d. thalamus and the hypothalamus.

11. The most important structures of the limbic system are the limbic cortex, the

    a. hippocampus, and the amygdala.

b. basal ganglia, and the thalamus.

c. primary motor cortex, and the primary association cortex.

d. hypothalamus, and the medulla.

a. planning and execution of movement.

b. visual and auditory functions.

c. control of the endocrine system.

d. emotional behavior, learning, and memory.

12. The limbic system plays a role in

Lesson II: Some Structures of the Central Nervous System and The Peripheral Nervous System

Read the interim summary on pages 89-90 of your text to re-acquaint yourself with the material in this section.

Learning Objective 3-5   Describe the two major structures of the diencephalon.

Read pages 83-85 and answer the following questions.

1. a. The diencephalon is the second major division of the _____ and is located between the

_____ and the _____. The two most important structures of the diencephalon are

the _____ and the _____.

b. Study Figures 3.15 and 3.17 in your text and describe the location and appearance of the thalamus. Be sure to mention the massa intermedia in your answer.

2. Define *projection fibers* and *nuclei* in your own words and explain their relation to the function of the thalamus.

3. Where do these thalamic nuclei receive and relay their sensory information?

a. lateral geniculate nucleus

b. medial geniculate nucleus

c. ventrolateral nucleus

4. a. Describe the location and general functions of the hypothalamus. (Study Figures 3.17 and 3.18 in your text.)

b. What structure is attached to the base of the hypothalamus? What other structure lies just in front of it? (See Figure 3.18 in your text.)

c. The hypothalamus controls the anterior pituitary gland, and through it most of the _____

system, by secreting the hypothalamic _____, which are produced by specialized neurons called

_____ _____, located near the base of the _____ _____. (See

Figure 3.19 in your text.)

d. To explain why the anterior pituitary gland is often called the "master gland," briefly summarize the effects of some of the hormones it secretes.

e. Describe the production and secretion of the hormones of the posterior pituitary gland.

f. Now summarize the effects of some of the hormones secreted by the posterior pituitary gland

---

Learning Objective 3-6   Describe the two major structures of the midbrain, the two major structures of the hindbrain, and the spinal cord.

Read pages 85-89 and answer the following questions.

1. List the two major parts of the midbrain or mesencephalon.

   1.   2.

2. Then list the two principal structures of the tectum and the sensory systems they are a part of. (See Figure 3.20 in your text.)

   1.   2.

3. Continue by listing the structures of the brain stem.

   1.   2.   3.

4. Finally, list the principal structures of the tegmentum shown in Figure 3.20d.

   1.   4.

   2.   5.

   3.   6.

5. a. Briefly describe the composition and appearance of the reticular formation.

   b. List some of its functions.

6. a. What gives the periaqueductal gray matter its name?

   b. List a function of the

      1. periaqueductal gray matter.

      2. red nucleus.

      3. substantia nigra.

7. a. List the two divisions of the hindbrain.

      1.   2.

   b. Now list the two structures of the metencephalon.

      1.   2.

8. Briefly describe the location of the

   a. cerebellar cortex.

   b. deep cerebellar nuclei.

   c. cerebellar peduncles. (See Figure 3.20c.)

9. Briefly describe some of the functions of the cerebellum and the kinds of disability resulting from damage to this structure.

10. Describe the location of the pons and the function of several nuclei found there. (Look back at Figures 3.15 and 3.20a in your text.)

11. Describe the location and functions of the medulla oblongata, the major structure of the myelencephalon. (Look back once again at Figures 3.15 and 3.20 in your text.)

12. What is the principal function of the spinal cord?

13. How is the spinal cord protected?

14. Name the passage at the center of each vertebra through which the spinal cord passes. (See Figure 3.21 in your text.)

15. a. Explain why the spinal cord is only about two-thirds as long as the vertebral column.

    b. Describe the cauda equina and explain how it is possible to eliminate sensations from the lower part of the body using a caudal block. (Look back at Figure 3.3 in your text.)

    c. Study Figure 3.22 in your text and describe the dorsal roots and ventral roots and the axons they contain. Be sure to notice the location of the white matter and gray matter.

16. To review: The interim summary summarizes the development of the human brain and its principal divisions and structures.

Read the interim summary on page 95 of your text to re-acquaint yourself with the material in this section.

> *Learning Objective 3-7*   Describe the peripheral nervous system, including the two divisions of the autonomic nervous system.

Read pages 90-94 and answer the following questions.

1. List the two sets of nerves of the peripheral nervous system and describe their general functions.

   1.   2.

2. Look back at Figure 3.3 in your text and review the pathways of the spinal nerves throughout the body.

3. The cell bodies of _____ axons which bring sensory information into the brain and spinal cord are

    located _____the central nervous system with the exception of the _____

    _____ which is a part of the brain. Incoming axons are called _____ axons and the cell

    bodies from which they arise are found in the _____ _____ _____.

    _____ axons leave the spinal cord through the _____ _____ and control

    the muscles and glands. (See Figure 3.23 in your text.)

4. Study Figure 3.24 in your text and list the names, numbers, and functions of at least four of the twelve pairs of
    cranial nerves that leave the brain. Begin with the vagus nerve.

    1. vagus nerve (10)

    2.

    3.

    4.

5. List the two main divisions of the PNS and identify their functions.

    1.   2.

6. The autonomic nervous system is further divided into two parts. List them.

    1.   2.

7. a. Using examples, describe the kinds of activity mediated by the sympathetic division.

    b. Where are the cells bodies of sympathetic motor neurons located, and where do their axons exit the CNS?

    c. Where do these axons go?

    d. Study Figure 3.25 in your text and describe how the sympathetic ganglion chain is formed.

8. a. Axons of the ANS that leave the spinal cord are called _____ _____ and, with one

       exception, enter the ganglia of the _____ _____. The exception is the

       _____ _____ located in the center of the adrenal gland.

    b. Where do postganglionic neurons send their axons?

    c. Which hormones are secreted by the cells of the adrenal medulla and what are their effects on the body?

9. Using examples, describe the kinds of activity mediated by the parasympathetic division.

10. Name the two regions that give rise to preganglionic axons of the parasympathetic division.

    1.   2.

11. To review: Study Table 3.3 in your text.

Lesson II Self Test

1. The _____ surrounds the third ventricle and its two most important structures are the _____.
    a. forebrain; the telencephalon and the diencephalon
    b. diencephalon; thalamus and the hypothalamus
    c. limbic system; basal ganglia and the amygdala
    d. diencephalon; hippocampus and the amygdala

2. The thalamus is responsible for
    a. most of the neural input received by the cerebral cortex.
    b. emotional behavior.
    c. movement of a particular part of the body.
    d. behaviors related to survival of the species.

3. Neurons in the hypothalamus
    a. control the peripheral nervous system.
    b. send projection fibers through the optic chiasm.
    c. are controlled by hormones secreted by the anterior pituitary gland.
    d. are involved behaviors such as sleeping and drinking.

4. The anterior pituitary gland produces
    a. vasopressin.
    b. oxytocin.
    c. gonadotropic hormones.
    d. estrogen.

5. The principal structures of the tectum are the
    a. superior and inferior colliculi.
    b. hippocampus and amygdala.
    c. thalamus and hypothalamus.
    d. lateral and medial geniculate nuclei.

6. The reticular formation
    a. relays visual information from the retina to the rest of the brain.
    b. appears as four bumps on the brain stem.

    c. is one of two major fiber systems within the brain.
    d. plays a role in sleep and arousal.

7. The periaqueductal gray matter is so called because of its location and an abundance of
    a. fibers.
    b. cell bodies.
    c. synapses.
    d. axons.

8. The spinal cord is _____ the vertebral column.
    a. fused to
    b. longer than
    c. outside
    d. shorter than

9. Dorsal roots contain _____ axons and ventral roots contain _____ axons.
    a. unipolar; bipolar
    b. myelinated; unmyelinated
    c. afferent; efferent
    d. motor; sensory

10. The cranial nerve that controls the parasympathetic function of organs in the thoracic and abdominal cavities is the
    a. preganglionic nerve.
    b. hypoglossal nerve.
    c. vagus nerve.
    d. trigeminal nerve.

11. The two divisions of the autonomic nervous system are the
    a. brain and the spinal cord.
    b. somatic nervous system and the autonomic nervous system.
    c. sympathetic division and the parasympathetic division.
    d. spinal nerves and the cranial nerves.

12. _____ _____ leave the spinal cord through the ventral root.

    a. Preganglionic axons

    b. Postganglionic axons
    c. Sympathetic ganglia
    d. Cranial nerves

Answers for Self Tests

Lesson I				Lesson II		
1.	c	Obj. 3-1		1.	b	Obj. 3-5
2.	a	Obj. 3-1		2.	a	Obj. 3-5
3.	b	Obj. 3-2		3.	d	Obj. 3-5
4.	c	Obj. 3-2		4.	c	Obj. 3-5
5.	c	Obj. 3-2		5.	a	Obj. 3-6
6.	a	Obj. 3-3		6.	d	Obj. 3-6
7.	d	Obj. 3-3		7.	b	Obj. 3-6
8.	b	Obj. 3-3		8.	d	Obj. 3-6
9.	b	Obj. 3-3		9.	c	Obj. 3-7
10.	a	Obj. 3-4		10.	c	Obj. 3-7
11.	a	Obj. 3-4		11.	c	Obj. 3-7
12.	d	Obj. 3-4		12.	a	Obj. 3-7

CHAPTER 4
Psychopharmacology

Lesson I: Principles of Psychopharmacology and Sites of Drug Action

Read the interim summary on page 104 of your text to re-acquaint yourself with the material in this section.

Learning Objective 4-1   Describe the routes of administration and the distribution of drugs within the body.

Read pages 97-101 and answer the following questions.

1. Define these terms in your own words.

    a. psychopharmacology

    b. drug (as it will be used in the chapter)

    c. drug effects

    d. site of action

    e. pharmacokinetics

2. The most common route of drug administration for laboratory animals is _____.

3. Complete this table of the types of injections.

Type	Injection Site	Speed of Absorption	Comments
Intravenous (IV)			
Intraperitoneal (IP)			
Intramuscular (IM)			
Subcutaneous (SC)			
Intracerebral			
Intracerebroventricular (ICV)			

4. a. The most common route for administration of medical drugs for humans is _____

    _____.

    b. When is this the preferred form of drug administration?

5. List four other routes of drug administration for humans, noting when each route is most appropriate.

    1.

    2.

    3.

    4.

6. Figure 4.1 in your text illustrates the speed at which cocaine reaches the blood when taken in some of the ways you have just described.

7. a. Let's look at factors that affect how quickly a drug exerts its effects. Why does the lipid solubility of a drug affect the rate at which it reaches sites of action in the brain?

    b. Define *depot binding* in your own words.

    c. Go on to explain how this process can both delay and prolong the effects of a drug. Be sure to mention the role of albumin in your answer. (Study Figure 4.2 in your text.)

    d. In addition to albumin, what are some other sources of depot binding?

8. What eventually happens to all drugs that have been introduced into the body?

Learning Objective 4-2   Describe drug effectiveness, the effects of repeated administration, and the placebo effect.

Read pages 101-104 and answer the following questions.

1. Complete these sentences. (Study Figures 4.3 and 4.4 in your text.)

    a. The best way to measure the effectiveness of a drug is

    b. The most desirable drugs have

    c. One measure of a drug's margin of safety is

    d. The therapeutic index is

    e. The lower the therapeutic index is

2. a. Provide two reasons why drugs vary in their effectiveness.

    1.   2.

    b. How is the dosage of a drug affected by a high affinity for its binding site? a low affinity?

c. What is the most desirable pattern of affinity for a drug?

3. a. Define these two phenomena, which may occur with repeated administration of a drug.

   1. tolerance

   2. sensitization

   b. If a person who has reached tolerance suddenly stops taking the drug, how does the body react? Be sure to use the term *withdrawal symptoms* in your answer.

   c. Carefully explain how the body's compensatory mechanisms are linked to the body's reaction to continued drug use and its sudden cessation.

4. Discuss two types of compensatory mechanisms.

5. a. Using barbiturates as an example, explain how its sites of action are affected differently by continued drug use. Describe some of the dangers of drug tolerance.

   b. Why is sensitization less common than tolerance?

6. a. Define *placebo* in your own words.

   b. Why is it incorrect to say placebos have no effects?

7. a. How did subjects' sensitivity to pain change after they received a placebo they thought would reduce pain? (Levine et al., 1979)

   b. What was the effect of an injection of naloxone on their sensitivity to pain? (Be sure to explain how naloxone affects the brain. See Figure 4.5 in your text.)

   c. What do the results demonstrate about the effects of placebos in some situations?

8. Why must control groups that receive placebos be used in research with animal and human subjects?

Read the interim summary on pages 108-109 of your text to re-acquaint yourself with the material in this section.

Learning Objective 4-3   Describe the effects of drugs on neurotransmitters and presynaptic and postsynaptic receptors

Read pages 104-108 and answer the following questions.

1. Most drugs that affect behavior do so by affecting _____ _____. Those that block or inhibit the postsynaptic effects are called _____, and those that facilitate them are called _____.

2. Review the sequence of synaptic activity that you learned about in Chapter 2.

Figure 1 below illustrates eleven ways that drugs can affect synaptic transmission. As you answer the following questions, fill in the missing information. (Study Figure 4.6 in your text.)

3. Describe the two ways in which drugs can affect the production of a neurotransmitter. Put your answers in boxes 1 and 2 and indicate if the effects are those of an agonist or antagonist.

4. What effect can drugs have on the storage of a neurotransmitter in synaptic vesicles? Explain the process below, write a brief summary in box 3, and indicate if the drug is an agonist or antagonist.

5. What effect can drugs have on the release of a neurotransmitter? Explain the process, and write a summary statement in boxes 4 and 5. Indicate if the drug is an agonist or antagonist.

6. Describe how a drug acts as a direct agonist. Write a summary statement in box 6.

7. How do direct antagonists function? What is another name for drugs with this effect? Write a summary statement in box 7.

8. In contrast, how do indirect agonists function? Be sure to use the term *noncompetitive binding* in your answer. (Study Figure 4.7 in your text.)

9. Drugs can stimulate or block presynaptic autoreceptors. Describe these effects and write summary statements in boxes 8 and 9.

10. a. In an axoaxonic synapse, with what does the terminal button form a synapse?

 b. When the first terminal button is active, how may it affect the second one?

 c. What kind of receptors are found on the second terminal button?

 d. How do these receptors produce presynaptic inhibition? presynaptic facilitation? (Study Figure 4.8 in your text.)

 e. What effects can drugs have on presynaptic inhibition and facilitation?

11. a. Where are autoreceptors found and how are they affected by the neurotransmitter released by the dendrites?

 b. What is the effect of drugs that bind with and activate dendritic autoreceptors? bind with and block dendritic autoreceptors? (Study Figure 4.9 in your text.)

12. What two processes terminate the postsynaptic potential? How do drugs affect these processes? Write summary statements in boxes 10 and 11.

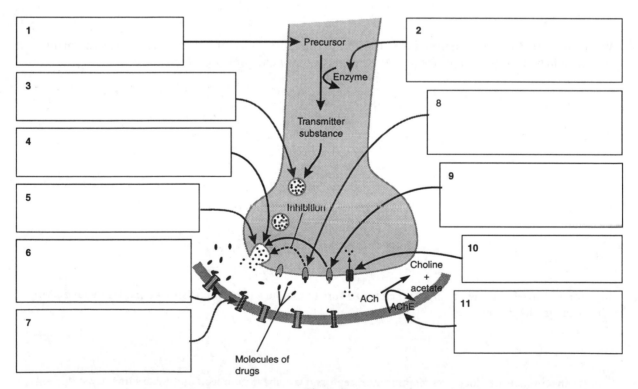

Figure 1

13. To review the effects of drugs that bind with receptor, study Table 4.1 in your text and then complete the one below.

Site of action	Effect of drug on receptor	Effect of activated receptor	Effect on synaptic transmission (agonist or antagonist)
Postsynaptic receptor	stimulate		
	block		
Presynaptic autoreceptor	stimulate		
	block		
Presynaptic heteroreceptor	stimulate		
	block		
Presynaptic heteroreceptor	stimulate		
	block		
Dendritic autoreceptor	stimulate		
	block		

Lesson I Self Test

1. The fastest way to have a drug reach the brain is to administer it through an

   a. intravenous injection.
   b. intraperitoneal injection.
   c. intramuscular injection.
   d. subcutaneous injection.

2. A(n) _____ is the most common route for administering drugs to small animals and a(n) _____ is never used with small animals.

   a. intramuscular injection; intrarectal administration
   b. intravenous injection; subcutaneous injection
   c. intraperitoneal injection; sublingual administration
   d. intracerebral injection; topical administration

3. Depot binding

   a. can halt the effects of a drug.
   b. prolongs or delays the effects of a drug.
   c. begins when albumin molecules are fully saturated with a drug.

   d. does not usually alter the initial effects of a drug.

4. The therapeutic index of a drug is

   a. is derived from the dose-response curve.
   b. the dose that produces desired effects in 50 percent of the animals.
   c. a measure of a drug's margin of safety.
   d. is an indication of the drug's affinity for its site of action.

5. Repeated administration of a drug

   a. can produce sensitization.
   b. can inhibit tolerance.
   c. contributes to the uniform effects of a drug over time.
   d. may prevent compensatory mechanisms from engaging.

6. A placebo effect

   a. varies with the strength of the drug.
   b. is always pleasurable.
   c. can have physiological causes
   d. has no role in neuroscience research.

7. Select the *incorrect* statement.

   a. When a drug acts as a precursor, it increases the production of a neurotransmitter, serving as an agonist.
   b. If a drug inactivates enzymes responsible for the production of a neurotransmitter, it acts as an agonist.
   c. Transporter molecules that fill synaptic vesicles may be blocked by a drug, which then serves as an antagonist.
   d. Some antagonist drugs prevent the release of the neurotransmitter from terminal buttons.

8. A drug that mimics the effects of a neurotransmitter acts as a

   a. receptor blocker.
   b. direct antagonist.
   c. direct agonist.
   d. indirect ligand.

9. Select the *incorrect* statement

   a. The terms *receptor blocker* and *direct antagonist* are synonyms.
   b. Receptor blockers can cause ion channels to close.
   c. A direct agonist attaches to an alternate binding site and facilitates the opening of the ion channel.

   d. Drugs that block presynaptic autoreceptors increase the release of the neurotransmitter.

10. Some neurons contain presynaptic heteroreceptors which are found in the

    a. nucleus.
    b. synaptic cleft between two neurons.
    c. first terminal button at an axoaxonic synapse.
    d. second terminal button at an axoaxonic synapse.

11. Drugs that bind with and block dendritic autoreceptors

    a. produce an inhibitory hyperpolarization.
    b. prevent noncompetitive binding.
    c. block the nodes of Ranvier.
    d. reduce the production of the neurotransmitter.

12. For most neurotransmitters, termination of the postsynaptic potential occurs when molecules of the neurotransmitter are

    a. encapsulated between branches of dendrites.
    b. destroyed by an enzyme.
    c. surrounded and absorbed by the synaptic vesicles.
    d. taken back into the terminal buttons.

Lesson II: Neurotransmitters and Neuromodulators

Read the interim summary on page 128 of your text to re-acquaint yourself with the material in this section.

Learning Objective 4-4   Review the general role of neurotransmitters and neuromodulators, and describe the acetylcholinergic pathways in the brain and the drugs that affect these neurons.

Read pages 109-112 and answer the following questions.

1. a. Most synaptic activity in the brain is accomplished by two neurotransmitters, _____ which has _____ effects and _____ which has _____ effects.

   b. What, then, do all the other neurotransmitters do? Provide two examples to support your answer.

2. List three sites in the body where synapses release acetylcholine. (See Figure 4.10 in your text.)

   1.   3.

   2.

3. Why was acetylcholine the first neurotransmitter to be discovered?

4. a. Use one word to describe the general effect of acetylcholine in the brain.

    b. List three sites in the brain with systems of acetylcholinergic neurons and the functions these neurons influence. (See Figure 4.10 in your text.)

Site	Function
1.	
2.	
3.	

5. a. Figure 2 illustrates the chemical reactions responsible for the production of acetylcholine. Label each component. (Study Figure 4.11 in your text.)

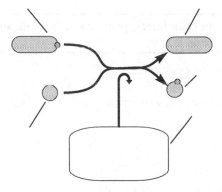

Figure 2

    b. Explain the details of this reaction in your own words.

6. List two drugs that affect the release of acetylcholine and describe their effects.

    1.

    2.

7. a. What happens to choline after acetylcholine is deactivated by acetylcholinesterase? Why? (Study Figure 4.11 in your text.)

    b. How can this process be prevented? (Study Figure 4.12 in your text.)

8. a. Describe the symptoms of the hereditary disorder myasthenia gravis.

    b. Identify the drug that is used to treat this disorder and explain its effects.

9. a. List two types of acetylcholine receptors and briefly describe their characteristics.

    1.

    2.

    b. Circle the type of receptor that predominates in the CNS.

10. *Belladonna* means "pretty lady." Explain why atropine is referred to as a belladonna alkaloid.

11. Within minutes of receiving curare, what physical changes occur in the body? Explain how the drug works and describe its use in surgery.

12. To review some of the drugs that affect acetylcholine release and its synapses, study Table 4.2 in your text.

Learning Objective 4-5   Describe the monoaminergic pathways in the brain and the drugs that affect these neurons.

Read pages 113-121 and answer the following questions.

1. List and group by subclass the four transmitter substances that belong to the monoamine family. (See Table 4.3 in your text.)

    1.   3.

    2.   4.

2. Why do the monoamines affect widespread regions of the brain?

3. What are some of the functions in which dopaminergic neurons play a role?

4. Outline the synthesis of the catecholamines. Study Figure 4.13 in your text and name the

    a. precursor of both dopamine and norepinephrine.

    b. chemical that results when a hydroxyl group is added to tyrosine.

    c. enzyme that facilitates this addition.

    d. neurotransmitter that results when L-DOPA then looses a carboxyl group.

    e. neurotransmitter that results when a hydroxyl group is added to dopamine.

    f. enzyme that facilitates this addition.

5. List the three are most important systems of dopaminergic neurons. Note where their axons project and their functions. (Study Figure 4.14 in your text.)

    1.

    2.

    3.

6. Name and describe a serious disorder caused by the degeneration of dopaminergic neurons. What drug is effective in the treatment of this disorder and how does it work?

7. How does the drug AMPT interfere with the synthesis of dopamine?

8. What monoamine antagonist was discovered over three thousand years ago in India? How does it function?

9. Identify the two most common dopamine receptors and briefly describe their characteristics.

    1.

    2.

10. How do presynaptic autoreceptors suppers the production of dopamine?

11. What are the effects of a low dose of apomorphine? a high dose? (Study Figure 4.15 in your text.)

12. Which drugs inhibit the reuptake of dopamine?

13. What is the role of monoamine oxidase (MAO) found in

    1. terminal buttons? What is the effect of deprenyl? (See Figure 4.16 in your text.)

    2. blood?

14. Which drugs are used in the treatment of schizophrenia? Which dopamine receptors may be affected?

15. To review some of the drugs that affect dopaminergic synapses, see Table 4.4 in your text.

16. Adrenaline and _____ are synonymous, as are noradrenaline and _____.

17. a. Where does the final step in the synthesis of norepinephrine take place? Go on to explain how the synthesis occurs with the aid of an enzyme.

    b. How is the amount of norepinephrine affected by fusaric acid? moclobemide?

18. a. The cell bodies of the most important noradrenergic system begin in the _____ _____ a nucleus located in the dorsal _____. (See Figure 4.17 in your text.)

    b. What is the primary behavioral effect of activation of these neurons?

19. From what structures do noradrenergic neurons release the neurotransmitter? What is their appearance?

20. What are the effects of activation of α_1, α_2, and β adrenergic receptors?

21. To review some of the drugs that affect noradrenergic synapses, see Table 4.5 in your text.

22. Now outline the synthesis of serotonin (also called 5-HT, or 5-hydroxytryptophan). (Study Figure 4.18 in your text.) Name the

    a. precursor for serotonin.

    b. enzyme that adds a hydroxyl group to tryptophan.

    c. chemical that results from this addition.

    d. enzyme that removes a carboxyl group from 5-HTP resulting in serotonin.

23. How does PCPA affect this synthesis?

24. Where are the cell bodies of serotonergic neurons found in the brain? Which are the most important clusters? (See Figure 4.19 in your text.)

25. The D system originates in the _____ raphe nucleus. Its axonal fibers are _____ with spindle-shaped _____. The M system originates in the _____ raphe nucleus. Its axonal fibers are _____ with rounded _____. (See Figure 4.20 in your text.)

26. How many types of serotonin receptors have been identified? What are some of their behavioral roles?

27. List three drugs that interact with serotonin and describe their effects.

    1.

    2.

    3.

28. To review some of the drugs that affect serotonergic synapses, see Table 4.6 in your text.

Learning Objective 4-6   Review the role of neurons that release amino acid neurotransmitters and describe drugs that affect these neurons.

Read pages 121-125 and answer the following questions.

1. a. Approximately how many amino acids may serve as neurotransmitters in the mammalian central nervous system?

    b. List three that are especially important.

        1.   3.

        2.

c. List the two thought to have evolved first.

   1.   2.

d. Circle the one that is the principal excitatory neurotransmitter in the brain and spinal cord.

2.   a. List the four types of glutamate receptors.

   1.   3.

   2.   4.

b. Circle the most common glutamate receptor.

3.   What is the function of the AMPA receptor?

4.   a. How many binding sites are found on the NMDA receptor. (See Figure 4.21 in your text.)

   b. Explain the statement: The NMDA receptor is a voltage- and neurotransmitter-dependent ion channel.

   c. When the ion channel controlled by the NMDA receptor is open, sodium and calcium flow into the cell. Why is the entry of calcium so important?

5.   Explain how PCP affects ion channels on the NMDA receptor. (Review the behavioral symptoms of PCP summarized in Table 4.7 in your text. Other drugs that affect glutamate receptors are summarized in Table 4.8.)

6.   a. GABA is a(n) _____ neurotransmitter which is synthesized from _____

   _____ by the action of _____, an _____. The synthesis of GABA can be

   halted by _____. Two receptors, _____ and _____ have been identified.

   b. Explain how GABA is presumed to maintain stability in the brain and what happens when an abnormality in GABA-secreting neurons or GABA receptors occurs.

7.   Let's look at some of the binding sites on the GABA$_A$ receptor, shown in Figure 4.22 in your text, and some of the substances that bind with them.

   a. The principal binding site is for GABA. Which drug serves as a direct agonist for this site? a direct antagonist?

   b. Which drug(s) or class of drugs binds with the

      1. second site?   3. fourth site?

      2. third site?   4. fifth site?

   c. Which site may alcohol bind with?

8.   What is a therapeutic effect of taking benzodiazepines?

9.   What is the effect of low doses of barbiturates? high doses?

10.   Which drug has an effect opposite to that of benzodiazepines and barbiturates?

11.   a. What chemical may be the natural ligand for the benzodiazepine binding site?

   b. What are its behavioral effects and what do these effect suggest about the evolution of neuromodulators?

12. When the GABA$_B$ receptor is activated, what changes occur in the cell?

13. a. Where is glycine found and what is its principal effect?

    b. What are the pharmacological and behavioral effects of the following drugs?
       1. tetanus toxin

       2. strychnine?

Learning Objective 4-7   Describe the effects of peptides, lipids, nucleosides, and soluble gases released by neurons.

Read pages 125-128 and answer the following questions.

1. Peptides are produced in the _____ from _____ _____, which are large _____, which are broken apart by _____. Vesicles containing these chemicals are delivered to the terminal buttons by _____ _____. Once released peptides are destroyed by _____.

2. Define *endogenous opioid* and *enkephalin* in your own words.

3. If opiate receptors are stimulated, what kinds of events are affected?

4. How does naloxone affect these receptors and what are its practical uses?

5. What may be the function of peptides which are released with the neurotransmitter in many terminal buttons? Describe research to support your answer. (Table 4.9 in your text lists many important CNS peptides.)

6. a. Identify the active substance is marijuana and describe some of its effects.

    b. Identify the receptors stimulated by THC and their location. (See Figure 4.23 in your text. Matsuda et al., 1990)

    c. What is one of the substances that serve as a natural ligand for these receptors? (Devane et al., 1992)

    d. What observation led to the use of THC to control chemotherapy induced nausea and vomiting in young children? (Fride and Mechoulam, 1996; Abrahamov et al., 1995)

7. A nucleoside is a compound that consists of a(n) _____ _____ bound with a(n) _____ or _____ base.

8. One of these compounds is adenosine.

   a. When is it released?

   b. Which structures appear to release it? Why is it difficult to be more precise?

   c. In general, how does adenosine affect neural activity? Why?

   d. What common drug blocks adenosine receptors? (See Table 4.10 in your text.)

9. a. List two soluble gases involved in neural communication.

   1.   2.

   b. Which bodily functions are affected by nitric oxide? (Culotta and Koshland, 1992)

   c. Where is nitric oxide produced, how quickly does it diffuse, and how long is it present in nearby cells?

Lesson II Self Test

1. Most neural communication involves the release of either _____, an inhibitory neurotransmitter or _____, an excitatory neurotransmitter.

   a. epinephrine; norepinephrine
   b. GABA; glutamate
   c. glycine; glutamate
   c. acetylcholine; GABA

2. Which of the following statements about acetylcholine is false?

   a. It was the first neurotransmitter to be discovered.
   b. All muscle movement is accomplished by the release of acetylcholine.
   c. It is deactivated by choline acetyltransferase (ChAT) into its components, acetate and choline.
   d. Once deactivated, choline is returned to the terminal buttons and recycled.

3. _____ blocks muscarinic receptors and _____ blocks nicotinic receptors.

   a. Curare; atropine
   b. Apomorphine; physostigmine
   c. Atropine; curare
   d. Tyrosine; atropine

4. The four monoamines are

   a. epinephrine, norepinephrine, dopamine, and serotonin.
   b. GABA, glycine, glutamate, and serotonin.
   c. dopamine, L-DOPA, epinephrine, and norepinephrine.
   d. tyrosine, glycine, reserpine, and catecholamine.

5. The precursor of dopamine and norepinephrine is _____, and their synthesis is interrupted by _____.

   a. atropine; reserpine
   b. tryptophan; deprenyl
   c. adenosine; neostigmine
   d. tyrosine; AMPT

6. Axonal varicosities _____ norepinephrine.

a. synthesize
b. release
c. recycle
d. deactivate

7. The hallucinogenic drug LSD produces its effect by interacting with the activity of

a. epinephrine.
b. serotonin.
c. GABA.
d. acetylcholine.

8. NMDA receptors, AMPA receptors, and kainate receptors all respond to

a. serotonin.
b. GABA.
c. glutamate.
d. glycine

9. One of the necessary conditions for the NMDA receptor to open is _____.

a. the presence of glycine
b. the presence of zinc
c. the binding of calcium with certain enzymes in the cell

d. the attachment of magnesium to the magnesium binding site

10. Benzodiazepines bind with _____ receptors and _____.

a. GABA$_A$; have an anxiolytic effect
b. glycine; and are anticonvulsive drugs
c. GABA$_B$; have a tranquilizing effect
d. glutamate; are used to treat seizure disorders

11. Many peptides that are released along with a neurotransmitter may serve to regulate the

a. sensitivity of presynaptic or postsynaptic receptors to the neurotransmitter.
b. reuptake of the neurotransmitter.
c. axoplasmic flow to the terminal buttons.
d. metabolism of the brain.

12. Endogenous opioids are

a. byproducts of neurotransmitter synthesis.
b. steroids synthesized from cholesterol.
c. neuromodulators produced in the brain.
d. hormones secreted not only by the brain but by many other tissues of the body.

Answers for Self Tests

Lesson I

1. a Obj. 4-1
2. c Obj. 4-1
3. b Obj. 4-1
4. c Obj. 4-2
5. a Obj. 4-2
6. c Obj. 4-2
7. b Obj. 4-3
8. c Obj. 4-3
9. c Obj. 4-3
10. d Obj. 4-3
11. a Obj. 4-3
12. d Obj. 4-3

Lesson II

1. b Obj. 4-4
2. c Obj. 4-4
3. c Obj. 4-4
4. a Obj. 4-5
5. d Obj. 4-5
6. b Obj. 4-5
7. b Obj. 4-5
8. c Obj. 4-6
9. a Obj. 4-6
10. a Obj. 4-6
11. a Obj. 4-7
12. c Obj. 4-7

CHAPTER 5
Methods and Strategies of Research

Lesson I: Experimental Ablation

Read the interim summary on pages 142-144 of your text to re-acquaint yourself with the material in this section.

> *Learning Objective 5-1*   Discuss the research method of experimental ablation: the rationale, the evaluation of behavioral effects resulting from brain damage, and the production of brain lesions.

Read pages 131-134 and answer the following questions.

1. Define *experimental ablation* in your own words. (Be sure to note a synonym for this term.)

2. Now explain its rationale.

3. a. Distinguish between *brain function* and *behavior* and explain why this distinction is important in interpreting research results.

    b. What anatomical difficulty do researchers encounter in interpreting results of lesion studies?

4. Briefly describe and compare research techniques used to produce brain lesions.

    a. Suction

       1. procedure

       2. selectivity

    b. Radio frequency (RF) current (See Figure 5.1 in your text.)

       1. procedure

       2. selectivity

    c. Excitatory amino acids such as kainic acid that produce excitotoxic lesions (See Figure 5.2 in your text.)

      1. procedure

      2. selectivity

    d. Drugs such as 6-hydroxydopamine (6-HD)

      1. procedure

      2. selectivity

5.   Whenever subcortical regions are destroyed, what other kind of damage is unavoidable?

6.   What procedure do researchers follow to try to determine whether this damage has affected their results? (Be sure to use the term *sham lesion* in your answer.)

7.   Now briefly describe how brain activity can be temporarily interrupted using local anesthetics or cooling techniques. (See Figure 5.3 in your text.)

Learning Objective 5-2   Describe stereotaxic surgery.

Read pages 134-136 and answer the following questions.

1.   Name the instrument and the reference book researchers use during stereotaxic surgery.

2.   a. Describe the contents and organization of a stereotaxic atlas.

    b. Now describe how a researcher uses the atlas to locate a subcortical brain structure. Be sure to use the term *bregma* in your answer. (See Figures 5.4 and 5.5 in your text.)

    c. Why are the locations described in stereotaxic atlases only approximate?

3.   Study Figure 5.6 in your text and describe a stereotaxic apparatus.

4. How is an animal prepared and positioned for surgery?

5. List several uses of stereotaxic surgery.

Learning Objective 5-3   Describe research methods for preserving, sectioning, and staining the brain and for studying its parts and interconnections.

Read pages 136-138 and answer the following questions.

1. Why do researchers use histological methods to prepare brain tissue for microscopic examination?

2. After the brain is removed from the skull, it is placed in a _____ such as _____, which _____ the tissue, halts _____ and kills any _____ that might destroy it.

3. Why is tissue usually perfused before placing it in a fixative?

4. Study Figure 5.7 in your text and describe a microtome and its function.

5. Briefly explain how neural tissue is prepared for staining.

6. Explain why brain tissue must be stained.

7. If a researcher stains neural tissue with cresyl violet, what kind of material will take up the stain? (See Figure 5.8 in your text.)

8. a. When do researchers use an electron microscope rather than a light microscope?

    b. In general, how do electron microscopes and scanning electron microscopes produce images?

    c. Study Figure 5.9 and 5.10 in your text and compare those images.

Learning Objective 5-4   Describe research methods for tracing efferent and afferent axons and for studying the living human brain.

Read pages 138-142 and answer the following questions.

1. Sometimes a researcher may wish to trace pathways of *efferent* axons—that is, those that leave a particular brain structure—in order to learn more about how that structure may ultimately influence behavior.

    a. What is the general name for all techniques used for this purpose?

    b. Write a description of the method that uses PHA-L using the following phrases, some of which are shown in Figures 5.12 in your text.

    travel by means of fast axoplasmic transport
    into the brain structure being studied
    examine tissue under the microscope
    molecules of PHA-L are taken up by dendrites
    to the terminal buttons
    transported through the soma to the axon

    cells are filled with molecules of PHA-L
    slice and mount the brain tissue
    use an immunocytochemical method
    inject a minute quantity of PHA-L
    kill the animal
    within a few days

    c. Carefully explain how immunocytochemical methods make use of our knowledge of the role of proteins, antibodies, and antigens in the immune system. (Study Figure 5.13 in your text.)

2. Researchers must also trace pathways of *afferent* axons; that is, those that lead to a particular brain structure.

    a. What is the general name for all techniques used for this purpose?

    b. Name a chemical used to trace afferent axons and the means by which it is transported to the cell bodies. Some results are shown in Figures 5.14 and 5.15 in your text.

3. How has the development of computerized tomography (CT) and magnetic resonance imaging (MRI) overcome some of the earlier difficulties inherent in studying the human brain? (See Figures 5.16 in your text.)

4. Compare and contrast computerized tomography and MRI. (An example of a CT scan in shown in Figure 5.17 in your text and an example of a MRI scan is shown in Figure 5.18.)

    a. procedure used to obtain a scan

    b. details shown in scans

5. To review: All the research methods discussed in this section are summarized in Table 5.1 in your text.

Lesson I Self Test

1. The results of lesion studies are often difficult to interpret because

   a. a particular neural circuit can perform only one behavior.
   b. directly or indirectly, all regions of the brain are interconnected.
   c. sometimes there is no clear difference between behavior and function.
   d. the effects of surgical anesthesia cannot be determined.

2. Which of these methods produces the most selective brain lesions?

   a. suction
   b. microdialysis
   c. excitatory amino acids
   d. radio frequency current

3. To account for incidental brain damage when lesions are produced, researchers

   a. increase the number of animals in the study.
   b. use equal numbers of male and female animals.
   c. produce sham lesions.
   d. repeat the study.

4. A temporary or "reversible" brain lesion can be produced using

   a. very low doses of an excitatory amino acid.
   b. a local anesthetic.
   c. electrical current on only one side of the brain.
   d. a very brief interruption in the blood supply.

5. Using a stereotaxic apparatus, researchers can

   a. assess loss of function resulting from brain lesions.
   b. slice brains for histological examination.
   c. make subcortical lesions in the brain.
   d. confirm the location of brain lesions.

6. Using a stereotaxic atlas, researchers can

   a. locate bregma.
   b. determine the approximate location of structures deep within the brain.
   c. calculate the correct amount of anesthesia required.

   d. determine which method of making brain lesions to use.

7. A fixative performs all these functions *except*

   a. attaching tissue to a microscope slide.
   b. halting autolysis.
   c. hardening tissue.
   d. killing destructive microorganisms.

8. Using a microtome, researchers can

   a. apply a mounting medium.
   b. dry and heat tissue.
   c. examine and photograph stained and mounted brain sections.
   d. slice tissue into thin sections.

9. Scanning electron microscopes produce

   a. moving images that can be preserved on video cassettes.
   b. images cast on glass slides that can also be examined with a light microscope.
   c. images of three dimensional structures.
   d. images of tissue that cannot be exposed to light.

10. _____ labeling methods are used to trace _____ axons which carry information _____ a brain structure.

    a. Retrograde; afferent; toward
    b. Anterograde; afferent; away from
    c. Retrograde; efferent; away from
    d. Anterograde; afferent; toward

11. Immunocytochemical methods are used to

    a. locate peptides and proteins.
    b. provide a view of a "slice" of the human brain.
    c. selectively destroy axons.
    d. inhibit fast axoplasmic transport.

12. Researchers using CT or MRI

    a. do not have to obtain permission from either the patient or the family.
    b. can study the living brain without operating on the patient.
    c. must first anesthetize the patient.
    d. must first shave the patient's head.

Lesson II: Recording and Stimulating Neural Activity, Neurochemical Methods, and Genetic Methods

Read the interim summary on pages 152-153 of your text to re-acquaint yourself with the material in this section.

Learning Objective 5-5   Describe how the neural activity of the brain is measured and recorded, both electrically and chemically.

Read pages 144-150 and answer the following questions.

1. To review: List the two types of electrical events in the brain that can be recorded.

    1.   2.

2. Compare the duration and behavioral state of the animal during chronic and acute recordings.

3. Explain what the phrase *single-unit recording* means.

4. Describe the preparation for recording the neural activity of individual neurons in the brain.

    a. How are microelectrodes of glass and tungsten wire made? (See Figure 5.19 in your text.)

    b. How are these electrodes implanted in the brain? (See Figure 5.20 in your text.)

    c. How are the electrical signals detected by the microelectrodes recorded?

5. How does the preparation change for recording the neural activity of a whole region of the brain? Be sure to describe macroelectrodes in your answer.

6. a. Describe two ways to measure the electrical activity of the human brain.

    b. By studying these records of electrical patterns, called electroencephalograms, what can researchers learn? (See Figures 5.21 and 5.22 in your text.)

7. a. In addition to the electrical activity of the brain, what other sign of neural activity can be measured?

    b. Explain the role of 2-deoxyglucose (2-DG) in measuring the metabolic activity of the brain.

    c. Explain how autoradiographs are prepared. (See Figure 5.23 in your text.)

8. a. How are nuclear proteins produced and what do they indicate?

    b. Describe the procedure that detects the presence of Fos and explain what is shown in Figure 5.24 in your text.

9. a. Explain how the metabolic activity of the human brain is measured using positron emission tomography (PET). (See Figure 5.25 in your text.)

    b. What is one of the reasons why PET scanners are expensive to use?

10. Explain several advantages of functional magnetic resonance imaging (fMRI). (See Figure 5.26 in your text.)

11. Study Figure 5.27 in your text and then carefully explain how neurochemicals can be detected using microdialysis.

12. How can neurochemicals be measured in the human brain by means of a noninvasive technique? (See Figure 5.28 in your text)

Learning Objective 5-6   Describe how neural activity in the brain is stimulated, both chemically and electrically and the behavioral effects of electrical brain stimulation.

Read pages 150-152 and answer the following questions.

1. List two ways that neurons can be artificially stimulated.

    1.   2.

2. Briefly explain both procedures, mentioning any advantages and disadvantages. (See Figure 5.29 in your text.)

3. a. Describe how extremely small quantities of a substance are discharged through a multibarreled micropipette which is illustrated in Figure 5.30 in your text.

    b. How is neural activity recorded during microiontophoresis?

4. List three uses of electrical brain stimulation.

    1.   3.

    2.

5. Identify and briefly discuss some of the difficulties in interpreting the significance of behavioral changes elicited by electrical brain stimulation.

6. a. Why are patients undergoing open-head surgery to remove a seizure focus not given a general anesthetic?

    b. How do surgeons determine the function of neural tissue near the seizure focus?

    c. How did Penfield, who developed this treatment for focal seizure disorder, use the data he obtained using electrical brain stimulation? (See Figure 5.31 in your text.)

7. To review: All the research methods discussed in this section are summarized in Table 5.2 in your text.

Read the interim summary on page 157 of your text to re-acquaint yourself with the material in this section

> *Learning Objective 5-7*   Describe research methods for locating particular neurochemicals, the neurons that produce them, and the receptors that respond to them.

Read pages 153-157 and answer the following questions.

1. Let's follow the example of the effects of organophosphate insecticides to learn how researchers look for a particular neurochemical and, at the same time, review information about acetylcholine.

    a. State the two hypotheses that could explain why organophosphate insecticides disrupt dreaming.

    b. Which one of these is correct?

    c. Carefully explain how acetylcholinesterase inhibitors such as the organophosphate insecticides affect the brain.

    d. Further research is still needed to determine in which region of the brain the acetylcholinergic synapses are affected. Outline three possible strategies to search for the affected region.

2. Now outline three ways to search for a particular neurochemical.

3. a. Briefly explain how brain tissue is prepared using immunocytochemical methods. (See Figure 5.32 in your text.)

    b. Which one of the ways outlined in question 2 can be studied using immunocytochemical methods?

c. Name the enzyme involved in the synthesis of acetylcholine and explain how it is identified using immunocytochemical methods. (See Figure 5.33 in your text.)

4. a. Which one of the ways outlined in question 2 can be studied using in situ hybridization?

b. Study Figures 5.34 and 5.35 in your text and briefly explain how in situ hybridization is used to find the location of a particular messenger RNA.

c. In addition to location, what other information does this method provide?

5. List and briefly describe two methods that are used to search for receptors. (See Figure 5.36 in your text.)

6. Explain how we can verify that neurons in the VMH contain receptors for ovarian sex hormones by using autoradiography or immunocytochemistry.

7. What kinds of information can be obtained using double labeling? (See Figure 5.37 in your text.)

8. To review: All the research methods discussed in this section are summarized in Table 5.3 in your text.

Read the interim summary on page 159 of your text to re-acquaint yourself with the material in this section.

| *Learning Objective 5-8*   Discuss research techniques to identify genetic factors that may influence behavior. |

Read pages 157-159 and answer the following questions.

1. List the two factors that interact to determine behavior.

   1.   2.

2. What method is particularly useful in estimating the role of heredity on a particular trait?

3. What do we mean when we say that a pair of twins is concordant for a trait? discordant for a trait?

4. Explain why monozygotic twins have a higher concordance rate for genetically controlled traits than do dyzygotic twins.

5. Let's look at another method of estimating the influence of heredity on a particular trait. In an adoption study,

   a. which two groups of people are adopted people compared with?

   b. what kinds of information must the researcher obtain in order to use this method?

6. What will researchers conclude about the factors that influence a trait if adopted people strongly resemble their biological parents? their adoptive parents? both sets of parents?

7. What are targeted mutations, and what are some of their "targets"?

Lesson II Self Test

1. 2-deoxyglucose is

   a. found in the membrane of cells.
   b. a nuclear protein.
   c. the preferred fuel of the brain.
   d. not metabolized by cells.

2. An electroencephalogram is a

   a. microscope slide of radioactivity in the brain.
   b. paper or computerized record of electrical activity in the brain.
   c. x-ray record of normal or abnormal brain tissue.
   d. treated photographic film showing receptor location.

3. The metabolic activity in the brain of a laboratory animal can be measured by giving an injection of _____ and analyzing the results using _____.

   a. Fos; PET scanner
   b. 2-DG; autoradiography
   c. fluorogold; high-performance liquid chromatography

   d. saline; electroencephalography

4. Microdialysis is used to measure the

   a. permeability of the cell membrane.
   b. intracranial pressure.
   c. secretions of the brain.
   d. electrical activity of the brain.

5. An advantage of chemical stimulation over electrical stimulation of the brain is that

   a. it requires less equipment.
   b. stereotaxic surgery is not necessary.
   c. the effects are more localized.
   d. no tissue is destroyed.

6. To study the effect of chemicals on the activity of a single cell researchers use

   a. microiontophoresis.
   b. in situ hybridization.
   c. single-unit recording.
   d. autoradiography.

7. One of the difficulties in using electrical brain stimulation as a research tool is stimulation

    a. sometimes causes neurotransmitters to be released.
    b. is difficult to localize.
    c. must always be administered during open head procedures.
    d. can never duplicate natural neural processes.

8. To identify neurons producing a particular peptide, researchers use _____ methods.

    a. immunocytochemical
    b. anterograde tracing
    c. autoradiographic
    d. retrograde tracing

9. To search for a particular messenger RNA, researchers use

    a. the Fos protein.
    b. autoradiography.
    c. in situ hybridization.
    d. 2-DG.

10. Double labeling techniques permit researchers to determine what chemicals a neuron contains and

    a. their connections with other neurons.
    b. the enzymes that produce them.
    c. the messenger RNA involved in their synthesis.
    d. nearby agonists or antagonists.

11. In adoption studies, the heritability of a particular behavioral trait is determined by comparing adopted people with

    a. other adopted people matched for that trait.
    b. other people matched for that trait, but who were raised by their biological parents.
    c. their biological and adoptive parents.
    d. their biological siblings, but not other children in their adoptive families.

12. Targeted mutations are deliberately mutated genes that

    a. interrupt the immune reaction.
    b. inactivate enzymes.
    c. fail to produce a functional protein.
    d. increase protein synthesis.

Answers for Self Tests

	Lesson I	
1.	b	Obj. 5-1
2.	c	Obj. 5-1
3.	c	Obj. 5-1
4.	b	Obj. 5-1
5.	c	Obj. 5-2
6.	b	Obj. 5-2
7.	a	Obj. 5-3
8.	d	Obj. 5-3
9.	c	Obj. 5-3
10.	a	Obj. 5-4
11.	a	Obj. 5-4
12.	b	Obj. 5-4

	Lesson II	
1.	d	Obj. 5-5
2.	b	Obj. 5-5
3.	b	Obj. 5-5
4.	c	Obj. 5-5
5.	c	Obj. 5-6
6.	a	Obj. 5-6
7.	d	Obj. 5-6
8.	a	Obj. 5-7
9.	c	Obj. 5-7
10.	a	Obj. 5-7
11.	c	Obj. 5-8
12.	c	Obj. 5-8

CHAPTER 6
Vision

Lesson I: Anatomy of the Visual System and Coding of Visual Information in the Retina

Read the interim summary on page 169 of your text to re-acquaint yourself with the material in this section.

> **Learning Objective 6-1** Describe the characteristics of light and color, outline the anatomy of the eye and its connections with the brain, and describe the transduction of visual information.

Read pages 161-169 and answer the following questions.

1. a. We receive information about the environment from sensory receptors. What is the name of the process by which stimuli are detected by these receptors? What is the name of the electrical change in the cells' membrane?

    b. If these receptors lack axons, how do they form synapses with other neurons?

2. _____ is that portion of the electromagnetic spectrum that we humans can see. Light travels at a

    constant speed of _____ per second and the wavelength of visible light determines one of the

    perceptual dimensions of color, the _____. When the intensity of the electromagnetic signal

    increases, we perceive that the _____ of the color has increased. The degree of _____ of

    a color depends on the purity of the light. (See Figures 6.1 and 6.2 in your text.)

3. List the three types of movement that eyes make and describe them briefly.

    1.

    2.

    3.

4. Begin a review of the anatomy of the eye by studying Figures 6.3 and 6.4 in your text.

    a. Name the bony pockets in the front of the skull that surround the eyes.

b. What holds the eyes in place and moves them.

c. Name the white outer layer of the eye.

d. Name the mucous membranes that line the eyelid.

e. Light enters through which layer of the eye?

f. Describe how the amount of light that enters the eye is regulated.

g. Describe the lens and explain the process of accommodation.

h. Name the substance between the lens and retina that gives the eye its volume.

i. Name the light-sensitive region of the back of the eye.

5. List the characteristics of the specialized photoreceptors—the rods and the cones—in Table 1 below. (See Table 6.1 in your text.)

	Cones	Rods
Number		
Location		
Sensitive to what kind of light?		
Role in visual acuity		
Role in color vision		

Table 1

6. Label the parts of the eye in Figure 1, below.

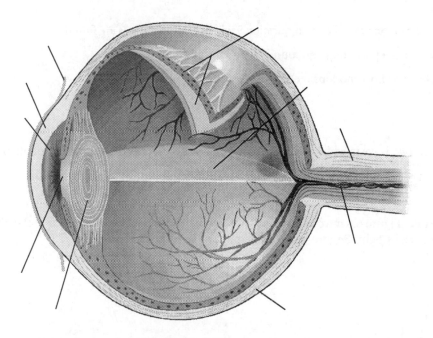

Figure 1

7. Explain why the optic disk is called the blind spot. Be sure to try the demonstration in Figure 6.5 in your text.

8. a. Study Figure 6.6 in your text and list the three primary layers of the retina.

    1.   3.

    2.

    b. Where are the photoreceptors located in relation to these layers and to the direction of entering light?

    c. Photoreceptors form synapses with _____ _____, which form synapses with _____ _____.

    d. Name two other kinds of cells found in the retina.

    1.   2.

9. Study Figure 6.7 in your text for a closer look at the anatomy of photoreceptors. Sketch a rod and a cone and label their parts.

10. Now let's follow the process of visual perception step by step. We will begin with the role of the photopigments.

    a. List the two components of photopigments.

    1.   2.

    b. Indicate on your sketch in question 9 where photopigments are found.

    c. Name the photopigment found in human rods.

    d. Describe how rhodopsin changes when it is exposed to light.

    e. List two ways in which the membrane of photoreceptors differs from that of other neurons. (Baylor, 1996)

    1.   2.

    f. Study Figure 6.8 in your text and carefully explain the changes that occur in the photoreceptor when it is struck by light. Be sure to use the term *transducin* in your answer.

11. Now let's continue by studying the neural circuit from the photoreceptors to the ganglion cells.

    a. Study Figure 6.9 in your text and list the first two types of cells in this circuit.

    1.   2.

b. Light _____ polarizes the photoreceptors and _____ polarizes the bipolar cells.

c. What happens to the firing rate of ganglion cells when this occurs?

12. Axons of the retinal ganglion cell ascend through the optic nerves to which part of the brain?

13. a. What is the name of the inner two layers of neurons in the lateral geniculate nucleus? the outer four layers? (See Figure 6.10 in your text.)

b. What do these names indicate about the size of the cells found there?

14. a. To what region of the cerebral cortex do axons of neurons in the dorsal lateral geniculate nucleus project?

b. Where is this region located?

c. Study Figure 6.11 in your text and explain why the primary visual cortex is sometimes called the striate cortex.

15. Study Figure 6.12 in your text to review the primary visual pathway in more detail. Describe the route of the optic nerves on the inner and outer halves of the retina to primary visual cortex.

16. a. If a person looks straight ahead, the right hemisphere receives information from the _____ side of the visual field and the left hemisphere receives information from the _____.

b. Explain why the previous statement is true. Be sure to explain the role of the lens in your answer.

17. Identify and briefly describe the functions of several other pathways from the retina.

Read the interim summary on pages 175-176 of your text to re-acquaint yourself with the material in this section.

Learning Objective 6-2   Describe the coding of visual information by photoreceptors and ganglion cells in the retina.

Read pages 169-175 and answer the following questions.

1. a. Define the *receptive field* of a neuron in your own words.

b. Using the term receptive field, explain why foveal vision is especially acute. (See Figure 6.13 in your text.)

2. List and describe

a. the response pattern of ganglion cells in the frog retina, discovered by Hartline (1938).

b. the response pattern of ganglion cells in the cat retina, discovered by Kuffler (1952, 1953). (See Figure 6.14 in your text.)

c. the connections of ON/OFF cells in the primate retina. (Schiller and Malpeli, 1977)

3. Why could the firing patterns of ON and OFF cells be described as efficient?

4. a. When monkeys were given an injection of APB, a drug that blocks synaptic transmission in ON bipolar cells, what kind of stimuli did they have difficulty detecting? did not have difficulty detecting? (Schiller et al., 1986)

    b. Explain why we can conclude that rod bipolar cells in the monkey retina must be ON cells. (Dolan and Schiller, 1989)

5. a. Describe a phenomenon that results from the center-surround organization of the receptive fields of ganglion cells. (Look at Figure 6.15 for an example.)

    b. Study Figure 6.16 and explain how this phenomenon works.

6. State two advantages of color vision. (Mollon, 1989)

7. Briefly state Thomas Young's theory of color vision.

8. Before continuing, study Figure 6.17 in your text and explain the difference between color mixing and pigment mixing.

9. Briefly state Ewald Hering's theory of color vision.

10. What two problems with the Young theory did Hering's theory overcome?

    1.

    2.

11. a. Later research with photoreceptors in the retina proved Young was right. Study Figure 6.18 in your text and explain the relationship between the particular opsins found in retinal photoreceptors and color vision.

    b. List the three types of cones found in the retina and compare their relative numbers.

    1.   3.

    2

12. Supply characteristics for these three genetic defects in color vision.

Defect	Description	Visual Acuity
Protanopia		
Deuteranopia		
Tritanopia		

13. Retinal ganglion cells respond to _____ of opposing primary colors, thus there are two kinds of

    color-sensitive cells _____-_____ and _____-_____.

14. Describe the typical response pattern of color-sensitive and "black and white" retinal ganglion cells. (Study Figure 6.19 in your text.)

15. Study Figure 6.20 in your text and describe how retinal ganglion cells code different wavelengths of light detected by the cones.

    a. How does red light affect

    1. red cones?   2. red-green ganglion cells?

    b. How does green light affect

    1. green cones?   2. red-green ganglion cells?

    c. How does yellow light affect

    1. red and green cones?   3. red-green ganglion cells?

    2. yellow-blue ganglion cells?

    d. How does blue light affect

    1. blue cones?

    2. yellow-blue ganglion cells?

16. Now explain why we can see (and imagine) a yellowish red but not a bluish yellow.

17. Explain why you will see a red and green radish on the right of Figure 6.21 after staring at the left side for thirty seconds.

Read the interim summary on pages 183-184 of your text to re-acquaint yourself with the material in this section.

Learning Objective 6-3   Discuss the striate cortex and discuss how its neurons respond to orientation and movement, spatial frequency, and texture.

Read pages 176-180 and answer the following questions.

1. Look back at Figure 6.11 and at Figure 6.22 and review the appearance of striate cortex.

2. a. What nucleus of the thalamus sends visual information to the middle layer (layer 4c) of striate cortex?

    b. What region sends visual information to layers 2 and 3?

3. Approximately what percentage of the striate cortex analyzes information from the fovea?

4. What discovery by Hubel and Wiesel (1977, 1979) revolutionized the study of the physiology of visual perception?

5. Study Figure 6.23 in your text and explain what is meant when we say, "Most neurons in the striate cortex are sensitive to orientation."

6. Study Figure 6.24 in your text and compare the responses of simple and complex cells to various line orientations and backgrounds as well as movement.

7. Explain the importance of sine-wave gratings in visual detection. (See Figure 6.25 in your text. De Valois et al., 1978)

8. a. Study Figure 6.26 in your text and explain the concept of visual angle.

    b. Go on to explain its relationship to the spatial frequency of a sine-wave grating.

9. Summarize research on the receptive fields of simple cells by Albrecht (1978).

    a. Describe or sketch the stimulus. (Study Figure 6.27 in your text.)

    b. How did the cells respond to the moving stimulus?

c. What did the response pattern resemble?

10. Compare the spatial frequencies that indicate small objects or large objects with sharp edges and large areas of light and dark.

11. a. The most important visual information for object recognition is contained in _____ spatial frequencies.

b. Compare the photographs of Abraham Lincoln in Figure 6.28 in your text and explain how the figure on the left was created. (Harmon and Julesz, 1973) You may want to try the demonstration as you answer this question.

c. Explain how these figures confirm the statement in question 11a.

12. a. Describe the stimuli that the new class of neurons in the monkey striate cortex respond to best? (See Figure 6.29 in your text. (von der Heydt et al., 1992)

c. What may be their function?

Learning Objective 6-4   Discuss how neurons in the striate cortex respond to retinal disparity and color; explain the modular organization of striate cortex and the phenomenon of blindsight.

Read pages 180-184 and answer the following questions.

1. a. List some of the cues we can observe using only one eye that help us determine depth.

b. Describe how we also determine depth through stereopsis, using cues that we observe with both eyes. Be sure to explain the concept of retinal disparity in your answer.

2. a. What observation led Wong-Riley (1978) to discover blobs?

b. Within the striate cortex, where are blobs found? See Figure 6.31 and describe their appearance.

c. How has the role of the parvocellular system in color vision been recently revised? (Hendry and Yoshioka, 1994; Martin et al., 1997; Komatsu, 1998)

3. The brain is most likely organized in _____. The striate cortex consists of approximately 2500

_____, each containing about _____ neurons. These modules consist of two segments

each centered around a _____. Each half of the module receives input from only _____

_____, but the module combines the information from both eyes making most of the neurons

_____.

4. What is the function of neurons within a CO blob? neurons outside the CO blobs? (Livingstone and Hubel, 1984; Born and Tootell, 1991; Edwards et al. 1995)

5. What have recordings revealed about the

   a. arrangement of the receptive fields of all the neurons of a module?

   b. region of the visual field that all the neurons of a module analyze?

   c. kinds of cells found in the interblob region?

   d. orientation sensitivity of cells in the interblob region?

   e. the percentage of input from each eye to each neuron in the interblob region? Be sure to use the term *ocular dominance* in your answer. (Study Figure 6.32 in your text.)

6. Summarize Blasdel's (1992a, 1992b) research on the organization of modules in monkeys.

   a. Briefly describe his preparations for electrical recordings.

   b. Describe his findings about the organization of orientation-sensitive cells shown in Figure 6.33a in your text.

   c. Explain the relationship between ocular dominance and orientation sensitivity of cells shown in Figure 6.33b.

7. Study Figure 6.34 in your text and explain how the response to spatial frequency by neurons found inside and outside the CO blobs varied. (Edwards et al., 1995)

8. a. What is the cause of cortical blindness and how does it affect vision?

   b. In spite of their affliction, how do these patients respond to a request to reach for an object in their blind field? (Weiskrantz et al., 1974; Weiskrantz, 1987)

   c. What is their response to their actions?

   d. What other stimuli do they respond to?

   e. What is a possible explanation for blindsight and what does it suggest about conscious awareness? (Cowey and Stoerig, 1991)

Lesson I Self Test

1. If a color is fully saturated, the radiation contains

    a. all wavelengths.
    b. one wavelength.
    c. wavelengths beyond the visible spectrum.
    d. a mixture of wavelengths from a specific band of the spectrum.

2. Optic nerves join together at the _____, where half of the axons cross to the opposite side of the brain.

    a. calcarine fissure
    b. optic chiasm
    c. optic disk
    d. striate cortex

3. The first step in visual perception occurs when light

    a. causes a photopigment to split into its two constituents.
    b. enters the sclera.
    c. reaches the brain through the optic chiasm.
    d. causes a change in the receptor potential of the photoreceptor.

4. Foveal vision is more acute than peripheral vision because

    a. the receptor-to-axon relationships are approximately equal in the fovea.
    b. its photoreceptors respond more quickly to changes in illumination.
    c. its receptive field is near the fixation point.
    d. its ganglion cells fire continuously.

5. Kuffler found that the receptive field of cat ganglion cells resembles

    a. a mosaic.
    b. a circle surrounded by a ring.
    c. staggered columns.
    d. CO blobs.

6. Retinal ganglion cells use a(n) _____ coding system.

    a. trichromatic
    b. relative brightness
    c. opponent-process
    d. black and white

7. Hubel and Wiesel first suggested that orientation-sensitive neurons in the visual cortex responds best to _____, but other research indicates the best stimulus is _____.

    a. lines and edges; spots
    b. low spatial frequencies; high spatial frequencies.
    c. lines and edges; sine-wave gratings
    d. sine-wave gratings; spots

8. When low frequency information is removed from an image of an object, it becomes

    a. easier to identify.
    b. more difficult to identify.
    c. easier to identify if it is moved closer.
    d. more difficult to identify if it is moved closer.

9. Neurons that respond to "periodic patterns" are probably used to perceive

    a. surface texture.
    b. depth.
    c. color.
    d. high contrast images.

10. CO blobs

    a. were discovered in the modules of prestriate cortex.
    b. are organized in ovals within a module.
    c. contain color sensitive neurons.
    d. analyze information from the entire visual scene.

11. Retinal disparity helps us to recognize

    a. shapes and patterns.
    b. depth.
    c. density.
    d. right and left.

12. The phenomenon of blindsight suggests that

    a. neurons sensitive to orientation can supply enough information to maintain skills such as reaching for an object.
    b. the ability to reach successfully for an object was an early evolutionary response that has survived somewhat independently of the primate visual system.
    c. damage to the primary visual cortex or optic radiations does not disrupt ocular dominance.
    d. visual information can control behavior without producing a conscious sensation.

Lesson II: Analysis of Visual Information: Role of the Striate Cortex and the Visual Association Cortex

Read the interim summary on pages 198-199 of your text to re-acquaint yourself with the material in this section.

Learning Objective 6-5   Describe the anatomy of the visual association cortex and discuss the location and functions of the two streams of visual analysis that take place there.

Read pages 184-185 and answer the following questions.

1.   a.   Both streams of visual analysis of visual association cortex begin in the _____ _____,

     but begin to diverge in the _____ _____.

     b.   Where does the ventral stream end? (Study Figure 6.35 in your text.) What is its primary function?

     c.   Where does the dorsal stream end? What is its primary function?

2.   Summarize the characteristics and functions of the parvocellular, magnocellular, and koniocellular divisions of the visual system by completing Table 2. (Study Table 6.2 in your text.)

Property	Magnocellular division	Parvocellular division	Koniocellular division
Color			
Sensitivity to contrast			
Spatial resolution			
Temporal resolution			

Table 2

3.   Which systems are found in all mammals? in only primates?

4.   From which system(s) do(es) the dorsal stream receive its information? the ventral stream? (Maunsell, 1992)

5.   a.   Describe the location of extrastriate cortex. (Zeki and Shipp, 1988)

     b.   Briefly describe the organization of extrastriate cortex. Beginning with the striate cortex, describe the flow of information through the visual association cortex. (Van Essen et al., 1992)

Learning Objective 6-6   Discuss the perception of color and the analysis of form by neurons in the ventral stream.

Read pages 185-189 and answer the following questions.

1. How do neurons in CO blobs in the striate cortex respond to color? neurons in subarea V4 of extrastriate cortex? Compare the response characteristics to color by neurons in the blobs and neurons in subarea V4 of extrastriate cortex in the monkey. (Zeki, 1980)

2. Describe the phenomenon of color constancy in your own words.

3. Now describe research on color constancy in neurons in subarea V4 in monkey extrastriate cortex. (Schein and Desimone, 1990).

    a. What kind of stimuli did neurons in the primary receptive field of area V4 respond to?

    b. How did stimuli in the secondary receptive field influence the response to stimuli in the primary receptive field of neurons in subarea V4?

    c. What do these responses suggest about color constancy?

4. What did Walsh et al. (1993) conclude after studying the response to color by damaged neurons in area V4?

5. a. Describe the location of area TEO.

    b. When area TEO was destroyed, what severe deficit did monkeys exhibit? (Heywood et al., 1995)

    c. What, then, may be the function of area TEO?

6. What may account for the fact that humans from many cultures as well as chimpanzees classify colors the same way? (Boynton and Olson, 1987; Uchikawa and Boynton, 1987; Matuzawa, 1985; Komatsu, 1997)

7. a. What kind of brain damage results in achromatopsia?

    b. How is vision affected? (Damasio et al., 1980; Kennard et al., 1995)

8. What region corresponding to area TEO in monkeys did Hadjikhani et al. (1998) identify using fMRI? (See Figure 6.36 in your text.)

9. Explain why the perception of color and shape is interrelated.

10. Complete these sentences.

    a. The analysis of form by the visual cortex begins with neurons in

    b. These neurons send information to

    c. Analyzed information is then sent

11. a. Describe the location of the inferior temporal cortex, which is shown in Figure 6.37 in your text.

    b. List the two major regions of the inferior temporal cortex.
        1.   2.

    c. What kind of analyses are performed here?

    d. Summarize some of the interconnections of areas of visual association cortex, which are shown in Figure 6.38 in your text.

12. Describe these characteristics of neurons in area TEO.

    a. size of receptive field (Boussaoud et al., 1991)

    b. inputs

    c. outputs

    d. degree of neural coding performed

    e. effects of lesions (For example, Iwai and Mishkin, 1969)

13. Now describe these characteristics of neurons in area TE.

    a. size of receptive field

    b. stimuli that do and do not evoke response (Rolls and Baylis, 1986; Kovács et al., 1995)

14. a. Describe the procedure, illustrated in Figure 6.39 in your text, which Tanaka and his colleagues used to find the stimuli that produced the best response in neurons of area TE of a cat. (reviewed by Tanaka, 1996)

   b. What do the results suggest about the way that neurons may perceive particular objects? (Figure 6.40 in your text illustrates the response of a single neuron.)

15. a. How did the recording technique used by Wang et al. (1996) differ from the one Blasdel used?

   b. What can we conclude from the complex response patterns of neurons in primate inferior temporal cortex? (See Figure 6.41 in your text.)

Learning Objective 6-7   Describe the two basic forms of visual agnosia: apperceptive agnosia and associative visual agnosia.

Read pages 189-193 and answer the following questions.

1. a. Define *agnosia* in your own words.

   b. What deficits are seen in

      1. apperceptive visual agnosia?

      2. associative visual agnosia?

   c. Would you expect a person with visual agnosia to be able to

      1. read the list of items in a first-aid kit?

      2. identify an adhesive bandage from among the other items in the kit by sight?

      3. identify an adhesive bandage by touch?

   d. Explain why visual agnosia is a deficit in perception and identification rather than simple vision or memory.

2. Why would it be inappropriate to give a patient with prosopagnosia the following directions: "Look for John. He'll give you a ride home."

3. Which disorder indicates more severe brain damage, agnosia for common objects or prosopagnosia?

   Let's look more closely at the ability to recognize faces.

4. a. How easily do subjects learn to recognize pictures of faces they have never seen before when the faces are oriented normally and turned upside-down? (Yin, 1970)

b. Name this effect. Does it apply to pictures of other stimuli too?

c. What does this effect suggest about the face recognition?

d. Where are these circuit apparently located? Which hemisphere is more important for face recognition?

5. a. Compare the performance of normal subjects and subjects with prosopagnosia on the inverted faces task. (Yin, 1970; Farah et al., 1995)

b. How did a man studied by Moscovitch et al. (1997) react to the picture in Figure 6.42 in your text?

c. What do all these studies suggest about face recognition?

6. Outline the discussion that a brain region for facial recognition developed through experience and not natural selection. Cite research to support your answer. (Diamond and Carey, 1986; Gauthier and Tarr, 1997. See Figure 6.43 in your text.)

7. a. Check the tasks that you would expect a patient with associative visual agnosia to be able to perform successfully. (Look at Figure 6.44 in your text.)

_____ draw a picture of a tree

_____ copy a picture of a tree

_____ explain what a tree is

b. How well did a patient with associative prosopagnosia match photos of different views of the same face? identify the faces? identify his own face? (Sergent and Signoret, 1992)

8. Carefully explain the underlying difficulty experienced by people with associative visual agnosia.

9. In general, which brain connections appear to be disrupted? spared?

Learning Objective 6-8   Describe how neurons in extrastriate cortex respond to movement and location, and discuss the effects of brain damage on perception of these features.

Read pages 193-198 and answer the following questions.

1. a. Name and describe the location of neurons that respond to movement. (Look back at Figures 6.37 and 6.38.)

b. List some of the regions that relay information to this area.

c. Compare the response speed to stimuli and the length of the response of areas V4 and V5 of extrastriate cortex by studying Figure 6.45 in your text. (Petersen et al., 1988)

d. What anatomical difference may account for the response rate?

e. What combination of brain damage disrupts sensitivity to movement in area V5? (Rodman et al., 1989, 1990)

2. a. Circle the kinds of stimuli that elicit the best response from neurons in area V5. (Albright et al., 1984)

   1. moving stimuli / stationary stimuli

   2. movements in any direction / movements in a particular direction

   b. Briefly outline the organization of area V5 and its receptive fields. (Raiguel et al., 1995)

3. Area V5 sends information about movement to an adjacent area the _____ _____ _____ (_____). Neurons here respond to _____ patterns of movement and appear to analyze _____ _____.

4. a. What kind of stimuli evoked a response from a group of neurons in the frontal cortex of monkeys? (Gallese et al., 1996; Rizzolatti et al., 1996)

   b. What name did the researchers give these neurons, and what may be their function?

5. a What kind of brain damage did patient L.M. receive? (Zihl et al., 1991)

   b. How was her perception of movement affected?

6. a. Research performed by Malach et al. (1995), suggests which region in the human brain may be most important for the perception of movement? (See Figure 6.46 in your text.)

   b. Describe the procedure Walsh and colleagues used to deactivate this area. (Walsh et al., 1998)

   c. How was the response of subjects to moving stimuli displayed on a computer screen disrupted?

7. a. Describe the technique Johansson (1973) and others have used to study the structure of motion.

   b. What did subjects who saw the movies report?

8. a. What kind of brain damage did patient R.A. receive? (reported by Vaina, 1998)

    b. Compare what patients L.M. and R.A. reported when they saw moving points of light. (McCleod et al., 1996; Zihl et al., 1991)

    c. What do their differing perceptions suggest about the neural control of the perception of motion and structure from motion?

9. What may be the function of human mirror neurons found in the prefrontal cortex? (Rizzolatti and Arbib, 1998)

10. a. Once again, study Figures 6.37 and 6.38 and note the regions that send information to area V5.

    b. What visual analysis is performed by the parietal lobe?

    c. What kind of deficits result from damage to this region? (Ungerleider and Mishkin, 1982)

11. a. Briefly describe the experimental tasks used by Haxby et al. (1994) and how they monitored subjects' performances.

    b. What relationship did they observe between the subjects' responses and cortical activity? (See Figure 6.47 in your text.)

12. When Mellet et al. (1996) asked subjects to image three-dimensional assemblies, what areas of the brain became active? (See Figure 6.48 in your text.)

13. a. People with Balint's syndrome have suffered brain damage to which part of the brain? (Balint, 1909; Damasio, 1985)

    b. List and describe the three major symptoms of this syndrome.

        1.

        2.

        3.

    c. What is the characteristic response when a person with Balint's syndrome is asked to

        1. reach for an object?

2. look around a room and describe its contents and their location? Why?

3. identify several objects held together?

14. a. What terms do Goodale and colleagues prefer to use to describe the functions of the dorsal and ventral streams of visual cortex?

b. Carefully state their reasons.

c. What kind of movements are impaired and remain intact as a result of brain lesions in this region? (Jakobson et al., 1991; Milner et al, 1991; Goodale et al., 1994)

15. Explain why associative visual agnosia may result from disconnection of the ventral stream and verbal mechanisms in the brain. Cite research to support your answer. (Sirigu et al., 1991)

Lesson II Self Test

1. The ventral stream of visual association cortex recognizes

   a. the distance of an object from the viewer.
   b. where an object is located.
   c. the identity of an object.
   d. the movement of an object.

2. Extrastriate cortex

   a. consists of several regions that each respond to a particular kind of visual information.
   b. receives information directly from the retina.
   c. performs the initial analysis of visual information.
   d. responds best to familiar stimuli.

3. Neurons in subarea V4 of extrastriate cortex

   a. have two independent receptive fields.
   b. respond to a variety of wavelengths of light.
   c. are especially sensitive to changes in illumination.
   d. cannot compensate for the source of illumination.

4. People with achromatopsia have

   a. difficulty tracking a moving object.
   b. lost some or all of their color vision.
   c. no peripheral vision.
   d. diminished visual acuity.

5. Inferior temporal cortex performs the analysis of

   a. form and function.
   b. figure and background.
   c. location and movement.
   d. form and color.

6. Neurons in area TE

   a. have the smallest receptive fields.
   b. send their primary outputs to area TEO.
   c. respond best to simple stimuli such as spots, lines, or sine-wave gratings.
   d. appear to participate in the recognition of objects.

7. Associative visual agnosias are

   a. disconnections between visual perceptions and verbal systems.
   b. failures in high-level perceptions.
   c. genetic abnormalities involving the cones.
   d. inabilities to integrate tactile and visual information.

8. People with prosopagnosia

a. have difficulty with visual accommodation.
b. do not have binocular vision.
c. do not recognize faces.
d. are color blind.

9. Neurons in area V5

a. appears to analyze optic flow.
b. are arranged in grids.
c. appear to perceive structure from motion.
d. respond to movement and show directional sensitivity.

10. Optic flow seems to be a function of the

a. mirror neurons.
b. MSTd.
c. superior colliculus.

d. visual association cortex.

11. Simultanagnosia, one of the symptoms of Balint's syndrome, is the inability to

a. reach for an object successfully.
b. scan the contents of a room and perceive object locations.
c. perceive more than one object in a group.
d. identify objects by sight alone.

12. The _____ stream is involved in the perception of _____.

a. dorsal; location
b. ventral; movement.
b. dorsal; objects
d. ventral; spatial orientation.

Answers for Self Tests

Lesson I

1.	b	Obj. 6-1
2.	b	Obj. 6-1
3.	a	Obj. 6-1
4.	a	Obj. 6-2
5.	b	Obj. 6-2
6.	c	Obj. 6-2
7.	c	Obj. 6-3
8.	b	Obj. 6-3
9.	a	Obj. 6-3
10.	c	Obj. 6-4
11.	b	Obj. 6-4
12.	d	Obj. 6-4

Lesson II

1.	c	Obj. 6-5
2.	a	Obj. 6-5
3.	b	Obj. 6-6
4.	b	Obj. 6-6
5.	d	Obj. 6-6
6.	d	Obj. 6-6
7.	a	Obj. 6-7
8.	c	Obj. 6-7
9.	d	Obj. 6-8
10.	b	Obj. 6-8
11.	c	Obj. 6-8
12.	a	Obj. 6-8

CHAPTER 7
Audition, the Body Senses, and the Chemical Senses

Lesson I: Audition and the Vestibular System

Read the interim summary on pages 217-218 of your text to re-acquaint yourself with the material in this section.

Learning Objective 7-1   Describe the parts of the ear and the auditory pathway.

Read pages 201-211 and answer the following questions.

1. a. What makes a sound? (See Figure 7.1 in your text.)

    b. What range of vibrations can humans hear?

2. Explain the following characteristics of sound. (See Figure 7.2 in your text.)

    a. pitch (Be sure to use the term *hertz* in your answer.)

    b. loudness

    c. timbre

3. Explain the difference between an analytic and a synthetic sense organ.

4. Study Figure 7.3 in your text and then describe the path of sound from your outer ear through your middle ear.

    a. When sound enters your external ear and moves through the external auditory canal what structure begins to vibrate?

    b. Describe the appearance and explain the function of the ossicles.

    c. Where is the oval window located?

5. Name the parts of the ear shown in Figure 1, below.

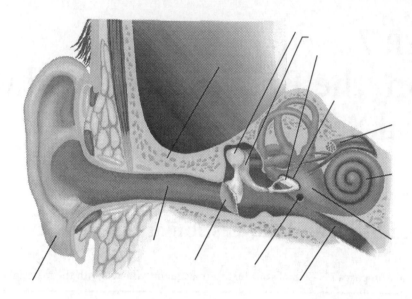

Figure 1

6. Briefly explain how airborne sound is transmitted to the cochlea.

7. a. List the names of the three sections of the cochlea shown in Figure 7.4 in your text.

    1.   2.   3.

    b. Now list the three structures that compose the organ of Corti.

    1.   2.   3.

8. Begin a description of the auditory hair cells.

    a. What is their function?

    b. What is their relation to the three membranes of the organ of Corti? Be sure to mention Deiters's cells in your answer.

9. a. What causes the basilar membrane to bend?

    b. Explain what von Békésy (1960) observed about the relationship between the portion of the basilar membrane that bends and the frequency of the sound.

10. Study Figure 7.5 in your text and explain the role that the round window plays in hearing.

11. Continue with your description of the auditory hair cells.

    a. Where are the inner and outer auditory hair cells found?

b. Describe their appearance and compare the number of each type. (See Figure 7.6 in your text.)

c. When the basilar and tectorial membranes bend in response to sound waves, how do the cilia move in response?

12. a. Let's examine the role of cilia in more detail. Describe the core of the cilia. (Flock, 1977)

b. How are they attached to each other and what are the points of attachment called? (See Figure 7.7 in your text.)

c. Study Figure 7.8 in your text and carefully explain how the direction of movement of the cilia affects their ion channels and results in a receptor potential.

d. Explain the procedure and results that confirmed the location of the ion channels at the end of the tip links. (Study Figures 7.9 and 7.10 in your text. Denk et al., 1995)

e. When Preyer and colleagues (Preyer et al., 1995) dissolved the tip links, what effect was seen on receptor potentials created by movement of the cilia?

f. What, then, causes the opening of these ion channels?

g. Describe this process which is shown in Figure 7.11 in your text. Be sure to mention the myosin motor in your answer. (Assad and Corey, 1992; Gillespie, 1995; Jaramillo, 1995)

13. a. Name the cranial nerve that connects the cochlea to the brain. Briefly describe the bipolar neurons that travel through this nerve. (Return to Figure 7.4.)

b. Where do the vast majority of incoming cochlear nerve axons synapse? the rest synapse?

c. What do the connections of the inner hair cells suggest about their function? the outer hair cells?

d. Briefly describe the olivocochlear bundle.

14. Trace the central auditory pathway with the help of Figure 7.12 in your text. Begin with the cochlear nucleus of the medulla. Where do neurons of the

a. cochlear nucleus send axons?

b. superior olivary complex send axons? Be sure to mention the lateral lemniscus in your answer.

c. inferior colliculus send axons?

d. medial geniculate nucleus send axons?

15. What other parts of the brain receive auditory information?

16. Describe the connections between the basilar membrane and the auditory cortex. How do we refer to the relationship between these two structures? Why?

17. List the two major regions of auditory association cortex and describe their location. (See Figure 7.13 in your text. Kaas et al., 1999)

1.

2.

Learning Objective 7-2   Describe the detection of pitch, loudness, timbre and the location of sound.

Read pages 211-217 and answer the following questions.

1. Explain the notion that moderate to high frequencies of sound are detected by place coding. Support your answer by referring to

a. the work of von Békésy. (See Figure 7.14 in your text.)

b. hearing loss induced by antibiotics. (Stebbins et al., 1969)

c. cochlear implants.

2. a. What discrepancy between the vibrations of the basilar membrane and the frequency of sounds that humans can detect became apparent from early research? Why?

b. What has more recent research discovered? (Evans. 1992; Ruggero,1992; Narayan et al., 1998)

c. Which cells in the organ of Corti affect the mechanical properties of the basilar membrane?

d. Carefully explain how they may do so. (Brownell et al., 1985; Zenner et al., 1985; Kemp, 1978)

3. Explain why the results obtained by Kiang (1965) suggested that low frequencies must be detected by some means other than place coding.

4. Describe the experiments by Pijl and Schwartz (1995a, 1995b) that provide evidence for rate coding.

5. Explain the means by which axons in the cochlear nerve inform the brain of the loudness of

a. a moderate to high frequency sound.

b. low-frequency sounds.

6. a. What characteristic of sound allows us to distinguish between a clarinet and a violin?

 b. Study Figure 7.15 in your text and explain the mathematical analysis of a complex tone such as the sound of a clarinet. Be sure to use the terms *fundamental frequency* and *overtones* in your answer.

 c. Explain how the basilar membrane responds to different overtones?

 d. Explain this statement: The coding of timbre is actually a complex frequency analysis.

7. By what means do we recognize

 a. the location of high frequency sounds?

 b. the location of low frequency sounds?

 c. whether a sound is in front of us or behind us?

  1.   2.

8. a. Imagine that you have spent the evening studying with a friend at her apartment. When she leaves you alone in the living room to go to the kitchen to make some tea, you notice the ticking of a clock. Explain how your eardrums will respond if the clock is

  1. on a table to the left.

  2. straight ahead of you on the mantle.

 b. You hear the insistent bass notes of some music playing in an adjacent apartment. You ask your friend if she knows the person who lives in the apartment to the right, and whether she can ask the person to turn the music down. How did you know the music was coming from the right? Study Figure 7.16 in your text and be sure to use the terms *phase differences* and *out of phase* in your answer.

9. a. Outline Jeffress's (1948) explanation of how the nervous system detects very short delays in the arrival time of two signals. (Study Figure 7.17 in your text.)

 b. Describe anatomical evidence from work with barn owls in support of this explanation. (Study Figure 7.18 in your text. Carr and Knoishi, 1989; 1990)

10. Why is it difficult for the auditory system to use binaural phase differences to detect the location of high-frequency sounds?

11. a. While you are driving, you suddenly hear the shrill wailing of a siren. It sounds like it is coming from the left, and you turn your head that way and watch for the emergency vehicle. Explain how you perceived which direction to turn.

b. Where are neurons that detect binaural differences in loudness found?

12. List the three primary functions of hearing. (Heffner and Heffner, 1990c; Yost, 1991)

    1.   3.

    2.

13. a. By what means does the auditory system appear to identify the sources of sounds?

    b. Where do the circuits of neurons involved in pattern recognition appear to be located?

    c. Cite research to illustrate some of the kinds of analyses performed by auditory cortex. (For example, Whitfield and Evans, 1965)

14. Describe some anatomical characteristics of neurons that carry auditory information that enable them to carry this information rapidly and accurately. (Trussel, 1999.)

15. What happens to the auditory abilities of monkeys following

    a. bilateral lesions of the auditory cortex? How is their behavior affected? (Heffner and Heffner, 1990a)

    b. lesions of the left auditory cortex? (Heffner and Heffner, 1990b)

Read the interim summary on pages 220-221 of your text to re-acquaint yourself with the material in this section.

Learning Objective 7-3   Describe the structures and functions of the vestibular system.

Read pages 218-220 and answer the following questions.

1. a. List the two components of the vestibular system, their location, and the particular stimulus to which they respond.

    1.   2.

   b. List the functions of the vestibular system.

    1.   3.

    2.

   c. List the two vestibular sacs.

    1.   2.

2. Study Figure 7.19 in your text and identify the bony labyrinths of the inner ear shown in Figure 2 on the next page.

3. The semicircular canal consists of a _____ canal floating within a _____ one. An enlargement called the _____ contains the organ in which the sensory receptors reside. The cilia of the sensory receptors are embedded in a gelatinous mass called the _____. (See Figure 7.20 in your text.)

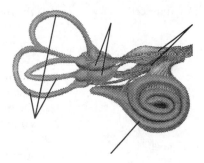

Figure 2

4. Carefully describe how angular acceleration of the head affects the fluid in the semicircular canals.

5. Study Figure 7.20 in your text and explain how the vestibular sacs provide information on the head's orientation. Be sure to mention the otoconia in your answer.

6. Study Figure 7.21 in your text and describe the appearance and function of the hair cells of the semicircular canals and the vestibular sacs.

7. Name the two branches of the eighth cranial nerve–the auditory nerve.

    1.   2.

8. a. What is the location of the bipolar cells that give rise to the afferent axons of the vestibular nerve?

    b. Where do most afferent axons form synapses?

    c. Where do neurons of the vestibular nuclei send their axons?

9. Explain the importance of the vestibulo-ocular reflex.

Lesson I Self Test

1. The frequency of vibration determines its

    a. pitch.
    b. loudness.
    c. timbre.
    d. complexity.

2. Because the cochlea is filled with fluid,

    a. its shape remains constant because liquids cannot be compressed.
    b. the ability to hear high frequencies diminishes with age as this liquid is absorbed by the body.
    c. sounds transmitted through air must be transferred to a liquid medium.
    d. it is most sensitive to rolling movements; thus we can experience seasickness.

3. Which of the statements about auditory hair cells is *not* true?

    a. The inner hair cells are more numerous than the outer hair cells.
    b. They contain cilia.
    c. They produce depolarizations when bent in one direction and hyperpolarizations when bent in the opposite direction.
    d. They contain actin filaments which make them stiff and rigid.

4. The membrane behind the round window moves in and out in opposition to movements of the

    a. Eustachian tube.
    b. cochlea.
    c. tectorial membrane.
    d. membrane behind the oval window.

5. Most of the neurons in the cochlear nuclei send axons directly to the

    a. auditory cortex.
    b. superior olivary complex.
    c. thalamus.
    d. medial geniculate nucleus.

6. Progressive hair cell damage from the use of certain antibiotics causes a parallel progressive hearing loss, which suggests that some sounds are detected through

    a. place coding.
    b. rate coding.
    c. synthetic coding.
    d. analytic coding.

7. Musical overtones are

    a. a series of complex waveforms.
    b. repetitions of the fundamental frequency at a constant intensity.
    c. multiples of the fundamental frequency.
    d. repetitions of the fundamental frequency at varying intensities.

8. The source of continuous low-pitched sounds is detected through *phase differences*, which refers to

    a. the time interval between the arrival at each ear of different portions of the oscillating sound wave.
    b. the time interval between the arrival at each ear of the same portion of the oscillating sound wave.
    c. the simultaneous arrival at each ear of the same portion of an oscillating sound wave.
    d. a or c, depending on the frequency of the stimulus.

9. Bilateral lesions of the auditory cortex of monkeys results in

    a. impaired ability to detect high frequency sounds.
    b. inability to detect intermittent, but not continuous sounds.
    c. gradual deafness.
    d. impaired ability to determine the source of a sound.

10. The semicircular canals

    a. respond to gravity.
    b. are part of the system of ossicles.
    c. are located in the sagittal, transverse, and horizontal planes in the head.
    d. respond to steady rotation of the head.

11. The vestibulo-ocular reflex depends upon vestibular connection to the

    a. third, fourth, and sixth cranial nerve nuclei.
    b. cerebellum.
    c. cortex.
    d. lower brain stem.

12. The gelatinous mass within the vestibular sacs shifts in response to movement of the

    a. cilia.
    b. otoconia.
    c. fluid in the cupula.
    d. fluid in the semicircular canal.

Lesson II: The Somatosenses, Gustation, and Olfaction

Read the interim summary on pages 229-230 of your text to re-acquaint yourself with the material in this section.

Learning Objective 7-4   Describe the cutaneous receptors and their response to touch, temperature, and pain.

Read pages 221-225 and answer the following questions.

1. Identify the kind of information each of the following senses provides.

   a. cutaneous senses

   b. kinesthesia

   c. organic senses

2. List five stimuli to which the cutaneous senses respond.

   1.   4.

   2.   5.

   3.

3. a. List two functions of the skin.

      1.   2.

   b. List the three layers of the skin.

      1.   3.

      2.

   c. Finally, list the two types of skin.

      1.   2.

4. What kind of stimuli are detected by these receptors found in hairy skin? (See Figure 7.22 in your text.)

   a. free nerve endings

   b. Ruffini corpuscles

   c. Pacinian corpuscles

5. In addition to the receptors found in hairy skin, glabrous skin contains other receptors. What kind of stimuli are detected by

   a. Meissner's corpuscles?

   b. Merkel's disks?

6. a. Explain why the Pacinian corpuscle responds to vibration and not steady pressure. (Loewenstein and Mendelson, 1965)

   b. How does the bending of the tip of a nerve ending in a Pacinian corpuscle produce a receptor potential? (Study Figure 7.23 in your text.)

7. Describe the phenomenon of adaptation, citing research by Nafe and Wagoner (1941).

8. Describe the cooperative roles played by the muscles and cutaneous receptors in detecting the physical characteristics of objects that a person touches.

9. Explain what we mean when we say that feelings of warmth and coolness are relative. (You may want to try the demonstration of adaptation to ambient temperature described in your text.)

10. List the two types of thermal receptors.

   1.   2.

11. a. Briefly explain Spray's hypothesis of how sensory transduction takes place in coolness receptors. (Spray, 1986)

   b. How did Bazett and colleagues determine the location of receptors for warmth and coolness? (Bazett et al., 1932)

12. There seems to be at least three types of nociceptors or pain receptors. List them and identify some of the stimuli to which they respond citing relevant research.

   1.

   2. (Kress and Zeilhofer, 1999)

   3. (Burnstock and Wood, 1996)

Learning Objective 7-5   Describe the somatosensory pathways and the perception of pain.

Read pages 225-229 and answer the following questions.

1. Trace the somatosensory pathways with the help of Figure 7.24 in your text.

   a. In general, how do most of the somatosensory axons from the skin, muscles, and internal organs enter the central nervous system?

   b. Where do somatosensory axons from the head and face enter the CNS?

   c. Axons carrying precisely localized information ascend the dorsal columns in the white matter of the spinal cord to which brain region?

   d. These axons then cross the brain and ascend to which region? Where do axons from the thalamus project?

   e. Axons carrying poorly localized information follow a different route. What pathway do these axons follow to ascend to the ventral posterior nuclei of the thalamus?

2. Describe the arrangement of cells within the somatosensory cortex and the kind of stimuli that evoke a response. (Mountcastle, 1957).

3. What did Dykes' (1983) review of research conclude about the divisions of primary and secondary somatosensory cortical areas?

4. Briefly describe the location of brain damage and the type of tactile agnosia experienced by

   a. Patient E.C., studied by Reed et al. (1996).

    b. Patient M.T., studied by Nakamura et al. (1998). (See Figure 7.25 in your text.)

5. a. Explain why the perception of pain is beneficial.

    b. Give an example of an environmental event that can alter a person's perception of pain. (Beecher, 1959)

6. a. When two groups of human subjects plunged their arms into ice water, which brain regions became active? (See Figure 7.26 in your text. Rainville et al., 1997)

    b. One group of subjects was hypnotized beforehand. How did hypnosis affect their reaction to pain and the regional activity of their brain?

    c. What do the results suggest about brain regions involved in the physical and emotional reaction to pain?

7. a. Describe some of the sensations reported by people who have had a limb amputated—the phantom limb phenomenon. (Melzak, 1992)

    b. Outline the classic explanation and treatment for this phenomenon.

    c. According to Melzak, what may account for phantom limb sensations? Cite the experiences of people with brain lesions or birth defects that support his suggestion.

8. a. List the two brain regions that effectively produce analgesia when electrically stimulated.

    1.   2.

    b. How has electrical stimulation been used to help humans suffering from chronic pain? (Kumar et al., 1990)

9. Study Figure 7.27 in your text and sketch and explain the neural circuit that mediates opiate-induced analgesia proposed by Basbaum and Fields (1978, 1984).

10. Describe two situations in which reduction of pain sensitivity is beneficial, thus suggesting the biological importance of analgesia.

11. Finally, summarize research on reduced sensitivity to pain.

    a. classically conditioned analgesia (Maier et al., 1982)

    b. defeat or threat (Lester and Fanselow, 1985; Kavaliers, 1985; Hendrie, 1991)

c. blocking the analgesic effects of acupuncture (Mayer et al., 1976) and the necessity of belief in the procedure (Lee and Beitz, 1992)

d. behaviors important to survival (Komisaruk and Larsson, 1971; Komisaruk and Steinman, 1987; Whipple and Komisaruk, 1988)

e. blocking the analgesic effects of a placebo (Levine et al., 1979)

Read the interim summary on pages 235-236 of your text to re-acquaint yourself with the material in this section.

Learning Objective 7-6   Describe the four taste qualities, the anatomy of the taste buds and how they detect taste, and the gustatory pathway and neural coding of taste.

Read pages 230-235 and answer the following questions.

1. List the four major qualities of taste.

    1.   3.

    2.   4.

2. How does flavor differ from taste?

3. Explain the biological significance of each of the taste qualities.

4. Let's look at the anatomy of the taste buds. (Study Figure 7.28 in your text.)

    a. The _____, _____, _____, and _____ all contain taste buds, but most of them are found on the _____ arranged around the _____. Taste buds consist of groups of 20-50 _____ _____.

    b. Indicate the location of the fungiform papillae, the foliate papillae, and the circumvallate papillae on a sketch of the tongue.

    c. Where are the cilia found?

    d. What is the function of the tight junctions between taste cells?

5. In general, how are different taste sensations produced by a molecule of a tasted substance?

6. List the best stimulus for the taste receptors for

    a. saltiness.   c. bitterness.

    b. sourness.   d. sweetness

7. Carefully study Figure 7.29 in your text and explain the changes that may occur when a tasted molecule binds with a taste receptor.

   a. salty

   b. sour

   c. bitter

   d. sweet

8. What evidence suggests that

   a. more than one kind of receptor is involved in the sensation of saltiness? (Schiffman et al., 1983; Ossebaard et al., 1997)

   b. receptors for bitterness and sweetness may be similar? (Horowitz and Gentili, 1974)

9. a. Describe the characteristics of molecules that taste bitter.

   b. Identify the G protein coupled to bitterness (and sweetness) receptors. (McLaughlin et al., 1993)

   c. What change does this protein initiate when a bitter molecule binds with a receptor?

   d. Go on to explain the rest of the process of the transduction of bitterness.

   e. When gustducin production was prevented by a "knock out" gene, how did affected mice respond to bitter and sweet tasting substances? (Wong et al., 1996)

10. What other two taste qualities have been proposed by researchers? Briefly summarize supporting research. (For example, Kurihara, 1987)

11. List the three cranial nerves that carry gustatory information to the brain and indicate which regions they serve.

   1.   3.

   2.

12. Begin with taste receptors on the tongue and continue to trace the gustatory pathway shown in Figure 7.30 in your text.

   a. Name the first station on this pathway.

   b. Where do the axons go from there?

   c. What other nerve sends information to this nucleus? (Beckstead et al., 1980)

   d. Where do thalamic taste-sensitive neurons project? (Pritchard et al., 1986)

   e. Where do neurons in the primary gustatory cortex project? (Rolls et al., 1990)

   f. Finally, what other brain regions receive gustatory information? (Nauta, 1964; Russchen et al., 1986)

13. Use one word to explain how taste is represented in the brain.

14. Summarize the results of research on the neural coding of taste in the

   a. chorda tympani. (See Figure 7.31 in your text. Nowlis and Frank, 1977)

   b. primary gustatory cortex (Smith-Swintosky et al., 1991)

15. How do taste-sensitive neurons appear to be organized in gustatory cortex?

Read the interim summary on page 240 of your text to re-acquaint yourself with the material in this section.

Learning Objective 7-7   Describe the major structures of the olfactory system, explain how odors may be detected, and describe the patterns of neural activity produced by these stimuli

---

Read pages 236-240 and answer the following questions.

1. Describe the location of the olfactory receptors cells and their supporting cells which is shown in Figure 7.32 in your text.

2. a. Where do olfactory receptor cells send processes?

   b. How do these processes divide and come in contact with odorous molecules?

   c. Where do axons of these cells enter the skull and where do they synapse?

   d. What may be the function of the free nerve endings of the trigeminal nerve axons in the olfactory mucosa?

   e. Where do the olfactory tract axons project?

   f. Where, in turn, do these structures project? (Buck, 1996; Shipley and Ennis, 1996)

   g. With regard to olfaction, what may be the function of the

     1. orbitofrontal cortex?

     2. hypothalamus?

3. a. What is the role of the G_{olf} protein? (For example, Jones and Reed, 1989; Nakamura and Gold, 1987)

b. Summarize research results that confirmed the connection between the receptor molecules on the olfactory cilia and the G protein. (Buck and Axel, 1991)

4. Why it is unlikely that each odor substance is detected by it own receptor?

5. Study Figure 7.33 in your text and review the relationship between the receptors, olfactory neurons, and the glomeruli.

    a. The cilia of each olfactory neuron contain _____ type of receptor. Each glomerulus receives

        information from approximately _____ different olfactory receptor cells.

    b. Summarize research results about the

        1. type of receptor molecules found on a particular glomerulus. (Ressler et al., 1994)

        2. location of particular types of glomeruli within an animal's olfactory bulbs.

6. How, then, can we use a relatively small number of receptors to detect so many different odorants? (Study Figures 7.34 and 7.35 in your text.)

Lesson II Self Test

1. We experience feelings of pressure through

    a. the cutaneous senses.
    b. kinesthesia.
    c. the organic senses.
    d. the vestibular senses.

2. The _____, which are found in _____ skin, are the largest sensory end organs in the body.

    a. Pacinian corpuscles; hairy
    b. Ruffini corpuscles; hairy
    c. Pacinian corpuscles; hairy and glabrous
    d. Ruffini corpuscles; glabrous

3. The reason why people ignore the pressure from a ring or a belt that they wear daily is that receptor cells

    a. become fatigued from constant information.
    b. adapt to constant stimulation.

    c. degenerate from constant pressure and are not replaced.
    d. are constricted by the constant pressure.

4. Somatosensory cortex

    a. is divided into maps that allocate the most tissue to the regions with the greatest surface area such as the skin of the back.
    b. is arranged in five horizontal layers.
    c. is arranged in columns that respond to a particular type of stimulus.
    d. has yet to be represented on functional maps.

5. The most effective locations for producing analgesia using electrical brain stimulation are the

    a. nucleus of the solitary tract and the nucleus raphe magnus.
    b. trigeminal nerve and the rostroventral medulla.

c. periaqueductal gray matter and the rostroventral medulla.
d. nucleus raphe magnus and the posterior nuclei of the thalamus.

6. Electrical brain stimulation apparently produces analgesia by stimulating the release of

a. prostaglandins.
b. morphine.
c. histamines.
d. endogenous opiates.

7. Sourness receptors respond best to

a. hydrogen ions.
b. plant alkaloids.
c. potassium ions.
d. glycerol.

8. The first relay station for taste is the

a. primary gustatory cortex.
b. basal forebrain.
c. chorda tympani.
d. nucleus of the solitary tract.

9. Studies have confirmed that _____ and _____ tastes are detected by receptors bound to _____.

a. sweet; bitter; gustducin
b. sweet; umami; hydrophobic residues

c. sour; salty; cyclic AMP
d. bitter; salty; potassium

10. Olfactory receptors are located in the

a. olfactory bulbs.
b. cribriform plate.
c. olfactory epithelium.
d. olfactory tracts.

11. Select the *incorrect* statement.

a. The cilia of each olfactory neuron contains only one type of receptor.
b. There are as many types of glomeruli as there are types of receptor molecules.
c. A particular odorant binds to only one receptor molecule.
d. The location of particular types of glomeruli appears to be the same in each of the olfactory bulbs of a particular animal.

12. The flow of olfactory information is as follows: olfactory receptor cell→olfactory glomerulus→olfactory tract→_____→_____ .

a. orbitofrontal cortex; entorhinal cortex
b. hippocampus; orbitofrontal cortex
c. amygdala; orbitofrontal cortex
d. amygdala; hypothalamus

Answers for Self Tests

Lesson I

1. a Obj. 7-1
2. c Obj. 7-1
3. a Obj. 7-1
4. d Obj. 7-1
5. b Obj. 7-1
6. a Obj. 7-2
7. c Obj. 7-2
8. b Obj. 7-2
9. d Obj. 7-2
10. c Obj. 7-3
11. b Obj. 7-3
12. b Obj. 7-3

Lesson II

1. a Obj. 7-4
2. c Obj. 7-4
3. b Obj. 7-4
4. c Obj. 7-5
5. c Obj. 7-5
6. d Obj. 7-5
7. a Obj. 7-6
8. d Obj. 7-6
9. a Obj. 7-6
10. c Obj. 7-7
11. c Obj. 7-7
12. d Obj. 7-7

CHAPTER 8
Control of Movement

Lesson I: Muscles and the Reflexive Control of Movement

Read the interim summary on page 247 of your text to re-acquaint yourself with the material in this section.

Learning Objective 8-1   Describe the three types of muscles found in the bodies of mammals, and explain the physical basis of muscular contraction.

Read pages 243-246 and answer the following questions.

1. List the three types of muscles found in the bodies of mammals.

    1.   2.   3.

2. How are skeletal muscles attached to the bones?

3. a. Describe flexion and give an example.

    b. Now describe extension and give an example.

4. Add labels to Figure 1 on the next page. (See Figure 8.1 in your text.)

5. List the two types of muscle fibers that are part of a skeletal muscle and note their location.

    1.   2.

6. Identify the functions of the following structures:

    a. extrafusal muscle fiber.

    b. alpha motor neuron.

    c. intrafusal muscle fiber

    d. sensory endings in the central region of the intrafusal muscle fiber.

    e. gamma motor neuron.

7. What is the relationship between precision of movement and the number of muscle fibers served by a single axon of the alpha motor neuron?

8. List the three components of a motor unit.

    1.   2.   3.

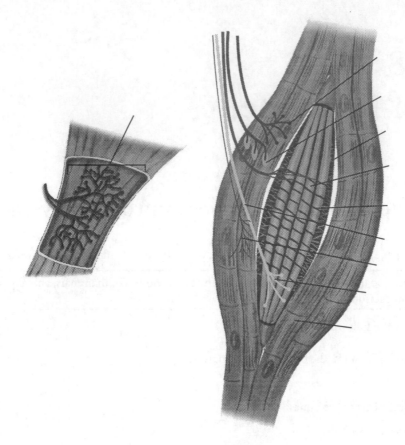

Figure 1

9. List the two kinds of protein filaments found in a myofibril and describe their function. (Return to Figure 8.1. See the marginal definitions.)

   1.   2.

10. Why is skeletal muscle called striated muscle?

11. A(n) _____ _____ is the synapse between the terminal button of a(n)

    _____ _____ and the membrane of a(n) _____ _____. The

    terminal buttons of the _____ synapse on _____ _____.

12. Identify the following events involved in a muscular contraction.

    a. the neurotransmitter that is released by the terminal buttons when an axon fires

    b. the change in the postsynaptic membrane that is produced by the transmitter substance

    c. the unalterable effect on the membrane of the muscle fiber by an endplate potential

    d. the effect on calcium channels and ionic movement

13. What is the role of actin and myosin in this process? (Study Figure 8.2 in your text.)

14. Cite two reasons why the physical effects of a muscular contraction last longer than the action potential. (See Figure 8.3 in your text.)

15. What determines the strength of a muscular contraction?

16. a. Explain the distinction between the functions of the stretch receptors of the intrafusal muscle fibers and those of the Golgi tendon organ.

    b. To be sure that you understand this distinction, describe the response of the intrafusal muscle fibers and the Golgi tendon organ to various kinds of movement which are illustrated in Figure 8.4 in your text.

       1. slow, passive lowering of arm

       2. arm is abruptly dropped

       3. weight is dropped into hand

17. There are two types of smooth muscle. List some of the places where each is found and note what initiates contractions.

    1. multiunit smooth muscle

    2. single-unit smooth muscle

18. a. What factors modulate heart rate?

    b. What initiates the heartbeat?

Read the interim summary on page 251 of your text to re-acquaint yourself with the material in this section.

Learning Objective 8-2   Explain the monosynaptic stretch reflex, the gamma motor system, and the contribution of the Golgi tendon organ.

Read pages 247-251 and answer the following questions.

1. a. Describe the patellar reflex.

   b. How do we know this reflex does not involve the brain?

2. Study Figure 8.5 in your text and trace the pathway of the monosynaptic stretch reflex.

   a. When a weight is placed in the hand, what happens to the activity of the muscle spindles?

   b. Where is the only synapse in this reflex circuit?

c. Briefly explain how the monosynaptic stretch reflex aides in the control of posture. (See Figure 8.6 in your text.)

3. Explain the relationship between activity of the gamma motor system and the degree of sensitivity to stretch by the intrafusal muscle fibers.

4. When the brain initiates limb movement

a. what two sets of motor neurons in the spinal cord are stimulated?

b. and there is little resistance, how will the extrafusal and the intrafusal muscle fibers respond? the afferent axons of the muscle spindle?

c. and unexpected resistance is encountered, how will extrafusal and intrafusal muscle fibers now respond?

5. a. What do the more sensitive afferent axons from the Golgi tendon organ detect? the less sensitive ones?

b. Now study Figure 8.7 in your text and trace this polysynaptic reflex circuit originating at the Golgi tendon organ. Where do the terminal buttons of these less sensitive axons synapse and what is their function?

c. Where do the terminal buttons of the interneurons form synapses?

d. What do they secrete and what is the effect of its release?

c. What is the function of this reflex pathway?

6. What may be the consequence of blocking the Golgi tendon organ with a local anesthetic?

7. a. Describe the cause and characteristics of decerebrate rigidity in a cat.

b. Outline the neural mechanism which affects the stretch reflex. Be sure to mention the clasp-knife reflex in your answer.

8. a. A stretch reflex excites the _____ and inhibits the _____.

b. Now study Figure 8.8 in your text and explain why this occurs.

Read the interim summary on page 268 of your text to re-acquaint yourself with the material in this section.

Learning Objective 8-3   Describe the organization of motor cortex, and describe the four principal motor tracts and the movements they control.

Read pages 251-257 and answer the following questions.

1. a. What do we mean when we say that the primary motor cortex shows somatotopic organization?

    b. Study Figure 8.9 in your text and explain why some features of the motor homunculus are exaggerated in size.

2. Let's examine some of the anatomical connections to the primary motor cortex.

    a. Identify the principal cortical input to the primary motor cortex and two other regions that also send information there.

    b. Compare the inputs, outputs, and functions of these adjacent regions.

    c. Review the anatomical connections from the temporal and parietal cortex and explain how they contribute to the control of movement. (Study Figure 8.10 in your text.)

    d. What is the anatomical and functional relationship between the primary motor cortex and the primary somatosensory cortex? Cite research to support your answer. (Asanuma and Rosén, 1972; Rosén and Asanuma, 1972)

3. a. What tasks did Evarts (1974) teach subject monkeys? (Study Figure 8.11 in your text.)

    b. What did single cell recordings indicate about the

        1. relationship between lever movement and the rate of firing by the cell?

        2. role of the postcentral gyrus in hand and finger movements?

4. Neurons in the _____ _____ _____ control movement through two

    groups of descending tracts located in the _____ _____ of the spinal cord. The

    _____ group consists of the _____ tract, the _____ tract, and the

    _____ tract and is principally involved in the control of _____ _____

    movements. The _____ group consists of the _____ tract, the _____

    tract, the _____ tract, and the _____ _____ tract and controls more

    _____ movements.

5. Let's trace these pathways, shown in Figures 8.12 and 8.13 in your text, through which the primary motor cortex controls movement beginning with the lateral group of descending pathways.

a. Where do axons in the corticospinal tract originate? terminate?

b. What other brain regions send axons through this pathway?

c. Describe the pathway that axons follow to the cerebral peduncles.

d. At what point do the axons of the corticospinal tract form the pyramidal tracts?

e. Most fibers now cross to the other side of the brain to form what tract?

f. The remaining fibers descend to form what other tract?

g. Where do the axons of the lateral corticospinal tract and the ventral corticospinal tract originate? synapse? (Study the light and dark blue lines in Figure 8.12.)

h. What kind of movement does each tract control?

6. Describe the recovery of movement and any difficulties Lawrence and Kuypers (1968a) observed in monkeys whose pyramidal tracts (corticospinal tracts) were cut.

a. 6-10 hours after recovery from anesthesia

b. the day after surgery

c. six weeks later

7. What do their results indicate about the organization of the control of fingers, posture, and locomotion? the same behavior in different circumstances?

8. a. Where does the corticobulbar tract terminate? (Study the green lines in Figure 8.12.)

b. What functions does it control?

9. a. Where does the rubrospinal tract originate and synapse? (Study the red lines in Figure 8.12.)

b. Which muscle groups are controlled by this pathway? are not controlled?

10. In another study Lawrence and Kuypers (1968b) destroyed the rubrospinal tract unilaterally in some of the monkeys who had previously received bilateral pyramidal tract lesions.

a. Describe the eating behavior of these monkeys.

b. What do the results suggest about the function of the rubrospinal pathway?

11. List again the four tracts that make up the ventromedial group of descending pathways. Next to each tract indicate where its cell bodies are located and its function.

1.

2.

3.

4.

12. Lawrence and Kuypers (1968b) also cut the ventromedial fibers of some of the monkeys who had previously received bilateral pyramidal tract lesions.

a. Describe the posture, locomotion, and eating movements of these monkeys.

b. What do the results suggest about the function of ventromedial pathways?

13. To review these pathways, their locations, and the muscle groups they control, study Table 8.1 in your text.

Lesson I Self Test

1. The number of muscle fibers that a single axon serves determines

   a. the size of the body part that must be moved.
   b. the precision with which a muscle can be controlled.
   c. whether the axon controls flexion or extension.
   d. the muscle's sensitivity to stretch.

2. The three components of a motor unit are

   a. an alpha motor neuron; its axon; and associated extrafusal muscle fibers.

   b. a gamma motor neuron; its axon; and associated intrafusal muscle fibers.
   c. an alpha motor neuron; its terminal buttons; and associated neurotransmitter.
   d. muscles; tendons; and associated stretch receptors.

3. During a depolarization of the muscle fiber, which event does *not* occur?

   a. Calcium enters the cytoplasm.
   b. The movement of actin causes the muscle fiber to shorten.
   c. The myosin cross bridges move, shortening the muscle fiber.

   d. Myofibrils extract energy provided by the mitochondria.

4. The Golgi tendon organ detects

   a. muscle length.
   b. strength of muscular contraction.
   c. contraction of the antagonistic muscle.
   d. rate of muscular contraction.

5. The monosynaptic stretch reflex

   a. initiates limb withdrawal in response to pain.
   b. helps compensate for changes in weight that cause limb movement.
   c. maintains muscles in a constant state of contraction.
   d. is the simplest neural pathway and has little utility.

6. A polysynaptic reflex

   a. can be demonstrated by tapping the patellar tendon.
   b. contain no interneurons between the sensory neurons and the motor neuron.
   c. simplifies the role of the brain in controlling movement.
   d. limits the amount of muscular contraction to prevent injury.

7. Muscle spindles are sensitive to changes in

   a. blood levels of calcium.
   b. tendon stretch.
   c. muscle tension.
   d. muscle length.

8. When a stretch reflex is elicited in the agonist muscle it _____quickly causing the antagonist to _____.

   a. contracts; lengthen
   b. lengthen; contract
   c. releases; release at the same rate
   d. releases; pull back

9. Stimulation studies of primary motor cortex indicate that the largest amount of cortical area is devoted to movements of

   a. arms and legs.
   b. head and neck.
   c. fingers and speech muscles.
   d. trunk and genitalia.

10. The principal cortical input to the primary motor cortex is

   a. temporal cortex.
   b. parietal cortex.
   c. frontal association cortex.
   d. posterior association cortex.

11. The fact that monkeys with bilateral pyramidal tract lesions had no trouble opening their hands when climbing but had difficulty opening their hands when eating indicates that

   a. these monkeys can still successfully forage for food.
   b. damaged neural pathways that mediate large movements can regenerate, but neural pathways that mediate precise movements cannot.
   c. the ability to use the hands to flee (climb) conveys a greater selective advantage to the species than feeding.
   d. the same behavior can be controlled by different brain mechanisms in different contexts.

12. The reticulospinal tracts controls

   a. movements of the fingers and hands.
   b. several autonomic functions such as respiration.
   c. movements of forelimb and hindlimb muscles.
   d. posture and righting reflexes.

Lesson II: Control of Movement by the Brain

Read the interim summary on page 268 in your text to re-acquaint yourself with the material in this section.

Learning Objective 8-4   Describe the symptoms and causes of limb apraxia and constructional apraxia.

Read pages 257-260 and answer the following questions.

1. Define *apraxia* in your own words and explain the difference between apraxia and paralysis.

2. List the four kinds of apraxia and the associated deficit.

1.   3.

2.   4.

3. a. More specifically, list the three kinds of movement difficulties patients with limb apraxia may exhibit.

1.   3.

2.

b. Describe how a patient with limb apraxia is tested orally, beginning with the easiest task.

c. If the patient cannot understand speech, how is the apraxia evaluated? (Heilman et al., 1983)

4. Summarize the cause and physical disabilities for each of the following types of limb apraxia.

a. Callosal apraxia

1. Lesion site (Study Figure 8.14, lesion A in your text.)

2. Affected neural circuits

3. Affected limb

b. Sympathetic apraxia

1. Lesion site (Study Figure 8.14, lesion B)

2. Affected limbs

c. Left parietal apraxia

1. Lesion site (Study Figure 8.14, lesion C)

2. Affected limbs

5. a. According to Mountcastle et al. (1975), what may be the primary motor function of the region of the parietal lobes?

b. What is the presumed function of the right parietal lobe? left parietal lobe?

6. Study Figure 8.15 in your text and then explain how the command to reach for an object is processed by the brain. Begin your explanation right after the person hears the request to do something.

7. a. What kind of lesion results in constructional apraxia?

b. What are some tasks that people with constructional apraxia can and cannot perform successfully? (See Figure 8.16 in your text.)

Learning Objective 8-5   Discuss the anatomy and function of the basal ganglia, and its role in Parkinson's disease and Huntington's chorea.

Read pages 260-265 and answer the following questions.

1.   a. List the motor nuclei of the basal ganglia. (Study Figure 8.17a in your text.)

     1.   2.   3.

    b. Now list some of the nuclei associated with the basal ganglia.

     1.   2.   3.

    c. Finally, list the afferent and efferent connections of the basal ganglia.

     1. afferent connections

     2. efferent connections

    d. Which motor systems do the basal ganglia thus influence?

     1.   2.

2.   Trace the connections between the basal ganglia and the cortex shown in Figure 8.17 b.

    a. Where do the frontal, parietal, and temporal cortex send axons?

    b. Where does the putamen send axons?

    c. And where does the globus pallidus send axons?

    d. What kinds of information, then, do the basal ganglia receive and how is it used?

3.   What do we mean when we say the information in this circuit is represented somatotopically?

4.   What other important structures send information to the basal ganglia?

5.   Let's look more closely at the nature of the connections in the cortical-basal ganglia loop that you have just traced.

    a. Which neurotransmitter is secreted by the excitatory neurons in this loop? the inhibitory neurons?

    b. What kind of input do the caudate nucleus and the putamen receive from the cerebral cortex?

    c. Where do they, in turn, send axons and what kind of synapses do they form?

    d. What is the name of the pathway that includes the GP_i? the GP_e?

    e. Where does the GP_i send axons and what kind of synapses do they form?

    f. And where does the VA/VL thalamus send axons and what kind of synapses do they form?

g. Carefully explain why the net effect of this loop is excitatory. (Study the arrows with solid lines in Figure 8.17b.)

h. Where in this loop does the GP$_e$ send axons? the subthalamic nuclei?

i. What is the net effect of this loop? (Study the arrows with broken lines in Figure 8.17b.)

j. Finally, where does the globus pallidus send axons?

6. Briefly describe the primary symptoms of Parkinson's disease and say how they disrupt such activities as getting up, walking, writing, and maintaining balance.

7. Explain how we know that tremor and rigidity are not the cause of slowness of motion.

8. Study Figure 8.17b in your text and then add labels to the ovals and the leader lines in Figure 2. Add the missing arrows, indicating excitatory connections with black lines and inhibitory connections with red or broken lines.

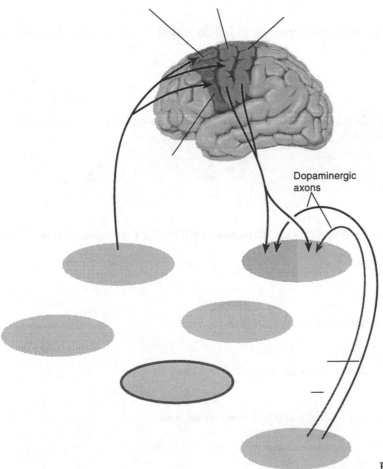

Dopaminergic axons

Figure 2

9. Why does treatment of Parkinson's disease with L-DOPA eventually become less effective?

10. a. Stereotaxic surgery may be a successful addition to management of this disease. What do neurosurgeons hope to achieve by transplanting fetal tissue into the brains of people who no longer respond to drug therapy?

    b. The _____ cells of the _____ _____ found on the _____ arteries on each side of the _____ may be an even better source of dopamine-secreting neurons.

    c. How did Luquin et al. (1999) destroy dopaminergic neurons of the nigrostriatal pathway in monkeys to produce symptoms of Parkinson's disease?

    d. And how did they alleviate these symptoms?

11. a. Explain why destruction of the GP$_i$ during a pallidotomy might relieve the symptoms of Parkinson's disease.

    b. What was a side effect of early operations?

    c. What developments caused this surgical procedure to be abandoned and then resumed?

    d. How have technological advances improved the outcome of pallidotomies? (Graybiel, 1996; Grafton et al., 1995)

12. Parkinson's disease may be caused by toxins. Identify three possible sources of toxins and cite evidence to support your answer. (Langston et al., 1983; Langston et al., 1984)

13. Carefully describe the effects of deprenyl to explain its promise as a treatment for Parkinson's disease. (Tetrud and Langston, 1989)

14. What is the cause of a rare genetic form of this disease? (Kitada et al., 1998)

15. a. What is the cause of Huntington's chorea. (See Figures 8.17b and 8.18 in your text.)

    b. Where does neural degeneration appear to begin and how does it progress?

    c. At what age do the symptoms usually begin?

d. How does progressive degeneration affect movement?

e. Briefly describe the location of the gene that causes Huntington's chorea, its particular defect, and how this defect may lead to the death of these neurons in the brain. Be sure to mention huntingtin in your answer.(Huntington's Disease Collaborative Research Group, 1993)

f. How may the abnormal huntingtin interact with other proteins? (Burke et al., 1996; Kuhl et al., 1995; Li et al., 1995; Li et al., 1996)

| *Learning Objective 8-6*   Discuss the role of the cerebellum and the reticular formation in the control of movement. |

Read pages 265-268 and answer the following questions.

1. In general, what kind of deficits occur if the cerebellum is damaged?

2. Describe neural circuits found in these regions of the cerebellum. Identify the input(s) and output(s) to each region, and the types of movements that are controlled. (Study Figures 8.19 and 8.20 in your text.)

    a. flocculonodular lobe

    b. vermis (Be sure to mention the fastigial nucleus.)

    c. intermediate zone (Be sure to mention the interposed nuclei.)

    d. lateral zone (Be sure to mention the pontine nucleus.)

3. When motor cortex initiates a movement, how does the cerebellum respond? (Be sure to mention the dentate nucleus. Study Figure 8.20.)

4. List some of the movement deficit resulting from damage to the

    a. flocculonodular lobe or vermis.

    b. intermediate zone.

    c. lateral zone (Be sure to describe decomposition of movement and ballistic movements.)

5. a. According to Kornhuber (1974) what may be a primary function of the cerebellum?

b. To illustrate this function of the cerebellum, compare the timing of the release of a ball by normal subjects and subjects with cerebellar lesions. (Timmann et al., 1999)

6. Describe research findings (Thach, 1978) that support earlier clinical observations (Holmes, 1939) that the cerebellum appears to integrate successive sequences of movements.

7. Where is the reticular formation located?

8. List some of the functions of the reticular formation.

   1.   3.

   2.

9. Describe the results of the following studies of the reticular formation.

   a. stimulation of the mesencephalic locomotor region (Shik and Orlovsky, 1976)

   b. recordings from single neurons in freely moving cats (Siegel and McGinty, 1977)

10. To review the movement of the motor system follow the description in the interim summary of your text.

Lesson II Self Test

1. Apraxia is the inability to

   a. properly execute a learned skilled movement.
   b. benefit from practicing a skilled movement.
   c. perceive sequences of skilled movements.
   d. resume performing a skilled movement that has been interrupted.

2. Limb apraxia is assessed by asking a patient to

   a. perform a movement.
   b. describe how he or she would move in a particular situation.
   c. teach someone else a movement.
   d. list components of a motion in sequential order.

3. Patients with callosal apraxia are able to perform a requested movement with their right arm, but not their left because

   a. the lesion has paralyzed the left arm.
   b. most people are right handed and the lesion does not affect "handedness."
   c. the anterior corpus callosum has been damaged and the right and left premotor areas can no longer communicate.

   d. Wernicke's area has been damaged and requests to perform a movement are only partially understood.

4. Patients with constructional apraxia have difficulty

   a. pantomiming particular actions.
   b. "constructing" the proper sequence of action when shown a series of pictures, in random order, of the components of a motion.
   c. controlling the movements of their hands and arms.
   d. building shapes using toy building blocks.

5. The primary deficit in constructional apraxia appears to involve

   a. motor impairment of the hands and arms.
   b. the ability to perceive and imagine geometric shapes.
   c. difficulty in sequencing of actions.
   d. the inability to follow instructions.

6. The components of the basal ganglia are the

a. ventrolateral nucleus, the ventral anterior nucleus, and the pontine nucleus.

b. premotor cortex, the primary motor cortex, and the supplementary motor area.

c. the globus pallidus, the substantia nigra, and the subthalamic nuclei.

d. caudate nucleus, the putamen, and the globus pallidus.

7. Parkinson's disease is characterized by _____ movements and Huntington's chorea is characterized by _____ movements.

a. slow; uncontrollable
b. smooth; slow
c. rigid; smooth
d. slow; smooth

8. A pallidotomy destroys the

a. substantia nigra.
b. internal division of the globus pallidus.
c. caudate nucleus
d. putamen.

9. Huntington's chorea is caused by a defective gene that

a. causes the faulty conversion of MPTP into toxic MPP.
b. results in abnormally high levels of GADPH.

c. halts nitric oxide synthesis.
d. produces a protein with an elongated stretch of glutamine.

10. The cerebellum consists of two _____ with the _____ located on the midline.

a. lobes; intermediate zone
b. zones; corpus callosum
c. sets of nuclei; interposed nuclei
d. hemispheres; vermis

11. If a patient complains to a physician that he or she has recently been having difficulty maintaining balance, the physician may suspect a lesion in the

a. basal ganglia.
b. lateral zone of the cerebellum.
c. red nucleus.
d. flocculonodular lobe of the cerebellum.

12. Stimulation of the mesencephalic locomotor region of the reticular formation causes cats to

a. sit down.
b. tremble.
c. pace.
d. stare.

Answers for Self Tests

Lesson I

1. b Obj. 8-1
2. a Obj. 8-1
3. b Obj. 8-1
4. b Obj. 8-1
5. b Obj. 8-2
6. d Obj. 8-2
7. d Obj. 8-2
8. a Obj. 8-2
9. c Obj. 8-3
10. c Obj. 8-3
11. d Obj. 8-3
12. c Obj. 8-3

Lesson II

1. a Obj. 8-4
2. a Obj. 8-4
3. c Obj. 8-4
4. d Obj. 8-4
5. b Obj. 8-4
6. d Obj. 8-5
7. a Obj. 8-5
8. b Obj. 8-5
9. d Obj. 8-5
10. d Obj. 8-6
11. d Obj. 8-6
12. c Obj. 8-6

CHAPTER 9
Sleep and Biological Rhythms

Lesson I: Sleep and its Functions

Read the interim summary on page 276 of your text to re-acquaint yourself with the material in this section.

Learning Objective 9-1   Describe the course of a night's sleep: its stages and their characteristics.

Read pages 271-275 and answer the following questions.

1.   Explain why sleep is properly considered to be a behavior.

2.   Briefly describe the appearance of a sleep laboratory.

3.   List the physiological functions that are monitored during a night of sleep in a sleep laboratory and explain how they are measured. (See Figure 9.1 in your text.)

4.   Name and describe the two activity patterns that characterize the waking EEG of a normal person and identify the behavioral state that each accompanies.

1.   2.

5.   Describe the characteristics of neural synchrony and desynchrony.

6.   Study Figure 9.2 in your text and fill in the table on the next page.

7.   Discuss the EEG record, the frequency, and the possible significance of sleep spindles and K complexes. (Bowersox et al., 1985; Steriade, 1992; Niiyama et al., 1995,1996; Wauquier et al., 1995)

8.   During which stage of sleep will a sleeping person who is awakened insist that he or she had not yet fallen asleep?

9.   a. What does the acronym REM stand for?

b. Summarize the changes that occur during REM sleep in the

    1. EEG   3. EOG

    2. EMG

Stage	Name of EEG pattern	Description of EEG pattern
Resting		
Alert		
Stage 1		
Stage 2		
Stage 3		
Stage 4		
REM sleep		

10. a. Which stages of sleep are called non-REM sleep? slow-wave sleep?

    b. Why do most investigators consider slow-wave sleep and REM sleep to be more important than stages 1 and 2 sleep?

    c. What stimuli will cause a sleeper to awaken from stage 4 sleep? REM sleep?

11. Compare dreams that occur during REM and slow-wave sleep.

12. Study Figure 9.3 in your text and describe the typical pattern of sleep stages that occurs during a night's sleep.

    a. Normal sleep alternates between what two kinds of sleep?

    b. Approximately how long is each cycle?

    c. How many periods of REM sleep occur each night?

    d. When does most slow-wave sleep occur?

13. a. What name did Kleitman give to the mechanism that regulates both the alternating pattern of REM and slow-wave sleep and the activity cycle during waking? (Kleitman 1982)

    b. What observation of infant behavior first suggested the existence of this 90-minute activity cycle? (Kleitman, 1961)

14. Explain how a response of male subjects that occurs during REM sleep has been used to assess the causes of impotence. (Karacan et al., 1978; Singer and Weiner, 1996)

15. Review by listing the principal characteristics of slow-wave and REM sleep that you have learned so far, and then compare your list with Table 9.1 in your text.

REM Sleep	Slow-Wave Sleep

16. Refute these incorrect assertions.

    a. Sleep is a state of unconsciousness.

    b. Some people never dream.

17. a. In which region of the brain is cerebral blood flow during REM sleep high? low? (Madsen et al., 1991).

    b. How may this pattern correlate with the content of dreams during REM sleep? (Hobson, 1988; Melges, 1982)

18. a. After recording eye movements during REM sleep, Roffwarg and colleagues awakened the sleepers and asked them to describe the dreams they had just had. How did their dream descriptions correlate with their recorded eye movements? (Roffwarg et al., 1962)

    b. What may a particular wave that accompanies eye movements made during REM sleep and when awake subjects scanned a scene suggest about the content of dreams? (Miyauchi et al., 1990)

    c. What other brain mechanisms may be active during a dream? (McCarley and Hobson, 1979; Hong et al., 1996)

19. During which stage of sleep do the most terrifying nightmares occur? (Fisher et al., 1970)

20. To review: Some of the most important characteristics of the stages of sleep are outlined in the interim summary.

Read the interim summary on pages 281-282 of your text to re-acquaint yourself with the material in this section.

Learning Objective 9-2   Review the hypothesis that sleep is an adaptive response.

Read pages 276-277 and answer the following questions.

1. Sleep is a _____ phenomenon among _____. However, only warm-blooded vertebrates experience _____ sleep.

2. Summarize evidence that sleep is more than an adaptive response and may be physiologically necessary.

    a. Describe the sleep patterns of the Indus dolphin. (Pilleri, 1979)

    b. Study Figure 9.5 in your text and describe the sleep patterns of the cerebral hemispheres of the bottlenose dolphin and the porpoise. (Mukhametov, 1984)

3. Explain why these unusual sleep patterns suggest that sleep is more than an adaptive response.

Learning Objective 9-3   Review the hypothesis that sleep serves as a period of restoration by discussing the effects of sleep deprivation, exercise, and mental activity.

Read pages 277-279 and answer the following questions.

1. Explain the rationale for using sleep deprivation to study the functions of sleep.

2. What did a review of over 50 sleep studies indicate about the effects of sleep deprivation on the ability to perform physical exercise, on physiological stress, and on cognitive abilities? (Horne, 1978)

3. Summarize the experience of a teenager who obtained a place in the *Guinness Book of World Records* by comparing

    a. the total number of hours of his enforced wakefulness with the number of hours he slept at the end of his record attempt.

    b. the percentage of recovery of stage 1 and 2 sleep, slow-wave (stage 4), and REM sleep. (Gulevich et al., 1966)

    c. the importance of each sleep stage.

4. Summarize research results that suggest that during stage 4 sleep the body is resting.

    a. cerebral metabolic rate and cerebral blood flow during stage 4 sleep (Sakai et al., 1979; Buchsbaum et al., 1989; Maquet, 1995)

    b. amount of activity during waking and the subsequent level of delta waves during stage 4 sleep

    c. behavior if awakened from stage 4 sleep

    d. effect of missing a night's sleep on cognitive abilities (Harrison and Horne, 1998, 1999)

5. a. Fatal familial insomnia, an inherited neurological disorder, results from damage to which part of the brain?

    b. What are the first symptoms of this disorder? the later symptoms? (Sforza et al., 1995; Gallassi et al., 1996)

6. a. Describe the apparatus, shown in Figure 9.6 in your text, and the procedure developed to keep rats awake and exercising. Be sure to use the term *yoked control* in your answer. (Rechtschaffen et al., 1983; 1989; Rechtschaffen and Bergman, 1995)

    b. How successful were the experimenters in producing sleep deprivation?

    c. Summarize the effects of sleep deprivation on both the experimental (sleep-deprived) rats and the yoked-control rats.

    d. How could the lives of the experimental animals be extended? (Everson and Wehr, 1993)

    e. What may have led to their eventual deaths? (Everson, 1995)

    f. What do these results suggest about the importance of sleep?

7. Explain the rationale for evaluating a possible restorative function of sleep by studying the affects of daytime activity on nighttime sleep.

8. Summarize changes in slow-wave sleep of

    a. healthy subjects after six weeks of bed rest. (Ryback and Lewis, 1971)

    b. completely immobile quadriplegics and paraplegics. (Adey et al., 1968)

9. When exercise does increase slow-wave sleep, what is an important variable? (Horne, 1981, 1988)

10. Describe how Horne and Moore (1985) studied the effect of body temperature during exercise on subsequent slow-wave sleep.

    a. What were the two experimental procedures?

    b. How did the experimental procedures affect the slow-wave sleep of subjects?

    c. What does Horne now believe is the more important variable?

11. Explain the results of follow-up research that tends to support his conclusion. (Horne and Harley, 1989)

12. a. What is the effect of tasks that demand mental activity and alertness on the brain? In what part of the brain is the effect most significant? (Roland, 1984)

    b. What do these results suggest about the function of sleep?

c. Describe other research that supports this interpretation. (Kattler et al., 1994)

13. a. Describe how Horne and Minard (1985) studied the effects on sleep of increased mental activity that did not increase physical activity.

   b. What changes were observed in their slow-wave sleep that night, and what do the results suggest about the function of sleep?

Learning Objective 9-4   Discuss the functions of REM sleep.

Read pages 279-281 and answer the following questions.

1. Review the physiological changes that occur during REM sleep to

   a. the eyes.

   b. the heart rate.

   c. breathing.

   d. the brain.

2. When subjects are deprived of REM sleep, what do researchers observe

   a. as deprivation progresses? (Dement, 1960)

   b. a few days later, when subjects are permitted to sleep normally? Be sure to use the term *rebound phenomenon* in your answer.

3. Briefly state the hypothesis concerning the function of REM sleep that falls into each of these categories.

   a. learning (Greenberg and Pearlman, 1974; Crick and Mitchison, 1983, 1995)

   b. brain development (Roffwarg et al., 1966)

4. Outline support for the development hypothesis by discussing the characteristics of the REM sleep of

   a. guinea pigs, rats, cats, and humans.

   b. humans from fetuses through old age. (Roffwarg et al., 1966; Petre-Quadens and De Lee, 1974; Inoue et al., 1986)

5. a. What were the physical and/or behavioral effects of

   1. suppressing the REM sleep of infant rats? (Mirmiran, 1995)

   2. brain lesions that disrupted one of the phenomena of REM sleep? (Marks et al., 1995)

b. Why must these results be interpreted carefully?

6. If the function of REM sleep is to promote brain development, why might adults have REM sleep?

7. Describe two experimental procedures used to study the effects of REM sleep on learning.

8. What may be the role of REM sleep in learning in studies using the first procedure? Cite research to support your answer. (Smith, 1996)

9. Describe how Bloch et al. (1977), using the second procedure, studied the effect of learning on the REM sleep of rats.

   a. What task were rat subjects taught to perform?

   b. Study Figure 9.7 in your text and describe how subsequent REM sleep was related to

      1. the training experience.

      2. daily performance.

      3. the well-learned task.

10 a. How does REM sleep deprivation affect human learning and remembering, and how does learning affect REM sleep?

   b. Compare the amount of REM sleep of retarded children, gifted children, and normal children. (Dujardin et al., 1990)

   c. How does the amount of REM sleep of college students change during exam week? (Smith and Lapp, 1991)

12. Outline two possible explanations for the relation between waking, slow-wave sleep and REM sleep shown in Figure 9.8 in your text. (Benington and Heller, 1994)

13. Finally, what evidence suggests REM sleep may not be necessary for survival? (Lavie et al., 1984)

Read the interim summary on page 292 of your text to re-acquaint yourself with the material in this section.

Learning Objective 9-5   Evaluate evidence that the onset and amount of sleep is chemically controlled, and describe the neural control of arousal.

Read pages 282-286 and answer the following questions.

1. Cite evidence that indicates that sleep is regulated. (Karacan et al., 1970)

2. Briefly explain how sleep might be triggered chemically by either a sleep-promoting substance or a wakefulness-promoting substance. (Study Figure 9.9 in your text.)

3. Let's look at some chemicals that may regulate sleep.

   a. Review research on the sleep patterns of bottlenose dolphins. What is the effect of depriving the dolphin of sleep in only one hemisphere? (Mukhametov, 1984; Oleksenko et al., 1992)

   b. If sleep is chemically controlled, what do these results suggest about where the chemicals are produced and where they circulate?

4. What evidence suggests that benzodiazepine-like substances may be involved?

5. Discuss the effects of anti-inflammatory drugs and the cytokines on body temperature and sleep that suggest they may indirectly affect sleep. (Murphy et al.,, 1994; Knefati et al., 1995; Krueger and Majde, 1995)

6. a. The primary nutrient of the brain is _____. If the brain uses it more quickly than it can be

      supplied in the blood, extra nutrients in the form of _____ are supplied by the

      _____. An increase in the metabolism of this substance causes a rise in the level of

      _____.

   b. When the level of adenosine rises, how is the next night's sleep affected? glycogen production affected?

   c. If wakefulness is prolonged, what other changes now occur?

   d. What evidence supports the adenosine hypothesis? (Benington et al., 1995)

7. Define *arousal* in your own words.

8. Electrical stimulation of the reticular formation produces arousal. (Moruzzi and Magoun, 1949)

   a. Where is the reticular formation located? (See Figure 9.10 in your text.)

   b. How does it receive sensory information and what effect does it have?

c. How does the reticular formation, in turn, affect the cerebral cortex? through which pathways? (Jones, 1990)

9. List the four systems of neurons that play a role in arousal and wakefulness. (Wada et al., 1991; McCormack, 1992; Marrocco et al., 1994)

1.   3.

2.   4.

10. Where are groups of acetylcholinergic neurons that produce activation located? (Jones, 1990; Steriade, 1996)

11. What were the results of a comparison of acetylcholine levels in the striatum, hippocampus and frontal cortex and the level of an animal's arousal? (Day et al., 1991)

12. How did electrical stimulation of a region of the dorsal pons affect the level of acetylcholine in the cerebral cortex? (Rasmusson et al., 1994)

13. Explain why the neurons of the locus coeruleus are affected by drugs like amphetamine. (To see the location of the locus coeruleus, study Figure 9.11 in your text.)

14 a. Study Figure 9.12 in your text and either describe or draw the changes in the firing rate of noradrenergic neurons in the locus coeruleus during various stages of sleep and waking. (Aston-Jones and Bloom, 1981a)

b. What do these differences in firing rate suggest about the control of arousal and REM sleep?

c. What kind of environmental stimuli produced the highest firing rate in noradrenergic LC neurons? What was the animals' behavioral state at that time? (Aston-Jones and Bloom, 1981a, 1981b)

d. Describe the task Aston-Jones et al. (1994) taught monkeys.

e. How did their performance correspond to the rate of firing of noradrenergic LC neurons?

f. What conclusion do these results support?

15. a. Almost all of the brain's serotonergic neurons are found in the _____ _____. (See Figure 9.13 in your text.)

b. Where do their axons project?

16. a. How is cortical arousal affected by stimulation of the raphe nuclei? administration of PCPA? (Peck and Vanderwolf, 1991)

    b. Compare the response of noradrenergic and serotonergic neurons to external stimuli that produce pain or induce stress. (Jacobs et al., 1990)

17. According to Jacobs and Fornal (1993, 19970, how may serotonergic neurons be involved in an animal's ongoing activities?

18. Study Figure 9.14 in your text and either describe or draw the changes in the firing rate of serotonergic neurons during waking and slow-wave and REM sleep. (Trulson and Jacobs, 1979)

19. a. Where are histaminergic neurons located?

    b. Where do they project and how do they influence these regions? (Khateb et al., 1995)

    c. What is the effect on waking and sleep of injections of drugs that prevent the synthesis of histamine, drugs that block histamine H_1 receptors (Lin et al., 1988) or antihistamine drugs?

Lesson I Self Test

1. The waking EEG is characterized by

   a. occasional delta activity.
   b. periods of alpha and beta activity.
   c. regular changes in heart rate, blood pressure and respiration.
   d. bursts of K complexes.

2. A bout of REM sleep

   a. almost always follows a period of slow-wave sleep.
   b. occurs four or five times during an 8-hour sleep and lasts approximately 90 minutes.
   c. contains more than 50 percent delta activity.
   d. is the deepest stage of sleep.

3. Evidence suggests that many of the brain mechanisms that become active during a dream

   a. cease when the dream ends and are responsible for the general inability to recall dreams.
   b. occasionally become overactive resulting in terrifying dreams.
   c. are those that would become active if the events of the dream were actually occurring.
   d. are related to the duration rather than the content of a dream.

4. Which statement is *not* true?

   a. Sleep is a universal phenomenon among vertebrates.
   b. Only warm-blooded vertebrates exhibit unequivocal REM sleep.
   c. Some people never dream.
   d. The most important role of sleep is probably not rest and recuperation for the body.

5. When sleep-deprived subjects are permitted to sleep normally, they

   a. regain most of the stage 1 sleep they lost.
   b. do not regain all the sleep they lost.
   c. experience a nearly equal percentage of recovery for all stages of sleep.
   d. go directly into REM sleep from waking.

6. The effects of forced exercise using the yoked-control method

   a. increased subjects' needs for REM sleep on recovery nights following the experiment.
   b. reduced the total sleep time of experimental and control subjects by the same amount.
   c. include an increase in body temperature.
   d. are exaggerated when subjects are fed an enriched diet.

7. Subjects were treated to an interesting outing before spending the night in a sleep laboratory in order to

   a. increase mental activity without affecting physical activity.
   b. eliminate effects of external stress.
   c. reduce fluctuations in metabolic rate.
   d. maintain a constant level of alertness.

8. The rebound phenomenon

   a. indicates that REM sleep has the same function as slow-wave sleep.
   b. occurs when REM sleep-deprived subjects are permitted to sleep normally.
   c. results when aspects of REM sleep intrude into wakefulness.
   d. suggests that REM sleep deprivation causes physiological harm.

9. The REM sleep of rats who were trained to run a complex maze

   a. increased until the maze was mastered and then returned to baseline levels.
   b. decreased until the maze was mastered and then returned to baseline levels.
   c. increased each day during training.
   d. decreased each day during training.

10. The level of adenosine in the brain increases

    a. when glycogen is used to fuel the brain.
    b. when astrocytes renew their stock of glycogen.
    c. if the amount of delta activity during a night's sleep increases.
    d. if the amount of glucose in the blood supply increases.

11. Monkeys trained to follow a particular stimulus on a video display performed best when

    a. a noradrenergic antagonist was injected into the LC.
    b. sudden environmental stimuli heightened their state of vigilance.
    c. their level of arousal and vigilance decreased.
    d. the rate of firing of LC neurons was high.

12. _____ neurons are found in the _____, and _____ neurons are found in the _____.

    a. Noradrenergic; locus coeruleus; serotonergic neurons; tuberomammilary nucleus
    b. Acetylcholine; pons; histaminergic; basal forebrain
    c. Acetylcholine; locus coeruleus; noradrenergic; raphe nuclei
    d. Serotonergic; raphe nuclei; histaminergic; tuberomammilary nucleus

Lesson II: Physiological Mechanisms of Sleep and Waking, Disorders of Sleep, and Biological Clocks

Read the interim summary on page 292 to re-acquaint yourself with the material in this section.

Learning Objective 9-6   Discuss the neural control of slow-wave and REM sleep.

Read pages 286-292 and answer the following questions.

1. Summarize research results using a variety of experimental procedures that strongly suggest that the ventrolateral preoptic area (VLPA) of the basal forebrain is involved in the control of sleep.

   a. Let's begin with lesion studies. How did the destruction of the basal forebrain region affect the sleep and health of rats? (Nauta, 1946) of cats? (McGinty and Sterman, 1968)

b. How did infusions of kainic acid into the preoptic area affect sleep? (Szymusiak and McGinty, 1986b; John et al., 1994)

c. Turn now to stimulation studies. How did electrical stimulation of this region affect the behavior of freely moving cats? (Sterman and Clemente, 1962a, 1962b)

d. How did warming, a more natural stimulation, affect sleep? (McGinty et al., 1994; Alam et al., 1995; Steininger et al., 1999)

e. Offer two experiences that support the role of link between thermoregulation and sleep.

f. What were the results of recording studies in

1. clusters of neurons in the VLPA during sleep? (Sherin et al., 1996)

2. single neurons in the VLPA during slow-wave and REM sleep and after sleep deprivation? (Szymusiak et al., 1998)

g. Finally, what did anatomical and histochemical studies indicate about

1. inhibitory secretions of these neurons and where they project? (Sherin et al., 1998)

2. adenosine levels during wakefulness and sleep? (Porkka-Heiskanen et al., 1997)

2. To review: Study Figure 9.15 in your text.

3. List again the characteristics of REM sleep that you have already studied.

1.   4.

2.   5.

3.

4. a. What is the earliest component of REM sleep recorded from laboratory animals?

b. Describe PGO waves and explain the name. (See Figure 9.16 in your text.)

c. Why can we only speculate that PGO waves occur in humans?

d. Where is the mechanism that initiates REM sleep located? the mechanism that inhibits it during waking and slow-wave sleep?

5. a. Why do people who have been exposed to organophosphate insecticides engage in more REM sleep? (Stoyva and Metcalf, 1968)

b. How was the REM sleep of human subjects affected by an acetylcholinergic agonist? an acetylcholinergic antagonist? (Sitaram et al., 1978)

6. a. When are the levels of acetylcholine released by the terminal buttons in the cerebral cortex of the cat highest? lowest? (Jasper and Tessier, 1969)

b. Use one word to describe the rate of glucose metabolism during REM sleep in brain regions that contain ACh-secreting neurons or receive input from them. (Lydic et al., 1991)

c. What do these results suggest is the role of these neurons in REM sleep?

7. _____ neurons in the dorsolateral pons play a central role in triggering the onset of REM sleep. Contained primarily in two _____, this region is referred to as the _____ _____. (Jones and Beaudet, 1987. See Figure 9.17 in your text.)

8. a. Describe the activity of *REM-ON* cells shown in Figure 9.18 in your text.

b. What might the increased activity of these acetylcholinergic cells signify?

9. What effect do lesions of the peribrachial area have on REM sleep? (Webster and Jones, 1988)

10. List three regions to which acetylcholinergic neurons of the peribrachial area project. (Cornwall et al., 1990; Bolton et al., 1993)

1.   3.

2.

11. a. Locate the MPRF which is shown in Figure 9.19 in your text.

b. Which part of the MPRF is often called the cholinoceptive region? Why? (Be sure to refer to carbachol in your answer. Quattrochi et al.,1989; Garzón et al., 1998)

c. What is the effect of lesions of the MPRF on REM sleep? (Siegel, 1989)

12. What parts of the brain are responsible for the following components of REM sleep?

a. arousal and cortical desynchrony

b. PGO waves (Sakai and Jouvet, 1980; Steriade et al., 1990)

c. rapid eye movements (Webster and Jones, 1988)

13. a. When Jouvet (1972) made a lesion just caudal to the peribrachial area of the dorsolateral pons of a laboratory cat, what behavioral change did he observe?

b. What is the location of the neurons whose axons are responsible for the muscular paralysis of REM sleep?

c. Where do their axons project caudally? (Sakai, 1980)

d. And where do axons from the magnocellular nucleus project? What kind of synapses do they form here? (Morales et al., 1987)

14. Review research that supports the role of this pathway in REM sleep paralysis.

   a. How do lesions of the subcoerulear nucleus affect REM sleep and its accompanying paralysis? (Shouse and Siegel, 1992)

   b. What happens to single neurons in the magnocellular nucleus during REM sleep? (Kanamori et al., 1980)

   c. What is the effect of electrical stimulation of the magnocellular nucleus? (Sakai, 1980) lesions? (Schenkel and Siegel, 1989)

   d. Identify the inhibitory transmitter substance found in the magnocellular nucleus and its likely function. (Fort et al., 1990)

15. What does this presence of this inhibitory mechanism suggest about the importance of the motor components of dreaming?

16. a. Immediately review the neural circuitry of REM sleep shown in Figure 9.20 in your text.

   b. The first event preceding REM sleep is the activation of _____ neurons in the _____ area of the _____ _____.

   c. How do these neurons, either directly or through their projections, produce

   1. rapid eye movements?

   2. PGO waves?

   3. atonia?

   4. cortical activation?

17. Even though the MPRF is responsible for only one component of REM sleep, infusion of an ACh agonist induces REM sleep. Explain how this probably occurs. (Reinoso-Suàrez et al., 1994)

18. What kind of neural activity might be responsible for the rebound effect seen after REM sleep deprivation? (Mallick et al., 1989)

19. How does brain temperature change during slow-wave sleep and what does it suggest about the function of this sleep stage? (Jouvet, 1975)

20. Briefly explain how the activity of neurons in the locus coeruleus and the dorsal raphe nucleus may be involved in REM sleep. (Study Figure 9.21 in your text. For example, Lydic et al., 1983).

Read the interim summary on pages 295-296 of your text to re-acquaint yourself with the material in this

Learning Objective 9-7   Discuss insomnia, sleeping medications, and sleep apnea.

Read pages 292-293 and answer the following questions.

1. Describe insomnia, including its incidence, problems of definition, and most important cause.

2. Explain how the use of sleeping medication often leads to

   a. drug tolerance.

   b. a withdrawal effect. (Weitzman, 1981)

   c. drug dependency insomnia. (Kales et al., 1979)

3. What is the appropriate goal of sleeping medication?

4. a. Describe sleep apnea. Carefully explain the change in blood levels of carbon dioxide and its effect.

   b. What is a frequent cause of sleep apnea and how is it corrected? (Sher, 1990; Westbrook, 1990)

Learning Objective 9-8   Discuss problems associated with REM and slow-wave sleep.

Read pages 293-295 and answer the following questions.

1. Describe the four symptoms of narcolepsy.

   a. sleep attack

   b. cataplexy

   c. sleep paralysis

   d. hypnagogic hallucination

2. Describe research to discover brain abnormalities that interfere with aspects of REM sleep to produce narcolepsy.

    a. the sleep patterns of narcoleptic subjects. (Rechtschaffen et al., 1963)

    b. narcolepsy resulting from brain damage. (Plazzi et al., 1996; Frey and Heiserman, 1997)

    c. abnormalities in the brains of narcoleptic dogs. (Be sure to mention orexin in your answer. See Figure 9.23 in your text. Lin et al., 1999)

3. Which kinds of drugs are used to treat the symptoms of narcolepsy? (Vgontzas and Kales, 1999; Mitler, 1994; Hublin, 1996)

4. a. What happens when people suffering from REM without atonia dream? (Schenck et al., 1986)

    b. What are two causes of this condition? (Schenck et al., 1996)

    c. Why do drugs that are used to treat cataplexy aggravate REM without atonia? How is it treated? (Schenck and Mahowald, 1992; Schenck et al., 1996)

5. Describe three maladaptive behaviors that may occur during slow-wave sleep, noting any association with sleep stages, who is most susceptible, and what the best treatments are.

Read the interim summary on pages 302-303 of your text to re-acquaint yourself with the material in this section.

> *Learning Objective 9-9*   Describe circadian rhythms; discuss research on the neural and physiological bases of biological clocks.

Read pages 296-299 and answer the following questions.

1. Define *circadian rhythms* in your own words.

2. Study the record of wheel-running activity of a rat under various conditions of illumination presented in Figure 9.24 in your text. Use this example to continue your explanation of daily rhythms.

    a. During which portion of a normal day/night cycle is the rat active?

    b. When the "day" was artificially advanced 6 hours, what happened to the rat's activity cycle?

    c. What effects did constant dim light have on the rat's activity?

    d. Because there were no stimuli in the rat's environment that varied throughout the day, what must have been the source of rhythmicity?

3. a. What term describes the effect of light on daily activity cycles?

   b. How do pulses of light affect the activity cycles of animals kept in constant darkness? (Aschoff, 1979)

4. Describe the circadian rhythm of a modern human and how it changes under constant illumination.

5. Circadian rhythms are controlled by biological clocks. Name the structure that contains the primary biological clock of the rat. (Moore and Eichler, 1972; Stephan and Zucker, 1972.)

6. How do lesions of the SCN affect

   a. running, drinking, and hormonal secretions?

   b. the timing of sleep cycles? (Ibuka and Kawamura, 1975; Stephan and Nuñez, 1977)

   c. total amount of sleep?

7. Let's look at the anatomy of the SCN more closely. (See Figure 9.25 in your text)

   a. Approximately how big is the SCN of the rat? (Meijer and Rietveld, 1989)

   b. What is exceptional about the dendrites of neurons found here?

   c. What physical evidence suggests that a group of neurons near capillaries that serve the SCN may be neurosecretory cells? (Card et al., 1980; Moore et al., 1980)

   d. And what does the presence of these neurosecretory cells suggest about the way the SCN functions?

   e. What region projects fibers to the SCN? (Hendrickson et al., 1972; Aronson et al., 1993) What is the name of the pathway? (Again, look at Figure 9.25.)

8. a. Why are the circadian rhythms of mice with a genetic disorder that causes degeneration of retinal photoreceptors particularly interesting? (Foster et al., 1991; Jiminez et al., 1996)

   b. Cite supporting research using targeted mutations. (Freedman et al., 1999)

   c. Where may the responsible photochemicals and the receptive cells be located? (Provencio et al., 2000)

9. a. What protein is produced when light pulses reset an animal's circadian rhythm?

   b. What does the presence of this protein further indicate about the effects of light? (Rusak et al., 1990, 1992)

   c. If the glutamate receptors in the connections between the retina and the SCN are blocked by drugs, how are the effects of a period of bright light altered? (Abe et al. 1991; Vindlacheruvu et al., 1992)

10. a. List the direct and indirect pathway through which the SCN receive visual information.

    1. direct pathway   2. indirect pathway

    b. Now list two substances coreleased by the terminal buttons of the neurons that connect the IGL to the SCN.

    1.   2.

    c. What appears to be the role of both the direct and indirect pathway? Cite research to support your answer. (Albers and Ferris, 1984; Rusak et al., 1989; Harrington and Rusak, 1986)

11. a. In addition to light, what other stimuli reset an animal's circadian rhythms?

    b. How do bursts of activity change a hamster's circadian rhythm, and how is this effect abolished? (Reebs and Mrosovsky, 1989; Wickland and Turek, 1991, 1994)

    c. Describe research that shows that zeitgebers can be classically conditioned. (Amir and Stewart, 1996)

12. a. To which parts of the brain do neurons of the SCN connect in order to control drinking, eating, sleeping, and hormone secretion?

    b. If these connections are severed by knife cuts, what is the effect on circadian rhythms? (Meijer and Rietveld, 1989)

    c. Why must we be cautious in our assumptions about the role of these severed efferent axons of the SCN?

13. a. How did Lehman et al., (1987) abolish the circadian rhythms of subject animals and then reestablish them?

    b. If the placement of the grafts is not critical, what does that suggest about the way the SCN controls circadian rhythms? (Aguilar-Roblero et a., 1984)

14. a. After destroying the SCN of hamsters to abolish their circadian rhythms, Silver and her colleagues transplanted SCN tissue in semipermeable capsules in to the subjects. Why did they encapsulate the transplants? (Silver et al., 1996)

    b. What changes, if any, occurred in the subjects' circadian rhythms?

    c. What notion about the control of circadian rhythms do these results support?

    d. Briefly summarize subsequent research that the circadian clock is located in a particular subregion of the SCN. (See Figure 9.26 in your text. LeSauter and Silver, 1999)

Learning Objective 9-10   Discuss the time base of the circadian clock, changes in seasonal rhythms, and changes in circadian rhythms caused by work schedules and travel.

Read pages 299-302 and answer the following questions.

1. a. Compare autoradiographs of rats, shown in Figure 9.27 in your text, who were injected with 2-DG either during the day or at night. (Schwartz and Gainer, 1977)

   b. Which rats showed a higher metabolic rate of the SCN and what does that indicate?

   c. Now compare these results with results obtained using the same experimental procedure but using diurnal squirrel monkeys as the subjects. (Schwartz et al., 1983)

   d. What do these results suggest is and is not the function of the SCN?

2. a. Study the graphs of the electrical activity of individual SCN cells kept alive in a tissue culture shown in Figure 9.28 in your text. (Welsh et al., 1995)

   b. What do these results suggest about the location of the "ticking" of the biological clock?

3. What is the most likely explanation for the synchronized activity of SCN neurons?

4. a. Explain the experimental procedure Bouskila and Dudek (1993) used to show this explanation is incorrect.

   b. What, then, is the most likely source of cellular synchrony in the SCN?

5. Summarize the research on the intracellular ticking in the common fruit fly. (See Figure 9.29 in your text.)

   a. When the *per* and *tim* genes in the SCN of fruit flies become active, what substances do they produce?

   b. Go on to describe the interaction between the genes and their products that may be responsible for the intracellular ticking.

   c. How do the genes controlling the circadian clock of rodents differ from those of fruit flies?

6. Review the physiological control of seasonal rhythms.

   a. What is the relationship between the male hamster's testosterone cycle and light?

   b. What effect do lesions of the SCN have on this cycle? What is a possible explanation for this effect? (Rusak and Morin, 1976)

   c. Identify the gland and the hormone it secretes that control seasonal rhythms. (See Figure 9.30 in your text. Bartness et al., 1993; Moore, 1995)

d. Briefly describe how the SCN and this gland interact to control seasonal rhythms.

e. What kind of procedures can disrupt seasonal rhythms?

7. a. Shift work or travel across several time zones produce a desynchrony between the internal _____

and the external _____.

b. In general, what is the best way to ease the transition? (Dijk et al., 1995; Boulos et al., 1995)

c. What specific treatments have been developed? (Houpt et al., 1996; Eastman et al., 1995)

8. a. What is the rationale for the use of melatonin to regulate circadian rhythms?

b. How does it affect receptors in the SCN? (Gillette and McArthur, 1995; Starkey et al., 1995)

c. If melatonin is used to regulate circadian rhythms, what is the best time to administer it? Why?

Lesson II Self Test

1. Warming of one region of the basal forebrain induces _____.

   a. REM sleep
   b. slow-wave sleep
   c. insomnia
   d. vigilance

2. The acetylcholinergic neurons that play the most central role in the triggering of REM sleep are found in the

   a. peribrachial area.
   b. raphe nuclei.
   c. medial pontine reticular formation.
   d. magnocellular nucleus.

3. Neurons from the _____ send axons to the spinal cord, and this pathway may be responsible for the atonia that accompanies REM sleep.

   a. peribrachial area
   b. locus coeruleus
   c. magnocellular nucleus
   d. ventrolateral preoptic area

4. The right amount of sleep is

   a. only obtained by infants.
   b. whatever seems to be enough.
   c. assured with sleeping medication.
   d. infrequently obtained by insomniacs.

5. Sleep apnea is

   a. a form of drug dependency insomnia.
   b. a side affect of sleeping medications.
   c. a period of sleep without dreams.
   d. the inability to sleep and breathe at the same time.

6. During a cataplectic attack, the individual

   a. awakens gasping for breath.
   b. tries to act out dreams.
   c. is unconscious.
   d. is overcome by muscular paralysis.

7. REM without atonia is a disorder is which the person

   a. is not paralyzed during dreaming and acts out the dream.
   b. dreams while lying awake paralyzed.

c. becomes paralyzed or remains paralyzed for several minutes just before or just after otherwise normal REM sleep.
d. experiences profound REM sleep paralysis and does not exhibit the characteristic rapid eye movements that accompany dreaming.

8. How did the daily behavior of a rat change with constant dim illumination?

a. Periods of activity increased and periods of sleep decreased.
b. Food consumption increased with activity levels.
c. The biological clock ran slower; activity began about one hour later each day.
d. Body temperature increased slightly with constant light.

9. The primary biological clock of the rat is located in the

a. suprachiasmatic nucleus.
b. reticular formation.
c. locus coeruleus.
d. pons.

10. Researchers transplanted encapsulated donor SCN tissue into animals whose SCN had been destroyed and

a. failed to reestablish circadian rhythms because synaptic connections with surrounding tissue were not established.
b. successfully reestablished circadian rhythms even though synaptic connections with surrounding tissue were not established.
c. failed to reestablish circadian rhythms because the donor tissue was rejected even though it had been encapsulated.
d. successfully reestablished circadian rhythms only when transplants were placed in the normal location of the SCN

11. The "ticking" of the biological clock

a. and the control sleep and waking cycles are complementary functions of the SCN.
b. occurs in the glial cells that surround the neurons of the SCN.
c. occurs in individual neurons of the SCN.
d. is a characteristic of circuits of neurons, not individual neurons.

12. Taking melatonin _____ may help people adjust to the effects of shift work or jet-lag.

a. in the morning
b. at bedtime
c. beginning several days before a time change
d. whenever drowsiness occurs

Answers for Self Tests

Lesson I

1. b Obj. 9-1
2. a Obj. 9-1
3. c Obj. 9-1
4. c Obj. 9-2
5. b Obj. 9-3
6. c Obj. 9-3
7. a Obj. 9-3
8. b Obj. 9-4
9. a Obj. 9-4
10. a Obj. 9-5
11. d Obj. 9-5
12. d Obj. 9-5

Lesson II

1. b Obj. 9-6
2. a Obj. 9-6
3. c Obj. 9-6
4. b Obj. 9-7
5. d Obj. 9-7
6. d Obj. 9-8
7. a Obj. 9-8
8. c Obj. 9-9
9. a Obj. 9-9
10. b Obj. 9-9
11. c Obj. 9-10
12. b Obj. 9-10

CHAPTER 10
Reproductive Behavior

Lesson I: Sexual Development and Hormonal Control of Sexual Behavior

Read the interim summary on pages 311-312 of your text to re-acquaint yourself with the material in this section.

Learning Objective 10-1   Describe mammalian sexual development and explain the factors that control it.

Read pages 305-311 and answer the following questions.

1. Define *sexually dimorphic behavior* in your own words and list several examples.

2. a. How many pairs of chromosomes do cells other than sperms and ova contain?

    b. Explain why gametes contain only one member of each pair of chromosomes.

3. How many types of sex chromosomes are there? What is the sex chromosome pattern for a male? for a female?

4. a. At what point is the sex of an offspring normally determined?

    b. The gamete from which parent determines the sex of an offspring? (See Figure 10.1 in your text.)

5. What event is responsible for sexual dimorphism?

6. a. List the three categories of sex organs.

    1.   2.   3.

    b. Now list the gonads.

    1.   2.

    c. What are their dual functions?

    d. What factor determines whether the initially identical gonads become ovaries or testes? (Sinclair et al., 1990; Smith, 1994; Warne and Zajac, 1998)

7. Explain the difference between organizational effects and activational effects of sex hormones.

8. Name the precursors of the male and female internal sex organs and the organs that develop from them. (Study Figure 10.2 in your text to see how the precursors of the internal sex organs continue to develop.)

   a. male

   b. female

9. a. List the two types of hormones secreted by the testes that determine whether the Müllerian system or the Wolffian system continues to develop and describe their effects.

   1.   2.

   b. List the specific androgens responsible for masculinization.

   1.   2.

10. Be sure that you understand how hormones exert their effects on the body and then explain the cause and consequences of

   1. androgen insensitivity syndrome. (See Figure 10.3 in your text. Money and Ehrhardt, 1972; MacLean et al., 1995))

   2. persistent Müllerian duct syndrome. (Warne and Zajac, 1998)

11. What do people with Turner's syndrome reveal about the hormones necessary for the development of female internal and external sex organs? Explain your answer. (See Figure 10.4 in your text. Knebelmann et al. 1991)

12. Stop now and review what you have learned. Cover the right half of Figure 10.5 in your text (including the triple arrows). Identify the hormones that are secreted by the newly developed testes or ovaries and describe their effect on the development of the internal sex organs and external genitalia.

13. Complete these statements. (See Figure 10.6 in your text.)

   a. The primary sex characteristics include

   b. The secondary sex characteristics include

   c. Puberty begins when cells in the hypothalamus

   d. Gonadotropin-releasing hormones in turn stimulate

   e. The two gonadotropic hormones are

   f. Although the gonadotropic hormones are named for the effects they produce in the female,

14. a. What is the presumed reason for the fall in the age of puberty in developed countries? (Foster and Nagatani, 1999)

   b. What are the characteristics of girls who tend to reach puberty earlier than normal? later than normal? (Frisch, 1990)

   c. What tissue secretes the peptide leptin?

   d. In addition to signaling the brain to suppress appetite, what appear to be another function of leptin? Cite research to support your answer. (Chehab et al. 1997)

15. Summarize the changes in the bodies of males and females that are initiated by gonadal hormones at puberty.

16. What evidence confirms that the bipotentiality of some secondary sex characteristics is lifelong.

17. To review: Table 10.1 in your text summarizes information about sex steroid hormones.

Read the interim summary on pages 326-327 of your text to re-acquaint yourself with the material in this section.

Learning Objective 10-2 Describe the hormonal control of the female reproductive cycle and of male and female sexual behavior.

Read pages 312-317 and answer the following questions.

1. What is the chief difference between the human menstrual cycle and the estrous cycle of other female mammals?

2. Study Figure 10.7 in your text and follow the menstrual cycle from beginning to end.

   a. Name the principal hormone that stimulates the growth of ovarian follicles.

   b. Name the hormone secreted by the maturing ovarian follicle.

   c. What changes begin to occur in the uterus in response to this hormone?

   d. What effect does this hormone have on the anterior pituitary gland?

   e. What does the hormone from the anterior pituitary gland do?

   f. After the ovum is released, what happens to the ruptured follicle?

   g. What hormones does this structure release?

   h. If the ovum is not fertilized or is fertilized too late, what changes occur?

3. List the three features common to all male sexual behavior.

   1.   2.   3.

4. What is the refractory period?

5. What is the Coolidge effect and what may be its evolutionary importance?

6. What evidence indicates the importance of testosterone in male sexual behavior? (Bermant and Davidson, 1974)

7. a. Through aromatization _____ is converted to _____ through the action of _____. Briefly explain this process illustrated in Figure 10.8 in your text.

   b. What is the role of this aromatized hormone during puberty? (Warne and Zajac, 1998)

   c. What happens to sexual behavior of adult male monkeys if they are given a drug that blocks aromatase? (Zumpe et al., 1993)

8. a. Where is oxytocin produced?

   b. When is it released in males and females?

   c. What are the effects of its release in females? in males? (Carter, 1992; Carmichael et al., 1994)

9. a. Where is prolactin produced and what are the effects of its release in females? in males?

   b. When is it released in males? (Oaknin et al., 1989)

   c. What is one of the symptoms of hyperprolactinemia—the oversecretion of prolactin? (Foster et al., 1990)

   d. What was the effect on male sexual behavior of

      1. transplanting a pituitary gland into male rats? (Doherty et al., 1986)

      2. injecting small amounts of prolactin into the MPA of male rats? (Mas et al., 1995)

10. a. Unlike other endogenous opioids, what kind of receptors does dynorphin stimulate?

    b. What is the effect on male sexual behavior of

       1. injections of a drug that stimulates kappa receptors? (Leyton and Stewart, 1992)

       2. a drug that blocks opiate receptors? (Rodriguez-Manzo and Fernandez Guasti, 1995)

    c. When do dynorphin-secreting neurons in the male hamster brain become particularly active? (Parfitt and Newman, 1998)

    d. What, therefore, may be their function?

11. a. Name the position that receptive females of many four-legged species will assume to facilitate copulation.

    b. What two hormones are required for the sexual response of a female rodent?

c. Which hormone "primes" the other? Explain. (Takahashi, 1990)

d. Describe the response to males of female mice without estrogen receptors. (Rissman et al., 1997) without progesterone receptors. (Lydon et al., 1995)

12. List and briefly explain the effects that the sequence of estradiol followed by progesterone have on the female rat.

    1.

    2.

    3.

13. Define *behavioral defeminization* and *behavioral masculinization* in your own words.

14. Using these terms, explain the effects of the following treatments on sexual behavior.

    a. an adult male, castrated at birth and given no hormones, then given estradiol and progesterone in adulthood (Blaustein and Olster, 1989)

    b. an adult male, castrated in adulthood, then given estradiol and progesterone in adulthood

    c. an adult female, ovariectomized at birth and given testosterone, then given estradiol and progesterone in adulthood

    d. an adult female, ovariectomized at birth and given testosterone, then given testosterone in adulthood (Breedlove, 1992; Carter, 1992b)

15. Check your understanding of the organizational effects of androgens by studying Figure 10.9 in your text and then completing the blanks in the table on the next page.

    a. Circle the entry that indicates the activational effect of estradiol and progesterone. Label it AE.

    b. Circle the entry that indicates evidence of behavioral defeminization. Label it BDF.

    c. Circle the entry that indicates evidence of behavioral masculinization. Label it BM.

16. a. If male rats are treated early in life with drugs that block aromatization, how is their sexual behavior later affected? (Brand et al., 1991; Houtsmuller et al., 1994; Bakker et al., 1996)

    b. What do these results indicate about the hormonal control of behavioral defeminization?

Hormone Treatment		Resulting Sexual Behavior	
Immediately after birth	*When rat is fully grown*		
None	Estradiol + progesterone	Female: _____	Male: _____
None	Testosterone	Female: _____	Male: _____
Testosterone	Estradiol + progesterone	Female: _____	Male: _____
Testosterone	Testosterone	Female: _____	Male: _____

17. Outline two explanations of why all fetuses, both male and female, do not become masculinized and defeminized from exposure to estrogens. (Breedlove, 1992)

18. a. Female rats lick the genital region of their offspring. Why is this a useful behavior for both mother and pups?

    b. Why do rat mothers spend more time licking their male offspring? (reviewed by Moore, 1986)

    c. When the mothers' ability to smell was destroyed, how did their behavior toward their male offspring change?

    d. How was the adult sexual behavior of these males affected by reduced attention from their mothers? by genital stroking by the researchers?

    e. What do these results suggest about some of the masculinizing effects of androgens?

Learning Objective 10-3 Describe the role of pheromones in reproductive and sexual behavior.

Read pages 317-320 and answer the following questions.

1. Pheromones transmit chemical messages from one _____ to another, unlike hormones, which transmit messages from one part of the _____ to another. Pheromones are usually detected through _____ . They can affect reproductive _____ or _____ .

2. Describe each of the following phenomena, which affect reproductive physiology.

    a. Lee-Boot effect (van der Lee and Boot, 1955)

    b. Whitten effect (Whitten, 1959)

    c. Vandenbergh effect (Vandenbergh et al., 1975)

    d. Bruce effect (Bruce, 1960a, 1960b)

3. a. Name and describe the location of the sensory organ that mediates the effects of pheromones.

b. Where do afferent axons from this organ project? (Wysocki, 1979. See Figure 10.10 in your text.)

c. What kind of compounds does the vomeronasal organ most likely detect? Cite research to support your answer. (Meredith and O'Connell, 1979; Meredith, 1994)

d. What is the effect of removal of the accessory olfactory bulb? (Halpern, 1987)

4. Trace the neural circuit responsible for the effects of these pheromones beginning with the region to which the accessory olfactory bulb projects. (Study Figure 10.11 in your text.)

5. Review research to understand why pregnant females do not abort if they later encounter the odor of the male with which they mated.

a. Which axons appear to play a role in learning to identify a particular odor?

b. Following destruction of these axons, how well did the female recognize the odor of her mate? What was the subsequent effect on her pregnancy? (Keverne and de la Riva, 1982)

c. How might copulation facilitate this learning?

d. How are the noradrenergic axons affected by vaginal stimulation? (Rosser and Keverne, 1985)

e. What neurotransmitter is necessary for olfactory learning to occur? (Gray et al., 1986; Leon, 1987)

6. a. By what two means may pheromones that affect male reproductive behavior be detected?

b. Under what circumstances is this mating behavior abolished? (Powers and Winans, 1975; Winans and Powers, 1977; Lehman and Winans, 1982)

c. What do these results indicate about the neural control of the effects of pheromones on sexual behavior of male hamsters?

d. If aphrodisin, a sex-attractant pheromone of female hamsters, is swabbed on the hindquarters of a male hamster, how do test males react? (Singer et al., 1986; Singer, 1991)

e. Where is the gene responsible for aphrodisin production located? (Magert et al., 1999) an odorant-binding protein similar to aphrodisin? (Pes et al., 1998)

7. a. How does destruction of the vomeronasal organ of female rats affect their

1. preference for normal males and castrated males? (Romero et al., 1990)

2. sexual receptivity? (Rajendren et al., 1990)

b. What do these results suggest about the production of sex-attractant pheromones by males?

8. a. Describe the timing of the menstrual cycle of women who spent large amounts of time together. (McClintock, 1971; Russell et al., 1980; Stern and McClintock, 1998)

b. Compare the length of menstrual cycle of women who spent time in the presence of men and those who rarely did so.

c. How did menstruation affect the odor of female vaginal secretions and sexual attractiveness? (Doty et al., 1975)

9. How did exposure to androstenol, a substance normally produced by males, affect the social interactions of males and females? (Crowley and Brookshank, 1991)

10. a. What did the examination of the olfactory mucosae of surgical patients reveal? (See Figure 10.12 in your text. Garcia-Velasco and Mondragon, 1991)

b. What were the results of research to determine whether particular chemicals serve as pheromones in humans? (Monti-Bloch et al., 1998)

Learning Objective 10-4   Discuss the activational effects of gonadal hormones on the sexual behavior of women and men.

Read pages 320-322 and answer the following questions.

1. Ovarian hormones control both the _____ and the _____ to mate of most estrous female mammals other than primates. (Wallen, 1990)

2. Compare the sexual receptivity of women throughout the menstrual cycle with that of other female mammals throughout the estrous cycle.

3. a. What have most studies of the influence of ovarian hormones on women's sexual interest concluded? (Adams et al., 1978; Morris et al., 1987)

b. What did Wallen (1990) point out about the sexual interest and sexual activity of women in these studies?

c. When does sexual activity of lesbian couples tend to increase and what does this pattern suggest about the role of ovarian hormones? (Matteo and Rissman, 1984)

4. Now compare the sexual activity across the menstrual cycle of small numbers of monkeys living in small cages with that of large numbers of monkeys living in a large cage. (Study Figure 10.13 in your text. Wallen et al., 1986)

5. How do oral contraceptives affect fluctuations in a woman's secretion of ovarian hormones and her sexual interest? (Alexander et al., 1990)

6. Describe research on the activational effects of androgens on female sexual behavior in human couples.

   a. frequency of intercourse and female sexual gratification (Persky et al., 1978; Morris et al., 1987)

   b. female sexual desire (Alexander and Sherwin, 1993; Sherwin et al., 1985)

   c. occurrence of first intercourse (Halpern et al., 1997)

7. What roles, still speculative, may oxytocin play in female sexual response? (Anderson-Hunt and Dennerstein, 1995)

8. Compare the activational effects of testosterone on the sexual behavior of human males and other male mammals.

9. a. If a man is castrated, what changes occur in his interest in sexual activity?

   b. What factor appears to influence the decline in sexual ability after castration? (Money and Ehrhardt, 1972)

   c. Cite research with cats that also suggests the importance of experience.(Rosenblatt and Aronson, 1958a, 1958b)

10. Describe research that confirms that testosterone levels are affected by sexual arousal.

    a. the beard growth of an isolated scientist (Anonymous, 1970)

    b. watching erotic films (Hellhammer et al., 1985)

11. What roles, again still speculative, may oxytocin and prolactin play in male sexual response?

> **Learning Objective 10-5** Discuss sexual orientation, the prenatal androgenization of genetic females, and the failure of androgenization of genetic males.

Read pages 322-326 and answer the following questions.

1. Explain sexual orientation in your own words.

2. _____ homosexuality occurs only in humans. (Ehrhardt and Meyer-Bahlberg, 1981)

3. a. What belief concerning the cause of homosexuality was dispelled by a large-scale study by Bell et al. (1981)?

   b. What factor did they find to be the best predictor of homosexuality?

   c. What do these results suggest is a more likely cause for homosexuality than childhood social interactions?

4. a. Compare the levels of sex hormones during adulthood of male and female homosexuals with male and female heterosexuals. (Meyer-Bahlberg, 1984)

    b. What do the results of a few studies indicate about the testosterone levels of about 30 percent of female homosexuals?

    c. What, then, can we conclude about the levels of sex hormones as a biological cause of homosexuality?

    d. What is a more likely biological cause?

5. a. What is the cause of congenital adrenal hyperplasia (CAH)?

    b. How does prenatal masculinization affect males and females fetuses?

    c. Once diagnosed, how are human females medically treated?

    d. What do females with this syndrome report about their sexual orientation? (Money et al., 1984; Kinsey et al., 1943)

    e. Outline an explanation of how abnormally high levels of androgens may exert a behavioral effect.

6. Describe how Goy et al., (1988) studied the lasting effects of prenatal androgenization in female monkeys.

    a. How did the researchers create the conditions for prenatal androgenization?

    b. What variable influenced the degree of genital masculinization?

    c. Compare the sociosexual behavior of normal female monkeys and androgenized female monkeys with normal genitals.

    d. What do these results suggest?

7. a. What did researchers measure by placing a small microphone in the ears of homosexual, bisexual, and heterosexual men and women? (McFadden and Pasanen, 1999)

    b. Compare the frequency of otoacoustic emissions between men and women, homosexual and bisexual women, and three groups of men shown in Figure 10.14 in your text.

    c. What do the results suggest about biological differences between women with different sexual orientations?

8. a. Briefly describe how the internal and external genitalia of males with androgen insensitivity syndrome develop.

b. What is the best treatment of this condition, and how is this confirmed at the time of puberty?

c. What is the sexual orientation and behavior of these adults? (Money and Ehrhardt, 1972)

d. Carefully explain what this syndrome suggests about the role of testosterone and aromatized testosterone in normal male development.

9. Briefly summarize some of the documented differences between men's and women's brains. (Breedlove, 1994; Swaab et al., 1995 for specific references.)

   a. shared functions of the hemispheres

   b. overall brain size

   c. size and shape of particular regions

10. What do most researchers believe accounts for the sexual dimorphism of the human brain?

11. a. Identify the three subregions of the brain that differ in size in heterosexual and homosexual men and heterosexual women. (Swaab and Hofman, 1990; LeVay, 1991; Allen and Gorski, 1992)

   b. Compare the size of the bed nucleus of the stria terminalis (BNST) of

      1. males and females.

      2. male transsexuals and females.

      3. male homosexuals and male heterosexuals.

   c. Explain why the size of the BNST appears to be related to sexual identity and not sexual orientation by referring to these size comparisons. (Zhou et al., 1995; Study Figure 10.15 in your text.)

   d. What limited conclusions can we draw from these results?

12. a. Briefly explain the circumstances that necessitated John's parents raise him as a girl. (Money and Ehrhardt, 1972)

   b. What did the psychologists who studied the child first conclude about the success of the sex reassignment?

   c. In reality, how successful was it? (Diamond and Sigmundson, 1997)

   d. When, as an adolescent, Joan threatened suicide, what steps did her parents take?

   e. How has John now adjusted?

   f. How successful was sex reassignment for a child whose experience was similar to John's. (Bradley et al., 1998)

g. What can we therefore conclude about the effects of prenatal exposure to androgens on a person's sexual orientation and sexual identity?

13. a. What event could interfere with the prenatal androgenization of males?

b. Explain how maternal stress during pregnancy may have affected the

  1. sexual behavior of male rats (Ward, 1972).

  2. play behavior of juvenile male rats (Ward and Stehm, 1991).

  3. brain development of male rats (Anderson, et al., 1986).

c. What do the results of these studies suggest about a biological cause of male homosexuality?

14. a. What did a study of the siblings of homosexual and heterosexual men and homosexual and heterosexual women indicate? (Blanchard and Bogaert, 1996; Blanchard et al., 1998)

b. What is a possible explanation of the results and how do they contribute to an understanding of sexual orientation?

15. What were the results of twin studies to determine the role of heredity in male and female homosexuality? (Bailey and Pillard, 1991; Bailey et al., 1993; Pattatucci and Hamer, 1995)

16. To review: List the two biological factors that research indicates may affect sexual orientation.
  1.   2.

Lesson I Self Test

1. Which example illustrates the activational effects of sex hormones?

   a. development of ovaries and uterus
   b. production of sperm
   c. differentiation of the primordial gonads
   d. changes in brain development caused by androgens

2. The precursor of the _____ sex organs is the _____ system which develops _____.

   a. female; Wolffian; without any hormonal stimuli
   b. male; Wolffian; only if the testes secrete the appropriate hormones
   c. male; Müllerian; without any hormonal stimuli
   d. female; Müllerian; only if the ovaries secrete the appropriate hormones

3. Which event first marks the beginning of puberty?

   a. release of gonadotropic hormones by anterior pituitary gland
   b. secretion of gonadotropin-releasing hormones by hypothalamus

c. appearance of secondary sex characteristics

d. production of estrogens by ovaries or androgens by testes

4. The LH surge causes

a. estrus.

b. the refractory period.

c. the release of milk.

d. ovulation.

5. During aromatization _____ is converted into _____.

a. prolactin; oxytocin

b. aromatase; testosterone

c. estrogen; estradiol

d. testosterone; estradiol

6. The sexual behavior of female rodents depends on the presence of _____.

a. testosterone

b. estrogen

c. prolactin and oxytocin

d. estradiol and progesterone

7. The acceleration of the onset of puberty in a female rodent caused by the odor of a male is known as the _____ effect.

a. Whitten

b. Bruce

c. Vandenbergh

d. Lee-Boot

8. Removal of the _____ disrupts the Lee-Boot, Bruce, Vandenbergh, and Whitten effects.

a. pituitary gland

b. ventromedial nucleus of the hypothalamus

c. accessory olfactory bulb

d. adrenal glands

9. The frequency of intercourse throughout the menstrual cycle is at least moderately correlated with the woman's peak level of

a. testosterone.

b. progesterone.

c. estradiol.

d. oxytocin.

10. Castrated male cats remained potent longer if they

a. were introduced to a different female each time.

b. had previously engaged in high levels of sexual activity.

c. were housed with intact males.

d. did not have to compete with other males for the right to mate.

11. A large-scale study of male and female homosexuals found that

a. homosexuality results from unhappy parent-child relationships.

b. self-report was the best predictor of adult homosexuality.

c. only children were more likely to be homosexual than children with siblings.

d. homosexuality is often the result of poor interpersonal relationships with peers.

12. The biological basis of homosexuality may be differences in the

a. organizational affects of prenatal hormones.

b. activational affects of prenatal hormones.

c. degree of sexual dimorphism of the prenatal brain.

d. hormone levels of adult heterosexuals and homosexuals.

Lesson II: Neural Control of Sexual Behavior and Parental Behavior

Read the interim summary on pages 331-332 of your text to re-acquaint yourself with the material in this section.

Learning Objective 10-6 Discuss the neural control of male sexual behavior.

Read pages 327-329 and answer the following questions.

1. a. Let's look first at the spinal mechanisms that play a role in male sexual behavior. List the two male sexual reflexes that are controlled by spinal mechanisms.

1.   2.

b. Explain how men with spinal cord damage may still become fathers. (Hart, 1978) may still experience orgasm. (Money, 1960; Comarr, 1970)

2. a. What is the function of the spinal nucleus of the bulbocavernosus (SNB) of rats?

b. Why is it larger in male rats than female rats? (Breedlove and Arnold, 1980, 1983; Arnold and Jordan, 1988)

3. a. What stimulates a mother rat to lick the anogenital region of her male pups?

b. If the mother's sense of smell is destroyed and the amount of licking diminishes, what structural change results in the brains of the male pups? (Moore et al., 1992)

c. Why is maternal licking important for the brain development of male rats?

4. Now let's look at the brain mechanisms that play a role in male sexual behavior. Name and describe the location of the forebrain brain region most important for male sexual behavior.

5. a. If the medial preoptic area (MPA) is electrically stimulated, what kind of behavior is elicited in a male rat? (Malsbury, 1971)

b. How does sexual activity affect the

1. electrical activity of the neurons in the MPA? (Shimura et al., 1994; Mas, 1995)

2. metabolic activity of a male's MPA? (Oaknin et al., 1989; Robertson et al., 1991; Wood and Newman, 1993)

c. What profound effect does the destruction of the MPA have on male sexual behavior? (Heimer and Larsson, 1966/1967)

6. a. Where is the sexually-dimorphic nucleus (SDN) located? Compare its size in males and females rats. (See Figure 10.16 in your text. Gorski et al., 1978)

b. What factor during prenatal development determines the size of the SDN?

c. How is the volume of the SDN of an individual male rat related to the animal's sexual activity? (Anderson et al., 1986)

d. And how do lesions of the SDN affect male sexual activity? (De Jonge et al., 1989)

7. Like the _____ _____ _____, the _____ _____ is

    sexually dimorphic in rats.

8. a. How does mating affect chemical secretions of the medial amygdala? (Wood and Newman, 1993)

    b. How is male sexual behavior altered if it is destroyed? (DeJonge et al. 1992)

    c. How does the medial amygdala receive chemosensory information? sensory information? (See Figure 10.17 in
        your text.)

    d. How can sexual behavior in a castrated male rodent be restored? (Sipos and Nyby, 1996; Coolen and Wood,
        1999)

9. a. Where are the motor neurons that innervate pelvic organs involved in copulation located?

    b. Trace the anatomical connections between these neurons and the medial amygdala. Be sure to mention the
        nucleus paragigantocellularis of the medulla (PGi) in your answer. (Murphy et al., 1999; Shen et al., 1990;
        Marson and McKenna, 1996)

10. Immediately review what you have learned by studying Figure 10.18 in your text.

_____
| *Learning Objective 10-7* Discuss the neural control of female sexual behavior. |
_____

Read pages 329-331 and answer the following questions.

1. The most important forebrain region for male sexual behavior is the _____ _____

    _____ and the most important forebrain region for female sexual behavior is the _____

    _____ of the _____. (The location is shown in Figure 10.19 in your text.)

2. What are the behavioral effects of

    a. bilateral lesions of the VMH in female rats?

    b. electrical stimulation of the VMH? (Pfaff and Sakuma, 1979)

    c. injections of estradiol and progesterone in the VMH of ovariectomized females? (Rubin and Barfield, 1980;
        Pleim and Barfield, 1988)

    d. injections of a chemical that blocks the production of progesterone receptors? (Ogawa et al., 1994)

3. How does production of Fos protein in the VMH change with copulation or mechanical stimulation of the
    genitals or flanks? (Pfaus et al., 1993; Tetel et al., 1993)

4. a. Let's look at the mechanisms responsible for these behaviors. When female hamsters are given injections of
        estradiol and then progesterone, what change occurs in the activity of neurons in the VMH? (Rose, 1990)

    b. What kind of receptors are found on neurons in the VMH that increase Fos production in response to genital
        stimulation? (Tetel et al., 1994)

c. Where, then, do the effects of estradiol and stimulation converge?

d. Explain how estradiol increases the effectiveness of progesterone and affects female sexual behavior. Cite research to support your answer. (Study Figure 10.20 in your text. Blaustein and Feder, 1979)

5. a. Where do axons of neurons in the VMH project?

   b. Summarize changes in female sexual behavior resulting from

      1. electrical stimulation of the PAG and lesions of the PAG? (Sakuma and Pfaff, 1979a, 1979b)

      2. lesions that disconnect the VMH from the PAG? (Hennessey et al., 1990)

      3. estradiol treatment or electrical stimulation of the VMH. (Sakuma and Pfaff, 1980a, 1980b)

6. a. Where do axons of neurons in the PAG project? Where do neurons there project? (Daniels et al. 1999)

   b. What may be the function of this pathway?

7. Immediately review what you have just learned by studying Figure 10.21 in your text.

Read the interim summary on pages 337-338 of your text to re-acquaint yourself with the material in this section.

> *Learning Objective 10-8*   Describe the maternal behavior of rodents and explain how it is elicited and maintained.

Read pages 332-335 and answer the following questions.

1. Why is the attentive maternal behavior of a female rodent necessary for the survival of her offspring?

2. Describe the maternal behavior of a female rodent

   a. during pregnancy. (See Figure 10.22 in your text.)

   b. at the time of parturition.

3. Following birth, how does the mother

   a. assist elimination? Be sure to explain the procedure Friedman and Bruno (1976) used to determine the mutually beneficial nature of this behavior.

   b. retrieve pups outside the nest? (See Figure 10.23 in your text.)

4. When does maternal behavior begin to decrease?

5. Offer two reasons why maternal behavior is somewhat different from other sexually dimorphic behaviors.

6. a. Describe how a virgin female rat normally responds when she encounters a rat pup.

    b. Explain what the sensitization of virgin female rats means in your own words.

    c. Describe evidence that confirms the role of olfaction in sensitization. (Fleming and Rosenblatt, 1974; Fleming et al., 1979)

    d. In addition to olfaction, what physical sensations at the time of parturition also plays an important role? Cite research to support your answer (Graber and Kristal, 1977; Yeo and Keverne, 1986)

7. Describe two situations that cause mouse pups to emit ultrasonic calls and indicate how female mice respond to these calls. (Noirot, 1972; Hofer and Shair, 1993; Ihnat et al., 1995)

8. To illustrate the importance of tactile stimulation in the maintenance of maternal behavior, explain behavioral changes that occur if the region around the mouth of the mother is desensitized. the mouths of the pups. (Stern, 1989a, 1989b)

9. To review: What are the two most important sense modalities in the initiation of rodent maternal behavior, and what other sense modalities play a role in its control?

Learning Objective 10-9 Explain the hormonal and neural mechanisms that control maternal behavior and the neural control of paternal behavior.

Read pages 335-337 and answer the following questions.

1. Identify the hormones that facilitate nest building in nonpregnant female mice. (Lisk et al., 1969; Voci and Carlson, 1973)

2. Explain how the blood levels of these three hormones change with insemination, pregnancy, and parturition. (Study Figure 10.24 in your text.)

    a. estradiol

    b. progesterone

    c. prolactin

3. a. If ovariectomized virgin rats are given estradiol and progesterone in the pattern that duplicates the normal sequence, what behavioral change occurs? (Moltz et al., 1970; Bridges, 1984)

    b. What effects do these hormones have on a rat's responses to

       1. novel odors? (Fleming et al., 1989)

       2. preference for bedding material from a lactating female and her pups?

3. the strength of the long-term effects of sensitization? (Fleming and Sarker, 1990)

4. Summarize some research results on the importance of lactogenic hormones for maternal behavior.

   a. What treatment was necessary before virgin female rats who had received infusions of minute quantities of prolactin in the lateral ventricles or MPA responded? (Bridges et al., 1990)

   b. How did Lucas et al. (1998) disrupt rodent maternal behavior?

   c. What did an analysis of CSF for lactogenic hormones reveal? (Bridges et al., 1996)

   d. What does their presence in CSF suggest about the way in which they influence maternal behavior?

   e. How was the sensitization of virgin female mice affected by infusions of placental lactogenic hormones into the MPA?

5. a. Name the brain region critical for maternal behavior in rodents.

   b. How do lesions of the MPA affect maternal behavior and female sexual behavior? (Numan, 1974)

   c. What change occurs in the MPA as a result of

      1. parturition? (Del Cerro et al., 1995)

      2. exposure to pups?

   d. List the two regions of the midbrain where axons of the MPA that are activated by maternal behavior send axons. (Numan and Numan, 1997)

      1.   2.

   e. Where do some of these axons continue to project?

   f. If these connections are cut, how is maternal behavior affected? (Numan and Smith, 1984)

6. a. What kind of hormone receptors are found in the medial preoptic area? (Pfaff and Keiner, 1973)

   b. How does pregnancy affect these receptors? (Giordano et al., 1989)

   c. What is the effect on maternal behavior of

      1. estradiol implants in the MPA? (Numan et al., 1977)

      2. antiestrogen chemical injections in the MPA? (Adieh et al., 1987)

      3 prolactin infusions in the MPA? (Bridges et al., 1990)

      4. lesions of the medial amygdala or the stria terminalis? How? (Fleming et al., 1980)

      5. low-level electrical stimulation of the MPA? medial amygdala? (Morgan et al., 1999)

7. Study Figure 10.25 in your text and describe how estradiol may exert its effects on maternal behavior.

8. Finally let's look at some research on the neural control of paternal behavior.

   a. Compare the parental behavior and the MPA of monogamous prairie voles with that of promiscuous montane voles. (Shapiro et al., 1991)

   b. If male prairie voles are exposed to pups, what change occurs in the MPA and what does this change suggest about the role of the MPA? (Kirkpatrick et al., 1994)

   c. How is the paternal behavior of male rats affected by

      1. lesions of the MPA? (Rosenblatt et al., 1996; Sturgis and Bridges, 1997)

      2. implants of estradiol into the MPA?

   d. What do these research results suggest about the neural control of the maternal and paternal behavior of rodents?

Lesson II Self Test

1. Human males with spinal cord damage

   a. never again have an erection or experience an orgasm.
   b. can only experience an orgasm through mechanical stimulation.
   c. can experience "phantom erections" and orgasms.
   d. experience a decline in the ability to have an erection and orgasm similar to the effects of castration.

2. The size of the sexually dimorphic nucleus of the _____ is _____.

   a. medial amygdala; reduced in pups whose mother was prenatally sensitized
   b. left temporal lobe; directly related to level of prenatal stress
   c. preoptic area; controlled by the amount of androgens present during fetal development
   d. ventral tegmental area; directly related to fertility

3. An important connection between the MPA and the motor neurons of the spinal cord is through the

   a. nucleus paragigantocellularis (PGi).
   b. central tegmental field.
   c. medial amygdala.
   d. bed nucleus of the stria terminalis (BNST).

4. The brain region most critical for female sexual behavior is the _____ and the brain region most critical for male sexual behavior is the _____.

   a. ventromedial nucleus of the hypothalamus; ventral tegmental area
   b. medial preoptic area; sexually dimorphic nucleus
   c. ventromedial nucleus of the hypothalamus; medial preoptic area
   d. medial amygdala, medial preoptic area

5. The priming effect of estradiol is caused by

   a. the LH surge.
   b. an increase in progesterone receptors.
   c. increased release of norepinephrine in the hypothalamus.
   d. an increase in the firing rate of neurons in the periaqueductal gray matter.

6. Electrical stimulation of the periaqueductal gray matter facilitates

   a. ovulation.
   b. lordosis.
   c. hormonal priming.
   d. lactation.

7. Female rodents lick the anogenital region of their young. What is one of the results of this behavior?

a. assures identification of pups by scent
b. recycles water
c. reduces detection of pups' odor by intruders
d. regulates pups' metabolic rate

8. Virgin female rats can be made to care for infants if they are

a. caged with an experienced mother.
b. allowed to observe pups through a glass partition.
c. given injections of progesterone.
d. placed with young pups for several days.

9. Ultrasonic calls from a rodent pups signals that the pup is

a. cold.
b. hungry.
c. threatened by an intruder.
d. unable to move.

10. If ovariectomized virgin female rats are given a sequence of doses of estradiol and progesterone, they will

a. build brood nests.
b. begin to lactate.
c. fail to retrieve pups.

d. be sensitized to care for young more quickly.

11. Just before parturition the level of estradiol

a. rises; the level of progesterone begins to fall; and the level of prolactin rises.
b. and progesterone begin to fall and the level of prolactin rises.
c. falls, the level of progesterone rises, and the level of prolactin falls
d. rises, the level of prolactin falls, and then the level of progesterone rises.

12. When monogamous species of voles in which the male and female both care for the offspring are compared to promiscuous species that do not share parental responsibility

a. there are fewer connections between the MPA and the ventral tegmental area in monogamous males.
b. Fos production in the MPA of monogamous males is lower.
c. the sexual dimorphism of the MPA is less pronounced in the monogamous species.
d. the vasopressin levels in the MPA of monogamous males are lower.

Answers for Self Tests

Lesson I

1. b   Obj. 10-1
2. b   Obj. 10-1
3. b   Obj. 10-1
4. d   Obj. 10-2
5. d   Obj. 10-2
6. d   Obj. 10-2
7. c   Obj. 10-3
8. c   Obj. 10-3
9. a   Obj. 10-4
10. b   Obj. 10-4
11. b   Obj. 10-5
12. a   Obj. 10-5

Lesson II

1. c   Obj. 10-6
2. c   Obj. 10-6
3. a   Obj. 10-6
4. c   Obj. 10-7
5. b   Obj. 10-7
6. b   Obj. 10-7
7. b   Obj. 10-8
8. d   Obj. 10-8
9. a   Obj. 10-8
10. d   Obj. 10-9
11. a   Obj. 10-9
12. c   Obj. 10-9

CHAPTER 11
Emotion

Lesson I: Emotions as Response Patterns, Expression and Recognition of Emotions, and Feelings of Emotions

Read the interim summary on pages 350-351 of your text to re-acquaint yourself with the material in this section.

> **Learning Objective 11-1** Discuss the behavioral, autonomic, and hormonal components of an emotional response and the role of the amygdala in controlling them.

Read pages 340-347 and answer the following questions.

1. List and define the three components of an emotional response in your own words.

    1.

    2.

    3.

2. In general, what is the role of the amygdala in the neural control of emotional responses?

3. List the four major nuclei of the amygdala and their connections. (Study Figure 11.1 in your text.)

Nucleus/Nuclei	Receives information from	Sends information to

4. Underline the nucleus that is most important for expressing emotional responses provoked by aversive stimuli.

5.   What behavioral and/or physiological changes occur

   a. to the central nucleus in the presence of aversive stimuli? (Pascoe and Kapp, 1985; Campeau et al., 1991)

   b. if the central nucleus is destroyed? (Coover et al., 1992; Davis, 1992b; LeDoux, 1992)

   c. from short-term and long-term stimulation of the central nucleus? (Davis, 1992b; Henke, 1982)

6.   List several other regions which receive information from the central nucleus and the responses they control, which are summarized in Figure 11.2 in your text.

7.   A classically conditioned response is produced when a(n) _____ stimulus is paired with a stimulus that _____ produces a response and a conditioned emotional response is produced by a(n) _____ stimulus that is paired with a(n) _____-_____ stimulus. The first or _____ response elicited by a painful stimulus is aimed at _____ the stimulus and the second or _____ response involves physiological changes controlled by the autonomic nervous system.

8.   a. Define *coping response* in your own words.

   b. What is its effect on a conditioned emotional response?

9.   a. Study Figure 11.3 in your text, which diagrams how LeDoux and his colleagues classically conditioned an emotional withdrawal response in rats, and identify the warning stimulus and the emotion-producing stimulus. (reviewed by LeDoux, 1995)

   b. On the day following conditioning, how did the rats respond when they heard the warning tone? What additional response did they make? Be sure to use the term *freezing* in your answer.

   c. What brain region appears to be necessary for a conditioned emotional response to occur? (LeDoux, 1995)

   d. Which response components of conditioned emotional responses are disrupted by lesions of the lateral hypothalamus? the caudal periaqueductal gray matter? (LeDoux et al., 1988)

   e. In addition to auditory stimuli, what other kinds of sensory stimuli evoke conditioned emotional responses?

10. a. Explain how Davis and his colleagues produced and measured the startle response of rat subjects. (Study Figure 11.4 in your text. Davis, 1992a, 1992b; Davis et al., 1994)

b. Once the startle response was established, how did they augment it?

c. Trace the pathway of the augmented startle response by completing Figure 1. (Study Figure 11.5 in your text.)

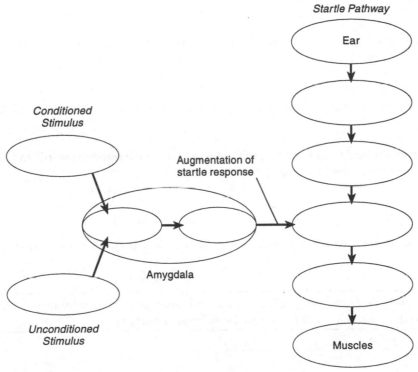

Figure 1

11. Where in the amygdala do anxiolytic drugs and opiates appear to exert their anxiety-reducing effects? (Knapp et al., 1982; Davis, 1992a; Sanders and Shekhar, 1995)

12. Summarize evidence that suggests the amygdala, which contains CCK-secreting neurons, plays a role in some of the behavioral effects of this hormone. (Ingram et al., 1989; Schiffmann and Vanderhaeghen, 1991)

a. injections of CCK_B agonists and antagonists and signs of anxiety (Frankland et al., 1997)

b. situations that increase fear and endogenous levels of CCK in the amygdala (Pavlasevic et al., 1993)

c. injections of an indirect antagonist for the benzodiazepine receptor and anxiety (Pratt and Brett, 1995)

13. Summarize evidence suggesting the amygdala plays a role in human emotional responses.

a. Under what circumstances did seizure disorder patients report feeling afraid? (White, 1940; Halgren et al., 1978; Gloor et al., 1982)

b. How do lesions of the amygdala affect a person's

    1. acquisition of a conditioned emotional response? (LeBar et al., 1995; Bechara et al., 1995)

    2. startle response? (Angrilli et al., 1996)

c. Compare the memories of normal subjects and people with amygdala damage for emotional story details? (Cahill et al., 1995)

d. Compare the PET scans of people when they recalled neutral films and emotionally arousing films they had seen. (Cahill et al., 1996)

e. Now compare the PET scans of people working on solvable and unsolvable anagrams. (Schneider et al., 1996)

f. Finally, compare the PET scans of normal subjects when they saw threatening words and neutral words. (See Figure 11.6 in your text. Isenberg et al., 1999)

14. How does CCK affect both anxiety and blood flow to the amygdala? (Benkelfat et al., 1995)

Learning Objective 11-2 Discuss the role of the orbitofrontal cortex in the analysis of social situations and the effects of damage to this region, including those produced by psychosurgery.

Read pages 347-350 and answer the following questions.

1. Study Figure 11.7 in your text and describe the location of the orbitofrontal cortex. How did this region get its name?

2. List the direct inputs and the outputs from the orbitofrontal cortex.

Direct Inputs	Outputs
1.	1.
2.	2.
3.	3.
4.	4.
5.	5.

3. a. What kind of information is received through the inputs?

    b. What kinds of activities are influenced through the outputs?

4. Summarize early case histories that suggested the role of the orbitofrontal cortex in emotional behavior.

    a. What part of Phineas Gage's brain was largely destroyed as a result of his accident and how did his injury affect his behavior? (See Figure 11.8 your text. Damasio et al., 1994)

    b. To discuss the case of Becky the chimpanzee, begin by describing the experimental task. (Jacobsen et al., 1935)

    c. How did Becky react to this task?

    d. What kind of lesion did she receive and how did it affect her behavior during subsequent training sessions?

    e. How did the medically necessary removal of the frontal lobes of a human appear to affect the patient? (Bricker, 1936)

5. a. What human application did these last two case studies suggest to Egas Moniz? (Fulton, 1949)

    b. Following prefrontal lobotomy, what emotional changes were observed in patients?

    c. What were some of the unexpected side effects of this surgery?

    d. Why was this procedure eventually abandoned? (Valenstein, 1986)

6. a. Study Figure 11.9 in your text and briefly describe "ice-pick" surgery using a transorbital leucotome.

    b. What specific objections did physicians raise to the use of this procedure to perform human brain surgery?

7. a. How well did a patient who had had surgery for the removal of a benign tumor of the orbitofrontal cortex assess hypothetical social situations? (Eslinger and Damasio, 1985)

    b. How well did this same patient conduct his personal affairs following surgery?

    c. What does this clinical evidence suggest about the role of the orbitofrontal cortex in making judgments and conclusions?

8. a. Briefly describe the card game that normal subjects, subjects with ventromedial prefrontal lesions and subjects with amygdala lesions were taught. (Bechara et al., 1997. 1999)

    b. How did normal subjects react just before choosing a card from the "bad" deck? How did their emotional response change their strategy?

c. In contrast, how did subjects with prefrontal lesions react to cards from the "bad" deck? subjects with lesions of the amygdala?

d. What, then, do emotional responses contribute to the process of making appropriate decisions?

9. a. What kind of connections bring environmental information to the orbitofrontal cortex?

b. And what kind of connections permit the orbitofrontal cortex to influence behavior and the ANS?

10. a. More specifically, what may be the role of the cingulate gyrus in making appropriate decisions?

b. If the human cingulate gyrus is electrically stimulated, what kinds of feelings occur? (Talairach et al., 1973)

c. If this region is damaged, what syndrome results? (Amyes and Nielsen, 1955)

11. What is the affect on the anterior cingulate gyrus of listening to
    a. narrations of life events that would be expected to arouse anger? (Dougherty et al., 1999)
    b. unpleasant music? (Blood et al., 1999)

12. Why may introverts show less activation of the anterior cingulate cortex than extroverts, but more activation of the prefrontal cortex? (Johnson et al., 1999)

Read the interim summary on page 358 of your text to re-acquaint yourself with the material in this section.

Learning Objective 11-3 Discuss cross-cultural studies on the expression and comprehension of emotions.

Read pages 351-352 and answer the following questions.

1. Why is the expression and recognition of emotions a beneficial social behavior?

2. a. State Darwin's hypothesis concerning the origin of human facial expression of emotion. (Darwin, 1872/1965)

b. What evidence did he obtain to support his conclusion?

3. Describe modern research by (Ekman and Friesen, 1971; Ekman, 1980) that tends to confirm Darwin's hypothesis.
    a. Who were the subjects?

b. How easily did they recognize the facial expression of Westerners?

c. How easily did Westerners recognize the facial expressions of a man from this tribe shown in Figure 11.10 in your text?

4. Explain the rationale for and the results of research comparing the facial expressions of young blind and sighted children, but not of blind and sighted adults. (Woodworth and Schlosberg, 1954; Izard, 1971)

5. What do the consistent patterns of the facial expression of emotion supported by cross-cultural studies and studies with the blind suggest about their basis?

6. a. List two factors that influence the expression of emotions.

   1.   2.

   b. Define *display rules* in your own words.

   c. According to Ekman and Friesen (1975), how do display rules affect emotional expression?

7. a. During the showing of a coming-of-age rite how did American and Japanese students react when they were alone? with others? (Ekman et al., 1972; Friesen, 1972)

   b. What do these findings suggest about the influence of culture on the display of emotion?

Learning Objective 11-4   Discuss the neural control of the recognition of emotional expression in normal people and people with brain damage.

Read pages 352-355 and answer the following questions.

1. a. What were some of the situations in which Kraut and Johnston (1979) observed the emotional expression of subjects?

   b. When did the subjects show the greatest reaction?

   c. What does this study suggest about emotional expression and communication?

2. If the right hemisphere plays a more important role in the comprehension of emotion, why is it advantageous to receive emotional stimuli in the left ear or left visual field?

3. Briefly review some of the tasks for which the right and the left hemisphere is better suited. (reviewed by Bryden and Ley, 1983)

4. a. Which recognition tasks did patients with right-hemisphere lesions find difficult? did not find difficult? (Blonder et al., 1991; Bowers et al., 1991)

b. What do these responses suggest about the role of the right-hemisphere in the comprehension of emotions conveyed by real or imagined facial expression or hand gestures?

5. a. Describe the three situations George et al. (1996) used to test comprehension of emotion.

    b. As recorded by PET scans, when did the right and left hemispheres of the brain show increased activity? (See Figure 11.11 in your text.)

6. a. What kind of brain damage had been received by subjects in a study by Heilman et al. (1975)?

    b. Describe the experimental task and the accuracy of the subjects' response.

    c. How accurately did a man with pure word deafness identify the emotional content of speech? (Heilman et al., 1983)

    d. What do these studies suggest about the components of comprehension of emotion?

7. What kind of brain damage did patients who had difficulty recognizing facial expressions of negative emotions suffer? (See Figure 11.12 in your text. Adolphs et al., 1996)

8. What are some of the combinations of recognition deficits for faces and facial expressions of emotion experienced by people with damage to visual association cortex? (Bowers and Heilman, 1981; Humphreys et al., 1993)

9. a. What characteristic of the face do neurons in a monkey's superior temporal sulcus appear to recognize? (Study Figure 11.13 in your text. Perrett et al., 1992)

    b. Why is gaze important in the recognition of emotions?

    c. How do lesions of the superior temporal sulcus affect monkeys' gaze recognition? (Campbell et al., 1990; Heywood and Cowey, 1992)

    d. Which neural connections may play a role in this recognition? (Harries and Perrett, 1991)

10. Summarize evidence that the amygdala may also plays an important role in the recognition of emotion.

    a. How do lesions of the amygdala affect the ability to recognize facial expressions of emotion? (For example, Adolphs et al., 1994; 1995)

    b. What other impairment do these lesions sometimes produce?

c. Compare the activity of the amygdala, as recorded by PET scans, when people viewed photographs of sad and happy faces. (Morris et al., 1996; Whalen et al., 1998)

11. a. After looking at photographs of unfamiliar people, what kind of judgements were normal subjects and subjects with lesions of the amygdala asked to make? (Adolphs et al., 1998)

b. How prudent were the judgements of each group of subjects?

c. What do the results suggest about the role of the amygdala in the recognition of facial expression of negative emotions and signs of untrustworthiness? (Adolphs et al., 1999)

12. a. Damage to the basal ganglia affects a person's ability to recognize an expression of _____.

b. Name two medical afflictions that impair the ability to recognize disgust. (Sprengelmeyer et al., 1996; 1997)

Learning Objective 11-5 Discuss the neural control of emotional expression in normal people and people with brain damage.

Read pages 355-358 and answer the following questions.

1. What does it mean to say that it is impossible to voluntarily produce a genuine smile? (Duchenne, 1862/1990)

2. a. What kind of voluntary and involuntary facial movements can patients with volitional facial paresis make? patients with emotional facial paresis. (Representative facial movements are shown in Figure 11.14 in your text. Hopf et al., 1992; Topper et al., 1995; Urban et al., 1998)

b. What kind of brain damage causes each of these syndromes?

c. What do these syndromes indicate about the movement of facial muscles and the genuine expression of emotion?

3. The _____ hemisphere appears to be specialized for both the _____ of emotion and the _____ of emotion.

4. a. How are chimerical faces, shown in Figure 11.15 in your text, created?

b. Why is the left half of the face more expressive?

c. What more natural observations confirmed this? (Moscovitch and Olds, 1982; Borod et al., 1998)

d. When the chimerical faces technique was used with rhesus monkeys, what did the analysis of the videotapes indicate about hemispheric specialization

1. of emotional expression? (Study Figure 11.16 in your text.)

2. in the evolution of emotional expression? (Hauser, 1993)

5. Compare the ability of patients with Wernicke's aphasia and patients with right-hemisphere lesions to express emotions using tone of voice.

6. a. When and how does a physician perform a Wada test? Be sure to note any changes in patients' descriptions of intense emotional events that occur.

b. What do Ross and his colleagues suggest is the role of the right hemisphere? the left? (Ross et al., 1994)

Read the interim summary on pages 360-361 in your text to re-acquaint yourself with the material in this section.

Learning Objective 11-6   Discuss the James-Lange theory of feelings of emotion and evaluate relevant research.

Read pages 358-360 and answer the following questions.

1. Outline the James-Lange theory in your own words. (James, 1884; Lange, 1887)

2. Carefully study Figure 11.17 in your text that diagrams the James-Lange theory. Check your understanding by describing the process.

3. According to the theory, in what order do these two events produce feelings of emotion?

"I'm more nervous than I thought I was." / Her stomach felt queasy as she waited to be interviewed for a second time for the job.

4. In what way does the James-Lange theory appear to contradict personal experience?

5. a. Explain two of Cannon's objections to the James-Lange theory. (Cannon, 1927)

b. Now refute his objections.

6. Why is the theory difficult to verify?

7. a. Describe the subjects interviewed by Hohman (1966).

    b. Explain how he tested the James-Lange theory by studying these subjects.

    c. What was the relationship between the level of injury and the intensity of feelings of emotion? Explain.

8. a. Why did Ekman and his colleagues ask subjects to move particular facial muscles, but gave them no further information? (Ekman et al., 1983; Levenson et al., 1990)

    b. What, according to the physiological monitoring, happened to the subjects while they made these movements?

    c. Suggest two explanations for the results you have just described.

9. Study Figure 11.18 in your text to see the facial expressions posed by adults in front of infants and the infants' responses. What do their responses suggest about the tendency to imitate? (Field et al., 1982)

Lesson I Self Test

1. If an animal learns how to avoid, escape from, or minimize an aversive stimulus, it has learned a(n)

    a. conditioned emotional response.
    b. coping response.
    c. offensive emotional response.
    d. defensive emotional response.

2. If the central nucleus of the amygdala is destroyed,

    a. autonomic and behavioral components of conditioned emotional responses are disinhibited.
    b. conditioned emotional responses to visual and olfactory, but not auditory, stimuli are disrupted.
    c. positive and negative feelings associated with conditioned emotional responses are disrupted.
    d. conditioned emotional responses cannot be learned.

3. An augmented startle response occurs through a connection between the central nucleus of the amygdala and the

    a. ventral nucleus of the lateral lemniscus.
    b. caudate nucleus.
    c. nucleus reticularis pontis caudalis.
    d. dorsolateral nucleus of the thalamus.

4. People who have suffered damage to the orbitofrontal cortex

    a. suffer from compulsive behaviors.
    b. do not exhibit normal timidity in strange situations.
    c. respond appropriately to hypothetical social situations, but not when these situations apply to them.
    d. show a tendency to express emotional feelings using gestures and facial expressions rather than verbally.

5. What may be the function of the orbitofrontal cortex?

a. to control voluntary activity

b. to organize hormonal responses to emotional stimuli

c. to make judgments and conclusions

d. to translate judgments into appropriate feelings and behaviors

6. Accurate identification of the facial expressions of Westerners by members of an isolated New Guinea tribe tends to confirm Darwin's hypothesis that emotional expressions

a. are innate, unlearned responses.

b. consists of four responses: fear, anger, sorrow, and surprise.

c. are immune to the effects of socialization.

d. are identical, whether posed or spontaneous.

7. The _____ hemisphere is involved in _____ emotions and the _____ hemisphere is involved in _____ emotions.

a. left; genuine; right; posed

b. right; negative; left; positive

c. left; fleeting; right; longer lasting

d. right; verbal expression of; left; nonverbal expression of

8. Following right hemisphere damage, patients

a. have difficulty determining the correct emotion conveyed in a situation.

b. can still imagine and describe mental images of emotions.

c. have difficulty expressing emotion with the face and voice.

d. can answer questions about emotional and nonemotional situations.

9. People with emotional facial paresis cannot _____ facial expressions of emotion.

a. imagine

b. mimic

c. spontaneously produce

d. distinguish between different

10 Research results using the chimerical faces technique suggest that the _____ half of the _____ is _____ expressive.

a. left; brain; more

b. left; face; less

c. right; brain; more

d. right; face; more

11. According to the James-Lange theory, emotional feelings

a. result from sensory feedback from the responses of emotion-producing situations.

b. are a direct response to emotion-producing situations.

c. are a product of both sensory feedback and acquired social behavior.

d. result in emotional behavior.

12. The results of research on patients with spinal cord injuries suggests that the intensity of their emotional states is related to the

a. frequency of social contact.

b. level of injury to the spinal cord.

c. length of time following injury

d. perception of self-worth.

Lesson II: Aggressive Behavior

Read the interim summary on page 369 in your text to re-acquaint yourself with the material in this section.

| *Learning Objective 11-7* Discuss the nature, functions, and neural control of aggressive behavior. |

Read pages 361-364 and answer the following questions.

1. Complete these statements.

a. Aggressive behaviors are species-typical; that is

b. Many aggressive behaviors are related to

2. List the three basic forms of aggressive behavior and give an example of each kind of behavior.

1.

2.

3.

3. a. Define *predation* in your own words.

   b. Compare the level of arousal and activity of the autonomic nervous system of animals engaged in offensive or defensive behaviors and predatory behaviors.

4. a. The neural control of aggressive behavior is _____.

   b. In general, where are the neural circuits for the particular movements an attacking or defending animal makes located?

   c. Which structures appear to control these circuits?

   d. What controls the activity of the limbic system?

5. a. What task did Roberts and Kiess (1964) teach laboratory cats?

   b. What was the only situation in which these cats would seek out a rat?

   c. If brain stimulation was turned on while a hungry cat was eating, what did it do? what did it not do?

   d. What do these results suggest about the neural control of eating and attack?

6. Brain stimulation that elicits _____ attack appears to be aversive, and brain stimulation that elicits

   _____ attack appears to be reinforcing. (Panksepp, 1971)

7. a. What forms of aggressive behavior can be elicited through electrical or chemical stimulation of the periaqueductal gray matter (PAG)?

   b. What other brain structures may play a role in these behaviors? (reviewed by Siegel et al., 1999)

8. a. How is defensive rage affected

      1. if, while the dorsal PAG is being stimulated, the medial hypothalamus is also stimulated? (Schubert et al., 1996)

      2. if AP-7 is infused into the dorsal PAG?

   b. How did the researchers establish that there is a connection between the dorsal PAG and the medial hypothalamus?

   c. Study Figure 11.19 in your text and note the regions of the amygdala and the hypothalamus that are involved in defensive rage and predation.

9. Why are serotonergic drugs sometimes used to treat violent behavior in humans?

10. If serotonergic axons in the forebrain are destroyed, how is aggressive attack affected? (Vergnes et al., 1988)

11. a. How did researchers assess the level of serotonergic activity in the brains of monkeys living in a free-ranging colony? (Mehlman et al., 1995; Higley et al., 1996a, 1996b.)

    b. To be sure that you understand what happens when serotonin (5-HT) is released in the brain, explain the relationship between the level of 5-HIAA in cerebrospinal fluid and the level of 5-HT.

    c. What kinds of activities did young male monkeys with low levels of 5-HIAA engage in?

    d. What was their survival rate? (Study Figure 11.20 in your text.)

    e. What do these results suggest about the role of serotonin in aggressive behavior?

12. a. How did dominance patterns in a vervet monkey colony change when the dominant males were removed and lower ranked males received either a serotonin agonist or antagonist? (Raleigh et al., 1991)

    b. Carefully explain why these results suggest that dominance and aggression are not synonymous.

13. a. In targeted mutation studies with mice, how did mice

       1. lacking receptors for 5-HT1B and normal mice react to an intruder? (Saudou et al., 1994)

       2. with decreased release of serotonin in the dorsal raphe nucleus react? (Chen et al., 1994)

    b. What do the results confirm about the effect of serotonin on aggression?

14. a. In humans, what is the relationship between serotonergic activity and

       1. aggressiveness and antisocial tendencies? (Brown et al., 1979; 1982)

       2. behavioral problems among other close relatives? (Coccaro et al., 1994)

    b. What was the effect of Prozac, a serotonin agonist, on behavior? (Coccaro and Kavoussi, 1997)

15. Briefly summarize research on a Dutch family to determine the role of MAO type A in aggressive behavior, noting the puzzling results. (Brunner et al., 1993)

16. a. To what extent is alcohol a factor in serious criminal activity in North America? (Murdoch et al., 1990)

    b. When mice are given low doses of alcohol how do some of them react? how do others react? (Miczek et al., 1998)

    c. What may account for their different reactions?

17. According to Hoaken et al. (1998), how may alcohol affect the brain and therefore aggressive behavior?

18. Summarize the effect on aggressive behavior of some monkeys if they are given

    a. free access to a 8.4 percent solution of alcohol.

    b. a serotonin agonist.(Higley et al., 1998)

19. Review evidence that alcohol and serotonin interact by explaining what did

    a. low sensitivity to the intoxicating effects of alcohol predict about the subsequent behavior of young men? (Heinz et al., 1998)

    b. low levels of 5-HIAA in the CSF of monkeys indicate about their behavior?

Learning Objective 11-8 Discuss the hormonal control of aggression in males, aggression in females, and maternal aggression.

Read pages 364-367 and answer the following questions.

1. a. Define *intermale aggression* in your own words.

   b. Now explain what the emergence of intermale aggression at puberty suggests about the control mechanisms of aggressive behaviors. Cite research to support your answer. (Beeman, 1947)

2. a. Briefly review the organizational and activational effects of early androgenization that influences both intermale aggression and male sexual behavior.(Study Figure 11.21 in your text.)

   b. Early androgenization _____ neural circuits, and the earlier the androgenization the

      _____ effective the _____.

3. If pregnant mice are subjected to prenatal stress, what two behavioral changes are observed in their male offspring at adulthood? (Kinsley and Svare, 1986)

4. What treatment restores intermale aggression in castrated cats? (Bean and Conner, 1978)

5. a. What technique abolishes intermale aggression in mice? What technique had no effect? (Study Figure 11.22 in your text. Bean, 1982)

   b. What is the probable stimulus for intermale aggression and what brain region may play a role?

c. What other type of aggressive behavior appear to be controlled by pheromones? (Dixon and Mackintosh, 1971; Dixon, 1973)

6. Discuss evidence that interfemale aggression is dependent on testosterone.

    a. How did ovariectomized female rats respond to injections of testosterone? (Study Figure 11.23 in your text. Van de Poll et al., 1988)

    b. Study Figure 11.24 in your text and be sure you understand the difference between 0M, 1M, and 2M females.

    c. Which of these females have the highest levels of prenatal testosterone and later exhibit the most interfemale aggression? (Vom Saal and Bronson, 1980)

7. At what time in the estrous cycle are some primates most likely to engage in aggressive behavior with males? (Carpenter, 1942; Saayman, 1971) with females? (Sassenrath et al., 1973; Mallow, 1979)

8. Summarize some of the findings of a literature review (Floody, 1983) on premenstrual syndrome.

    a. At what times in the menstrual cycle did observed aggressiveness increase and decrease?

    b. How widespread do mood shifts and actual aggressiveness appear to be?

    c. Which women were more likely to experience them? (Persky, 1974)

9. a. Compare the latency to attack an intruder by a lactating female with that of two strange males encountering each other. (Svare, 1983)

    b. When do pregnant mice begin to become aggressive? What is the stimulus? (Mann et al., 1984)

    c. What change in aggressiveness occurs immediately after giving birth? Why? (Ghiraldi and Svare, 1989; Svare, 1989)

    d. How can this period of docility be interrupted? restored?

    e. What two stimuli provided by offspring activate aggressive behavior?

    f. How can one of these stimuli be eliminated? (Svare and Gandelman, 1976; Gandelman and Simon, 1980)

    g. Briefly summarize how prenatal exposure to androgens appears to affect maternal aggression. (Vom Saal and Bronson, 1980a; Kinsley et al. 1986)

Learning Objective 11-9 Discuss the effects of androgens on human aggressive behavior.

Read pages 367-369 and answer the following questions.

1. Explain why the study of human male aggression must consider the effects of both socialization and androgenization.

2. a. Briefly describe the effects of castration of convicted male sex offenders. (Hawke, 1951; Sturup, 1961; Laschet, 1973)

    b. In what way were these studies flawed?

3. What alternative treatment for human sexual aggression is preferable and how effective is it? (Walker and Meyer, 1981; Zumpe et al., 1991)

4. a. What was the conclusion of a literature review concerning the relationship between men's testosterone levels and the level of aggression? (Archer, 1994)

    b. What were the results of a study of nearly 4500 US military veterans? (Dabbs and Morris, 1990)

    c. Summarize the relationship between measures of violence and the testosterone levels of

       1. male prisoners and female prisoners.

       2. female prisoners who engaged in unprovoked violence. (Dabbs et al., 1987; Dabbs et al., 1988)

    d. According to Mazur and Booth (1998), what may be the primary social effect of androgens?

5. Carefully explain why we cannot conclude that high testosterone levels cause increased aggression. Cite research to support your explanation. (Mazur and Lamb, 1980; Elias, 1981; McCaul et al., 1992; Bernhardt et al., 1998)

6. a. Now explain the ethical concerns that prevent the study of the effects of testosterone by giving experimental subjects androgen supplements.

    b. What is the only kind of experimental evidence on this subject available? Cite several examples.

7. a. How did anabolic steroids affect the aggressive behavior of male weight lifters? (Yates et al., 1992)

    b. Why is it incorrect to conclude that steroids are responsible for increased aggressiveness?

8. a. How and when does alcohol intake affect intermale aggression in dominant male squirrel monkeys? subordinate monkeys? (Study Figure 11.25 in your text. Winslow and Miczek, 1985, 1988)

    b. What do these effects suggest about factors that influence aggressive behavior?

    c. What did tests during the nonmating season confirm? (Winslow et al., 1988)

Lesson II Self Test

1. Predatory attack

    a. is usually accompanied by a strong display of rage.
    b. and eating are organized by different neural mechanisms.
    c. elicited by electrical stimulation appears aversive to laboratory animals.
    d. on rats by laboratory cats is a spontaneous behavior.

2. If AP-7 is infused into the periaqueductal gray matter, the effects of medial hypothalamic stimulation are

    a. increased.
    b. blocked.
    c. delayed.
    d. inconsistent.

3. Increased activity of serotonergic synapses _____ aggression.

    a. increases
    b. inhibits
    c. initiates
    d. has no effect on

4. Monkeys in a free-ranging colony with the lowest levels of a metabolite of serotonin

    a. showed increased risk-taking behavior.
    b. had the longest survival rates.
    c. usually became the dominant monkeys.
    d. had the highest levels of social competency.

5. As adults, the male offspring of prenatally stressed females exhibited

    a. less intermale aggression.
    b. more intermale aggression.
    c. less affect during predatory attack.

    d. a marked aversion to all forms of aggressive behavior.

6. Females who were next to a male fetus in the uterus _____than females located between two females.

    a. had significantly higher levels of testosterone in their blood
    b. were less likely to display female sexual behavior.
    c. were more likely to attack a male
    d. exhibited less maternal behavior

7. Females of some primate species are more likely to engage in fights

    a. during interruptions of menstruation caused by events such as pregnancy or low food supply.
    b. just before and just after menstruation.
    c. around the time of ovulation and just before menstruation.
    d. following ovulation if pregnancy does not occur.

8. Immediately after giving birth, female mice

    a. exhibit heightened irritability and aggressiveness.
    b. are more hostile toward rival females than males.
    c. will attack only males.
    d. are docile for approximately 48 hours.

9. Which of the following statements about alcohol and aggression is *not* true?

    a. Some, but not all, mice become aggressive when given low doses of alcohol.
    b. Alcohol may interfere with the inhibitory effects of the frontal lobes on aggression.

c. Monkeys with low levels of 5-HIAA display lower sensitivity to alcohol and higher levels of aggression.

d. Serotonin antagonists decrease both alcohol intake and aggression.

10. Studies of the effects of castration on human aggression

a. are the only way to determine the effects of androgens on aggression.

b. usually do not measure aggressive behavior directly.

c. do not need to include control groups.

d. usually do not correct for the effects of age at the time of castration on aggressive behavior.

11. Studies to correlate blood levels of testosterone and aggression

a. indicate that high levels of testosterone cause increased aggressive behavior.

b. are more reliable for male subjects than female subjects.

c. must take into account a person's environment in making conclusions.

d. cannot be undertaken because of ethical concerns.

12. Alcohol increases intermale aggression

a. among all male squirrel monkeys.

b. among dominant male squirrel monkeys but only during the mating season.

c. among subordinate male squirrel monkeys.

d. among subordinate male squirrel monkeys engaged in a defensive attack.

Answers for Self Tests

Lesson I

1. b Obj. 11-1
2. d Obj. 11-1
3. c Obj. 11-1
4. c Obj. 11-2
5. d Obj. 11-2
6. a Obj. 11-3
7. b Obj. 11-4
8. c Obj. 11-4
9. c Obj. 11-5
10. c Obj. 11-5
11. a Obj. 11-6
12. b Obj. 11-6

Lesson II

1. b Obj. 11-7
2. b Obj. 11-7
3. b Obj. 11-7
4. a Obj. 11-7
5. a Obj. 11-8
6. a Obj. 11-8
7. c Obj. 11-8
8. d Obj. 11-8
9. d Obj. 11-8
10. b Obj. 11-9
11. c Obj. 11-9
12. b Obj. 11-9

CHAPTER 12
Ingestive Behavior: Drinking

Lesson I: Fluid Balance, Drinking, and Salt Appetite

Read the interim summary on page 377 of your text to re-acquaint yourself with the material in this section.

Learning Objective 12-1   Explain the characteristics of a regulatory mechanism.

Read pages 372-373 and answer the following questions.

1.   Define *homeostasis* and *ingestive behavior* in your own words and explain their importance.

2.   What is the function of a regulatory mechanism?

3.   List and explain the functions of the four essential features of a regulatory mechanism. (See Figure 12.1 in your text.)

   1.   3.

   2.   4.

4.   Using the example of the room thermostat, explain the process of negative feedback.

5.   a. What role do ingestive behaviors play in homeostasis?

   b. Study Figure 12.2 in your text and explain the relation of the satiety mechanism to the correctional mechanism in the control of drinking.

Learning Objective 12-2   Describe the fluid compartments of the body and describe how the kidneys control the excretion of water and sodium.

Read pages 373-377 and answer the following questions.

1. There are _____ major fluid compartments in the body—one for _____ fluid and _____ for _____ fluid. The intracellular fluid is the fluid portion of the _____ of cells and contains approximately _____ percent of the body's water. The extracellular fluid includes the _____ fluid or blood plasma, the _____ fluid of the brain, and the _____ fluid between our cells. (Study Figure 12.3 in your text.)

2. Use the terms *isotonic, hypertonic,* and *hypotonic* to explain why the concentration of the interstitial fluid must remain constant. (Study Figure 12.4 in your text.)

3. a. Explain why the volume of blood plasma must be closely regulated by describing the consequences of hypovolemia.

    b. What limited correctional mechanism does the body use when blood volume is too low?

4. Explain why the volume of the interstitial fluid need not be regulated so closely, but it's tonicity must be.

5. a. Why are intracellular fluid and blood volume monitored by two different sets of receptors?

    b. What correctional mechanisms are controlled by these receptors?

6. What is the general function of the kidneys and the specific function of the nephrons and the ureter? (See Figure 12.5 in your text.)

7. a. Which steroid hormone regulates sodium excretion?
    b. Where is it produced?
    c. What is the effect of high levels of this hormone on the kidneys? low levels? (See Figure 12.6 in your text.)

8. a. Which peptide hormone regulates water excretion by the kidneys?
    b. Where is it produced, stored, and released?
    c. What is the effect of high levels of this hormone on the kidneys? low levels?

    d. If this hormone is lacking, what disease results?

Read the interim summary on page 383 of your text to re-acquaint yourself with the material in this section.

Learning Objective 12-3 Explain the control of osmometric thirst.

Read pages 377-380 and answer the following questions.

1. _____ thirst occurs when the tonicity of the interstitial fluid _____.

2. Study Figures 12.7 and 12.8 in your text and explain how the size and firing rate of an osmoreceptor changes as the surrounding interstitial fluid becomes more concentrated. Be sure that you understand the movement of water in osmosis. (Verney, 1947)

3. Now study Figure 12.9 in your text and explain how our bodies loose water from three fluid compartments through evaporation, and the accompanying changes that occur.

4. Describe what happens, step by step, to the fluid compartments of the body when we eat a salty meal.

5. a. Why did Fitzsimons (1972) begin his study of the stimulus for osmometric thirst by removing the kidneys of laboratory rats?

   b. One group of subject rats was injected with a substance that could enter cells and another group was injected with a substance that could not enter cells. Which group drank excessively and why?

   c. What, then, is the stimulus for osmometric thirst?

   d. When Fitzsimons injected subject rats with urea, how was drinking affected and why?

   e. What do these results suggest about a general location for osmoreceptors?

6. Which more specific locations had been suggested by earlier research by Andersson (1953)?

7. a. Where do most researchers believe the osmoreceptors in the brain are located?

   b. List four circumventricular organs. (See Figure 12.12 in your text.)

      1.   3.

      2.   4.

   c. Describe their blood supply; their location, especially in relation to the blood-brain barrier; and its significance.

8. a. What was the effect on osmometric thirst of

      1. destroying the OVLT of dogs? (Thrasher and Keil, 1987)

2. lesions of the OVLT alone and with destruction of additional brain tissue around the AV3V of rats? (see Johnson and Edwards, 1990)

b. What do the results of the studies indicate about the location of the osmoreceptors in dogs? in rats?

c. What additional evidence supports Johnson and Edwards conclusions?

9. a. Tissue from the AV3V including the OVLT of rats was removed and kept alive in the laboratory. What was the effect of infusions of

   1. hypertonic solutions on the OVLT?

   2. hypotonic solutions? (Nissen et al., 1993; Bourque et al., 1994; Richard and Bourque, 1995)

   b. What do these results suggest about the membrane of the neurons in the OVLT?

10. In addition to the circumventricular organs, what other locations outside the blood-brain barrier, may contain osmoreceptors?

11. Food and water from the stomach enter the first part of the _____ _____ or _____. Through _____ in the small intestine, water and nutrients enter the blood supply. The _____ collect into larger veins and eventually join the _____ _____ _____ which travels to the liver. The liver is the first organ to receive substances from the digestive system through the _____ _____ _____. (See Figure 12.10 in your text.)

12. a. If a hypertonic saline solution is infused into the stomach, what change occurs in the animal's behavior? (Kraly et al., 1995)

   b. How can this change be blocked?

   c. Why is it difficult to determine whether osmoreceptors are located in the stomach or duodenum?

   d. And why are the osmoreceptors in the liver probably not involved in the production of thirst? (Baertschi and Vallet, 1981; Kobashi and Adachi, 1992)

Learning Objective 12-4 Explain the control of volumetric thirst.

Read pages 380-383 and answer the following questions.

1. _____ thirst occurs when the volume of blood plasma _____.

2. a. Why does evaporation produce both osmometric and volumetric thirst?

b. Identify three conditions that cause volumetric thirst.

    1.   2.   3.

3. a. Now describe a procedure for initiating volumetric thirst in experimental animals. What kind of substance is injected into the animal?

b. What property of colloids draw extracellular fluid and sodium out of tissue gradually creating a vacant space?

c. What fluid begins to move into this vacant space and why?

d. In response to changing blood volume, what changes occur in the posterior pituitary gland and in the kidneys?

e. Throughout this procedure, what changes, if any, took place in the cells?

4. a. After injecting subject rats with polyethylene glycol, a colloid, what did Fitzsimons (1961) do?

b. Describe how rats drank after the draining procedure and the next day.

c. The lost of sodium induced a _____ _____ in the rats.

5. Where are the detectors for initiating volumetric thirst and a salt appetite located?

6. a. What is the primary cause of a reduced flow of blood to the kidneys?

b. How do the cells in the kidneys that detect a reduction respond?

c. Briefly explain how angiotensin II (AII) is produced.

7. a. List three physiological effects of AII.

    1.

    2.

    3.

b. Now list two behavioral effects.

    1.

    2.

8. Review what you have just learned by studying Figure 12.11 in your text and completing Figure 1, on the next page.

9 Briefly explain how atrial baroreceptors in the heart detect changes in blood volume.

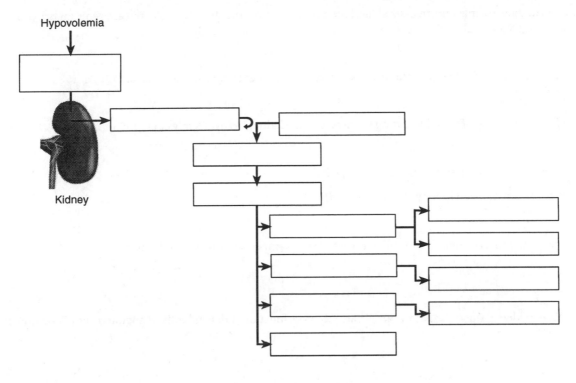

Figure 1

10. a. How did Fitzsimons and Moore-Gillon (1980) restrict the flow of blood to the hearts of subject dogs?

    b. In response to the reduced blood volume, what did the dogs begin to do?

    c. What is the pharmacological effect of an injection of saralasin?

    d. What effect did the drug have on the dogs' behavior, and what did this effect confirm?

11. a. In a different study with dogs, where did Moore-Gillon and Fitzsimons (1982) implant the balloon?

    b. When they inflated the balloon, what changes occurred in blood flow to the heart, the left atrium, and the animals' behavior?

12. When, after cutting the nerves connecting the atrial baroreceptors with the brain, the blood flow to the heart was temporarily reduced, what did the dogs do? (Quillen et al. 1990)

13. a. Why do eating and drinking usually occur together?

    b. How did a change in diet gradually affect the drinking behavior of rats? (Fitzsimons and Le Magnen, 1969)

14. a. Explain how eating a normal-sized meal soon leads to thirst and drinking. Cite research to support your answer. (Nose et al., 1986; Rowland, 1995; Kraly and Corneilson, 1990)

b. What may be the role of histamine in food-related drinking? (For example, Kraly and June, 1982)

c. How is drinking affected by cutting the nerves to the kidney? Why? (Kraly et al., 1995)

15. a. What is the primary stimulus for a salt appetite?

b. What two other signals may also be involved?

c. Why is the role of angiotensin still uncertain? (For example, Weisinger et al., 1996)

d. What evidence suggests that the atrial baroreceptors function independently of angiotensin? (Thornton et al., 1994)

Lesson I Self Test

1. The role of the detector in a regulatory mechanism is to

   a. monitor the value of the system variable.
   b. recognize stimuli that might change the value of the system variable.
   c. establish the value of the set point in response to environmental conditions.
   d. restore the system variable to the set point.

2. An essential feature of all regulatory mechanisms is

   a. a satiety mechanism.
   b. negative feedback.
   c. continuous feedback.
   d. a neural control mechanism.

3. Satiety mechanisms

   a. monitor system variables.
   b. replenish depleted stores of food, fluid, or nutrients.
   c. are a second correctional mechanism if detectors fail to work properly.
   d. monitor the activity of correctional mechanisms.

4. If the fluid inside a cell is isotonic to the interstitial fluid

   a. their volumes are equal.
   b. water will not tend to move in or out.
   c. water will diffuse out of the cells through osmosis.
   d. osmotic pressure may cause the membrane to rupture.

5. The _____ of the interstitial fluid must be closely regulated, but its _____ usually remains within normal limits.

   a. production; excretion
   b. excretion; volume
   c. tonicity; volume
   d. volume; tonicity

6. If we drink more water than we need, _____ secretion of _____ causes the kidneys to excrete more _____.

   a. decreased; vasopressin; water
   b. deceased; aldosterone; water
   c. increased; vasopressin; sodium
   d. increased; aldosterone; sodium

7. Osmometric thirst occurs when the

   a. tonicity of the interstitial fluid increases.
   b. volume of the intravascular fluid decreases.

c. blood flow to the kidneys decreases.

d. blood level of renin increases.

8. The stimulus for osmometric thirst is

    a. renin secretion.

    b. a decrease in urine production.

    c. hypovolemia.

    d. cell dehydration.

9. Osmoreceptors in the _____ initiate drinking in response to an infusion of a hypertonic saline solution, but osmoreceptors in the _____ do not.

    a. liver; OVLT

    b. stomach; kidneys

    c. stomach; liver

    d. OVLT; AV3V

10. The easiest way to produce volumetric thirst in an experimental animal is to give an injection of

    a. a colloid.

    b. a saline solution.

    c. saralasin.

    d. losartan.

11. A behavioral effect of angiotensin II is

    a. aversion to a high protein diet.

    b. stimulation of a salt appetite.

    c. near cessation of drinking.

    d. an absence of food-related drinking.

12. The detectors for volumetric thirst are located in the

    a. posterior pituitary gland and the hypothalamus.

    b. kidneys and the bladder.

    c. kidneys and in the heart.

    d. stomach and large intestine.

Lesson II: Brain Mechanisms of Thirst and Salt Appetite and Mechanisms of Satiety

Read the interim summary on page 388 in your text to re-acquaint yourself with the material in this section.

Learning Objective 12-5   Describe the neural control of thirst and a salt appetite.

Read pages 383-388 and answer the following questions.

1. a. Describe the location of the nucleus of the solitary tract.

    b. Which parts of the body send information to it and where does it send its efferent axons? (Johnson and Edwards, 1990)

2. Briefly summarize research that the region of the AV3V may play a role in fluid regulation in

    a. rats. (Thornton et al., 1984)

    b. humans. (McIver et al., 1991).

3. a. What property of angiotensin suggests that it may produce thirst through one of the circumventricular organs?

    b. Which circumventricular organ appears to be the site of action of blood angiotensin? Cite research to support your answer (For example, Smith et al., 1995. See Figure 12.12 in your text.)

4. a. What is the primary role of the subfornical organ (SFO)?

    b. The outputs of the SFO can be divided into three categories (Miselis et al., 1987). List them, their projections, and their functions.

Category	Projections	Functions
1.		
2.		
3.		

5. Review the five major effects of angiotensin, noting which ones involve the brain.

6. a. What kind of connections are destroyed by lesions of the ventral stalk of the SFO?

    b. How do these lesion affect drinking induced by injections of AII into a vein? (Lind et al., 1984) into the third ventricle?

    b. What can we conclude from these results about the location and function of other angiotensin receptors?

7. a. Outline Lind and Johnson's (1982) explanation for the presence of angiotensin receptors in the median preoptic nucleus.

    b. Summarize some research results that support their explanation.

      1. If the median preoptic nucleus is destroyed and AII is then injected into the blood or the third ventricle, what is the effect on drinking? (Johnson and Cunningham, 1987)

      2. If saralasin is injected directly into the median preoptic nucleus, how is drinking caused by an injection of AII directly into the SFO affected? (See the insert in Figure 12.12. Tanaka and Nomura, 1993)

8   Now outline the explanation suggested by Thrasher and his colleagues (Thrasher, 1989) of the role of the region in front of the third ventricle in osmometric and volumetric thirst. (See Figure 12.13 in your text.)

9. a. How do neurotoxic lesions of the median preoptic nucleus affect drinking caused by angiotensin and hypertonic saline? (See Figure 12.14 in your text. Cunningham et al., 1992)

    b. What do these results suggest about other controls of drinking?

10. Summarize research, using various techniques, to learn more about the role of the following structures in drinking.

   a. lesions of the lateral hypothalamus (Teitelbaum and Epstein, 1962)

   b. electrical stimulation of the rostral zona incerta (Huang and Mogenson, 1972)

   c. lesions of the zona incerta (Walsh and Grossman, 1978)

   d. recordings of single neurons in the zona incerta (Mok and Mogenson, 1986)

   e. injections of angiotensin into a cerebral ventricle (Czech and Stein, 1992)

11. Outline the neural control of salt appetite.

   a. Once again, what condition stimulates the adrenal glands to secrete aldosterone and produce a salt appetite?

   b. Where does this hormone exert its behavioral effects? (Coirini et al., 1985)

   c. How can these effects be abolished? (See Figure 12.15 in your text. Schulkin et al., 1989)

   d. What evidence suggested that aldosterone is not the only stimulus for salt appetite. Be sure to mention furosemide in your answer.

   e. Finally, what evidence suggests that the SFO, the OVLT, and the zona incerta all play a role in salt appetite? (Weisinger et al., 1990; Fitts et al., 1990; Grossman and Grossman, 1978; Gentil et al., 1971)

Read the interim summary on pages 390-391 of your text to re-acquaint yourself with the material in this section.

Learning Objective 12-6 Describe satiety mechanisms activated by drinking and satiety mechanisms activated by ingestion of sodium chloride.

Read pages 388-390 and answer the following questions.

1. Summarize evidence that receptors in the mouth and throat play a role in satiety for drinking.

   a. What is the delay between a thirsty dog drinking its fill and the water level of the blood plasma being replenished? (Adolph, 1939; Ramsay et al., 1977)

   b. In research by Miller et al., (1957), some thirsty rats were permitted to drink water, but how did others receive water?

   c. Which rats later drank more water? (See Figure 12.16 in your text.)

d. What do these results suggest about the function of receptors in the mouth and throat?

2. a. Describe an esophageal fistula.

   b. What does the drinking pattern of an animal fitted with this device indicate about satiety produced by receptors in the mouth and throat?

3. a. Why did researchers place a noose around the pylorus of subject rats as illustrated in Figure 12.17 in your text? (Hall, 1973; Hall and Blass, 1977)

   b. When the noose was tightened, what happened to the contents of the stomach?

   c. Thirsty rats then continued to drink. Why?

4. What is known about the role of receptors in the duodenum in satiety?

5. a. What substances are transported by the hepatic portal vein?

   b. How did infusions of water into the hepatic portal vein affect
      1. osmometric drinking initiated by injections of hypertonic saline (Kozlowski and Drzewiecki, 1973)?
      2. drinking by water-deprived rats?

   c. What do these results suggest about the role of the osmoreceptors in the liver?

   d. What nerve may carry inhibitory signals for thirst to the brain? (Kobashi and Adachi, 1993)

6. Finally let's look at satiety receptors for salt appetite. Discuss research that mouth, stomach or duodenal receptors may not be important in satiety for salt appetite? (Mook, 1969; Wolf et al., 1984)

7. a. How did injections of a hypertonic sodium chloride solution into the hepatic portal vein affect the amount of a salt solution an animal would drink? (Tordoff et al., 1987)

   b. What do the results suggest about the role of receptors in the liver?

8. a. Where is the hormone atrial natriuretic peptide (ANP) secreted? (De Bold et al., 1981; De Bold, 1985)

   b. Under what circumstances is it secreted?

   c. Begin a list of its functions. (Tarjan et al., 1988, for a review)

d. Where are ANP receptors found? (Quirion et al., 1984)

e. What is the presumed role of these receptors? (Quirion, 1989) Cite research to support your answer (Ehrlich and Fitts, 1990).

9. What structure plays a role in the inhibitory effect of ANP on drinking? (Quirion et al., 1984; Nermo-Lindquist et al., 1990; Ehrlich and Fitts, 1990)

Lesson II Self Test

1. The region around the anteroventral third ventricle of the brain including the OVLT

   a. monitors evaporation rate through skin temperature receptors.
   b. contains osmoreceptors that stimulate thirst and vasopressin secretion.
   c. initiates hypovolemia.
   d. is the weakest portion of the blood-brain barrier.

2. Angiotensin is _____ , and _____ the blood brain barrier.

   a. both a peptide and a hormone; does not cross
   b. a peptide; crosses
   c. both a hormone and a transmitter substance; crosses
   d. an enzyme; does not cross

3. Angiotensin

   a. blocks vasopressin secretion.
   b. lowers blood pressure.
   c. stimulates aldosterone secretion.
   d. increases urine production.

4, The subfornical organ

   a. does not appear to have any angiotensin receptors.
   b. secretes saralasin which blocks angiotensin.
   c. is a site of action of angiotensin.
   d. breaks down angiotensin.

5. The effects of the subfornical organ on drinking occur through its _____ outputs.

   a. autonomic
   b. behavioral
   c. endocrine
   d. metabolic

6. The angiotensin receptors in the median preoptic nucleus

   a. are stimulated when angiotensin crosses the blood brain barrier.
   b. detect angiotensin secreted as a transmitter substance by terminal buttons there.
   c. are an example of the redundant systems that have evolved in the brain.
   d. control the secretion of vasopressin.

7. Lesions of the zona incerta

   a. have no effect on the stimuli for volumetric thirst.
   b. stimulate salt intake.
   c. abolish drinking in response to injections of the colloid polyethylene glycol.
   d. produce a profound deficit in osmometric drinking.

8. Where does aldosterone appear to exert its behavioral effects?

   a. medial nucleus of the amygdala
   b. lateral hypothalamus
   c. zona incerta
   d. median preoptic nucleus

9. Rats who received preloads of water in the mouth drank _____ than rats who received the preloads in the stomach.

   a. more
   b. less
   c. the same amount of water
   d. the same amount of water, but more slowly

10. Research that used an esophageal fistula to prevent water from reaching the stomach suggest that satiety receptors in the mouth and throat

   a. play a greater role that first believed.
   b. have a short-lived effect.
   c. cannot signal satiety if connections with stomach receptors are blocked.

d. and stomach are of equal importance.

11. When the pylorus of an experimental animal is constricted by a noose stomach contents

    a. back up into the esophagus and throat.
    b. fall to the ground.
    c. continue to diffuse into the blood through the capillaries.

d. cannot leave the stomach.

12. Atrial natriuretic peptide stimulates the

    a. excretion of sodium.
    b. secretion of renin.
    c. retention of water.
    d. elevation of blood volume.

Answers for Self Tests

Lesson I

1. a Obj. 12-1
2. b Obj. 12-2
3. d Obj. 12-2
4. b Obj. 12-2
5. c Obj. 12-2
6. a Obj. 12-2
7. a Obj. 12-3
8. d Obj. 12-3
9. c Obj. 12-3
10. a Obj. 12-4
11. b Obj. 12-4
12. c Obj. 12-4

Lesson II

1. b Obj. 12-5
2. a Obj. 12-5
3. c Obj. 12-5
4. c Obj. 12-5
5. b Obj. 12-5
6. b Obj. 12-5
7. d Obj. 12-5
8. a Obj. 12-5
9. b Obj. 12-6
10. b Obj. 12-6
11. d Obj. 12-6
12. a Obj. 12-6

CHAPTER 13
Ingestive Behavior: Eating

Lesson I: Some Facts About Metabolism and What Starts and Stops a Meal

Read the interim summary on page 396 in your text to re-acquaint yourself with the material in this section.

Learning Objective 13-1 Describe characteristics of the two nutrient reservoirs and the absorptive and fasting phases of metabolism.

Read pages 393-396 and answer the following questions.

1. a. Why do we eat?

    1.   2.

    b. How do our bodies use most of the food we eat?

2. What is the location of the short-term nutrient reservoir and what is stored there?

3. Explain how glycogen is produced and the mechanism that stimulates its release.

    a. Cells in the _____ are stimulated by _____, produced in the _____, to

       convert _____ into glycogen and store it.

    b. What causes the level of glucose in the blood to fall and how is it detected?

    c. What two changes occur in the pancreas in response to a fall in glucose?

    d. What is the effect of glucagon release?

    e. Immediately review what you have just learned by studying Figure 13.1 in your text and completing Figure 1.

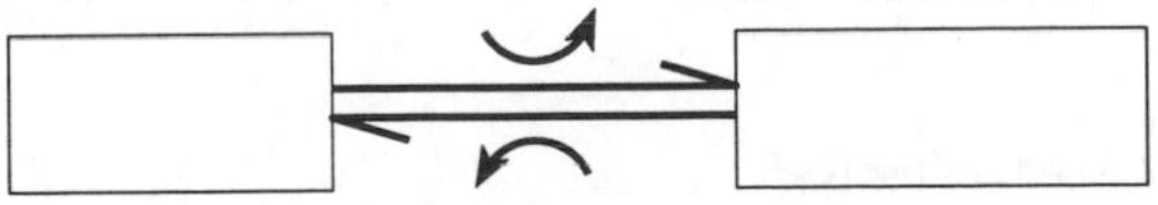

Figure 1

4. a. The short-term carbohydrate reservoir in the liver is the principal fuel supply for what part of the body?

   b. If the short-term reservoir is depleted, what is its next source of reserved fuel?

5. a. The long-term reservoir of _____ tissue is found beneath the _____ and in the

   _____ _____. It is filled with _____, complex molecules that contain

   _____ combined with three _____ _____.

   b. Briefly describe the cells of the adipose tissue.

6. What factors initiate the breakdown of triglycerides into glycerol and fatty acids?

7. Describe the mechanism that saves glucose for the brain during the fasting phase of metabolism. Be sure to mention the role of glucose transporters.

8. To review the fasting phase of metabolism study Figure 13.2 in your text. Continue your review by summarizing the effects of

   a. a fall in the blood glucose level on the pancreas.

   b. the absence of insulin on the cells of the body.

   c. the presence of glucagon on the liver.

   d. and the presence of glucagon and increased activity of the sympathetic nervous system on fat cells.

9. When does the absorptive phase of metabolism begin?

10. What three nutrients are supplied by a well-balanced meal?

11. Describe the changes that occur as each of these nutrients is absorbed.

   a. As carbohydrates break down, what change occurs in the level of glucose in the blood and how is this change detected?

   b. What change occurs in the pancreas as a result of the change in the level of glucose?

   c. How does insulin affect the cells of the body?

   d. What happens to any extra glucose?

e. As proteins break down, how are the amino acids used?

f. How are fats used?

12. To review the absorptive phase of metabolism again study Figure 13.2 in your text.

Read the interim summary on pages 400-401 of your text to re-acquaint yourself with the material in this section.

Learning Objective 13-2   Discuss social and environmental factors that begin a meal and long-term and short-term hunger signals.

Read pages 396-400 and answer the following questions.

1. Explain why the signals that start and stop a meal are undoubtedly different.

2. a. List factors that encourage us to eat even when we have no physiological need to do so.

   b. Explain how classical conditioning was used to study eating by hungry laboratory rats. (Weingarten,1983)

      1. Which stimulus triggered eating behavior? which did not?

      2. What do the results, shown in Figure 13.3 in your text, suggest about the kind of stimuli that can provoke eating?

   c. What is the relation between meal size and

      1. a fixed meal schedule? (Jiang and Hunt, 1983; de Castro et al., 1986)

      2. the presence of other people? (de Castro and de Castro, 1989)

   d. What, then, is the relationship between social factors and metabolic factors that lead to eating?

3. a. Let's look now at those metabolic factors that produce hunger. What initiates short-term hunger signals and how are they detected? long-term hunger signals?

   b. Under what conditions does the brain become less sensitive to short-term hunger signals and more sensitive to satiety signals? more sensitive to short-term hunger signals and less sensitive to satiety signals?

4. Carefully explain why hunger can be stimulated by an injection of

   a. insulin. What do we call this condition?

b. 2-deoxyglucose (2-DG). What do we call the condition caused by hypoglycemia or 2-DG?

c. methyl palmoxirate (MP) or mercaptoacetate (MA). What do we call this condition?

5. Why is less known about the importance of amino acids to metabolism?

6. a. Describe the experimental procedure that Friedman and his colleagues (Friedman et al., 1986) used to produce moderate glucoprivation and moderate lipoprivation in rats?

b. Study Figure 13.4 in your text and explain the effects on food intake under each of the experimental conditions.

c. What do the results suggest about the stimuli that cause hunger? Why?

7. There appear to be two sets of detectors for metabolic fuels. Where are they located and what do they monitor?

8. a. What was the effect on food intake of infusions of 2-DG into the hepatic portal vein of rats that had been eating a high-carbohydrate, low-fat diet? (Novin et al., 1973)

b. How was this effect abolished?

c. What do the results suggest about the location of detectors for glucoprivation?

9. a. And what was the effect on food intake of infusions of 2,5-AM into the hepatic portal vein of rats? (Lutz et al., 1996)

b. How did this effect alter the activity of afferent axons in the hepatic branch of the vagus nerve?

c. What do the results confirm about the location of detectors for glucoprivation?

10. a. How was lipoprivic hunger induced and then abolished? (Ritter and Taylor, 1990)

b. What is an additional effect of an infusion of MA into the hepatic portal vein? (Lutz et al., 1997)

c. What do these experiments suggest about the location of detectors for glucoprivation and lipoprivation and how information from them is transmitted to the brain?

11. a. Despite their high levels of blood glucose, untreated diabetics are chronically hungry. Why?

    b. What does this symptom suggest about where available fuels are monitored by detector cells?

12. One group of laboratory rats was fed a low-fat/high-carbohydrate diet while a second group was fed a high-fat/low-carbohydrate diet.

    a. Which group increased their food intake in response to administration of 2,5 AM? administration of MP?

    b. Why? (See Figure 13.5 in your text. Horn and Friedman, 1998)

13. _____ is the fuel for cell activity.

14. In addition to 2-DG and 2,5 AM, identify a third drug that causes eating and explain how it does so. (Rawson et al., 1994)

15. Outline the ischymetric hypothesis of hunger proposed by Nicolaïdis. (Nicolaïdis, 1974; 1987)

16. a. How did Ritter et al. (1981) block communication between the third and fourth ventricles of the brain?

    b. When 5-TG, a drug similar in action to 2-DG, was then injected into each ventricle how was eating affected?

    c. What is the presumed reason?

17. Finally, summarize evidence that suggests that

    a. hindbrain nutrient receptors may be located in either the area postrema (Bird et al., 1983) or the nucleus of the solitary tract (Yettefti et al., 1997).

    b. glucose infused into the ventricular system affects nutrient receptors in the brain. (Singer and Ritter, 1996)

    c. no single set receptors controls eating. (Tordoff et al., 1982; Ritter et al., 1992)

18. To review the probable location of nutrient receptors responsible for hunger signals study Figure 13.6 in your text.

Read the interim summary on page 405 of your text to re-acquaint yourself with the material in this section.

Learning Objective 13-3 Discuss the head, gastric, and intestinal factors responsible for stopping a meal.

Read pages 401-405 and answer the following questions.

1. a. Where in the body should we look for the source of short-term and long-term satiety signals?

    b. What effect does this information have on the brain?

2. Define *head factors* in your own words, including the kind of information they detect and their most important role.

3. Rats learn to eat less of a food with a particular flavor that is accompanied by intravenous infusions of glucose. (Mather et al., 1978) What does their behavior suggest about how head factors influence satiety?

4. Why do researchers believe that the stomach is less important in producing hunger and more important in producing satiety? (Ingelfinger, 1944; Davis and Campbell, 1973)

5. a. Explain why Deutsch and Gonzalez (1980) fit rats with pyloric cuffs.

    b. The rats were permitted to eat once a day. Sometimes, the researchers removed 5 ml of food from their stomachs. Sometimes, they added 5 ml of a saline solution. What did they observe? (See Figure 13.7 in your text.)

    c. What can we conclude from the results about the role of the stomach in short-term satiety?

    d. What conclusion is not justified?

6. a. Explain why Greenberg and colleagues (Greenberg et al., 1990) attached gastric fistulas to rats. Be sure to refer to sham feeding in your answer.

    b. How was sham feeding affected by an infusion of Intralipid into the duodenum? Intralipid combined with a local anesthetic?

    c. What does the inhibition of sham feeding indicate about the location of short-term satiety signals?

    d. Using radioactively labeled Intralipid, what did Greenberg et al. (1991) establish about the timing of the satiating effect?

7. Before studying the role of cholecystokinin (CCK) in satiety, note some information about this hormone.

    a. Where and when is it secreted?

b. What is its effect on the gallbladder? the pylorus?

c. How do injections of CCK affect eating? (Gibbs et al., 1973; Smith et al., 1982; West et al., 1984)

d. Why has it been studied as a satiety signal?

e. What property of CCK restricts the search for its site of action?

8. Summarize evidence that CCK acts peripherally.

   a. If the gastric branch of the vagus nerve is cut, how is the suppressive effect of CCK on eating altered? (Smith et al., 1982.)

   b. Moran and colleagues (Moran et al., 1989) removed the pyloruses of rats, a region rich in CCK receptors. What change in eating behavior did they observe immediately after surgery and 2-3 months later? (See Figure 13.8 in your text.)

9. a. What observation suggested to Russek (1971) that the liver might contain satiety detectors?

   b. When he injected glucose into the jugular vein and then the hepatic portal vein, what did he observe?

10. a. How did infusion of small amounts of glucose and fructose into the hepatic portal vein affect rats' appetites for food? (Tordoff and Friedman, 1988)

    b. Why did they conclude that it is the liver that signals satiety to the brain?

11. Finally review research on the mechanisms of long-term body fat regulation.

    a. If an animal gains weight through forced feeding and is later permitted to choose its food, how is subsequent food intake affected? (See Figure 13.9 in your text. Wilson et al., 1990)

    b. If an animal loses weight through enforced dieting, how are satiety factors affected? (Cabanac and Lafrance, 1991)

12. a. What are some of the characteristics of the ob mouse? Be sure to mention leptin in your answer. (Campfield et al., 1995; Halaas et al., 1995; Pelleymounter et al., 1995)

    b. If ob mice are given injections of leptin, what physical changes occur? (See Figure 13.10 in your text.)

c. And if normal animals are given injections of leptin, what physical changes occur? (See Figure 13.11 in your text. Eckel et al., 1998; Kahler et al., 1998)

d. How may leptin affect the brain?

e. In combination, how did leptin and CCK affect food intake?

Lesson I Self Test

1. The short-term fuel reservoir is located in
    _____ and is filled with _____.

    a. adipose tissue; triglycerides
    b. digestive tract; amino acids
    c. pancreas; glucose
    d. the cells of the liver and muscles; glycogen

2. Glucagon

    a. stimulates the conversion of glycogen into glucose.
    b. is secreted by the pancreas in response to a rise in glucose levels.
    c. has the same effect as insulin.
    d. combines with fatty acids and glycerol to form triglycerides.

3. During the fasting phase of metabolism

    a. supplies of glucose are abundant.
    b. most cells live on fatty acids.
    c. all cells of the body use glucose as a fuel.
    d. excess nutrients are stored in the liver, muscles, and adipose tissue.

4. During the absorptive phase of metabolism

    a. the blood level of glucose rises.
    b. the pancreas ceases to secrete insulin.
    c. proteins, carbohydrates, and fats are used to fuel the cells of the body.
    d. glucose dissolves in fats and is stored in adipose tissue.

5. As recorded in their diaries, subjects ate the most food when

    a. the food was familiar.
    b. the food had a sweet taste.
    c. other people were present.

    d. they ate alone.

6. Lipoprivation can be induced by injections of

    a. ATP.
    b. 2-DG.
    c. 2,5-AM.
    d. methyl palmoxirate (MP).

7. Cutting the hepatic branch of the vagus nerve

    a. quickly depletes stored nutrient reserves in the liver.
    b. prevents hunger signals originating in the liver from reaching the brain.
    c. prevent the satiating effect of lipoprivation.
    d. prevents detectors in the liver from responding to changes in nutrient levels.

8. Detectors in the liver that signal lipoprivic hunger appear to be sensitive to

    a. changes in their own internal rate of metabolism.
    b. blood level of particular nutrients.
    c. availability of insulin.
    d. the amount of lipids stored in adipose tissue.

9. Using a pyloric cuff, researchers demonstrated that the

    a. volume of stomach contents is more important than its nutritive content for satiety.
    b. stomach contains receptors that prevent overeating.
    c. stomach contains receptors that monitor the nutritive value of its contents.
    d. stomach communicates information about satiety through the vagus nerve.

10. Injections of cholecystokinin (CCK)

a. activate stretch receptors in the stomach.

b. promote stomach emptying.

c. inhibit the contraction of the gallbladder.

d. suppress eating.

11. By injecting glucose and fructose into the hepatic portal vein, researchers confirmed that the liver

a. contains receptors that respond when the liver receives nutrients from the intestines.

b. metabolizes sugars.

c. is the first organ to signal satiety.

d. breaks down fatty acids.

12. If ob mice are given an injection of leptin

a. they lose weight rapidly because they develop diabetes and cannot metabolize glucose.

b. they eat even greater quantities of food.

c. their weight returns to normal.

d. eating behavior is not affected.

Lesson II: Brain Mechanisms of Food Intake and Metabolism and Eating Disorders

Read the interim summary on pages 413-414 of your text to re-acquaint yourself with the material in this section.

Learning Objective 13-4 Describe research on the role of the brain stem and hypothalamus in hunger.

Read pages 405-411 and answer the following questions.

1. a. Briefly explain the surgical procedure of decerebration shown in Figure 13.12 in your text.

b. What are the consequences of this procedure?

c. Describe research results that demonstrate even decerebrate animals perform ingestive behaviors. How do decerebrate rats respond to

1. food in their mouths?

2. different tastes?

3. hunger and satiety signals?

2. a. What kind of sensory information does the AP/NST receive? detect?

b. Where is all this information then transmitted?

3. Summarize research on the importance of the AP/NST to hunger.

a. How is eating and/or Fos production in the AP/NST affected by

1. injections of 2,5-AM?

2. severing the branch of the vagus nerve that connects the liver to the brain? (Ritter et al., 1994)

b. How is lipoprivic hunger and glucoprivic hunger affected by lesions of AP/NST? (See Figure 13.13 in your text. Ritter and Taylor, 1990)

c. How did injections of glucose or glucagon alter the response of neurons in the NST to a sweet taste? (Giza et al., 1992) What does this finding suggest about the ingestive behavior of decerebrate rats?

4. a. Where does the AP/NST relay information received from the tongue and internal organs?

    b. How do changes in glucose or fatty-acid metabolism in the liver affect this nucleus? (Horn and Friedman, 1998)

    c. How do lesions of the lateral parabrachial nucleus of the pons affect

        1. hunger signals detected by the liver?

        2. lipoprivic feeding and feeding elicited by 2,5-AM? (Calingasan and Ritter, 1993; Grill et al., 1995)

        3. eating produced by 2-DG? What does this finding suggest about neural circuits? (See Figure 13.14 in your text.)

5. Briefly summarize conclusions that prevailed for a long time about the role of the lateral and ventromedial hypothalamus in hunger and satiety. (See Figure 13.15 in your text. Anand and Brobeck, 1951; Teitelbaum and Stellar, 1954; Hetherington and Ranson, 1942)

6. a. Decades later, researchers noted other behavioral changes resulting from these lesions. Describe some of them.

    b. What did Stricker and Zigmond (1976) suggest caused these behavior changes?

    c. Review later research that confirmed that the lateral hypothalamus does play a role in eating. What were the behavioral effects of

        1. neurotoxic lesions of the lateral hypothalamus? (Stricker et al., 1978; Dunnett et al.,1985)

        2. injections of excitatory amino acids that stimulated the lateral hypothalamus? (Stanley et al., 1993a)

        3. injections of a glutamate antagonist into the lateral hypothalamus? (Stanley et al., 1996. See Figure 13.16 in your text.)

7. These injections activate two populations of neurons in the lateral hypothalamus.

    a. What are some of their functions?

    b. What two peptide neurotransmitters do they secrete? (See Figure 13.17 in your text.)

8. a. What is the behavioral effect of injections of MCH or orexin into the lateral ventricles or various other regions of the brain?

b. If rats are deprived of food, how are messenger RNA levels for MCH and orexin affected? (Qu et al., 1996; Sakurai et al., 1998; Dube et al., 1999)

c. How are mice with targeted mutations against the MCH gene affected? (Shimada et al., 1998)

d. Trace the connections between MCH and orexin neurons and other brain structures shown in Figure 13.18 in your text. (Sawchenko, 1998; Nambu et al., 1999)

9. Let's review more research on the role of the lateral hypothalamus in eating, this time involving the neurotransmitter, neuropeptide Y (NPY).

a. To begin, how does NPY affect food intake? (Clark et al., 1984) How do infusions of this substance into the hypothalamus affect eating? Be sure to mention the kinds of behaviors that rats will engage in to obtain food. (Flood and Morley, 1991; Jewett et al., 1992)

b. NPY appears to have two sites of action. What changes result from infusions of NPY into the

1. lateral hypothalamus? (Stanley et al., 1993b)

2. into the paraventricular nucleus in the medial hypothalamus? (Wahlestedt et al., 1987; Abe et al., 1989; Currie and Coscina, 1996)

c. Hypothalamic levels of NPY are increased by _____ _____ and decreased by _____. (Sahu et al., 1988)

d. If NPY receptors are blocked, how is eating affected? (Myers et al., 1995)

e. What does this last finding suggest about NPY and normal eating?

10. a. Where are neurons that secrete NPY located? (Look back at Figure 13.15.)

b. Where do these NPY-containing neurons send a dense projection of axons? (Bai et al., 1985;) another projection? (Broberger et al., 1998; Elias et al., 1998)

c. What is known about the connections between these neurons and other parts of the brain? (Li et al., 1999)

11. a. Briefly summarize some of the multiple effects of NPY. How does NPY affect

1. energy expenditure? (Egawa et al., 1991)

2. ovulation and sexual behavior? (Clark et al., 1985)

b. Explain how temporary infertility conserves energy. (Wade et al., 1996)

c. By what means may NPY-secreting neurons interrupt reproduction?

12. All of the changes to the body that are produced by NPY appear to serve what purpose?

13. To review these neural connections, study Figure 13.19 in your text.

Learning Objective 13-5   Describe research on the role of the hypothalamus in satiety

---

Read pages 411-413 and answer the following questions.

1. Restate the most striking behavior of animals with a lesion of the ventromedial hypothalamus (VMH) and the long-accepted explanation for the VMH syndrome.

2. Carefully explain how VMH lesions disrupt the control of the autonomic nervous system and why food intake is increased by referring to their effect on the

   a. parasympathetic activity of the vagus nerve.

   b. subsequent stimulation of inhibition of the secretion of insulin, glucagon and adrenal catecholamines. (Weingarten et al., 1985)

   c. availability of the contents of nutrient reservoirs.

3. VMH lesions destroy not only the ventromedial hypothalamus but also axons that connect the paraventricular nucleus of the hypothalamus (PVN) with structures in the brain stem. According to Kirchgessner and Sclafani (1988), why might the destruction of these axons cause overeating?

4. a. Once again, where is leptin secreted? How did infusions of leptin into the cerebral ventricles affect eating and secretion of NPY by neurons in the arcuate nucleus? (Schwartz et al. 1996.)

   b. Where do the NPY-secreting neurons in the arcuate nucleus project?

   c. What is the significance of leptin receptors found in the NPY-secreting neurons of the arcuate nucleus? (Hakansson et al., 1996; Mercer et al., 1996. See Figure 13.20 in your text.)

   d. How do infusions of glutamate affect the NPY-secreting neurons of the arcuate nucleus? infusions of leptin? (Glaum et al., 1996)

5. a. Where is the peptide known as CART secreted and what does the acronym stand for? (Douglass et al., 1995)

   b. What is the presumed function of CART neurons?

   c. How does either CART production or CART level change with

      1. administration of cocaine or amphetamine?

2. food deprivation?

3. injections of leptin in the cerebral ventricles of ob mice?

d. And how does CART affect feeding stimulated by NPY?

e. Finally, how does an infusion of a CART antibody affect feeding?

6. a. What are some of the locations where CART neurons of the arcuate nucleus send their axons.

   b. Through which connections may CART neurons increase metabolic rate? suppress eating?

   c. What is the significance of leptin receptors found on CART neurons? (Elias et al., 1998b)

7. Explain how injections of gold thioglucose (GTG) affect the brain and behavior of mice? (Brecher and Waxler, 1949; Fei et al., 1997)

8. Immediately review some of the connections of CART neurons of the arcuate nucleus and the behavioral effects of leptin that are summarized in Figure 13.21 in your text. Complete Figure 2.

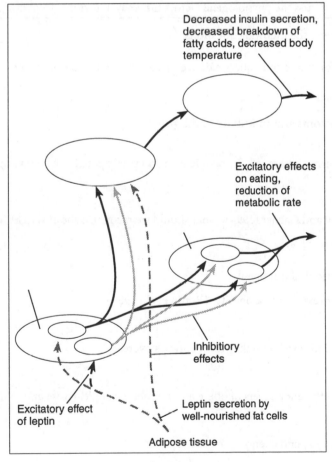

Figure 2

9. How is eating affected if

   a. serotonin (5-HT) is infused into various parts of the brain? (Leibowitz et al., 1990)

   b. serotonin antagonists are administered? (Blundell and Halford, 1998)

    c. drugs that destroy serotonergic neurons, inhibit 5-HT synthesis, or block 5-HT receptors are administered? (Breisch et al., 1976; Saller and Stricker, 1976; Stallone and Nicolaïdis, 1989)

10. What evidence suggests that serotonergic neurons

    a. inhibit the activity of NPY neurons? (Dryden et al., 1995)

    b. play a role in the satiating effects of CCK? (Grignaschi et al., 1993; Poeschla et al., 1993; Voigt et al., 1995; Voigt et al., 1998)

11. What is a possible site of action for the suppressive effects of 5-HT?

12. To review the peptide neurotransmitters involved in the control of eating and metabolism study Table 13.1 at the end of Chapter 13 in your text.

Read the interim summary on pages 420-421 of your text to re-acquaint yourself with the material in this section.

Learning Objective 13-6 Discuss the physiological factors that may contribute to obesity.

Read pages 414-417 and answer the following questions.

1. a. What may be an unfortunate consequence of urging children to finish everything on their plates? (Birch et al., 1987)

    b. What other social customs also contribute to this problem?

2. a. What was the long-term success rate for people who had participated in a behavioral weight loss program? (Kramer et al., 1989)

    b. According to Wooley and Garner (1994), what should we recognize about weight loss programs and what should be done?

3. Refute these misconceptions about obesity.

    a. Unhappiness and depression cause obesity. (Rodin et al., 1989)

    b. Obese people would loose weight if they didn't always overeat.

4. Explain how metabolic efficiency differs in obese and nonobese people. (Rose and Williams, 1961)

5. List the two ways that we expend energy.

    1.   2.

6. a. Nonoebese people in a research project ate more food than they needed to maintain their weights. How did their bodies use about

    1. two thirds of the calories they ingested?

2. one third of them? (Levine et al., 1998)

b. What does the distribution of the calories suggest about metabolic efficiency? Be sure to use the term *NEAT* in your answer.

7. a. According to twin studies, approximately how much of the variability in body fat is due to genetic differences? (Price and Gottesman, 1991; Allison et al., 1996; Comuzzie and Allison, 1998)

b. How did the body weight of a sample of people who had been adopted correlate with

1. their biological and adoptive parents? (Stunkard et al., 1986)

2. their full or half siblings with whom they had not been raised? (Sørensen et al., 1989)

8. a. State James and Trayhurn's (1981) hypothesis concerning the origin of genetic differences in metabolic efficiency.

b. Summarize the conclusions of research with the inhabitants of Nauru (Gibbs, 1996) and two groups of Pima Indians (Ravussin et al., 1994) that support James and Trayhurn's hypothesis.

9. Let's look again at the role of leptin in human obesity.

a. Familial obesity can result from a faulty gene for the production of leptin. How often does this kind of mutation occur?

b. Is there a relationship between plasma levels of leptin and the total body fat of obese and lean people? (Schwartz et al., 1996)

c. If leptin plays a role in human obesity, the mechanism may be reduced _____ to the hormone and not decreased _____.

10. Summarize evidence that leptin insensitivity may result from

a. a faulty leptin receptor gene in rats and humans. (Gura, 1997; Clément et al., 1998).

b. differences in the transport of leptin molecules into the brain. (Banks et al., 1996; Golden et al., 1997; Caro et al., 1996)

c. eating a high fat diet. (See Figure 13.22 in your text. Lu et al., 1998; Havel et al., 1999)

11. a. How does a genetic defect affect the agouti mouse? Be sure to mention the agouti protein and its role in your answer.

b. The agouti protein is an _____ of the MC-4 receptor, binding with the receptor causing

_____ and _____.

c. Where are MC-4 receptors found? (Mountjoy et al., 1994)

d. List the two natural ligands for the MC-4 receptor.

    1.   2.

e. What effects do these two proteins have on MC-4 receptors and on feeding?

f. In what kinds of neurons are the proteins found?

g. What effects does leptin have on the neurons that secrete these proteins?

h. What is the effect on eating of a targeted mutation against the gene responsible for the production of the MC-4 receptor? (Huszar et al., 1997)

i. Why may an understanding of the function of the MC-4 receptor benefit humans? (Vaissse et al., 1998; Yeo et al., 1998)

12. a. Where is uncoupling protein (UCP) found? (Nicholls and Wenner, 1972)

    b. Carefully explain how this protein affects the membranes of mitochondria.

    c. What, then, may be its role in weight control?

13. a. Where has a gene for a second uncoupling protein (UCP2) been found? (Fleury et al., 1997)

    b. Cite research that it may play a role in human metabolism. (Bouchard et al., 1997; Walder et al., 1998)

Learning Objective 13-7 Discuss the mechanical, surgical, and pharmacological treatments of obesity.

Read pages 417-419 and answer the following questions.

1. a. When people who have had their jaws wired together to help them loose weight have the wiring removed, what almost always happens?

    b. In an attempt to help patients maintain their losses, what did some therapists do?

    c. And what did about half their patients eventually do?

2. a. Describe gastroplasty, a surgical treatment for obesity.

b. Following surgery, how should patients feel after eating a small amount of food? Unfortunately, how do they often feel? (Be sure to mention *nimiety* in your answer.)

3. Briefly summarize some of the common side effects of intestinal bypass surgery.

4. a. What is the "Gastric Bubble" and why did some therapists suggest it for their patients?

   b. Why was it later taken off the market in the United States? (Kral, 1989)

5. Summarize the benefits of regular exercise in the treatment of obesity by noting how exercise programs affected middle-age men and children. (Bunyard et al., 1998; Gutin et al., 1999)

6. a. Explain why fenfluramine was used to treat obesity. (Bray, 1992)

   b. Although effective, why was the drug withdrawn from the market in the United States? (Blundell and Halford, 1998)

Learning Objective 13-8 Discuss the physiological factors that may contribute to anorexia nervosa and bulimia nervosa.

Read pages 419-420 and answer the following questions.

1. Describe the symptoms of anorexia nervosa.

2. Now describe the symptoms of bulimia nervosa and its aftermath. (Mawson, 1974; Halmi, 1978)

3. a. Study Figure 13.23 in your text and compare the effects of the sight and smell of warm cinnamon rolls on the insulin levels of anorexic women and lean but not anorexic women. (Broberg and Bernstein, 1989)

   b. What do the results indicate about the interest of anorexics in food?

4. a. To combat their intense fear of becoming obese, what do many anorexics do?

   b. What do studies with animals suggest may be a reason for increased exercise? (Routtenberg, 1968; Wilckens et al., 1992)

5. Which explanation for anorexia nervosa—biological or social—is favored by most psychologists?

6. a. Twenty years after treatment for anorexia, what percentage of a group of patients showed good recovery? (Ratnasuriya et al., 1991)

b. What had happened to almost 15 percent of them?

7. How does anorexia affect

   a. bone density?

   b. menstruation?

   c. the brain? (Artmann et al., 1985; Herholz, 1996; Kingston et al., 1996)

8. a. What do twin studies suggest about the cause of anorexia? (Russell and Treasure, 1989; Walters and Kendler, 1995)

   b. Summarize the biochemical changes in the brain associated with anorexia and bulimia reported in a literature review by Fava et al. (1989).

   c. Why are endocrine system changes probably effects rather than causes of this disorder?

9. a. Describe the levels of neuropeptide Y in the cerebrospinal fluid of patients with severe anorexia and the same patients after they have regained their normal weight. (Kaye et al., 1990; Kaye, 1996)

   b. What symptoms of anorexia may be affected by this neuropeptide?

10. a. Now describe the level of leptin in the cerebrospinal fluid of underweight anorexics and the same patients before their weight returns to normal. (Mantzoros et al., 1997)

    b. What aspect of recovery may be affected by this hormone?

11. Why has research to determine a biochemical basis for anorexia nervosa been difficult?

12. a. Which kind of drugs have been found to be ineffective in treating anorexia? (Mitchell, 1989; Attia et al., 1998)

    b. Summarize the limited success of treatment with cyproheptadine. (Halmi et al., 1986)

    c. What class of drugs may be useful in treating bulimia nervosa? (Kennedy and Goldbloom, 1991; Advokat and Kutlesic, 1995)

Lesson II Self Test

1. Lesions of the area postrema and nucleus of the solitary tract (AP/NST)

   a. stimulate a carbohydrate appetite.
   b. reduce the ability to distinguish between flavors.
   c. stimulate fos production.
   d. abolish both glucoprivic and lipoprivic feeding.

2. Lesions of the _____ produce _____ and lesions of the _____ abolish _____.

   a. lateral hypothalamus; hunger; ventromedial hypothalamus; satiety
   b. ventromedial hypothalamus; overeating; lateral hypothalamus; eating.
   c. paraventricular nucleus; overeating; ventromedial hypothalamus; undereating
   d. ventromedial hypothalamus; satiety; paraventricular nucleus; obesity

3. Neuropeptide Y , which is secreted by neurons whose cell bodies are located in the _____, _____.

   a. area postrema; controls hormones that regulate the fasting phase of metabolism
   b. paraventricular nucleus; causes a rapid decline in blood glucose levels
   c. arcuate nucleus; stimulates ravenous eating
   d. ventromedial hypothalamus; abolishes eating

4. CART

   a. levels decrease if animals are deprived of food.
   b. infusions into the cerebral ventricles stimulate eating.
   c. neurons do not contain leptin receptors.
   d. production can be stimulated by injections of NPY into the cerebral ventricles.

5. Appetite can be suppressed by the activation of receptors for

   a. CCK, serotonin, and MCH.
   b. NPY, leptin, and MC-4.
   c. leptin, serotonin, and CART.
   d. CCK, NPY, and CART.

6. People with an efficient metabolism

   a. must eat more food to maintain their body weight.
   b. have difficulty losing weight even on a reduced calorie diet.

   c. have difficulty matching food intake to physical activity.
   d. do not have any calories left over for deposit in long-term nutrient reservoirs.

7. The agouti mouse has a mutation of the gene responsible for the production of _____ receptors.

   a. neuropeptide Y (NPY)
   b. leptin
   c. melanocortin-4
   d. serotonin

8. The uncoupling protein may be one of the factors in determining

   a. metabolic efficiency.
   b. sensitivity to leptin.
   c. sensitivity to long-term satiety signals.
   d. weight gain in middle age.

9. Gastroplasty, a surgical procedure to help obese people loose weight, results in

   a. feelings of satiety when a small amount of food is eaten.
   b. nausea when too much time elapses between meals.
   c. an inability to distinguish between short-term and long-term satiety signals.
   d. nimiety when a small amount of food is eaten.

10. Fenfluramine and sibutramine, a similar but safer replacement drug, stimulate the release of

    a. NPY.
    b. insulin.
    c. serotonin.
    d. leptin.

11. Anorexics

    a. are unresponsive to the effects of food.
    b. do not experience hunger.
    c. have an intense fear of becoming obese.
    d. attempt to reduce their need for calories by reducing physical activity.

12. The cerebrospinal fluid of anorexics contains elevated levels of

    a. neuropeptide Y.
    b. cholecystokinin (CCK).
    c. fenfluramine.
    d. leptin.

Answers for Self Tests

Lesson I

1. d Obj. 13-1
2. a Obj. 13-1
3. b Obj. 13-1
4. a Obj. 13-1
5. c Obj. 13-2
6. d Obj. 13-2
7. b Obj. 13-2
8. a Obj. 13-2
9. c Obj. 13-3
10. d Obj. 13-3
11. a Obj. 13-3
12. c Obj. 13-3

Lesson II

1. d Obj. 13-4
2. b Obj. 13-4
3. c Obj. 13-4
4. a Obj. 13-5
5. c Obj. 13-5
6. b Obj. 13-6
7. c Obj. 13-6
8. a Obj. 13-6
9. d Obj. 13-7
10. c Obj. 13-7
11. c Obj. 13-8
12. a Obj. 13-8

CHAPTER 14
Learning and Memory: Basic Mechanisms

Lesson I: The Nature of Learning, Learning and Synaptic Plasticity, and Perceptual Learning

Read the interim summary on page 428 of your text to re-acquaint yourself with the material in this section.

> *Learning Objective 14-1* Describe the four basic forms of learning: perceptual learning, stimulus-response learning, motor learning, and relational learning.

Read pages 424-427 and answer the following questions.

1. _____ physically change the structure of our _____ _____ and thereby

    change our _____. This process is called _____ and these changes are called

    _____.

2. State the primary function of the ability to learn.

3. List four of the basic forms of learning.

    1.   3.

    2.   4.

4. Define *perceptual learning* in your own words.

5. State its primary function.

6. a. Use one word to indicate how many of our sensory systems are capable of perceptual learning.

    b. Where does perceptual learning appear to take place?

7. Define *stimulus-response learning* in your own words, noting its two major categories.

8. Which neural circuits are presumably involved?

9. In your own words, briefly explain what happens during classical conditioning.

10. Let's examine how the species-typical defensive eyeblink response of a rabbit can be conditioned to a tone. Identify the

    a. unconditional stimulus (US).   c. conditional stimulus (CS).

    b. unconditional response (UR).   d. conditional response (CR).

11. Study Figure 14.1 in your text and then complete Figure 1, which illustrates the kinds of changes that may take place in the brain during classical conditioning.

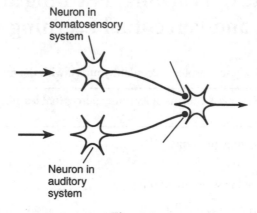

Figure 1

12. State the Hebb rule in your own words. (Hebb, 1949)

13. a. Briefly explain what happens during instrumental conditioning. Be sure to use the terms *reinforcing stimuli* and *punishing stimuli* in your answer.

    b. Explain why it is incorrect to say that reinforcement causes a particular behavior to become more frequent.

14. Study Figure 14.2 in your text and then complete Figure 2 on the next page, which illustrates the kinds of changes that may take place in the brain during instrumental conditioning.

15. Now that you have described classical and instrumental conditioning, discuss three ways in which they differ.

16. Define *motor learning* in your own words, and explain why it is considered a form of stimulus-response learning. (Study Figure 14.3 in your text.)

17. Define *relational learning* in your own words.

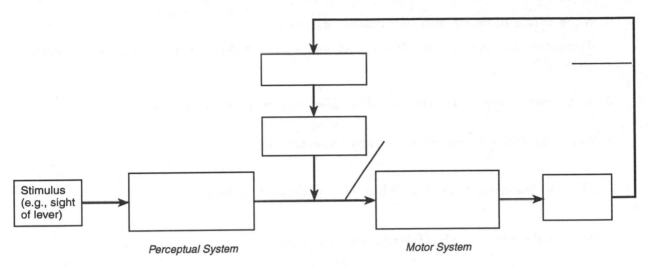

Figure 2

18. Briefly describe these forms of relational learning.

   a. spatial learning

   b. episodic learning

   c. observational learning

Read the interim summary on pages 440-441 of your text to re-acquaint yourself with the material in this section.

Learning Objective 14-2 Discuss research on how learning affects neural structures, the induction of long-term potentiation, and the role of NMDA receptors.

Read pages 428-434 and answer the following questions.

1. Define *synaptic plasticity* in your own words.

2. a. Which axons did Lømo (1966) electrically stimulate? What was the result?

    b. What is this increase called?

3. a. Return to Figure 3.16 in your text and review the location of the hippocampus in the human brain.

    b. List the structures that comprise the hippocampal formation.

       1.   3.

       2.

    c. Identify the structure through which the primary inputs and outputs of the hippocampal formation pass.

4. Let's trace the pathway of incoming information through the hippocampal formation.

    a. Where do neurons in the entorhinal cortex relay incoming information? Be sure to identify the route this information takes.

b. Where, in turn, do the neurons of this structure send axons?

c. What are the two major divisions of the hippocampus proper? Which one of these receives axons from the dentate gyrus?

d. Briefly describe the attachment of axon and dendrites to pyramidal cells in field CA3.

e. Why are dendritic spines important for long-term potentiation?

f. CA3 axons branch in two directions. Where does each of these branches travel?

g. Where do the pyramidal cells of field CA1 send their axons?

h. Finally, what is the function of CA1 pyramidal cells?

5. To review this pathway study Figure 14.4 in your text.

6. Study Figures 14.5 and 14.6 in your text and explain a typical procedure for producing long-term potentiation.

a. Where is a stimulating electrode placed? a recording electrode?

b. Define *population EPSP* in your own words.

c. What event triggers a population EPSP and what does the size of the first one indicate?

d. How is long-term potentiation induced?

e. What evidence confirms that long-term potentiation has occurred?

7. a. Briefly describe how long-term potentiation is induced in isolated slices of the hippocampal formation. (See Figure 14.7 in your text.)

b. What are some of the advantages of this procedure?

8. a. Define *associative long-term potentiation* in your own words. (Study Figure 14.8 in your text.)

b. How does this phenomenon appear to confirm the Hebb rule?

9. Explain why long-term potentiation occurs if

a. a series of pulses is given at a high rate all in one burst, but not if the same number of pulses are delivered at a slow rate. (See Figure 14.9 in your text.)

b. artificially depolarized axons are stimulated, but not if depolarization and stimulation occurred at different times. (See Figure 14.10 in your text. Kelso et al., 1986)

10. To review: What two events are necessary if long-term potentiation is to occur?

1.   2.

11. Study Figure 14.11 in your text and explain the role of NMDA receptors in long-term potentiation.

a. Where are NMDA receptors found?

b. What kind of ion channel does an NMDA receptor control?

c. Carefully explain what two conditions must occur in order for calcium to enter cells through the ion channels controlled by NMDA receptors?

d. Therefore, the NMDA receptor is a _____- and _____-dependent channel.

12. a. Briefly explain why research with drugs such as AP5 that block NMDA receptors supports their importance in long-term potentiation. (Brown et al., 1989)

b. Which receptors are responsible for synaptic transmission in the newly strengthened synapses?

13. a. How did an injection of EGTA affect

1. hippocampal pyramidal cells at the injection site?

2. long-term potentiation in these cells and neighboring cells? (Lynch et al., 1984)

b. What do these results suggest about the role of calcium in long-term potentiation?

14. Let's look now at the role of dendritic spikes that occur in some kinds of pyramidal cells during long-term potentiation. Carefully explain

a. what triggers dendritic spikes.

b. how the membrane potential of the cell and dendrites then changes.

c. and how the amount of calcium in the dendrites changes. (See Figure 14.12 in your text. Yuste and Denk, 1995; Yuste et al., 1999)

15. Using TTX, which prevents the formation of dendritic spikes, what did researchers confirm about the necessary conditions for long-term potentiation? (See Figure 14.13 in your text. Magee and Johnston, 1977)

16. Finally, study Figure 14.14 in your text and carefully explain why both weak and strong synapses on a dendritic spine must be active at the same time in order for ion channels controlled by NMDA receptors in the weak synapse to open and for associative long-term potentiation to occur.

Learning Objective 14-3 Discuss the mechanisms responsible for the increase in synaptic strength that occurs during long-term potentiation.

Read pages 434-440 and answer the following questions.

1. Outline the changes that may be responsible for synaptic strengthening.

2. Let's look at these changes more carefully.

    a. How did Tocco et al., (1992) establish long-term potentiation in intact laboratory animals?

    b. Describe how brain slices were prepared for histological examination and the results of the examination.

    c. What do the results suggest about the mechanism of synaptic strengthening?

3. When researchers controlled whether NMDA receptors were blocked by the magnesium ion, what kind of receptors increased in field CA1, presumably as a result of long-term potentiation? (Liao et al., 1995)

4. When the number of AMPA receptors increases, how are the effects of glutamate released by the terminal button changed?

5. a. Using a two-photon laser scanning microscope, researchers studied the movement of AMPA receptors on the dendritic spines of CA1 neurons during long-term potentiation. Where were these receptors found

    1. before long-term potentiation was induced?

    2. fifteen minutes afterwards? (Study Figures 14.15 and 14.16 in your text. Shi et al., 1999)

    b. How can this movement be prevented?

6. a. What term is used to refer to synapses altered by long-term potentiation? (Geinisman et al., 1991, 1996; Buchs and Muller, 1996))

    b. Briefly summarize Edwards' (1995) explanation of why the number of postsynaptic AMPA receptors increases. (Study Figure 14.17 in your text.)

7. a. After inducing long-term potentiation in hippocampal slices, how did researchers treat and prepare the slices so they could identify any changes that occurred? (Toni et al., 1999)

    b. What change did they see at first? later? (See Figures 14.18 and 14.19 in your text.)

    c. If the slices were treated with a chemical that prevented long-term potentiation, then what did they observe?

8. a. Define *protein kinase* in your own words.

    b. Explain why they become active.

    c. Once activated, how do protein kinases affect protein molecules?

    d. Where are high concentrations of the protein kinase CaM-KII found?

9. a. After researchers introduced a targeted mutation of a gene responsible for the production of the protein kinase CaM-KII into mice, how successful were they in inducing long-term potentiation? (Silva et al., 1992a)

    b. What does this finding suggest about the importance of CaM-KII in long-term potentiation?

10. a. Once CaM-KII has added a _____ group to itself in a process called _____, it no longer requires the presence of _____ to remain active.

    b. What is the effect of the autophosphorylation of CaM-KII on AMPA receptors? and the receptors on the synapse?

    c. If this unusual process is prevented by a targeted mutation, do attempts to establish long-term potentiation through NMDA receptor stimulation succeed? (Giese et al., 1998)

11. After long-term potentiation occurs, where do molecules of CaM-KII migrate? (See Figure 14.20 in your text. Shen and Meyer, 1999)

12. a. By what means might long-term potentiation affect the presynaptic terminal buttons? Be sure to use the term *retrograde messenger* in your answer.

    b. Cite evidence that hippocampal slices exposed to NMDA produce NO. (East and Garthwaite,1991)

    c. How do drugs that block the production of nitric oxide affect the establishment of long-term potentiation? (O'Dell et al., 1991; Schuman and Madison, 1991; Bon et al., 1992; Haley et al., 1992)

13. a. How is long-lasting long-term potentiation affected if a drug that blocks protein synthesis, is administered

    1. before, during, or immediately after a burst of stimulation?

    2. one hour after stimulation? (Frey et al., 1988; Frey and Morris, 1997)

    b. What, then, is a necessary condition if long-lasting long-term potentiation is to occur?

14. Discuss evidence that suggests that protein synthesis takes place in the dendrites. (Tiedge and Brosius, 1996)

15. Review the biochemical changes that occur during long-term potentiation by studying Figure 14.21 in your text.

16. a. Define *long-term depression* in your own words.

    b. How does AP5 affect the establishment of long-term potentiation and long-term depression? (See Figure 14.22 in your text. Dudek and Bear, 1992)

    c. Describe several patterns of electrical stimulation that produce long-term depression. (Stanton and Sejnowski, 1989; Debanne et al., 1994; Thiels et al., 1996)

    d. Outline evidence that long-term potentiation and long-term depression involve two different subtypes of NMDA receptors. (Hrabetova and Sacktor, 1997)

    e. How do long-term potentiation and long-term depression affect

    1. the number of AMPA receptors? (Carroll et al., 1999)

    2. phosphorylation of AMPA receptors and sensitivity to glutamate? (Lee et al., 1998)

    f. What do these findings suggest about the Hebb rule and learning?

17. a. List some areas of the brain other than the hippocampal formation where long-term potentiation has been successfully demonstrated.

    b. What does successful long-term potentiation in these other locations indicate about the role of NMDA receptors? (Monaghan and Cotman, 1985; Lynch et al., 1991)

    c. What are some of the implications of finding that long-term potentiation can be produced in several different brain locations?

Read the interim summary on page 450 of your text to re-acquaint yourself with the material in this section.

Learning Objective 14-4 Describe research on the role of the primary visual cortex in visual perceptual learning.

Read pages 441-447 and answer the following questions.

1. Define *perceptual learning* in your own words.

2.   Review the flow of information in primary visual association cortex. (Study Figure 14.23 in your text.)

3.   a. List the two divisions of the second level of visual association cortex.

      1.   2.

    b. What is their common beginning?

    c. Where does each end?

    d. What is the function of each in visual perception?

4.   a. What kind of brain damage disrupted the monkeys' ability to perform a visual discrimination task? (Study Figure 14.24 in your text. Mishkin, 1966)

    b. What do the results suggest about the flow of information necessary for successful visual pattern discrimination?

5.   What kind of stimuli may neurons near the superior temporal sulcus detect? (Baylis et al., 1985; Rolls and Baylis, 1986)

6.   How did Rolls et al., (1989) demonstrate changes in the response patterns of neurons in inferior temporal cortex when new stimuli are presented?

7.   Use one word to describe the capacity of visual perceptual learning.

8.   a. Describe one of the visual displays, shown in Figure 14.25 in your text, that Moscovitch and colleagues asked people to memorize. (Moscovitch et al., 1995)

    b. Now describe the two retrieval tasks they used to test recall.

    c. Study Figure 14.26 in your text and summarize testing results.

    d. What do the findings suggest about the location for recall of perceptual memories for identities and locations of objects?

9.   Define *short-term memory* in your own words.

10. a. Study Figure 14.27 in your text and describe the delayed matching-to-sample procedure that Fuster and Jervey (1981) used to test short-term memory.

    b. Study Figure 14.28 in your text which shows the response of a single representative neuron in inferior temporal cortex during this task.

      1. Describe the response of this neuron to red light and green light.

2. What are the implications of the sustained response to red light?

11. a. Let's look at other brain regions that are involved in short-term memory. Where do both major regions of visual association cortex form connections with prefrontal cortex? (See Figure 14.29 in your text. Wilson et al., 1993)

   b. If the activity of the prefrontal cortex is disrupted by damage or temporary deactivation, recognition of what kinds of stimuli are affected? (For example, Bodner et al., 1996)

   c. Within prefrontal cortex, what are the locations of neurons that become active during the delay interval of different kinds of delayed matching-to-sample tasks? (Study Figure 14.30 in your text. Wilson et al., 1996)

   d. What do these results indicate about the pattern of connections in the monkey brain and the human brain?

12. a. Trace the changes in neural activity during testing on a delayed matching-to-sample task in which the stimuli were presented one at a time. (See Figure 14.31 in your text. Miller et al., 1996) How did the visual association cortex and the prefrontal cortex respond when

   1. there was no stimulus (the delay interval)?

   2. a test stimulus that did not match the sample stimulus was presented?

   3. a test stimulus that matched the sample stimulus was presented?

   b. What does this response pattern suggest about the role of prefrontal cortex in short-term memory?

13. a. Briefly describe a paired-associate task.

   b. Describe the shift in the activity of neurons in prefrontal cortex that occurred during the delay interval of a paired-associate task. (Rainer et al., 1999)

   c. What may be the benefit of this shift?

14. a. Describe the delayed responding task Quintana and Fuster (1992) taught monkey subjects.

   b. During testing, what kinds of information did some neurons in dorsolateral prefrontal cortex appear to encode? other neurons?

   c. What do the results suggest about the aspects of a task subjects remember?

Learning Objective 14-5 Describe research on the role of acetylcholine in auditory learning.

Read pages 447-449 and answer the following questions.

1. How do we use the wealth of information we obtain and store through perceptual learning?

2. What kind of events appear to facilitate perceptual learning? which neurotransmitter?

3. What may be the cause of the memory loss that is one of the first symptoms of Alzheimer's disease? Cite research to support your answer. (Nakano and Hirano, 1982; Whitehouse et al., 1982)

4. a. Outline how researchers classically conditioned an emotional response in guinea pigs. (Bakin and Weinberger, 1990; Edeline and Weinberger, 1991a; 1991b; 1992; Weinberger, 1998))

    b. Study Figure 14.32 in your text and compare the response pattern of neurons in the auditory system before and after training.

    c. What do the results suggest about the effects of auditory learning on neurons in the auditory system?

    d. How long do these changes last?

    e. Study Figure 14.33 in your text and explain the important role of acetylcholine in this kind of leaning. Be sure to refer to the nucleus basalis in your answer.

5. a. If the nucleus basalis is stimulated at the same time a tone of a particular frequency is presented, how is the response of the neurons in the auditory cortex affected? Why? (Bakin and Weinberger, 1996)

    b. How can this effect be blocked?

    c. How did Cruikshank and Weinberger (1996) demonstrate a similarity between this response and long-term potentiation?

    d. What do their results indicate about an important element of classical conditioning?

Lesson I Self Test

1. In classical conditioning, the unconditional stimulus

    a. elicits the species-typical response.
    b. is a neutral stimulus.

    c. elicits the species-typical response if it has previously been paired with the conditional stimulus.
    d. initially has little effect on behavior.

2. Instrumental conditioning results from an association between

a. two stimuli.
b. a stimulus and a response.
c. a conditional and an unconditional stimulus.
d. two responses.

3. The Hebb rule states that a synapse will be strengthened if it repeatedly become active _____ the _____ neuron fires.

a. at the same time; presynaptic
b. soon after; presynaptic
c. about the same time; postsynaptic
d. before; postsynaptic

4. In order for long-term potentiation to occur

a. the presynaptic membrane must be depolarized at the same time that the synapses are active.
b. the postsynaptic membrane must be depolarized at the same time that the synapses are active.
c. the postsynaptic membrane must be hyperpolarized at the same time that the synapses are active.
d. a series of electrical pulses must be delivered at a slow rate.

5. The size of the

a. population EPSP was predicted by the Hebb rule.
b. first population EPSP indicates the strength of synaptic connections before long-term potentiation takes place.
c. population EPSP decreases if long-term potentiation has taken place.
d. population EPSP slowly increases for up to 40 hours if long-term potentiation has taken place.

6. NMDA receptors

a. control calcium ion channels.
b. are found in highest concentration in the mossy fibers of field CA3.
c. detect the presence of magnesium.
d. are blocked by glutamate.

7. One of the effects of long-term potentiation is a(n)

a. increase in the number of calcium-dependent enzymes.
b. increase in the amount of postsynaptic thickening of neurons in the hippocampal formation.
c. decrease in protein synthesis in the cell body.
d. increase in the number of postsynaptic AMPA receptors.

8. Nitric oxide

a blocks the effects of calcium.
b. may increase the number of glutamate receptors.
c. may be produced in the dendritic spines.
d. lasts for a long time and can diffuse the entire length of a postsynaptic axon.

9. Long-term depression may result from

a. sustained increases in protein synthesis in the cell body.
b. the gradual atrophy of the dendrites that transmit chemical messages to the cell.
c. low-frequency stimulation of the synaptic inputs to a cell.
d. increased sensitivity of protein kinases to calcium.

10. In a delayed matching-to-sample task, the "delay" is the interval

a. between teaching the subject the task and testing to see whether it has learned it.
b. between the sample stimulus and the choices.
c. between successive trials.
d. a subject must pause before responding.

11. In a delayed matching-to-sample task, neurons in inferior temporal cortex continued to respond during the delay interval, which suggests that these neurons are parts of circuits

a. involved in instrumental conditioning.
b. responsible for reinforcement.
c. involved in excitation rather than inhibition.
d. that remember that a particular stimulus was presented.

12. The release of _____ from _____ causes neurons in the auditory cortex _____.

a. acetylcholine; neurons in the nucleus basalis; to become more sensitive to the auditory input they are receiving
b. glutamate; neurons in the medial geniculate nucleus of the thalamus; to fail to differentiate between tones of different frequencies
c. calcium; NMDA receptors; to respond more vigorously to the presence of nitric oxide
d. nitric oxide synthase; presynaptic neurons; to increase protein synthesis necessary for long-term potentiation.

Lesson II: Classical Conditioning, Instrumental Conditioning and Motor Learning

Read the interim summary on page 452 in your text to re-acquaint yourself with the material in this section.

> *Learning Objective 14-6*   Discuss the physiology of the classically conditioned emotional response to aversive stimuli.

Read pages 450-452 and answer the following questions.

1. a. When the central nucleus of the amygdala is activated, it stimulates the release of _____ in the cerebral cortex.

    b. Explain how this release may facilitate perceptual learning.

2. A hypothetical neural circuit of the changes in synaptic strength resulting from a classically conditioned emotional response is diagrammed in Figure 14.34 in your text.

    a. In this example, what is the CS? the US?

    b. Where is information about the CS sent? the US?

    c. Where does information from the CS and US converge?

    d. When a rat does encounter a painful stimulus that is paired with a tone, how are the synapses in the MGm and basolateral amygdala strengthened according to the Hebb rule?

3. Let's look at experimental support that the basolateral amygdala and the MGm are involved in learning. What kind of lesions disrupt conditioned emotional responses established with a tone followed by a foot shock? (Iwata et al., 1986; LeDoux et al., 1986, 1990; Sananes and Davis, 1992)

4. What evidence suggests synaptic changes do occur in the MGm? (reported by Weinberger, 1982)

5. a. Summarize the changes in neurons in the lateral amygdala recorded during pairings of a tone with a footshock. (Study Figure 14.35 in your text. Quirk et al., 1995)

    b. Explain why these researchers believe the amygdala to be a more important site for learning than the MGm?

6. a. What is the result of stimulation of the axons that bring auditory information to the MGm (Gerren and Weinberger, 1983) and those that connect the medial geniculate nucleus to the lateral amygdala (Clugnet and LeDoux, 1990)?

b. Following long-term potentiation of the lateral nucleus of the amygdala, what changes are seen in the response of neurons in this nucleus to auditory stimuli? (Rogan and LeDoux, 1995)

7. a. How is acquisition of a classically conditioned emotional response affected if AP5 is injected directly into the basolateral amygdala of a rat before training begins? (Be sure you understand the pharmacological effect of AP5.)

    b. What is the effect of the drug if it is injected after training has taken place?. (Campeau et al., 1992; Fanselow and Kim, 1994)

    c. What do the results suggest about the role of NMDA receptors?

8. a. Define *extinction* in your own words.

    b. Is extinction affected if AP5 is injected into the amygdala just before extinction training takes place? (Falls et al., 1992)

Read the interim summary on pages 464-465 to re-acquaint yourself with the material in this section.

> *Learning Objective 14-7* Describe the role of the basal ganglia and premotor cortex in instrumental conditioning and motor learning.

Read pages 452-456 and answer the following questions.

1. To review: Instrumental conditioning involves the strengthening of connections between _____ _____ that detect a particular _____ and those that produce a particular _____. These _____ _____ begin in various regions of _____ association cortex and end in _____ association cortex. The two major pathways between them are direct _____ connections and connections through the _____ _____ and the _____.

2. Describe some of the functions of each of these pathways along with a task that illustrates each function.

3. Discuss how we learn a complex behavior through instrumental conditioning and the effects of practice on the basal ganglia and transcortical circuits.

4. a. List the nuclei that comprise the neostriatum.

    1.   2.   3.

    b. Which regions send information to them and where do they, in turn, send information? (See Figure 14.36 in your text.)

c. What kind of lesions do and do not disrupt a visual discrimination task? (Divac et al., 1967; Gaffan and Harrison, 1987; Gaffan and Eacott, 1995)

5. a. List the kinds of learning tasks that McDonald and White (1993) taught laboratory rats.

    1.

    2.

    3.

    b. Next to each kind of learning, note the location(s) of lesions that disrupted it.

6. During testing, monkeys were required to remember either the _____ or the _____ of visual stimuli. Remembering the _____ of the stimuli increased activity of the neurons in the _____ of the caudate nucleus, which receives information from the _____ _____ _____ , and remembering information about the _____ of the stimulus increased the activity in the _____ of the caudate nucleus, which receives information from the _____ . (Levy et al., 1997)

7. What do these results of the two studies you have just described indicate about the role of particular neural pathways and particular kinds of learning?

8. a. Briefly outline the neural degeneration that causes Parkinson's disease.

    b. Why can the symptoms of Parkinson's disease be viewed as motor deficits *and* failures of remembering how to do something? Cite research to support your answer. (Owen et al., 1992; Partiot et al., 1996)

9. a. Describe the patterns for predicting the weather that researchers showed both people with Parkinson's disease and unaffected people. (See Figure 14.37 in your text. Knowlton et al., 1996)

    b. Compare the results for all subjects. (See Figure 14.38 in your text.)

    c. What do these results suggest about the eventual effects of Parkinson's disease on the basal ganglia and learning?

10. Let's look at some motor learning that is disrupted by damage to premotor cortex and the supplementary motor area which is shown in Figure 14.39 in your text.

    a. Describe the instrumental learning task, shown in Figure 14.40 in your text, that researchers taught normal monkeys and monkeys with lesions of the supplementary motor cortex. (Thaler et al., 1995)

    b. How well did monkeys with lesions learn the task? a task cued by an auditory stimulus?

    c. What was the nature of their deficit?

11. What other kind of task does this kind of lesion impair? (See Figure 14.41 in your text. Chen et al., 1995)

12. a. When monkeys are performing a memorized series of responses, how do neurons in the supplemental motor area respond? (Mushiake et al., 1991)

    b. When the task was later cued with a visual stimulus, how did the response of the neurons change?

13. Which brain regions were active when human subjects learned a sequence of button presses? when they performed the task? (Hikosaka et al., 1996)

Learning Objective 14-8 Describe the role of dopamine in reinforcing brain stimulation; discuss the effects of systemic administration of dopamine antagonists and agonists.

Read pages 457-460 and answer the following questions.

1. Briefly recount the discovery of reinforcing brain stimulation by Olds and Milner (1954). (See Figure 14.42 in your text.)

2. a. The most reliable location for producing reinforcing brain stimulation is the _____

    _____ _____ which is a bundle of _____ that travels from the

    _____ to the _____ _____ _____.

    b. Where do most researchers place the tips of their electrodes?

3. a. In which midbrain structures do the major pathways of neurons whose terminal buttons secrete dopamine begin? (Lindvall, 1979; Fallon 1988)

    b. Explain why the activity of the compact clusters of the cell bodies of these neurons has a surprisingly widespread effect.

4. Complete the following table of the projections of the mesolimbic system and the mesocortical system.

Mesolimbic System	Mesocortical System
Begins in:	Begins in:
Projections	*Projections found in rats*
1.	1.
2.	2.
3.	3.
4.	*Additional projections found in primates*
5.	1.
	2.

5. a. Name and describe the location of the structure that has been the focus of much of the research on the physiology of reinforcement. (See Figure 14.43 in your text.)

   b. Research with Parkinson's patients suggests what other brain region may be involved in reinforcement?

6. Rats will press a lever in order to receive electrical brain stimulation in several brain regions. Name some. (Routtenberg and Malsbury, 1969; Crow, 1972; Olds and Fobes, 1981)

7. a. What task did subject rats have to perform in order to obtain reinforcing electrical stimulation? (Stellar et al., 1983)

   b. How did injections of a dopamine receptor blocker affect the reinforcing value of electrical brain stimulation? (Study Figure 14.44 in your text.)

8. a. If you do not remember the microdialysis technique, review the description in Chapter 5.

   b. Which neurotransmitter, verified using this technique, is released at the time of reinforcing electrical brain stimulation? (Moghadam and Bunney, 1989; Nakahara et al., 1989; Phillips et al., 1992. See Figure 14.45 in your text.)

   c. What other kinds of stimuli trigger this release? (Salamone, 1992)

   d. What do these results indicate about the function of dopaminergic neurons?

Learning Objective 14-9 Discuss how the reinforcement system may detect reinforcing stimuli and strengthen synaptic connections.

Read pages 460-464 and answer the following questions.

1. Why, according to most researchers, is electrical stimulation of some regions of the brain reinforcing?

2. What two functions must be performed by the reinforcement system if a stimulus is to become reinforcing?

1.   2.

3. Nick, having taken advantage of a special offer at the video store, watched three movies in two days. When a friend called to see if he wanted to get together and rent a movie, Nick suggested they go out for pizza instead. Use this example to explain one of the difficulties in determining what is a reinforcing event.

4. Name the brain structure that appears to be an important focal point in reinforcement.

5. Briefly describe how researchers demonstrated that dopaminergic neurons in the ventral tegmental area respond to both primary reinforcing stimuli and conditioned stimuli. (Ljungberg et al., 1992)

6. Once again, review how neutral stimuli become conditioned reinforcers or conditioned punishers through classical conditioning.

7. List the three inputs to the ventral tegmental area that may play the most important role in reinforcement.

1.   2.   3.

8. Summarize the possible roles of each of these three inputs in detection of reinforcing stimuli.

   a. Let's look first at the role of the amygdala in conditioned reinforcement. How does destruction of the amygdala or its disconnection from the visual system disrupt a monkey's recognition of visual stimuli? memory for paired stimuli? (Spiegler and Mishkin, 1981; Gaffan et al., 1988)

   b. How do neurotoxic lesions of the basolateral amygdala affect the reinforcing value of stimuli? (Cador et al., 1989; Everitt et al., 1989)

9. a. How did the firing rate of some neurons in the lateral hypothalamus and substantia innominata change as a monkey ate and drank more and more?

   b. What may be the role in reinforcement of the connections between the lateral hypothalamus and the ventral tegmental area? (See Figure 14.46 in your text. Burton et al., 1976; Rolls et al., 1986)

10. a. How does glutamate secreted by the terminal buttons of axons that connect the prefrontal cortex and the ventral tegmental area affect the secretion of dopamine in the ventral tegmental area and the nucleus accumbens? (Gariano and Groves, 1988)

    b. What are some of the functions of the prefrontal cortex? (Mesulam, 1986) How may the role of the prefrontal cortex in reinforcement compliment these functions?

11. Study Figure 14.47 in your text and then carefully explain when and how dopamine (and perhaps other neurotransmitters) may strengthen synaptic connections during instrumental conditioning.

12. a. Why did researchers infuse neurons in field CAI of the hippocampus with dopamine or dopamine agonists? (Stein and Belluzzi, 1989)

   b. Study the graphs in Figure 14.48 in your text and summarize their results.

   c. What conclusions may be drawn from the results about the effect of dopamine and the timing of infusions?

13. List some of the natural reinforcers that cause the release of dopamine in the nucleus accumbens.

14. Study Figure 14.49 in your text and explain how increasing sexual contact affected the level of extracellular dopamine in the nucleus accumbens of a male rat. (Pfaus et al., 1990)

15. a. When does the taste of saccharine cause an increase in the release of dopamine? a decrease? (Mark et al., 1989)

   b. Explain why the same stimulus had two different effects.

16. a. Researchers injected a dopamine receptor block into the nucleus accumbens of rats while they were pressing a lever to obtain some highly preferred food even though other food was freely available. How was their behavior affected? their hunger? (Salamone et al., 1991)

   b. Rats were trained to obtain food by running through a T maze. If they chose one arm of the maze what did they have to do and how much food did they receive? if they chose the other arm? (Cousins et al., 1996)

   c. And how did an injection of 6-HD affect their behavior? their motor skills?

   d. What do the findings of these studies suggest is the effect of dopamine release in the nucleus accumbens on behavior reinforced by appetitive stimuli?

17. Describe evidence that suggests that the basal ganglia and the prefrontal cortex may be involved in the reinforcing effects of dopamine on behavior. (Scheel-Krüger and Willner, 1991; Stein and Belluzzi, 1989)

Lesson II Self Test

1. When an animal is trained to make a classically conditioned emotional response by pairing a tone and a foot shock, the tone is the

   a. US.
   b. CS.
   c. US.
   d. UR.

2. The synaptic changes that produce a classically conditioned emotional response occurs in the

   a. substantia nigra and the ventral tegmental area.
   b. auditory cortex and the nucleus accumbens.
   c. MGm and the basolateral amygdala.
   d. medial forebrain bundle.

3. A classically conditioned response will disappear if the

   a. US is not associated with a biological need.
   b. CS is repeatedly presented by itself.
   c. CR was originally a behavior the animal had never made before.
   d. CR does not have favorable outcomes.

4. The principal nuclei of the basal ganglia are the

   a. caudate nucleus, the putamen, and the globus pallidus.
   b. amygdala, the substantia nigra, and the putamen.
   c. neostriatum and the substantia nigra.
   d. caudate nucleus, globus pallidus, and subthalamic nucleus.

5. People with Parkinson's disease who participated in an experiment to predict the weather from a set of cards

   a. performed as well as normal subjects.
   b. learned the task, but never improved their performance.
   c. learned the task more slowly than normal subjects.
   d. never learned the task.

6. Monkeys with lesions of the supplementary motor cortex never learned to extend their arm through an opening in the cage because they

   a. had lesion-induced difficulties with coordination.
   b. were no longer able to learn a response through instrumental conditioning.

   c. could not learn to make a self-initiated response.
   d. had lesion-induced deficits in visual perception.

7. If you wished to have the best chance of an animal pressing a lever to receive reinforcing brain stimulation, where would you place an electrode?

   a. medial forebrain bundle
   b. MGm
   c. nucleus accumbens
   d. premotor cortex

8. When rats trained to go through a runway to receive reinforcing electrical brain stimulation were given a drug that blocks dopamine receptors, the drug _____ the reinforcing effects of brain stimulation.

   a. increased
   b. replaced
   c. reduced
   d. abolished

9. The effects of reinforcing brain stimulation are _____ those of natural reinforcers.

   a. weaker than
   b. greater than
   c. similar to
   d. not as long-lasting as

10. An appetitive stimulus

    a. reinforces behavior only under certain conditions.
    b. facilitates the synthesis of acetylcholine.
    c. inhibits the release of dopamine.
    d. activates the reinforcement system only when the animal is not engaging in an appetitive behavior.

11. Infusion of dopamine or cocaine through a micropipette _____ the rate of firing of CA1 pyramidal neurons if the infusions occurred _____ spontaneous bursts of action potentials.

    a. increased; during
    b. increased; after
    c. decreased; during
    d. decreased; after

12. Injections of a dopamine blocker into the nucleus accumbens appears

a. to make animals less motivated to perform an instrumentally conditioned response.
b. to alter animals' ability to respond to natural reinforcers, such as food.
c. to make animals less sensitive to biological drives.
d. to prevent animals from recognizing familiar stimuli.

Answers for Self Tests

Lesson I

1. a   Obj. 14-1
2. b   Obj. 14-1
3. c   Obj. 14-1
4. b   Obj. 14-2
5. b   Obj. 14-2
6. a   Obj. 14-2
7. d   Obj. 14-3
8. c   Obj. 14-3
9. c   Obj. 14-3
10. b   Obj. 14-4
11. d   Obj. 14-4
12. a   Obj. 14-5

Lesson II

1. b   Obj. 14-6
2. c   Obj. 14-6
3. b   Obj. 14-6
4. a   Obj. 14-7
5. d   Obj. 14-7
6. c   Obj. 14-7
7. a   Obj. 14-8
8. c   Obj. 14-8
9. c   Obj. 14-8
10. a   Obj. 14-9
11. b   Obj. 14-9
12. a   Obj. 14-9

CHAPTER 15
Relational Learning and Amnesia

Lesson I: Human Anterograde Amnesia

Read the interim summary on pages 481-482 of your text to re-acquaint yourself with the material in this section.

Learning Objective 15-1   Describe the nature of human anterograde amnesia and the type of brain damage that causes it.

Read pages 467-472 and answer the following questions.

1. Explain the difference between anterograde amnesia and retrograde amnesia in your own words or draw a time line to illustrate the difference. (See Figure 15.1 in your text.)

2. If you are asked to describe Korsakoff's syndrome, how will you respond to the following questions?

    a. What is the most important symptom?

    b. Is speech affected?

    c. What is the usual cause of Korsakoff's syndrome and how does it lead to a vitamin deficiency? (Adams, 1969; Haas, 1988)

    d. When patients with Korsakoff's syndrome are asked about recent events, what tactic do they take? What is the formal name for this behavior?

3. a. Why did patient H.M. undergo bilateral removal of the medial temporal lobe? (Corkin et al., 1997)

    b. Although the operation was successful in treating his condition, what unexpected side effect became apparent?

    c. Why did this side effect go undetected in other patients who had previously undergone this procedure?

d. When this deficit occurs, what brain structure has been removed during surgery?

e. How has the procedure been modified to lessen the side effects and what test is administered prior to surgery as a further safeguard? (Wada and Rasmussen, 1960)

4. Briefly describe the case of patient H.M. following surgery.

a. Why has H.M. has been studied so thoroughly?

b. Place an *N* or an *I* in each blank to indicate whether H.M.'s ability in the following areas remains *normal* or has been *impaired* by his surgery.

_____ intellectual ability   _____ memory of events a few years before surgery

_____ memory for older events   _____ immediate verbal memory for numbers

_____ memory for events after surgery   _____ immediate verbal memory for words

_____ personality   _____ mental arithmetic computation

c. What has H.M. said that indicates that he is aware of his condition?

d. Under what conditions, and for how long, can H.M. remember small amounts of verbal information?

e. Why does H.M. work well at repetitive tasks?

5. After studying H.M., what conclusions did Milner and her colleagues make about the role of the hippocampus in memory formation.

1.

2.

3.

6. a. What is the capacity and duration of short-term memory? long-term memory?

b. What is the role in memory formation of rehearsal? consolidation? (See Figure 15.2 in your text.)

c. For patients with anterograde amnesia such as H.M., what does not appear to occur?

7. H.M. and other people with anterograde amnesia are not completely unable to learn. What categories of learning have they demonstrated under careful testing conditions?

1.   2.   3.

8. a. Describe how Milner (1970) demonstrated that H.M. still has the ability to form perceptual memories. (See Figure 15.3 in your text.)

   b. Why is the broken drawings task called a priming task?

   c. Compare H.M.'s performance and that of other people with anterograde amnesia with the performance of normal subjects on a priming task. (Cave and Squire, 1992; Hamann and Squire, 1997)

9. How did researchers demonstrate that patients with anterograde amnesia can learn to recognize melodies? faces? (Johnson et al., 1985)

10. Describe some of the stimulus-response tasks associated with sensory-response learning that amnesic subjects including H.M. have been taught. (Woodruff-Pak, 1993; Sidman et al., 1968)

11. a. Describe the mirror-drawing task that Milner (1965) used to demonstrate that H.M. is still capable of motor learning. (See Figure 15.4 in your text.)

    b. How successful at mirror drawing is H.M?

12. a. Describe the button-pressing task, shown in Figure 15.5 in your text, that Reber and Squire (1998) used to demonstrate motor learning in people with anterograde amnesia.

    b. Compare the performance of amnesic subject with that of normal subjects.

Learning Objective 15-2 Discuss the distinction between declarative memories and nondeclarative memories and their relation to anterograde amnesia.

Read pages 472-475 and answer the following questions.

1. When H.M. and other amnesic subjects are asked if they remember anything about experiments they have participated in, how do they respond?

2. a. Subjects in a study of the development of episodic and emotional memories each had a particular kind of brain damage. Note it in the table below. (Bechara et al., 1995)

Subject	Region of Brain Damage	Conditioned Emotional Response	Recall of Task
S.M.			
W.C.			
R.H			

b. Describe the task and note the conditioned emotional response of each subject when the blue light went on.

c. Note the subjects' response when they were asked about the experimental procedure.

d. Explain why the results are consistent with the kind of brain damage each subject suffered.

3. Researchers who study anterograde amnesia distinguish between two kinds of memories. Identify and define each. (Eichenbaum et al., 1992; Squire, 1992; Squire et al., 1989)

1.

2.

4. Classify these kinds of memories as declarative (D) or nondeclarative (ND)

_____ catching a ball   _____ programming a VCR

_____ swinging a golf club   _____ reminiscing at a high school reunion

_____ listing all the places you have lived   _____ getting up on water skis

5. a. Why did Graf et al. (1984) ask amnesic and nonamnesic subjects to rate how much they liked particular six-letter words?

b. Describe the explicit (declarative) memory and the implicit (nondeclarative) memory tests that followed and how well both groups of subjects performed. (Study Figure 15.6 in your text.)

6. a. What did Squire and his colleagues ask subjects to study? (Squire et al., 1992)

b. How did the researchers measure regional cerebral blood flow during testing?

c. Carefully describe the differing instructions to the subjects and the type of task each set of instructions represented.

d. Describe regional blood flow, especially in the hippocampus, during the declarative memory task and the priming task. A PET scan of regional blood flow during testing conditions is shown in Figure 15.7 in your text.

e. What do the results suggest about the role of the hippocampus?

7. To review these memory tasks study Table 15.1 in your text.

8. Anterograde amnesia appears to disrupt the ability to establish new _____ memories, but the ability to establish new _____ memories remains unchanged.

9. How did researchers demonstrate that one of the components of the anterograde amnesia of H.M. is a verbal memory deficit? (Gabrieli et al., 1988)

10. a. What do episodic memories consist of?

    b. When we want to retell them, what do we remember?

    c. What role may the hippocampal formation play in helping us to retell our experiences?

11. Why is it useful to consider the consequences of anterograde amnesia as a failure of relational learning?

Learning Objective 15-3   Review the connections of the hippocampal formation with the rest of the brain and describe evidence that damage to the hippocampal formation and related structures causes anterograde amnesia.

Read pages 475-481 and answer the following questions.

1. Complete these sentences.
    a. The hippocampal formation consists of
    b. The most important input to the hippocampal formation is
    c. The outputs of the hippocampal formation are primarily from
    d. Most of the outputs of the hippocampal formation are relayed back through

2. Summarize the cortical connections of the entorhinal cortex. (Study Figure 15.8 in your text.)

3. Immediately review what you have just learned by completing Figure 1.

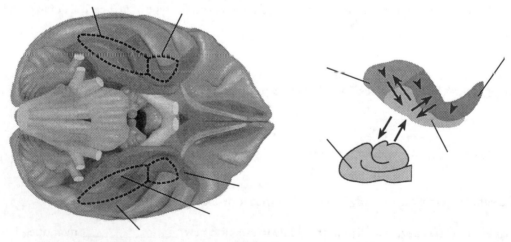

Figure 1

4. Briefly explain the role that the hippocampal formation is thought to play in forming declarative memories.

5. a. What kind of information activates the right side of the hippocampal formation? the left side?

    b. Researchers used functional MRI to record brain activity while subjects studied pictures for the first time. Which pictures were the subjects most likely to remember? (Brewer et al., 1998)

    c. And which words from a previously studied list were subjects most likely to remember? (See Figure 15.9 in your text. Alkire et al., 1998)

6. Name the region through which the hippocampal formation receives

    a. input from subcortical regions. What may be their function?

    b. dopaminergic input.

    c. noradrenergic input.

    d. serotonergic input.

    e. acetylcholinergic input.

7. When these neurotransmitters are released, how do they affect the function of the hippocampal formation?

8. What kind of information may the mammillary bodies receive from the hippocampal formation and where is this information sent on to?

9. Review these connections by studying Figure 15.10 in your text.

10. a. A temporary interruption in blood flow caused by cardiac arrest left patient R.B. with permanent anterograde amnesia. Following his death, a histological examination of his brain indicated which region of the brain was damaged? (Zola-Morgan et al., 1986)

    b. Damage to field CA1 from anoxia is shown in Figure 15.11 in your text. (Rempel-Clower et al., 1996)

    c. In addition to humans, what other species suffer anterograde amnesia when field CA1 is damaged? (Auer et al., 1989; Zola-Morgan et al., 1992)

11. a. What kind of receptors are found in abundance in field CA1?

    b. What kinds of disturbances stimulate glutamatergic terminal buttons to release high levels of glutamate?

    c. Carefully describe how a high level of glutamate affects NMDA receptors and thus explains why field CA1 is so sensitive to a lack of oxygen.

    d. How can the damaging effects of a lack of oxygen be reduced? (Rothman and Olney, 1987)

12. What other structures, when damaged, contribute to amnesia? (Zola-Morgan et al., 1989b, 1993)

13. Scientists are trying to determine whether the limbic cortex of the medial temporal lobe has any functions relating to memory that are independent of the hippocampus. (See Figure 15.12 in your text.) What do results from animal studies suggest? human studies?

14. a. Let's look more closely at evidence from three human patients who received brain damage at an early age. (Vargha-Khadem et al., 1997) In each patient, which area was damaged? undamaged?

    b. Provide some examples of the spatial, temporal, and episodic memory deficits these patients suffered.

    c. However, memory for what kind of information remained good?

    d. What does Vargha-Khadem suggest is the reason why their episodic memory is impaired and their semantic memory unimpaired?

    e. Why should this suggestion be viewed cautiously? (Zola et al., 2000)

15. a. What brain structure is almost always severely degenerated in patients with Korsakoff's syndrome? (See Figure 15.13 in your text. Kopelman, 1995)

    b. What other brain structures, that when damaged, cause amnesia? Cite research with patients suffering from brain damage resulting from conditions other than Korsakoff's syndrome. (Calabrese et al., 1995; D'Esposito et al., 1995; McMackin et al., 1995; Malamut et al., 1992)

    c. According to most researchers, what may be the physical change that results in amnesia? What is an alternate explanation?

16. a. Summarize the results of a series of PET scans of a patient with Korsakoff's syndrome that suggest the physiological cause of confabulation. (Benson et al., 1996)

    b. What kind of brain damage did a patient with amnesia who suddenly began confabulating suffer? (O'Connor et al., 1996)

17. a. Describe the recognition task Schacter et al. (1996) and colleagues taught a man with right frontal lobe damage.

    b. When did the man make the most "false alarms?"

c. What do these results suggest about the role of the frontal lobes?

18. When information is uncertain, what may be the function of the frontal lobes? (Johnson and Raye, 1998)

19. When anterograde amnesia occurs without retrograde amnesia, which brain structures have been damaged? (Rempel-Clower et al., 1996; Calabrese et al., 1995; Kapur et al., 1996)

Lesson I Self Test

1. Anterograde amnesia can best be described as

   a. a failure of short-term memory.
   b. a failure to establish new nondeclarative memories.
   c. the loss of relational learning.
   d. a diminished sense of time.

2. Korsakoff's syndrome sometime results from _____that accompanies chronic alcoholism.

   a. a thiamine deficiency
   b. glucose intolerance
   c. a folic acid deficiency
   d. the pyruvate deficiency

3. Patient H.M. is

   a. aware of his disorder.
   b. bored by repetitive tasks.
   c. unable to learn any new information.
   d. frustrated by his difficulty in following a conversation.

4. When patients with anterograde amnesia are retested on an incomplete drawing task they

   a. showed a priming effect but did not remember the context.
   b. showed a priming effect for geometric patterns but not for real objects.
   c. remembered the context but did not recognize the particular stimuli they had seen.
   d. showed no signs of learning.

5. Patients who showed a conditioned emotional response to a blue light that preceded a loud boat horn had bilateral damage to the

   a. hippocampus.
   b. amygdala.
   c. mammillary bodies.
   d. thalamus.

6. Nondeclarative memories

   a. are a form of perceptual memory.
   b. are usually expressed in writing.
   c. fade more quickly than declarative memories.
   d. do not require deliberate efforts to learn information.

7. What we remember about an episode that permits us to retrieve it later

   a. are a few striking details.
   b. are the events and the context in which they occur.
   c. is the information that is inconsistent with what we already know.
   d. is the information about it that we rehearse.

8. You looked up the telephone number, but went to let the dog in before making the call and found you had forgotten the number. This occurred because

   a. of the phenomenon of retrograde amnesia.
   b. long-term memories are difficult to retrieve.
   c. the phone number exceeded the capacity of short-term memory.
   d. insufficient rehearsal did not enable short-term memory to be converted into long-term memory.

9. The most important input to the hippocampal formation is the

   a. anterior thalamus.
   b. locus coeruleus
   c. entorhinal cortex.
   d. subiculum.

10. Neurons in field CA1 of the hippocampus are easily damaged when metabolic disturbances set off a series of events that include the

   a. rapid proliferation of NMDA receptors.

b. desynchronized firing of presynaptic axons.

c. entry of calcium into the neurons resulting in excessively high levels of intracellular calcium.

d. release of abnormally high levels of serotonin.

11. Confabulation, a symptom of Korsakoff's syndrome, may be caused by damage to the

   a. prefrontal cortex.
   b. mammillary bodies.
   c. perirhinal cortex

d. amygdala.

12. During testing, a patient made many more "false alarms" when the

   a. researcher distracted him.
   b. incorrect stimulus resembled one he had previously seen or heard.
   c. length of time between training and testing increased.
   d. number of choices increased.

Lesson II: Relational Learning in Laboratory Animals

Read the interim summary on page 493 to re-acquaint yourself with the material in this section.

Learning Objective 15-4   Describe the role of the hippocampus in relational learning including spatial learning.

Read pages 482-484 and answer the following questions.

1.   a. Describe the radial maze shown in Figure 15.14 in your text.

     b. Now describe the task used by Olton and Samuelson (1976) and the performance of the rats.

     c. In later research, how did normal rats perform if they were prevented from visiting the arms in a particular order? (Olton et al., 1977)

     d. What abilities, tested by the radial maze task, must rats have in order to survive?

     e. What kind of lesions severely disrupt the ability to avoid revisiting a place where food was just found. (reviewed by Olton, 1983)

     f. Describe how Olton and Papas (1979) used a different radial maze, shown in Figure 15.15 in your text, to test the implicit and explicit learning skills of subject rats.

     g. What kind of lesions disrupted performance and how was it disrupted?

     h. Explain why the rats' performance in both mazes can also be explained in terms of relational memory.

2. Describe research by Morris et al., (1982) on the effect of hippocampal lesions on spatial abilities.

    a. Describe the "milk maze" the researchers used.

    b. How were rat subjects trained in the maze?

    c. What was the only kind of information rats could use to find the submerged platform?

    d. How successfully did normal rats, control rats with neocortical control lesions, and rats with hippocampal lesions maneuver through the maze? (See Figure 15.16 in your text.)

    e. What do the results suggest about the importance of the hippocampal formation in relational learning?

3.   a. How can the milk maze be modified to test stimulus-response learning, which is nonrelational?

    b. How easily do rats with hippocampal lesions now find the platform?

4. Summarize research on other species that confirms the importance of the hippocampus in spatial learning.

    a. Specifically, how do hippocampal lesions affect the navigation skills of homing pigeons? (Gagliardo et al., 1999)

    b. Compare the size of the hippocampus of

        1. homing pigeons with other breeds of pigeons lacking good navigational abilities. (Rehkämper et al., 1988)

        2. birds and rodents that store food with those who do not. (Sherry et al., 1992)

        3. black-capped chickadees throughout the year. (Smulders et al., 1995)

Learning Objective 15-5   Discuss the function of place cells in the hippocampal formation and the role of the limbic cortex of the medial temporal lobe.

Read pages 484-489 and answer the following questions.

1.   a. In general, how did single pyramidal cells in the hippocampus respond as rats moved around their environment? (Be sure to mention spatial receptive fields in your answer. O'Keefe and Dostrovsky, 1971)

    b. What were these neurons named?

2. a. Describe how hippocampal place cells respond to environmental cues as a rat navigates the maze shown in Figure 15.17 in your text.

    b. If the maze is rotated, how do the place cells respond?

    c. In a symmetrical chamber, what kind of cues do rats use to orient themselves?

    d. How do place cells respond when these cues are moved as a group? interchanged?

3. Describe research by Hill and Best (1981) on how rats determine location using internally generated stimuli.

    a. How were subject rats prevented from using external cues to determine location?

    b. How did the spatial receptive fields of rats respond when they were

        1. placed in a maze that was rotated?

        2. first spun around and then placed in the maze?

4. Outline a different procedure leading to the same results used by McNaughton et al., (1989).

5. a. How did researchers guide normal rats and rats with fornix lesions to food? (See Figure 15.18 in your text. Whishaw and Gorny, 1999)

    b. Once they had obtained the food, what did the rats do?

    c. How did normal rats and rats with fornix lesions return to their home cages in the dark?

    d. What do the results suggest about the importance of the hippocampus in spatial guidance provided by one's own movements?

6. a. Describe the apparatus, shown in Figure 15.19 in your text, and how Skaggs and McNaughton (1998) used it to study the firing of hippocampal place cells in rats.

    b. When a rat was placed in its customary chamber, how did some of its hippocampal place cells respond? how did others respond? What did these patterns seem to indicate?

    c. On the last day of the experiment what change occurred to alter the firing patterns of the place cells of a least half of the rats?

    d. What evidence indicates that a rat "realized" it had made a mistake?

e. What, then, may the firing patterns of hippocampal place cells indicate?

7. After human subjects were familiar with a "virtual reality" computer game, researchers measured regional brain activity using a PET scanner. Study the results shown in Figure 15.20 in your text to determine when the right hippocampal formation became active. (Maguire et al., 1998)

8. a. The hippocampus appears to receive its spatial information through the _____

   _____.

   b. What property do neurons in entorhinal cortex, hippocampal pyramidal cells, and single granule cells in the dentate gyrus all share to varying degrees? (Quirk et al., 1992; Rose, 1993)

9. a. Why is it incorrect to conclude that each neuron in a spatial receptive field encodes a particular location?

   b. According to most researchers, how do rats learn their way through a new environment?

   c. Cite research on the stability of these "maps." (Thompson and Best, 1990)

10. a. Although some neurons in the hippocampus of monkeys respond to location, most of them respond to a different cue. Name it.

    b. What name do Rolls and his colleagues use to refer to these neurons and why do they think they are present? (Rolls,, 1996; Georges-François et al., 1999)

11. a. Define *paired-associate learning* in your own words.

    b. Which brain region is involved? is not involved?

12. a. Before continuing be sure that you know the locations of inferior temporal cortex, limbic cortex of the medial temporal lobe, and perirhinal cortex, which are shown in Figures 14.23 and 15.8 in your text.

    b. Now briefly describe the task and stimuli, shown in Figure 15.21 in your text, that Sakai and Miyashita (1991) used to assess paired-associate learning in monkeys.

    c. How did neurons in inferior temporal cortex respond to the various stimuli? (See Figure 15.22 in your text.)

    d. What else did the researchers observe about the response patterns?

    e. When stimuli are paired, how may neural circuits be altered?

f. What role in the establishment of paired-associate learning does inferior temporal cortex play? perirhinal cortex?

13. a. Perirhinal cortex receives information from which region? sends information to which region?

b. What kind of lesions

1. disrupted paired-associate learning?

2. had no effect?

3. abolished the "pairing" of neurons in inferior temporal cortex? (Murray et al., 1993)

Learning Objective 15-6 Describe how changes in synaptic strength and monoaminergic and acetylcholinergic input may affect hippocampal functioning.

Read pages 489-491 and answer the following questions.

1. a. What physical changes were observed in the hippocampal formation of rats that

1. had been raised in a complex environment? (Green and Greenough, 1986)

2. learned a radial-arm maze? (Mitsuno et al., 1994)

b. Changes in the hippocampal formation resemble what phenomenon that you have already studied?

2. Summarize the results of research using a method that interferes with long-term potentiation and affects learning. How do targeted mutations of the NMDA receptor gene affecting only CA1 pyramidal cells affect

a. receptor development? (See Figure 15.23 in your text. McHugh et al., 1996, Tsien et al., 1996)

b. the establishment of long-term potentiation?

c. the spatial receptive fields of CA1 pyramidal cells?

d. learning the Morris milk maze?

3. Researchers used genetic manipulation to increase the production of a particular subunit of the NMDA receptor in mice. (Tang et al., 1999)

a. How were the EPSPs produced by the altered NMDA receptor different from those of unaltered receptors?

b. Describe how the changed EPSPs affected long-term potentiation observed in hippocampal slices from subject mice.

c. Compare the speed with which subject mice and normal mice learned the Morris milk maze, and then explain what these differing rates indicate about the importance of the hippocampus in relational learning.

4. Why is it inadvisable to attempt to use this technique to produce smarter animals or people?

5. How do targeted mutations of genes responsible for the production of PKC and CaMKII affect long-term potentiation? the ability to learn the Morris milk maze? (Grant et al., 1992; Silva et al., 1992b)

6. How do acetylcholinergic, noradrenergic, dopaminergic, and serotonergic neurons indirectly affect long-term potentiation in the hippocampal formation?

7. Describe the effects of these neurotransmitters on the establishment of long-term potentiation.

   a. serotonin (Sandler and Ross, 1999)

   b. norepinephrine (For example, Dahl and Sarvey, 1989)

   c. dopamine (Stein and Belluzzi, 1989; Gasbarri et al., 1996)

8. Define hippocampal *theta rhythms* in your own words.

9. Let's look more closely at theta rhythms and the establishment of long-term potentiation in the hippocampal formation. What happens to synaptic strengthening if

   a. bursts of electrical stimulation coincide with the peaks of theta activity? (Pavlides et al., 1988)

   b. depolarizing stimulation coincides with the peaks of theta activity? with the troughs? (See Figure 15.24 in your text. Huerta and Lisman, 1996)

   c. animals receive injections of scopolamine suppressing theta rhythms? (Givens and Olton, 1990)

   d. animals receive low doses of alcohol that disrupt theta rhythms? (Givens, 1995)

10. a. What procedure appears to reduce some of the effects of damage to cholinergic inputs to the hippocampal formation?

    b. How do these transplants affect

       1. theta activity and spatial receptive fields? (Buzsáki et al., 1987; Shapiro et al., 1989)

       2. performance in the Morris milk maze? (Nilsson et al., 1987; Ridley et al., 1991)

11. Give several examples of theta behaviors and non-theta behaviors.

12. a. When a rat is exploring the environment, its rate of sniffing is synchronized with waves of _____
_____ _____. (Wiener et al., 1989)

b. What the rat has finished exploring and theta rhythms have ceased, what may then happen to environmental information that the rat gathered? (Buzsáki, 1989, 1996)

Learning Objective 15-7   Outline a possible explanation of the role of the hippocampal formation in learning and memory.

Read pages 491-493 and answer the following questions.

1. What have many investigators concluded about the deficit in spatial learning caused by hippocampal lesions? (For example, Wiener et al., 1989; Sutherland and Rudy, 1989; Rudy and Sutherland, 1995)

2. What may have been the original function of the hippocampus?

3. a. Draw on your own experiences to explain how moving from place to place depends on recognizing the context of the stimuli you encounter and their relationship to each other.

b. While your neighbors are away, you've been watering their houseplants every other day. Before you left for work this morning, you did so. Explain the contextual stimulus that accounts for the fact that you do not water the plants the next morning.

4. Review the inputs to the hippocampal formation that may explain how events are placed in their proper context.

5. Now refer to the learning experiences of a normal person and patients like H.M. to explain how anterograde amnesia might be an inability to distinguish and relate different contextual stimuli to each other.

6. Outline the hypothetical model concerning the role of the hippocampal formation in learning and memory proposed by Rolls (1989; 1996)

   a. Where in the brain does he believe that perceptual learning takes place?

   b. To which region does the neocortex send information about events and episodes?

   c. And where does this region then send the information, which has now been analyzed further?

   d. Trace the circuit that ends with the information being returned to the neocortex.

   e. What kind of axons are found in field CA3?

f. Explain how the network of neurons in field CA3 might function as an autoassociator.

7. What capability of the hippocampal formation may permit us to recall our actions with accuracy?

Lesson II Self Test

1. Rats with hippocampal lesions could not efficiently visit the arms of a radial maze because they could not

   a. distinguish between the many arms of the maze.
   b. learn which arms never contained food.
   c. establish an initial bearing.
   d. remember where they had just been.

2. Rats are trained in a milk maze

   a. to reduce the effects of tactile stimulation.
   b. to test their spatial perception and memory.
   c. to avoid using food as a reinforcing stimulus.
   d. to assess their stimulus-response learning.

3. How do rats in a symmetrical chamber react when researchers move environmental stimuli as a group?

   a. Rats move toward the center of the chamber.
   b. Rats tend to remain in one location.
   c. Rats run constantly around the perimeter of the chamber.
   d. Rats reorient their responses accordingly.

4. On the last day of testing, rats were switched from one nearly identical chamber to another. While inside the chamber, the firing of hippocampal place cells indicated that _____, but once outside the chamber _____.

   a. some rats "thought" they were in the usual chamber; the response pattern changed appropriately as if to correct a mistake
   b. rats "thought" they were in the usual chamber; the response pattern became erratic and only stabilized when rats returned to the chamber
   c. some rats "recognized" they were in a different chamber; the response pattern did not change and rats could not find their former chamber
   d. rats "recognized" they were in a different chamber; the response pattern of only about half the rats made the appropriate change

5. The hippocampus appears to receive its spatial information through the

   a. fornix.
   b. entorhinal cortex.
   c. amygdala.
   d. medial septum.

6. The exchange of information between the _____ and the _____ is essential for paired-associate learning.

   a. hippocampus; perirhinal cortex
   b. inferior temporal cortex; medial temporal cortex
   c. perirhinal cortex; inferior temporal cortex
   d. hippocampus; parahippocampal cortex

7. A targeted mutation that increased the production of NMDA receptors with a particular subunit _____ leading to enhanced long-term potentiation.

   a. caused production of slightly longer EPSPs,
   b. caused development of an increased number of calcium channels,
   c. that is less likely to cause damage from seizures or anoxia,
   d. that causes production of increased levels of CaM-KII,

8. What is the source of theta rhythms?

   a. glutamatergic axons from the dentate gyrus
   b. serotonergic axons from the fornix
   c. dopaminergic axons from the substantia nigra
   d. acetylcholinergic axons from the medial septum

9. Behaviors closely associated with the presence of hippocampal theta activity include

   a. wakefulness and sleep
   b. walking and running
   c. drinking
   d. reproductive behaviors

10. Depolarizing stimulation that coincided with the peaks of theta waves resulted in _____.

   a. depression
   b. disorientation of hippocampal place cells
   c. long-term potentiation
   d. disruption of working memory

11. The original function of the hippocampus may have been to

    a. regulate an animal's circadian rhythms.
    b. help an animal recognize new stimuli.
    c. regulate an animal's metabolism in response to environmental changes.
    d. help an animal navigate in its environment.

12. Rolls suggests that neurons in field CA3 function as an autoassociator—that is, they

    a. can produce the appropriate output from fragments of the original pattern.
    b. link together the structures that make up the hippocampal formation.
    c. can, along with the recurrent collaterals, provide an alternate system of connections that minimize the effects of brain damage.
    d. connect the hippocampal formation with the association cortex.

Answers for Self Tests

Lesson I

1.	c	Obj. 15-1
2.	a	Obj. 15-1
3.	a	Obj. 15-1
4.	a	Obj. 15-1
5.	a	Obj. 15-2
6.	d	Obj. 15-2
7.	b	Obj. 15-2
8.	d	Obj. 15-2
9.	c	Obj. 15-3
10.	c	Obj. 15-3
11.	a	Obj. 15-3
12.	b	Obj. 15-3

Lesson II

1.	d	Obj. 15-4
2.	b	Obj. 15-4
3.	d	Obj. 15-5
4.	a	Obj. 15-5
5.	b	Obj. 15-5
6.	c	Obj. 15-5
7.	a	Obj. 15-6
8.	d	Obj. 15-6
9.	b	Obj. 15-6
10.	c	Obj. 15-6
11.	d	Obj. 15-7
12.	a	Obj. 15-7

CHAPTER 16
Human Communication

Lesson I: Brain Mechanisms of Speech and Comprehension

Read the interim summary on pages 513-514 of your text to re-acquaint yourself with the material in this section.

> *Learning Objective 16-1* Describe the use of subjects with brain damage in the study of language and explain the concept of lateralization.

Read pages 496-497 and answer the following questions.

1. a. List some of the medical conditions that researchers often study to learn more about the effects that physical damage to the brain has on speech.

   b. Underline the most frequently studied of these conditions.

2. Why should conclusions about verbal communication based on studies of patients who have received seizure surgery be viewed cautiously?

3. Identify a third source of information about verbal communication.

4. Name and describe the most important category of speech disorders.

5. Explain this sentence: "Verbal behavior is a lateralized function."

6. a. Describe the Wada test and explain how it is used to determine hemispheric dominance for speech.

   b. Which hemisphere most often controls speech?

7. a. Explain why this hemisphere is particularly suited for speech.

b. Explain how the right hemisphere contributes to speech. (Gardner et al., 1983)

Learning Objective 16-2 Describe Broca's aphasia and the three major speech deficits that result from damage to Broca's area: agrammatism, anomia, and articulation difficulties.

Read pages 498-502 and answer the following questions.

1. Describe how Broca's aphasia affects

   a. speech production.

   b. production of meaningful speech.

   c. grammar, especially the use of function words and content words. (See Figure 16.1 in your text.)

   d. comprehension.

2. a. Broca's aphasia, named for Paul Broca, appears to result from damage to what region of the brain? (See Figure 16.2 in your text.)

   b. Describe more precisely the areas in the vicinity of Broca's area that, when damaged, do and do not produce Broca's aphasia. (H. Damasio, 1989; Naeser et al., 1989)

   c. What other region if damaged produces a Broca-like aphasia? (Study Figure 16.3 in your text. Damasio et al., 1984; Leblanc et al., 1992)

3. What did Wernicke (1874) suggest is the speech function of Broca's area?

4. a. List and briefly describe three deficits that are characteristic of Broca's aphasia, suggesting that the disorder is not a simple one.

   1.

   2.

   3

   b. Which of these deficits is the most elementary? the most complex?

c. Which deficit is characteristic of all forms of aphasia?

5. a. Describe the task and the cards that Schwartz and her colleagues used to test the speech comprehension skills of people with Broca's aphasia. (See Figure 16.4 in your text. Schwartz et al., 1980)

b. How well did their subjects do?

c. What do these results suggest about the ability of Broca's aphasics to use grammatical information?

6. a. What critical location for control of speech articulation did Dronkers (1996) find? (See Figure 16.5 in your text.)

b. How did she locate it? Be sure to mention apraxia of speech in your answer. (See Figure 16.6 in your text.)

7. a. What is another region of the brain that seems to be involved in speech production?

b. How is speech production affected if this region is stimulated? (Jürgens, 1998) damaged? (Esposito et al., 1999)

8. a. The agrammatism and anomia characteristic of Broca's aphasia are normally caused by damage to what area of the brain?

b. Describe how Stromswold et al. (1996) confirmed this location.

9. a. How well did Broca's aphasics respond to a sequence of verbal commands? (Boller and Dennis, 1979)

b. What do these results suggest about the functions of the left frontal lobe?

10. How does damage to the cerebellum affect speech production? (Adams and Victor, 1991) grammar? (Silveri et al., 1994).

Learning Objective 16-3 Describe the symptoms of Wernicke's aphasia, pure word deafness, and transcortical sensory aphasia and explain how they are related.

Read pages 502-506 and answer the following questions.

1. Return to Figure 16.2 and describe the location of Wernicke's area. What is its function?

2. List the two primary characteristics of Wernicke's aphasia.

    1.   2.

3. a. Compare the fluency, articulation, inflection, and grammar of the speech of patients with Broca's aphasia and Wernicke's aphasia.

    b. How is the speech comprehension of people with Wernicke's aphasia tested? Why?

4. Describe the reaction of patients with Wernicke's aphasia to their own speech difficulties.

5. a. What did Wernicke himself suggest is the function of the region that bears his name?

    b. What anatomical evidence appears to confirm the role of Wernicke's area in learning? (Jacobs et al., 1993)

6. List three characteristic deficits resulting from damage to Wernicke's area.
    1.   3.

    2.

7. Explain the distinction between recognizing and comprehending a word.

8. a. Describe how these abilities are affected in cases of pure word deafness.
    1. comprehension of speech

    2. comprehension of nonspeech sounds

    3. comprehension of emotion expressed through intonation

    4. speech production

    5. reading and writing

    b. How, therefore, do people with this disorder communicate with other people?

    c. Where does perception of speech sounds occur? (Binder et al., 1994; Belin et al., 2000)

9. Discuss the different functions of the left and right hemispheres in the analysis of speech sounds, noting which aspect of speech sounds is most critical for understanding.

10. Outline the hypothesis of Phillips and Farmer (1990) concerning the recognition of acoustical events of short duration.

11. Study Figure 16.7 in your text and discuss the two types of brain damage that cause pure word deafness. (Digiovanni et al., 1992; Takahashi et al.,1992)

12. a. Now study Figure 16.8 in your text and describe the location and the presumed function of the posterior language area. Be sure to note its proximity to Wernicke's area.

    b. Damage to the posterior language area results in the disorder _____ _____

       _____.

13. a. Describe how these abilities are affected in cases of transcortical sensory aphasia.

       1. speech comprehension

       2. speech recognition and repetition

       3. production of meaningful speech

    b. How do the deficits of people with transcortical sensory aphasia compare with those of people with Wernicke's aphasia?

14. Because patients can repeat what they hear, what kind of connection must exist within the brain? (Return to Figure 16.8.)

15. a. Describe how extensive brain damage resulting from carbon monoxide affected the patient's speech recognition, comprehension and production. (Geschwind et al., 1968)

    b. What does this case confirm about the brain mechanisms of speech?

Learning Objective 16-4 Discuss the brain mechanisms that underlie our ability to understand the meaning of words and to express our own thoughts and perceptions in words.

Read pages 506-507 and answer the following questions.

1. Words have meaning for us because they evoke particular _____, which are not stored in primary

   _____ _____, but in other parts of the brain.

2. Study Figure 16.9 in your text and follow the pathway responsible for recognizing and comprehending a spoken word.

3. a. Following a stroke that damaged part of the right parietal lobe, which plays a role in spatial perception, what kind of difficulty did a patient have in describing spatial relationships?

b. She could understand some meanings of particular words, but not other meanings. Explain and give examples.

4. Name and describe the specific comprehension difficulties associated with

a. damage to the association cortex of the left parietal lobe. Be sure to use the term *autotopagnosia* in your answer.

b. damage to the left temporal lobe. (McCarthy and Warrington, 1988)

c. widespread damage to the temporal and parietal lobes. (Damasio and Tranel, 1990; Hodges et al., 1992)

5. Explain the procedure and results of research to identify category-specific sites in the brain. (Spitzer et al., 1995)

6. What hemisphere is involved in the comprehension of abstract aspects of speech? How did researchers determine this? (Brownell et al., 1983,1990; Bottini et al., 1994; Nichelli et al., 1995)

Learning Objective 16-5 Describe the symptoms of conduction aphasia and anomic aphasia, including aphasia in deaf people.

Read pages 507-513 and answer the following questions.

1. a. The _____ _____ is a direct connection between Wernicke's area and Broca's area.

   b. What kind of information does it presumably convey?

2. a. Describe the brain damage that causes conduction aphasia. (Study Figure 16.10 in your text. Damasio and Damasio, 1980)

   b. Now describe its symptoms. Refer to specific examples from patients. (Margolin and Walker, 1981)

   c. What is the difference between the words such patients can and cannot repeat?

3. Study Figure 16.11 in your text and carefully describe the direct and indirect pathways that may connect the speech mechanisms of the temporal and frontal lobes suggested by the communication deficits of patients with transcortical sensory aphasia or conduction aphasia.

4. To review what you have learned, draw in and label the following regions in Figure 1: Broca's area, Wernicke's area, posterior language area, primary auditory cortex, the arcuate fasciculus, and the location of perceptions and memories. Draw in and label arrows responsible for the repetition of a perceived word and the translation of thoughts into words. The information needed to complete the figure is found in Figures 16.8, 16.9, and 16.11 in your text.

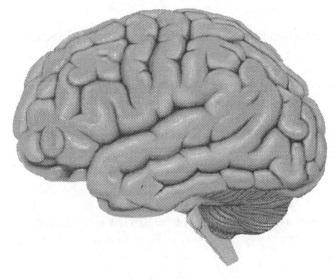

Figure 1

5. a. The symptoms of conduction aphasia suggest that the connection between Wernicke's area and Broca's area plays what role?

    b. Describe the circuit that Baddeley (1992) refers to as the phonological loop.

    c. Summarize research that supports this hypothesis. (See Figure 16.12 in your text. Paulesu et al., 1993; Fiez et al., 1996)

6. Read over the description of the picture in Figure 16.1 in your text given by the woman with anomic aphasia reported by Margolin and his colleagues. (Margolin et al., 1985)

    a. How did anomic aphasia affect her speech production and comprehension?

    b. When did she use circumlocutions?

    c. Which area of this woman's brain had been damaged? was spared?

    d. In follow-up informal testing, what word-finding difficulty became more apparent?

7. Begin a review of the range of verbal deficit patterns experienced by people with anomia.

    a. Describe the deficits experienced by people studied by

        1 Manning and Campbell (1992).

2. Semenza and Zettin (1989).

b. According to Damasio and colleagues (Damasio et al., 1991), which region has been damaged when patients have anomia for proper nouns? anomia for common nouns?

c. What do they suggest is an important distinction between the two types of words?

d. What, then, may be a function of the cortex of the temporal pole?

e. Anomia for verbs results from damage to the frontal cortex in and around Broca's area. Explain why this finding is consistent with our knowledge of the functions of the frontal lobes.

f. Study Figure 16.13 in your text and briefly describe research that confirms the importance of Broca's area and the surrounding region in the production of verbs. (Petersen et al., 1988; Wise et al., 1991; McCarthy et al, 1993; Fiez et al., 1996)

g. Which brain region(s) became active when people were asked to name pictures of animals and tools? just animals? just tools? (See Figure 16.14 in your text. Martin et al., 1996)

8. To review: Describe the probable flow of information through the brain for the

a. comprehension of speech.

b. production of spontaneous speech.

9. In what hemisphere might we expect to find damage in deaf people with aphasia? Why? Where are the lesions of aphasic deaf people? (Hickok et al., 1996)

10. Identify the hemispheres and the specific regions of the brain that are activated when lipreading. (See Figure 16.15 in your text. Campbell et al., 1996; Calvert et al., 1997)

11. Explain prosody in your own words.

12. How do we indicate some of the elements of prosody when we write?

13. Contrast the prosody of the speech of people with Wernicke's aphasia, fluent aphasia, and Broca's aphasia.

14. a. Which hemisphere plays the most important role in prosody?

    b. Name some of the other functions of this hemisphere that are probably related to prosody.

15. a. Describe the experimental tasks Weintraub et al. (1981) used to test the use and recognition of prosody by subjects with right-hemisphere damage.

    b. How well did subjects perform in these experiments?

16. To review your understanding of the deficits associated with each of the disorders covered in this lesson, fill in the blanks in the table below. Compare your answers with the information in Table 16.1 in your text.

Disorder	Area of lesion	Spontaneous speech	Comprehension	Repetition	Naming
Wernicke's aphasia					
Pure word deafness					
Broca's aphasia					
Conduction aphasia					
Anomic aphasia					
Transcortical sensory aphasia					

Lesson I Self Test

1. Most conclusions about the physiology of language have been made through work with subjects who have sustained

   a. head injuries.
   b. cerebrovascular accidents.
   c. brain tumors.
   d. infections.

2. When we say that verbal behavior is a lateralized function, we mean that

   a. both hemispheres of the brain are equally important for speech.
   b. both hemispheres of the brain have the capacity to perform all aspects of speech.
   c. one hemisphere is dominant for speech and the other hemisphere plays no role.

   d. one hemisphere is dominant for speech and the other hemisphere plays a smaller role.

3. People with Broca's aphasia

   a. speak fluently, but have anomia.
   b. speak fluently, but have poor comprehension.
   c. speak slowly, with difficulty, but grammatically.
   d. speak slowly, with difficulty, but with meaning.

4. Anomia is a difficulty in

   a. finding the correct word to describe an object, action, or situation.
   b. pronouncing abstract, but not concrete, words.

c. repeating sequences longer than three words.

d. using function and content words.

5. People with Wernicke's aphasia

a. speak fluently but without meaning and have poor comprehension.

b. speak haltingly but with meaning and have excellent comprehension.

c. can no longer speak but still comprehend the speech of others.

d. speak sporadically but to the point.

6. Research with people who have transcortical sensory aphasia suggests that

a. the ability to understand is necessary for accurate memorization.

b. recognition, repetition, and rhythm are inseparable aspects of speech production.

c. the ability to speak spontaneously is necessary in order to repeat what is heard.

d. brain mechanisms needed for recognition and comprehension of speech are different.

7. Pure word deafness is the inability

a. to comprehend the meaning of words.

b. to understand the speech of others.

c. to communicate orally with others.

d. to use grammatical constructions.

8. Damage to the posterior language area disrupts the ability to

a. recognize spoken words.

b. repeat spoken words.

c. understand words and produce meaningful speech.

d. understand particular categories of words.

9. Which is *not* true of the arcuate fasciculus?

a. It conveys meanings of words but not sounds.

b. It conveys sounds of words but not meanings.

c. It is an arch-shaped bundle that connects Wernicke's area and Broca's area.

d. Damage results in conduction aphasia.

10. Researchers suggest that people with conduction aphasia can repeat words only if they

a. are spelled regularly.

b. have meaning.

c. have no threatening emotional content.

d. are short.

11. Aphasia in deaf people

a. results in an inability to lipread, and is caused by damage to the right hemisphere, which is involved in recognizing faces.

b. is hard to determine, because sign language is not a full-fledged language.

c. is caused by right hemisphere damage, because sign language has a visual, spatial nature.

d. is caused by left hemisphere damage, as it is in hearing people.

12. Which of the following disorders is characterized by poor prosody?

a. Wernicke's aphasia

b. Broca's aphasia

c. anomic aphasia

d. conduction aphasia

Lesson II: Disorders of Reading and Writing

Read the interim summary on pages 525-526 of your text to re-acquaint yourself with the material in this section.

Learning Objective 16-6 Describe pure alexia and explain why this disorder is caused by damage to two specific parts of the brain.

Read pages 514-518 and answer the following questions.

1. a. Make a general statement about the relationship between the speaking and understanding skills and the reading and writing skills of people with aphasia.

2. To illustrate this general relationship, review the speech production, speech comprehension, and reading skills of people with the following aphasias which are summarized in tables is both your text and the study guide.

a. Wernicke's aphasia

    b. Broca's aphasia

    c. conduction aphasia

    d. transcortical sensory aphasia

3.   Briefly describe the abilities of a patient with severe fluent aphasia studied by Semenza et al. (1992) and explain what these rare exceptions suggest about neural organization.

4.   Describe how pure alexia affects

    a. reading.

    b. writing. (For an example, see Figure 16.16 in your text.)

    c. recognition of orally spelled words.

5.   a. If a patient suffered damage limited to the left primary visual cortex, how would reading ability be affected? Trace the flow of visual information paying special attention to the role of the corpus callosum.(Study Figure 16.17a in your text)

    b. If, however, a patient suffers damaged to both the left primary visual cortex and the posterior corpus callosum, how is reading ability now affected? (Study Figure 16.17b.)

    c. Finally, if a patient suffered damaged limited to the posterior corpus callosum, how is reading ability affected? (Study Figure 16.17c. Binder et al., 1992)

6.   a. Which of the four types of visual stimuli that patients saw while their regional cerebral blood flow was measured by a PET scanner activated the extrastriate cortex? which did not? (See Figure 16.18 in your text. Petersen et al., 1990)

    b. What do the results suggest about its function?

7.   Describe the disorder in deaf people that is similar to pure alexia. What brain damage causes this disorder? (Hickok et al., 1995)

8.   a. Is it plausible that natural selection has endowed the human brain with mechanisms that are devoted to reading? Explain.

b. How do researchers explain the fact that reading and recognition of real objects apparently evolved from different brain mechanisms? (Behrmann et al., 1998)

Learning Objective 16-7 Describe whole-word and phonetic reading and discuss five categories of acquired dyslexias.

Read pages 518-521 and answer the following questions.

1. a. Explain the distinction between whole-word reading and phonetic reading.

    b. Under what circumstances do we use the whole-word and phonetic methods?

    c. Look at Figure 16.19 in your text for an illustration of some elements of the reading process.

2. Contrast acquired dyslexia with developmental dyslexia.

3. Let's examine some of the reading disorders resulting from acquired dyslexia, beginning with surface dyslexia.

    a. Surface dyslexia is usually caused by damage to the _____ _____ _____ lobe.

    b. Why is this deficit called surface dyslexia?

    c. By what method do people with surface dyslexia read and understand what they have read? Be sure to mention the importance of listening to their own pronunciation. (Study Figure 16.20 in your text.)

    d. What kind of words do they read easily? with difficulty?

4. a. Phonological dyslexia is usually caused by damage to the _____ lobe. (Price, 1998; Fiez and Petersen, 1998)

    b. By what method do people with phonological dyslexia read? (Study Figure 16.21 in your text.)

    c. What kind of words do they read easily? with difficulty? (Beauvois and Dérouesné, 1979; Dérouesné and Beauvois, 1979)

5. Explain why the reading ability of people with phonological dyslexia is further evidence for a distinction between whole word reading and phonetic reading.

6. a. Continue to discuss this distinction by describing the way words expressed in Japanese kanji and kana symbols are read.

    b. What have studies of Japanese people with localized brain damage indicated about the reading process? (Iwata, 1984; Sakurai et al., 1994))

7. What reading methods appear to be lost in word-form or spelling dyslexia? (See Figure 16.23 in your text.)

8. Explain how people with word-form dyslexia read by describing their ability to recognize words if

    a. permitted to spell the word.

    b. someone else spells the word aloud.

    c. they spell the word incorrectly due to the severity of their deficit. (See Figure 16.22 in your text.)

9. Explain why direct dyslexia resembles transcortical sensory aphasia. (Schwartz et al., 1979; Lytton and Brust, 1989)

10. Describe how direct dyslexia affects the ability

    a. to read aloud and to understand what is read. Be sure to mention which reading method is lost.

    b. to communicate with others, and to understand what is said.

11. Describe how brain injury resulting from an automobile accident affected patient R.F.'s ability to

    a. read most words.

    b. name most common objects.

    c. communicate with others.

    d. choose words that matched a picture. (See Figure 16.23 in your text. Margolin et al., 1985)

12. a. What reading method appears to be lost? is still partially intact?

    b. What observation about spelling did R.F. make that confirms this assessment?

Learning Objective 16-8 Explain the relation between speaking and writing and describe the symptoms of phonological dysgraphia, orthographic dysgraphia and semantic (direct) dysgraphia.

Read pages 521-523 and answer the following questions.

1. Explain why people with speech difficulties may also have writing difficulties.

2. Describe some of the remarkably specific writing deficits related to difficulties in motor control. (Cubelli, 1991; Alexander et al., 1992; Margolin and Goodman-Schulman, 1992; Silveri, 1996)

3. Let's look at four ways of writing words. If you have not already tried the antidisestablishmentarianism experiment, try it now. Use you own experience to describe any difficulties that you had when you wrote the word

    a. without saying it softly to yourself.

    b. and softly sang a song at the same time.

4. Continue by describing three other writing methods. Be sure to note what type of sensory information is required.

    1.

    2.

    3.

5. Writing difficulties can also involve spelling difficulties. Let's examine research on phonetic and visual spelling. Describe how phonological dysgraphia affects the ability to write

    a. nonsense words by sounding them out.

    b. familiar and unfamiliar words by imagining how they look.

6. Describe how orthographic dysgraphia affects the ability to write

    a. regular words and pronounceable nonsense words.

    b. irregular words. (Beauvois and Dérouesné, 1981)

7. Phonological dysgraphia then is impaired _____ writing resulting from damage to the

    _____ _____ lobe and orthographic dysgraphia is impaired _____ writing

    resulting from damage to the _____ _____ lobe. (Benson and Geschwind, 1985)

8. How successfully did a patient who had suffered a left hemisphere stroke recognize words that were spelled aloud to him when he was permitted to make writing movements with his hands? when he was asked not to? (Cipolotti and Warrington, 1996)

9. Compare the writing deficits of Japanese patients with those of patients whose languages use the Roman alphabet. (Iwata, 1984; Yokota et al., 1990)

10. a. See Figure 16.24 in your text and then describe the writing skills of the Japanese man studied by Kawamura et al., (1989).

    b. What do these results suggest about the organization of writing in the brain? (Study Figure 16.25 in your text.)

11. What is the characteristic symptom of semantic agraphia? (Roeltgen et al, 1986; Lesser, 1989)

Learning Objective 16-9 Describe research on the neurological basis of developmental dyslexias.

Read pages 523-525 and answer the following questions.

1. Describe evidence that suggests there is a biological component of developmental dyslexia. (Pennington et al., 1991; Wolff and Melngailis, 1994; Grigorenko et al., 1997; Fisher et al., 1999; Gayán et al., 1999))

2. Describe the nature of the deficit by summarizing the results of a study of fifty-six dyslexia boys. (Castles and Coltheart, 1993)

3. a. Explain why we should not be surprised to find that developmental dyslexia is more than a reading deficit.

    b. Describe another deficit common among people with developmental dyslexia. (Eden and Zeffiro, 1998)

4. What did Filipek's (1995) literature review reveal about the location of brain damage that causes developmental dyslexia?

5. a. When Galaburda and Livingstone's (1993) studied the brains of deceased dyslexics where did they find an abnormality?

b. Specifically, what was wrong with this part of their brains?

c. Why might this damage result in dyslexia? Explain Stein and Walsh's (1997) hypothesis.

d. Summarize results of supporting research that studied

    1. problems dyslexics experience when they try to read. (Cornelissen et al., 1991)

    2. discrimination tasks attempted by monkeys. (Walsh and Butler, 1996)

    3. MRI scans of subjects looking at moving and stationary patterns. (See Figure 16.26 in your text. Eden et al., 1996)

6. a. Explain what is row blindness by describing the experiences of dyslexic subjects with the pattern of Xs and Os shown in Figure 16.27a,b in your text. (Lewis and Frick, 1999)

    b. How may this perceptual deficit contribute to difficulty reading?

7. a. When Geschwind and Behan (1984) compared the reading ability and incidence of immune diseases of a group of right- and left-handed people, what did they learn?

    b. What limited conclusion can be drawn from these results?

8. To review the reading and writing disorders you have just learned about, study Table 16.2 in your text.

Lesson II Self Test

1. Pure alexia is a(n) _____ disorder and patients _____.

    a. perceptual; can no longer read, but can still write
    b. motor; can no longer read or write
    c. sensory; can read but no longer write
    d. auditory; can read and write silently but cannot read or spell aloud

2. Research using a PET scanner to measure regional cerebral blood flow suggests that a region of extrastriate cortex is important for

    a. recognition of familiar combinations of letters.
    b. encoding acoustical information about the sounds of letters.
    c. associating words with their meanings.
    d. writing.

3. Surface dyslexia involves a deficit in

    a. phonetic reading.
    b. whole-word reading.
    c. letter-to-sound decoding.
    d. comprehension only; reading is intact.

4. People with phonological dyslexia will have difficulty reading

   a. function words.
   b. abstract words.
   c. nonwords.
   d. content words.

5. Phonological dyslexia is usually caused by damage to the

   a. left parietal lobe.
   b. corpus callosum.
   c. left frontal lobe.
   d. parvocellular layers.

6. In which form of dyslexia do people fail to comprehend what they read?

   a. word-form dyslexia
   b. phonological dyslexia
   c. direct dyslexia
   d. surface dyslexia

7. Studies of Japanese people with localized brain damage who have difficulty reading kana or kanji symbols provide evidence

   a. for reading forms based on the type of alphabet used in the language.
   b. for a universal reading form that involves brain mechanisms that existed before the invention of writing.
   c. that the brain contains redundant neural circuits involved in reading.
   d. for two different forms of reading that involve different brain mechanisms.

8. The fact that it is more difficult to write the word *antidisestablishmentarianism* while singing suggests that

   a. the "auditory image" of words expressed in music is stronger than the image of words expressed in speech.

   b. the ability to write some words depends on being able to articulate them subvocally.
   c. it is more difficult to understand the spoken (or sung) word than the written word.
   d. the ability to write words depends on the strength of the "auditory image" that is evoked.

9. People with phonological dysgraphia _____ words and then write them.

   a. visually imagine
   b. sound out
   c. finger-spell
   d. rehearse

10. People with orthographic dysgraphia have difficulty spelling and writing

   a. compound words.
   b. nonwords.
   c. regular words.
   d. irregular words.

11. Researchers have noted a relationship between developmental dyslexias,

   a. right-handedness, and muscular coordination.
   b. left-handedness, and immune disorders.
   c. right-handedness, and speech difficulties.
   d. ambidexterity, and longevity.

12. All of the following support the hypothesis that dyslexia can result from abnormal input to the parietal lobe caused by an abnormal magnocellular system, *except:*

   a. There is evidence of disorganized magnocellular layers in dyslexics.
   b. Dyslexics often have trouble with spatial perception and of movements in space.
   c. Differences have been recorded in the primary visual cortex of dyslexics.
   d. Dyslexics often complain that when they try to read, letters seem to move around.

Answers for Self Tests

Lesson I

1. b Obj. 16-1
2. d Obj. 16-1
3. d Obj. 16-2
4. a Obj. 16-2
5. a Obj. 16-3

6. d Obj. 16-3
7. b Obj. 16-3
8. c Obj. 16-4
9. a Obj. 16-5
10. b Obj. 16-5
11. d Obj. 16-5
12. b Obj. 14-5

Lesson II

1. a Obj. 16-6
2. a Obj. 16-6
3. b Obj. 16-7
4. c Obj. 16-7
5. c Obj. 16-7
6. c Obj. 16-7

7. d Obj. 16-7
8. b Obj. 16-8
9. a Obj. 16-8
10. d Obj. 16-9
11. b Obj. 16-9
12. c. Obj. 16-9

CHAPTER 17
Schizophrenia and the Affective Disorders

Lesson I: The Physiology of Schizophrenia

Read the interim summary on pages 542-544 of your text to re-acquaint yourself with the material in this section.

Read pages 528-530 and answer the following questions.

1.   Schizophrenia affects what percent of the world's population?

2.   Who first used the term schizophrenia? What does the term mean? What did he intend the term to signify?

3.   Explain the general difference between the positive and negative symptoms of schizophrenia.

4.   Describe these positive symptoms.

   a. thought disorders

   b. delusions of persecution, grandeur, and control

   c. hallucinations

5.   Describe some of the negative symptoms.

6.   Immediately review these symptoms by studying Table 17.1 in your text.

7.   What appears to be the cause of positive symptoms? negative symptoms?

8. Researchers use both twin studies and adoption studies to study the heritability of schizophrenia. What do adoption studies indicate about the incidence of schizophrenia among the children of schizophrenic parents raised by their parents or by nonschizophrenic adoptive parents? (Kety et al., 1968, 1994)

9. What do twin studies indicate about the concordance rate for schizophrenia in monozygotic and dizygotic twins. (Gottesman and Shields, 1982; Tsuang et al., 1991)

10. a. If schizophrenia is a simple trait produced by a single dominant gene, what percentage of the offspring of two schizophrenic parents would be schizophrenic?

    b. And if schizophrenia is a recessive trait, what percentage of the offspring of two schizophrenic parents would be schizophrenic?

    c. What is the actual incidence of this disease among these children?

    d. What does the incidence suggest about the transmission of schizophrenia?

11. a. If a susceptibility to schizophrenia is inherited, which group of people may carry the "schizophrenia gene" but not express it?

    b. Study Figure 17.1 in your text and compare the incidence of schizophrenia in the offspring of monozygotic and dizygotic twins both discordant for the disease. (Gottesman and Bertelsen, 1989)

    c. What do the incidence rates suggest about the heritability of schizophrenia and the inevitability of developing the disease?

12. Describe some of the research on the possible location of the "schizophrenia gene." What can we conclude from these studies? (For example, Dawson and Murray, 1996.)

Learning Objective 17-2 Discuss drugs that alleviate or produce the positive symptoms of schizophrenia; discuss research into the nature of a possible dopamine abnormality in the brains of schizophrenics.

Read pages 530-534 and answer the following questions.

1. State the dopamine hypothesis of schizophrenia in your own words.

2. In general, how do antipsychotic drugs such as chlorpromazine affect schizophrenia?

3. a. What is the pharmacological effect common to all drugs that relieve the positive symptoms of schizophrenia? (Creese et al., 1976) produce the positive symptoms of schizophrenia?

    b. Name four drugs that produce the positive symptoms of schizophrenia.

       1.   3

       2.   4.

4. Most researchers believe which part of the brain is most likely involved in schizophrenia?

5. Why might overactivity of dopaminergic synapses in the nucleus accumbens and amygdala produce the positive symptoms of schizophrenia? Cite research (Snyder, 1974; Fibiger, 1991) to support your answer.

6. List three possible abnormalities in dopamine transmission in the brains of schizophrenic patients, which are summarized in Table 17.2 in your text.

    1.

    2.

    3.

7. a. Examine these possibilities. How did an intravenous injection of amphetamine alter dopamine release in the striatum of schizophrenic patients? (See Figure 17.2 in your text. Laruelle et al., 1996)

    b. What was the relationship between dopamine release and changes in the positive symptoms these patients experienced?

8. Describe research to investigate another possibility—that there is an overabundance of dopamine receptors in the brain.

    a. What research methods have been used to study this possibility?

    b. Briefly summarize the inconclusive results of studies using these methods.

9. a. State two reasons why the dopamine hypothesis may still be valid.

       1.

       2.

    b. Let's look at these more closely. What is the site of action of the highly effective antipsychotic drug clozapine? (Kinon and Lieberman, 1966)

c. Therefore, which brain region may be more important in schizophrenia than the neostriatum?

d. Which dopamine receptors does clozapine have little affinity for? great affinity for? (Pickar, 1995; Van Tol et al., 1991)

e. What other dopamine receptor may be involved in schizophrenia and where is it found in high concentrations? (Murray et al., 1994)

f. What did researchers find with regard to the concentration of D_3 and D_4 receptors in the brains of deceased schizophrenics? (See Figure 17.3 in your text. Murray et al., 1995; Gurevich et al., 1997)

10. What evidence suggests that clozapine may have other pharmacological effects in addition to its affinity for particular dopamine receptors that may affect the positive symptoms of schizophrenia? (Kramer et al., 1997; Tarazi and Baldessarini, 1999)

11. a. What percentage of schizophrenic patients are not helped by antipsychotic drugs?

b. What are some of the serious side effects of many antipsychotic drugs that can affect drug use?

12. Describe tardive dyskinesia by completing the following sentences.

a. Tardive dyskinesia is a serious side effect of taking

b. It affects approximately

c. Some of the symptoms, which are the opposite of those of Parkinson's disease, are

d. Symptoms are made worse by (Cite two situations.)

13. If tardive dyskinesia is produced by an overstimulation of dopamine receptors, why should it be caused by antipsychotic drugs, which are dopamine antagonists? (Be sure to refer to supersensitivity and compensatory mechanisms in your answer. Baldessarini and Tarsy, 1980)

14. a. Why is clozapine referred to as an "atypical," but very effective, antipsychotic drug? (Davis et al., 1991)

b. What are some advantages and disadvantages of clozapine? (Lee et al., 1994; Meltzer et al., 1996)

Learning Objective 17-3 Discuss evidence based on population studies that the negative symptoms of schizophrenia may result from brain damage.

Read pages 534-537 and answer the following questions.

1. Describe some of the neurological symptoms of schizophrenia and explain why they suggest that the disease may result from brain damage. (Stevens, 1982)

2. a. Using CT and MRI scans, what did Weinberger and Wyatt (1982) discover about the relative ventricle size of chronic schizophrenics and normal control subjects of the same age? (Study Figure 17.4 in your text.)

    b. What is the best explanation for the difference in size?

3. a. What other kinds of abnormalities have been documented in later studies? (McCarley et al., 1999; Powers, 1999 for reviews.)

    b. What is the relationship between severity of brain abnormalities and severity of symptoms?

4. a. Define *epidemiology* in your own words.

    b. How may environmental factors increase the risk of schizophrenia in some individuals?

    c. List seven environmental factors that have been associated with the incidence of schizophrenia.

       1.   5.

       2.   6.

       3.   7.

       4.

5. a. Some people whose birthdays fall during the late _____ and early _____ months are more likely to develop schizophrenia later in life—a relationship called the _____

       _____. (See Figure 17.5 in your text. Kendell and Adams, 1991; Takei et al., 1995; Tam and Sewell, 1995)

    b. Is this a universal effect? Explain. (McGrath and Welham, 1999)

    c. What threat to a pregnant woman's health rises during these months?

    d. If the pregnant woman does contract a viral illness, how might her developing fetus be injured? (Pallast et al., 1994)

7. What is the relationship between population density and the incidence of schizophrenia? (Franzek and Beckmann, 1996)

8. a. In general, how is the incidence of schizophrenia affected by influenza epidemics?

    b. Summarize the results of research on the seasonality effect conducted in

       1. Finland. (Mednick et al., 1990)

       2. England and Wales. (See Figure 17.6 in your text. Sham et al., 1992)

c. What, therefore, is the period of greatest vulnerability for a fetus?

9. Describe the latitude effect and provide a possible explanation.

10. What did researchers (Susser and Lin, 1992; Susser et al., 1996) find when they studied the offspring of women who were pregnant during the Hunger Winter? Explain the role of a thiamine deficiency in your answer. (Davis and Bracha, 1996)

11. a. What is Rh incompatibility?

    b. How may it contribute to the development of schizophrenia? Which children are vulnerable? (Hollister et al., 1996)

12. Finally, what might explain a higher incidence of schizophrenia among the children of women who learned that their husbands had been killed in combat in World War II? (Huttunen and Niskanen, 1978)

Learning Objective 17-4   Discuss direct evidence that schizophrenia is associated with brain damage.

Read pages 537-542 and answer the following questions.

1. What were the conclusions of a review

    a. by independent observers of home movies from families with a schizophrenic child? (Walker et al., 1994; Walker et al., 1996)

    b. of the school work and social adjustment of children who later became schizophrenic? (Cannon et al., 1997)

2. Describe the anatomical differences in the MRI scans of the brains of monozygotic twins discordant for schizophrenia which are shown in Figure 17.7 in your text. (Suddath et al., 1990)

3. a. Study Figure 17.8 in your text and then explain why the prenatal environment of monozygotic twins is not always identical. Be sure to use the terms *monochorionic* and *dichorionic* in your answer.

    b. How do researchers determine whether a pair of twins is monochorionic or dichorionic?

    c. The concordance rate for schizophrenia is _____ for _____ monozygotic twins and _____ for _____ monozygotic twins. (Davis et al., 1995)

4. a. Why did Bracha et al. (1992) also examine the fingerprints of monozygotic twins concordant or discordant for schizophrenia? What did they find?

b. What were the findings of follow-up research on the lines in the twins' palms? (Davis and Bracha, 1996)

5. a. How do the total number of synapses in the brain change from birth until the age of fifteen or twenty?

   b. What may happen during this progression that ultimately leads to schizophrenia? (Squires, 1977; Woods, 1998)

6. To review: What does research suggest may be the

   a. most important cause of schizophrenia?

   b. cause of the positive symptoms?

   c. cause of the negative symptoms?

7. According to Weinberger (1988), what kind of brain damage causes the negative symptoms of schizophrenia?

8. a. Name and describe the most reliable test to determine the function of the dorsolateral prefrontal cortex. (See figure 17.9 in your text.)

   b. Compare the cerebral blood flow in the lateral prefrontal cortex of normal subjects and schizophrenic subjects while they were taking a computerized version of the WCST. (See Figure 17.10 in your text. Weinberger et al., 1986)

   c. What did Taylor's (1996) review of the literature confirm?

9. Provide an explanation for the widely observed hypofrontality by noting the behavioral effects of

   a. destruction of the dopaminergic input to the prefrontal cortex of monkeys. (Brozowski et al., 1979)

   b. injection of D_1 antagonists into the prefrontal cortex. (Sawaguchi and Goldman-Rakic, 1994)

   c. administration of amphetamine to schizophrenic patients. (Daniel et al., 1991)

10. What is the rationale for studying phencyclidine (PCP) to understand schizophrenia?

11. a. How does a single injection of PCP affect dopaminergic neurons and alter dopamine release in the nucleus accumbens to produce the positive symptoms of schizophrenia? (Deutch et al., 1987; Hertel et al., 1995; Jentsch et al., 1998)

    b. Does PCP affect these neurons directly or indirectly?

12. How does chronic PCP abuse appear to alter the brain to produce the negative symptoms? (Hertzmann et al., 1990; Wu et al., 1991)

13. a. To study chronic PCP abuse, how often were subject monkeys injected with the drug? (Jentsch et al., 1997)

b. Describe the task the animals learned to perform.

c. How successfully did normal monkeys perform when the box was rotated? subject monkeys? (See Figure 17.11 in your text.)

d. What were the physiological effects of PCP in the brain?

e. What treatment improved the task performance of subject monkeys?

14. In later research, what was the correlation between changes in level of dopamine transmission caused by PCP and behavioral impairment? (Jentsch et al., 1999)

15. Carefully explain how the hyperactivity of dopaminergic neurons and the hypoactivity of the prefrontal cortex may be linked. (Weinberger, 1988; Grace, 1991; Deutch, 1992)

16. How was dopamine activity in the nucleus accumbens affected by

a. infusing PCP directly into the prefrontal cortex?

b. lesions of the prefrontal cortex? (Jentsch et al., 1998)

c. destruction of dopaminergic axons and terminals in the prefrontal cortex? (King et al., 1997)

d. injections of clozapine? (Be sure to note how this drug affects another part of the brain. Youngren et al., 1999)

17. What physical abnormalities that have been observed in the brains of schizophrenics are consistent with the PCP model? (Okubo et al., 1997; Akil et al., 1999)

18. a. What is the site of action of PCP and how does it disrupt neural function?

b. Carefully explain why researchers have used glycine agonists to study the role of the NMDA receptor in schizophrenia.

c. Summarize the results of two double-blind studies using glycine agonists to reduce patients' symptoms. (See Figure 17.12 in your text. Goff et al., 1999; Hereseo-Levy et al., 1999)

19. What is the significance for research on schizophrenia of the failure of ketamine and MK-801 to affect the brains of prepubertal children? (Marshall and Longnecker, 1990; Farber et al., 1995)

Lesson I Self Test

1. If the tendency to develop schizophrenia is heritable

    a. the percentage of dizygotic twins concordant for schizophrenia will be higher than that of monozygotic twins.
    b. the incidence of schizophrenia in adopted children with biological schizophrenic parents will be higher than that of the general population.
    c. environment plays no role in the development of the disease.
    d. the disease will be milder if only one biological parent is schizophrenic.

2. The fact that not all children of two schizophrenic parents become schizophrenic suggests that

    a. schizophrenia results from a single faulty gene.
    b. having schizophrenic parents may increase susceptibility to the disease.
    c. the "schizophrenia gene" is recessive.
    d. schizophrenia is not caused by genetic factors.

3. Chlorpromazine, a dopamine _____ relieves the _____ symptoms of schizophrenia by _____.

    a. antagonist; negative; inhibiting dopamine release
    b. agonist; negative; stimulating dopamine synthesis
    c. antagonist; positive; blocking dopamine receptors
    d. agonist; positive and negative; stimulating dopamine release

4. Which of the following is *not* consistent with the suggestion that reinforcement pathways play a role in schizophrenia?

    a. Schizophrenics sometimes report feelings of elation and euphoria at the beginning of a schizophrenic episode.
    b. Cocaine and amphetamine release dopamine in reinforcement pathways and can cause psychotic symptoms.
    c. One of the most effective antipsychotic drugs, clozapine, inhibits dopamine in the nucleus accumbens, which is part of the reinforcement circuit.

    d. The neostriatum probably plays a more important role in schizophrenia than parts of the brain involved in reinforcement.

5. Tardive dyskinesia

    a. is relieved by decreasing the amount of antipsychotic medication.
    b. is most common after treatment with the drug clozapine.
    c. is a parkinsonian side effect of antipsychotic medications.
    d. may be caused by dopamine receptor supersensitivity.

6. Careful study of CT and MRI scans indicates that schizophrenics have

    a. enlarged ventricles.
    b. fewer convolutions in the cerebellum.
    c. atrophy of the neostriatum.
    d. a thicker corpus callosum.

7. The "seasonality effect" in schizophrenia refers to

    a. the increased likelihood that people born in the summer months develop schizophrenia.
    b. the increased likelihood that people born in the winter months develop schizophrenia.
    c. the intensification of schizophrenic symptoms in the winter months.
    d. the increased incidence of schizophrenia in countries farther from the equator.

8. If an Rh-negative woman is pregnant with an Rh-positive child the likelihood of schizophrenia is increased for

    a. only the first such child.
    b. all such daughters, but not sons.
    c. all such children except the first.
    d. all such children.

9. Monozygotic twins concordant for schizophrenia are most likely

    a. to be monochorionic twins.
    b. to be dichorionic twins.
    c. to have had unequal exposure to the maternal hormones of pregnancy.
    d. to have been exposed to the same predisposing environmental factors after birth.

10. Hypofrontality

a. decreases when subjects are mentally challenged by tests such as the WCST.

b. is decreased neural activity in the prefrontal cortex.

c. results when D1 receptors are stimulated.

d. is enhanced by drugs such as amphetamine.

11. Which statement about PCP is *incorrect?*

a. PCP elicits both positive and negative symptoms of schizophrenia.

b. PCP acts as an indirect antagonist for NMDA receptors.

c. PCP increases dopamine release in the nucleus accumbens.

d. PCP acts directly on dopaminergic neurons.

12. The negative symptoms of schizophrenia, which might be caused by disrupting the activity of NMDA receptors, can be relieved by administering

a. glutamate.

b. chlorpromazine.

c. a glycine agonist.

d. ketamine.

Lesson II: The Major Affective Disorders

Read the interim summary on page 555 of your text to re-acquaint yourself with the material in this section.

Learning Objective 17-5   Describe the two major affective disorders, the heritability of these diseases, and their physiological treatments.

Read pages 544-547 and answer the following questions.

1.   a. The primary symptom of schizophrenia is _____ _____ and the primary symptom

of the major affective disorders is _____ _____.

b. List the two principal types of major affective disorders.

1.   2.

2.   Describe bipolar disorder.

a. Name and describe the two alternating moods.

b. Approximately how long is each episode?

c. What is the incidence of bipolar disorder in men and women?

3.   Describe unipolar depression, including its incidence in men and women.

4.   Present a profile of patients suffering from affective disorders by describing the effect of the disease on

a. self-esteem.

b. personal safety.

c. energy level.

d. appetite.

e. sex drive.

f. sleep patterns.

g. body functions.

5. Explain the differences between mania and a normal enthusiasm for life.

6. State the results of these studies tracing the heritability of the affective disorders.

   a. incidence among close relatives of patients (Rosenthal, 1971)

   b. incidence in sets of monozygotic and dizygotic twins (Gershon et al., 1976) reared together or apart (Price, 1968)

   c. the existence of a gene responsible for susceptibility to bipolar disorder (Spence et al., 1995; MacKinnon et al., 1997; Berrettini, 1998)

7. a. List four effective biological treatments of unipolar depression.

   1.   3.

   2.   4.

   b. Now list two effective biological treatments for bipolar disorder.

   1.   2.

   c. What does the efficacy of drug therapy suggest about the cause of the affective disorders?

8. a. Explain how an early antidepressant drug, iproniazid, affects the brain. Be sure to state the function of monoamine oxidase (MAO).

   b. Describe and explain the most common serious side effect of MAO inhibitors.

9. a. Explain the pharmacological effects of the tricyclic antidepressant drugs.

b. In other words, both MAO inhibitors and the tricyclic antidepressant drugs are _____

_____.

c. Name a widely prescribed specific serotonin reuptake inhibitor.

10. Briefly describe the history of electroconvulsive therapy (ECT). (See Figure 17.13 in your text.)

11. a. Compare the speed with which MAO inhibitors and ECT relieve depression.

b. State a serious side effect of the excessive use of ECT. (Squire, 1974)

c. State two reasons why occasional use of ECT may be justified. (Baldessarini, 1977)

12. What may be the cause of cognitive impairment resulting from ECT and what preventative treatment is effective? (Prudic et al., 1999)

13. Explain transcranial magnetic stimulation and its effectiveness in treating depression. (George et al., 1995; Klein et al., 1999; Triggs et al., 1999)

14. a. Which phase of bipolar disorder is effectively treated with lithium? (Gerbino et al., 1978; Soares and Gershon, 1998)

b. What are some of the significant advantages of treating bipolar disorder with lithium? (Fieve, 1979)

c. Approximately what percentage of people suffering from this disorder are helped by lithium? (Price and Heninger, 1994)

d. Lithium is not without side effects. List some.

e. Why do some patients eventually stop taking this highly effective drug, and what risk do they run? (Suppes et al., 1991; Post et al., 1992)

15. a. State a tentative explanation of the effect of lithium on the brain. (Atack et al., 1995; Jope et al., 1996; Manji and Lenox, 1999)

b. What is an alternative medication to lithium? How effective is it? (See Figure 17.14 in your text. Post et al., 1984; Post et al., 1992)

Learning Objective 17-6 Summarize the monoamine hypothesis of depression and review the long-term changes in receptor sensitivity.

Read pages 547-552 and answer the following questions.

1.   Briefly explain the monoamine hypothesis of depression.

2.   Begin a review of evidence that supports this hypothesis. When reserpine was first used to treat high blood pressure, what side effect did physicians notice in about 15 percent of their patients? (Sachar and Baron, 1979)

3.   Explain how reserpine affects the membrane of synaptic vesicles and the release of monoamine transmitter substance in the brain.

4.   Explain how the pharmacological and behavioral effects of reserpine complement those of MAO inhibitors.

5.   Describe research on CSF levels of 5-HIAA and suicidal depression.

   a. Explain how 5-HIAA is produced in the brain.

   b. Compare the CSF levels of 5-HIAA in the brains of people who

      1. had attempted suicide and control subjects.

      2. were depressed and eventually committed suicide and those who did not.(Träskmann et al, 1981; Roy et al., 1989)

   c. What did analysis of the CSF of healthy, nondepressed volunteers reveal? (Sedvall et al., 1980)

   d. Explain how decreased levels of 5-HIAA in CSF support the notion that serotonin may play a role in aggression and suicide as well as depression. (Siever et al., 1991)

6.   a. How did Delgado et al. (1990) lower the tryptophan level in subjects' brains?

   b. What effect did the procedure have on the level of serotonin in the subjects' brains? Why?

   c. And what was the effect on their depression?

   d. How, then, may some drugs successfully relieve depression?

7. a. In addition, how does tryptophan depletion affect the mood of

    1. healthy people?

    2. people with a family history of depression? (Benkelfat et al., 1994)

    3. depressed people being treated with serotonin reuptake inhibitors and norepinephrine reuptake inhibitors?

    b. However, what happens if patients whose depression is successfully being treated with norepinephrine reuptake inhibitors are given AMPT? (See Figure 17.15 in your text. Heninger et al., 1996)

8. Using a PET scanner, Bremner et al. (1997) measured the regional cerebral metabolic rate of patients before and after they drank a placebo or the amino acid "cocktail." What did the scans indicate about the metabolic activity of people who relapsed and those who did not?

9. Outline a hypothesis to explain why antidepressant drugs do not relieve symptoms for many days. (Artigas et al., 1996)

10. Immediately review this hypothesis by studying Figure 17.16 in your text and completing this summary.

    When serotonergic neurons in the raphe nuclei become active, their dendrites release serotonin; thus, specific serotonin reuptake inhibitors cause _____ serotonin to accumulate around these dendrites. The serotonin binds with dendritic _____ _____ and _____ the firing rate of these neurons. After two to three weeks, the dendritic autoreceptors become _____, and the firing rate of the neurons goes back to _____. Now the drug starts producing its antidepressant effects. When the neurons fire, the drug causes _____ amounts of serotonin to accumulate in the clefts of the synapses formed by the terminals of these neurons, located primarily in the _____ cortex, _____ and _____ _____.

11. a. If this explanation is correct, what should be the effect of drugs that block these receptors? Cite supporting research. (Artigas et al, 1993; Blier and Bergeron, 1995; Zanardi et al., 1998)

    b. Now cite research findings from a double-blind study that do not support this explanation. (Berman et al., 1999)

12. a. What evidence suggests that dopamine may play a role in depression?

    b. If depressed patients are given dopamine agonists, how are they affected?

    c. How does chronic treatment with an antidepressant drug affect the sensitivity of D_1 and D_2 dopamine receptors in the nucleus accumbens? the release of dopamine by electrical stimulation?

d. What can we conclude from these findings about a role for dopamine in depression?

13. a. What is substance P and what evidence suggests that it may play a role in depression? (Mantyh et al., 1984; Shirayama et al., 1996)

  b. Summarize research results on the efficacy of MK-869 in the treatment of depression which are shown in Figure 17.17 in your text. (Kramer et al., 1998)

14. What is the location of brain abnormalities that are associated with

  a. unipolar depression? (Elkis et al., 1996; Drevets et al., 1992)

  b. bipolar disorder? (Drevets et al., 1992)

  c. depression? (Öngur et al., 1998)

15. Where have alterations in metabolic activity been observed in

  a. depressed people? (Drevets et al., 1992; Wu et al., 1992; Abercrombie et al., 1998)

  b. normal subjects experiencing sadness? (George et al., 1995; Beauregard et al.,1998; Mayberg et al., 1999)

  c. depressed people before and after ECT treatment. (Study Figure 17.18 in your text. Nobler et al., 1994)

16. To what degree do obstetric complications contribute to bipolar disorder? (Kinney et al., 1993; Kinney et al., 1998)

17. a. Define *silent cerebral infarctions (SCI)* in your own words.

  b. What is the relationship between have had SCIs and developing late-onset depression? (Fujikawa et al., 1993)

  c. If late-onset depression is not caused by SCIs, what, then, is the likely cause? (Fujikawa et al., 1994)

  d. How does the cause of late-onset depression affect treatment success? (Fujikawa et al., 1996)

Learning Objective 17-7 Explain the role of circadian and seasonal rhythms in affective disorders: the effects of REM sleep deprivation and total sleep deprivation, and seasonal affective disorder.

Read pages 552-555 and answer the following questions.

1. Describe how the sleep of people with depression is disrupted.

  a. amounts of slow-wave delta sleep and stage 1 sleep

b. fragmentation of sleep

c. changes in REM sleep patterns (See Figure 17.19 in your text. Kupfer, 1976; Vogel et al., 1980)

2. a. What is the effect on depression of selective deprivation of REM sleep? (Vogel et al., 1975, Vogel et al., 1990)

b. Approximately how long does it take for relief from depression to occur?

3. a. How did antidepressant drugs affect the sleep cycle of cats? (Scherschlicht et al., 1982)

b What is the primary physiological effect of all antidepressant drugs that suppress REM sleep? (Vogel et al., 1990)

c. What evidence suggests that these antidepressant drugs may have another pharmacological effect? (Vogel et al., 1998)

4. a. What change in REM sleep was observed in first-degree relatives of people with depression? (Giles et al., 1987)

b. Which family members had the highest risk of becoming depressed? (Giles et al., 1988)

c. What did a comparison of REM sleep patterns of the newborn infants of mothers with and without a history of depression indicate? (Coble et al., 1988)

5. Briefly describe some of the physical characteristics of the brains of the laboratory animals that Vogel et al. (1990) believe can serve as models of depression.

6. Describe research on the antidepressant effect of total sleep deprivation.

a. How quickly does total sleep deprivation relieve depression? (See Figure 17.20 in your text. Wu and Bunney, 1990)

b. According to Wu and Bunney (1990), why does sleep trigger depression in susceptible people? (See Figure 17.21 in your text.)

c. What characteristic of a depressed patient predicts a good response to total sleep deprivation? (Refer to Figure 17.21 and note how the mood of people who responded to sleep deprivation treatment changed during the day. Riemann et al., 1991; Haug, 1992; Wirz-Justice and Van den Hoofdakker, 1999)

d. Offer two explanations why naps, even ones as short as 90 seconds, reinstate the depression of some subjects.

7. Although total sleep deprivation is impossible and impractical, what patterns of partial sleep deprivation are practical and effective? (Szuba et al., 1991; Leibenluft and Wehr, 1992; Papadimitriou et al., 1993; Riemann et al., 1999)

8. a. Describe the symptoms of seasonal affective disorder, noting how they differ from the symptoms of major depression.

   b. Compare the symptoms of seasonal affective disorder and summer depression. (Wehr et al., 1987; Wehr et al., 1991)

   c. What evidence suggests a genetic basis for seasonal affective disorder? (Madden et al., 1996; Sher et al., 1999)

9. a. How is seasonal affective disorder best treated? (Rosentahal et al., 1985; Stinson and Thompson, 1990)

   b. Outline a possible explanation why phototherapy is effective against seasonal affective disorder. Be sure to use the term *zeitgeber* in your answer.

   c. Now summarize research results that conflicts with this explanation. (Wirz-Justice et al., 1993; Meesters et al., 1995; Lewy et al., 1998; Terman et al., 1998)

10. What other form of depression improves with phototherapy? (Neumeister et al., 1996)

11. a. What percentage of people are sensitive to seasonal changes in the hours of sunlight? What is an easy treatment for these "winter blahs?" (Kasper et al., 1989b)

    b. What is an alternative to phototherapy? (Wirz-Justice, 1996)

    c. What is the effect of exercise on depression? (Singh et al., 1997)

Lesson II Self Test

1. Bipolar disorder is characterized by

   a. unremitting or episodic depression without periods of mania and afflicts more women than men.

   b. mania without periods of depression and afflicts more women than men.

   c. alternating bouts of depression followed by periods of normal affect and afflicts more men than women.

d. alternating bouts of mania and depression and afflicts men and women about equally.

2. Studies of the genetic basis of affective disorders have shown that

a. there is little evidence in favor of a genetic component in these disorders.
b. concordance rates for monozygotic twins are considerably higher than concordance rates for dizygotic twins.
c. there is a genetic basis for unipolar depression but not bipolar disorder.
d. the responsible dominant gene is located on chromosome 11.

3. A serious side effect of frequent electroconvulsive therapy is

a. disturbances in biological rhythms.
b. elevated blood pressure.
c. long-lasting memory impairments.
d. suppression of normal feelings of emotion.

4. Lithium

a. is most effective in treating the manic phase of bipolar disorder.
b. has a harmful side effect referred to as the cheese effect.
c. has a high therapeutic index reducing the risk of accidental overdose.
d. works relatively quickly and very effectively so compliance is not a problem.

5. The monoamine hypothesis suggests that depression is a result of _____ of monoaminergic neurons.

a. insufficient activity
b. excessive numbers
c. overactivity
d. the proliferation

6. Depressed individuals fed a diet low in tryptophan and a "cocktail" high in other amino acids

a. become manic.
b. relapse into depression.
c. show changes in cognition but not affect.
d. have elevated levels of serotonin metabolites.

7. Short-term administration of specific serotonin reuptake inhibitors or MAO inhibitors

a. also inhibits dendritic autoreceptors.
b. is a more effective treatment for depression in combination with drugs that block receptors.

c. temporarily increases serotonin levels in the raphe nuclei.
d. prevents fluctuations in serotonin levels to reduce symptoms of depression.

8. Increased activity of _____ appears to be a consistent finding in depression.

a. the hippocampus
b. the prefrontal cortex
c. NK1 receptors
d. dopamine D_1 receptors

9. People whose depression is relieved by total sleep deprivation

a. begin to feel better immediately.
b. feel better in the morning than in the evening.
c. must limit their sleep to brief naps.
d. gradually feel better over the course of several weeks.

10. Wu and Bunney suggested that sleep deprivation causes an improvement in depressive symptoms because

a. during sleep a depressogenic substance is produced that needs to be metabolized during waking hours.
b. waking produces a substance with antidepressant effects.
c. REM sleep allows a person to actively rehearse the life events that may be causing depression.
d. it causes memory loss.

11. Seasonal affective disorder

a. appears to have a geographical rather than a genetic basis.
b. does not affect people who work indoors as often as it affects people who work outdoors.
c. develops about the time the temperature drops below freezing in the fall.
d. involves weight gain whereas major depression involves weight loss.

12. An effective treatment for seasonal affective disorder is

a. avoidance of temperature changes, especially at night.
b. infrequent naps to regulate the amount of REM sleep.
c. a fixed meal schedule to minimize changes in metabolic rate.
d. exposure to several hours of bright light each day.

Answers for Self Tests

Lesson I

1. b Obj. 17-1
2. b Obj. 17-1
3. c Obj. 17-2
4. d Obj. 17-2
5. d Obj. 17-2
6. a Obj. 17-3
7. b Obj. 17-3
8. c Obj. 17-3
9. a Obj. 17-4
10. b Obj. 17-4
11. d Obj. 17-4
12. c Obj. 17-4

Lesson II

1. d Obj. 17-5
2. b Obj. 17-5
3. c Obj. 17-5
4. a Obj. 17-5
5. a Obj. 17-6
6. b Obj. 17-6
7. c Obj. 17-6
8. b Obj. 17-6
9. a Obj. 17-7
10. a Obj. 17-7
11. d Obj. 17-7
12. d Obj. 17-7

CHAPTER 18
Anxiety Disorders, Autistic Disorder, and Stress Disorders

Lesson I: Anxiety Disorders and Autistic Disorder

Read the interim summary on pages 564-565 of your text to re-acquaint yourself with the material in this section.

Learning Objective 18-1 Describe the symptoms and possible causes of panic disorder.

Read pages 558-560 and answer the following questions.

1.   In general, what is the primary symptom of the anxiety disorders?

2.   a. Define *panic disorder* in your own words.

b. What is the incidence of panic disorder in the general population? (Robbins et al., 1984)

c. At what age does this disorder most commonly begin? (Woodruff et al., 1972)

3.   a. List some of the universal symptoms of a panic attack.

b. Explain the relationship between panic attacks, anticipatory anxiety, and agoraphobia.

4.   Why are people who suffer from panic disorder often convinced it is a medical, rather than a mental, condition?

5.   a. What is the incidence of panic disorder for monozygotic and dizygotic twins? (Slater and Shields, 1969) for first-degree relatives of people with panic disorder? (Crowe et al., 1983)

b. What does the familial pattern of panic disorder suggest about its origin? (Crowe et al., 1987)

6. How may a panic attack be induced? (Stein and Uhde, 1994)

7. a. After receiving an injection of sodium lactate, what percentage of a group of normal subjects experienced a panic attack? (Balon et al., 1989)

   b. What percentage of the relatives of the subjects who experienced a panic attack had a history of anxiety disorders?

8. What are the two components of the treatment for anxiety disorders?

   1.   2.

9. a. Once again, how do benzodiazepines agonists and antagonists affect the sensitivity of GABA binding sites?

   b. What possible causes of anxiety disorders are suggested by the effects of these drugs on GABA receptors?

10. a. If pregnant cats are given diazepam (Valium), what is the effect on the

    1. fearfulness of their offspring?

    2. level of benzodiazepine receptors in some parts of the brains of their offspring? (Marczynski and Urbancic, 1988)

    b. What, therefore, may be a cause of fearfulness?

11. Summarize research that suggests and questions the role of CCK in panic disorder. (Bradwejn et al., 1990; Csonka et al., 1988; Adams et al., 1995)

12. Serotonin agonists successfully treat panic disorder and obsessive-compulsive disorder after a delay of approximately six weeks. What does this delay suggest about the way the drug affects the brain?

13. a. What changes occurred in the brain(s) of

    1. a woman who had an unexpected panic attack while undergoing a PET scan? (Fischer et al., 1998)

    2. women with severe spider phobias who did and did not panic when they saw spider videos? (Johanson et al., 1998)

    b. What do these results suggest about the brain regions involved in panic attacks?

Learning Objective 18-2 Describe the symptoms and possible causes of obsessive-compulsive disorder.

Read pages 560-564 and answer the following questions

1. Define *obsessions* and *compulsions* in your own words.

2. a. What is the incidence of obsessive-compulsive disorder

      1. in the general population?

      2. among men and women?

   b. At what age does this disorder commonly begin? (Robbins et al., 1984)

   c. What does a comparison of symptoms in various racial and ethnic groups reveal? (Akhtar et al., 1975; Khanna and Channabasavanna, 1987; Hinjo et al., 1989)

   d. How does this disorder disrupt normal social contact?

3. List the four categories of compulsions and give an example of each. (Study Table 18.1 in your text.)

   1.

   2.

   3.

   4.

4. Discuss the possible relationship between compulsive behaviors and species-typical behaviors? (Wise and Rapoport, 1988)

5. Fiske and Haslam (1997) propose a particular explanation for the origins of obsessive-compulsive disorder. Summarize their hypothesis.

6. Review research on the possible causes of hereditary obsessive-compulsive disorder.

   a. What have family studies revealed about the incidence of obsessive-compulsive disorder and Tourette's syndrome? (Pauls and Leckman, 1986; Pauls et al., 1986)

   b. Briefly describe Tourette's syndrome especially any similarities with obsessive-compulsive disorder. (Leonard et al., 1992b, 1992c)

   c. What may be the cause of both obsessive-compulsive disorder and Tourette's syndrome?

7. Now review research on the possible causes of nonhereditary obsessive-compulsive disorder.

   a. What injuries or diseases may contribute to this disorder? (Berthier et al., 1966; Hollander et al., 1990)

b. Which brain regions appear to be damaged or dysfunctional? (Giedd et al., 1995; Robinson et al., 1995)

c. Describe Sydenham's chorea and its relationship to obsessive-compulsive disorder. (Swedo et al., 1989a; Cummings and Cunningham, 1992; Husby et al., 1976)

8. a. Which brain regions show increased activity in patients with OCD? (Saxena et al., 1998)

b. And which brain regions show decreased activity following successful behavior therapy or drug therapy? Why are these results surprising?

9. a. What interesting technique did Breiter et al. (1996) use to investigate the brain functions of people with obsessive-compulsive disorder?

b. Which brain regions became active during the testing?

10. a. What kind of surgery is often a successful treatment for this disorder? (Ballantine et al., 1987; Mindus et al., 1994; Baer et al., 1995)

b. Under what circumstances is surgery justified?

11. According to Saxena et al. (1998), what may be the cause of obsessive-compulsive disorder? (Refer to Figure 8.17 in your text.)

12. The most effective treatment of obsessive-compulsive disorder is _____ _____.

13. a. Outline the drug treatment schedule OCD research subjects followed. (Leonard et al., 1989)

b. Study Figure 18.1 in your text and compare the effectiveness of clomipramine and an antidepressant drug desipramine in relieving their symptoms.

c. When patients were switched from CMI to DMI, what happened to their symptoms?

14. How do all effective antiobsessional drugs affect the brain? What does this common effect suggest about a reason why the symptoms of OCD diminish?

15. Discuss findings that may explain why serotonergic agonists are only effective in treating OCD after a delay of several weeks. (El Mansari et al., 1995)

16. a. Briefly describe several other compulsive behaviors which afflict people and how they are successfully treated. (Rapoport, 1991; Leonard et al., 1992)

   b. Now describe a compulsive behavior seen in some breeds of large dogs and how it can be successfully treated. (Rapoport et al., 1992)

Read the interim summary on page 569 of your text to re-acquaint yourself with the material in this section.

Learning Objective 18-3   Describe the symptoms and possible causes of autism.

Read pages 565-569 and answer the following questions.

1.   What is the incidence of autism in the general population? between boys and girls?

2.   List some characteristic abnormalities of autistic disorder that fall into each of these categories.

   a. affective

   b. cognitive

   c. behavioral

3.   Now list and briefly describe three other pervasive developmental disorders.

   1.

   2.

   3.

4.   a. Outline the explanation of the symptoms of autism proposed by Frith and her colleagues (Frith et al., 1991).

   b. Describe the test administered to autistic children by Baron-Cohen et al. (1985) that supports this explanation. (See Figure 18.2 in your text.)

   c. What is a shortcoming of this explanation?

5.   Explain two approaches to understanding the basis of autism—one incorrect (Bettelheim, 1967) and one widely accepted. (Cox et al., 1975)

6. a. Cite evidence from family studies, especially the study of autism in siblings, that supports the role of genetics in this disorder. (Folstein and Piven, 1991; Bailey, 1993)

    b. Compare the concordance rates for autism in monozygotic and dizygotic twins. (Folstein and Piven, 1991; Bailey et al., 1995)

    c. What is unique about the twin who develops autism in monozygotic pairs who are discordant for autism? What does this suggest about the causes of this disorder?

7. Phenylketonuria (PKU) has been linked to autism. Describe this disorder, how it affects brain development, and how it may be treated. (Lowe et al., 1980; Folstein and Rutter, 1988)

8. a. Describe some of the symptoms that people with autistic disorder and people with Tourette's syndrome have in common. (Comings and Comings, 1991)

    b. What did Sverd et al. (1991) find in the family histories of patients with symptoms of autism and Tourette's syndrome? (See Table 18.2 in your text.)

    c. What do these finding suggest about the origins of both of these disorders?

9. Describe research to study links between autistic disorder and

    a. disease during pregnancy. (Chess et al., 1917)

    b. physical abnormalities. (Fernell et al., 1991)

    c. prenatal exposure to drugs. (Miller and Strömland, 1993; Strömland et al., 1994)

10. a. What part of the central nervous system is developing between prenatal days 20 and 24—the period in which some autistic people were exposed prenatally to thalidomide? (Rodier et al., 1996)

    b. What similar abnormalities, either induced by a targeted mutation or exposure to valproic acid, have been found in mice? (Mark et al., 1993; Rodier et al., 1997

11. Approximately what percentage of all cases of autism have definable biological causes?

12. Where have researchers found evidence for abnormalities in the brains of people with autistic disorder? (See Figure 18.3 in your text. DeLong, 1992; Happé and Frith, 1996; Kemper and Bauman, 1998; Courchesne, 1991; Holroyd et al., 1991; Hashimoto et al, 1995; Haas et al., 1996).

Lesson I Self Test

1. People with panic disorder suffer from anticipatory anxiety, which is

    a. a brief interval of unrealistic fear that precedes a panic attack.
    b. the first stage of a panic attack.
    c. often sufficient to trigger a panic attack.
    d. the fear that another panic attack will strike.

2. Studies concerning the genetic basis of panic disorder have shown that

    a. 50 percent of the first degree relatives of a person with panic disorder also have panic disorder.
    b. the concordance rate for monozygotic twins is similar to that found in dizygotic twins.
    c. panic disorder may be caused by a single, dominant gene.
    d. environmental factors outweigh genetic factors.

3. An injection of _____ may cause a panic attack in susceptible people.

    a. alcohol
    b. lactic acid
    c. benzodiazepine
    d. lithium carbonate

4. Drugs that are _____ have been used to successfully treat panic disorder.

    a. serotonin agonists
    b. serotonin antagonists
    c. benzodiazepine receptor antagonists
    d. CCK-receptor antagonists

5. People suffering from obsessive-compulsive disorder

    a. discuss their behavior openly.
    b. have periodic episodes of mania.
    c. recognize that their thoughts and behaviors are senseless.
    d. are often insomniacs.

6. Obsessive-compulsive disorder has been associated with all the following disorders except

    a. Tourette's syndrome.
    b. phenylketonuria.
    c. birth trauma.
    d. Huntington's chorea.

7. PET scans have recorded abnormal activity in all of the following regions of the brains of patients with obsessive-compulsive disorder except

    a. prefrontal cortex.
    b. cingulate cortex.
    c. basal ganglia.
    d. cerebellum.

8. All effective antiobsessional drugs

    a. block dopamine receptors.
    b. are MAO antagonists.
    c. increases the sensitivity of the GABA binding site.
    d. block the reuptake of 5-HT.

9. Which is not true of the language of autistic children?

    a. It is abnormal or even nonexistent.
    b. It often includes repetition of what others have said.
    c. It improves in late adolescence.
    d. It is often self-centered or self-interested.

10. Autistic disorder

    a. occurs in more girls than boys.
    b. has near 100 percent concordance in monozygotic twins.
    c. afflicts all siblings of parents carrying the faulty genes.
    d. results from nongenetic causes about 50 percent of the time.

11. Frith's hypothesis that autism is the inability to see the world from another's point of view does not explain why autistic people show

    a. abnormal social relationships.
    b. stereotyped movements.
    c. impaired imagination.
    d. an inability to predict and explain other people's behavior.

12. Which part of the brain develops between prenatal days 20 and 24 and may be implicated in autistic disorder?

    a. brain stem
    b. basal ganglia
    c. amygdala
    d. sensory cortex

Lesson II: The Stress Disorders

Read the interim summary on pages 580-581 in your text to re-acquaint yourself with the material in this section.

Learning Objective 18-4   Describe the physiological responses to stress and their effects on health.

Read pages 569-573 and answer the following questions.

1.   Define in your own words

   a. stress

   b. fight-or-flight response.

2.   The _____ and _____ responses to an emotion can have harmful effects on

   health. These responses are _____ and ready the body's _____ _____.

3.   a. Where is epinephrine secreted?

   b. What are some of its effects? Which effect of epinephrine and norepinephrine together contributes to cardiovascular disease?

   c. In stressful situations, what change occurs in the secretion of norepinephrine in the brain? (Yokoo et al., 1990; Cenci et al., 1992)

   d. If noradrenergic axons from the brain stem to the forebrain are destroyed, how is the response to social isolation stress affected? (Montero et al., 1990)

   e. Trace the brain circuit that appears to produce the release of norepinephrine. (Wallace et al., 1992)

4.   a. What is the other stress-related hormone and where is it secreted?

   b. List some of its effects.

1.	4.
2.	5.
3.	6.

   c. What is the presumed significance of the fact that nearly every cell of the body has glucocorticoid receptors?

d. The secretion of glucocorticoids is controlled by neurons of the _____ _____ of the _____ which secrete a peptide called _____-_____ _____, which, in turn, stimulates the anterior pituitary gland to secrete _____ _____. The _____ _____ secretes glucocorticoids in response to ACTH.

(The control of the secretion of glucocorticoids is illustrated in Figure 18.4 in your text.)

5. a. In which brain region does CRF serve as a neuromodulator/neurotransmitter?

    b. What are the effects of an intracerebroventricular injection of CRF? (Britton et al., 1982; Cole and Koob, 1988; Swerdlow et al., 1986) of a CRF antagonist? (Kalin et al., 1988; Heinrichs et al, 1994; Skutella et al., 1994)

6. a. What kind of injections did experimental and control rats receive before being subjected to restraint stress? (Smagin et al., 1999)

    b. Which rats showed a significant weight loss? (See Figure 18.5 in your text.)

    c. What do these results suggest about the role of CRF in stress?

7. a. What are the effects of stress on rats who have had their adrenal glands removed?

    b. What medical treatment do adrenalectomized human patients receive in times of stress? (Tyrell and Baxter, 1981)

8. Describe the incidence of hypertension in air traffic controllers in high-stress and low-stress airports shown in Figure 18.6 in your text. (Cobb and Rose, 1973)

9. a. According to Selye (1976), what event causes the harmful effects of stress?

    b. List some of the effects on health of prolonged stress.

    c. How were the effects of stress on healing demonstrated in subjects who cared for relatives with Alzheimer's disease? What were the results? (Kiecold-Glaser et al., 1995) (See Figure 18.7 in your text.)

10. a. List two changes that occur in neurons in field CA1 of the hippocampal formation as a result of long-term exposure to glucocorticoids. (Sapolsky, 1986; Sapolsky et al., 1986; Nair et al., 1998)

    1.   2.

    b. What kind of events can further weaken and destroy these neurons?

    c. What behavioral changes may then develop in old age? Cite research to support your answer. (Lupien et al., 1996)

11. a. Briefly describe the social structure of vervet monkey colonies.

    b. What changes were documented in the brains of monkeys who were subjected to constant stress and died? (See Figure 18.8 in your text. Uno et al., 1989)

    c. Cite evidence that stress induced brain degeneration occurs in humans as well. (Jensen et al., 1982)

12. a. State two effects of maternal prenatal stress on offspring. (Takahashi et al., 1992)

    b. How does long-term stress affect these forms of learning?

      1. the establishment of long-term potentiation in hippocampal slices (Foy et al., 1987)

      2. a spatial working memory task (See Figure 18.9 in your text. Mizoguchi et al., 2000)

13. Describe evidence that suggests that the effects of prenatal stress are mediated by the secretion of glucocorticoids. (See Figure 18.10 in your text. Barbazanges et al., 1996).

Learning Objective 18-5 Discuss some of the long term effects of stress: posttraumatic stress disorder, cardiovascular disease, and the coping response.

Read pages 573-576 and answer the following questions.

1. a. Describe *posttraumatic stress disorder* in your own words.

    b. Describe some of the symptoms.

    c. When may these symptoms occur?

2. What four factors increase the likelihood that a soldier subjected to combat stress will develop posttraumatic stress disorder? (Kulka et al., 1990)

3. What do MRI studies reveal about the effects of posttraumatic stress disorder on the hippocampus of combat veterans (Bremner et al., 1995; Gurvits et al., 1996)? adults who experienced severe childhood abuse (Bremner, 1999)?

4. a. What kind of pictures did researchers show veterans with and without posttraumatic stress disorder? (Shin et al., 1997)

    b. What brain regions became active in veterans with posttraumatic stress disorder, as recorded by PET scanners, when the researchers read sentences about the pictures and asked the subjects to imagine them?

5. Summarize the results of similar research with women with posttraumatic stress disorder caused by childhood sexual abuse. (Shin et al., 1999)

6. a. What event occurs when the blood vessels to the heart become blocked? when the blood vessels to the brain become blocked?

    b. List the two most important risk factors for cardiovascular disease.

        1.   2.

7. Review research to assess the relationship between cardiovascular disease and individual differences in stress reactions.

    a. Describe the cold pressor test.

    b. What were the results of a comparison of the subjects' reaction to this test as children and the incidence of high blood pressure later in life? (Wood et al., 1984)

    c. Which monkeys who had been subjected to a stressful situation later showed the highest rates of coronary artery disease? (Manuk et al., 1983, 1986)

    d. How was the blood pressure of normal rats affected by hypothalamic tissue transplants from hypertensive rats and from normal rats? (See Figure 18.11 in your text. Eilam et al., 1991)

    e. What may be one of the effects of these genetic differences? (Krukoff et al., 1999)

8. Explain how acute stress affects cardiovascular disease and mortality. (Rozanski et al., 1999; Leor et al., 1996)

9. Identify the individual differences that may determine the severity of a stressful situation.

10. What is one of the most important variables that determines whether an aversive stimulus will cause a stress reaction?

11. Compare the responses of rats and humans who are both permitted some degree of control in stressful situations. (Weiss, 1968; Gatchel et al., 1989; Shors et al., 1989)

12. a. What substance may play a role in coping responses? (Drugan et al., 1994)

    b. Study Figure 18.12 in your text and compare the levels of endogenous benzodiazepines in the brains of the "coping" group and home cage group of rats who were exposed to stress.

Learning Objective 18-6 Discuss psychoneuroimmunology and the interactions between the immune system and stress.

Read pages 576-580 and answer the following questions.

1. Define *psychoneuroimmunology* in your own words.

2. a. Let's construct an overview of the functions of the immune system. The white blood cells of the immune

    system develop in the _____ _____ and the _____ _____.

    Some of these cells circulate in the _____ or _____ _____ and others

    reside permanently in one _____.

    b. What triggers an immune reaction? What are the two types of reactions?

    c. Describe a nonspecific inflammatory reaction resulting from tissue damage.

    d. Describe a nonspecific reaction resulting from tissue infection from a virus. Be sure to mention *interferon* in your answer.

    e. Explain the role and importance of natural killer cells.

    f. Briefly describe a specific immune reaction—the chemically mediated reaction—by explaining the relationship between

        1. antigens and antibodies.

        2. B-lymphocytes and immunoglobulins.

3. immunoglobulins and antigens. (Study Figure 18.13a in your text.)

g. Briefly describe a second specific immune reaction—the cell-mediated reaction. Be sure to mention T-lymphocytes in your answer. (See Figure 18.13b.)

h. Explain the role of cytokines in both of these immune reactions.

i. Finally, how may glucocorticoids suppress this immune response? (Sapolsky, 1992)

3. What is the most important mechanism by which stress impairs the immune system?

4. a. State the general conclusion of research on stress and the immune system based on studies of the caregivers of family members with Alzheimer's disease (Kiecolt-Glaser et al., 1987; Vedhara et al., 1999), of husbands who lost their wives to breast cancer (See Figure 18.14 in your text. Schleifer et al., 1983), and of healthy subjects imagining past unpleasant situations (Knapp et al., 1992).

b. Keller et al. (1983) found decreased lymphocytes in rats who had experienced the stress of inescapable shock. How did they determine the cause? (See Figure 18.15a in your text.)

c. What type of immune response is not affected by adrenalectomy? (See Figure 18.15b.)

5. What role does the central nucleus seem to play in immunosuppression? (Sharp et al., 1991; Imaki et al., 1992)

6. Contrast the effects on the immune system of acute stress and chronic stress. (Dhabar and McEwen, 1997; Dhabar et al., 1995, 1996)

7. What other parts of the body may play a role in stress-induced immunosuppression not involving glucocorticoids?

8. a. List two effects of inescapable intermittent shock.

   1.   2.

   b. Which brain chemicals appear to mediate these effects and how can they be abolished in the laboratory? (Shavit et al., 1984)

c. How can natural killer cell activity also be suppressed? (Shavit et al, 1986)

9. What stress related responses sometimes occur to

a. a surviving spouse?

b. medical students during final examinations? (Glaser et al., 1987)

c. patients with rheumatoid arthritis? (Feigenbaum et al., 1979)

d. rats who are handled or exposed to a cat? (Rogers et al., 1980)

e. rats predisposed to diabetes and subjected to moderate chronic stress? (Lehman et al., 1991)

10. a. Explain the hypothesis of research on stress and upper respiratory illness. (Stone et al., 1987)

b. Summarize the results of records kept by volunteers who developed upper respiratory illness which are shown in Figure 18.16 in your text.

c. How did the researchers account for the effect? Be sure to refer to IgA in your answer.

d. Briefly describe research by Cohen et al. (1991) that confirmed this study. (See Figure 18.17 in your text.)

Lesson II Self Test

1. Select the correct statement about stress.

   a. Short-term exposure to stressors typically causes conditions such as ulcers.
   b. The fight-or-flight response is a maladaptive reaction to stressors.
   c. Emotional responses are generally useful and adaptive, but can be hazardous if continuous rather than episodic.
   d. The deleterious effects of stress on health generally have been over-emphasized; scientific research does not support this link.

2. Which of the following is not a stress-related hormone released by the adrenal glands?

   a. epinephrine
   b. cortisol
   c. ACTH
   d. norepinephrine

3. The secretion of glucocorticoids is controlled by neurons in the _____ and glucocorticoid receptors are _____.

   a. paraventricular nucleus of the hypothalamus; contained in almost every cell of the body.
   b. central nucleus of the amygdala; found in highest concentration in the adrenal glands.
   c. hippocampal formation; especially susceptible to the effects of stress.

d. hypothalamus; the first to signal a rise in blood pressure.

4. Long-term stress increases the secretion of _____ which may be responsible for _____.

   a. aldosterone; cardiovascular disease
   b. epinephrine; learning and memory deficits
   c. glucocorticoids; the harmful effects of stress
   d. antigens; autoimmune diseases

5. Young vervet monkeys near the bottom of the social hierarchy who experienced almost constant stress

   a. failed to learn normal group coping responses.
   b. engaged in more fight-or-flight responses than other young monkeys who were not subjected to stress.
   c. later showed the highest rates of coronary artery disease.
   d. sustained severe damage to the hippocampal formation.

6. Posttraumatic stress disorder

   a. is a delayed reaction that only develops months or years after the traumatic event.
   b. is sometimes associated with damage to the hippocampal formation.
   c. susceptibility does not appear to be influenced by genetic factors.
   d. occurs more often in persons from secure backgrounds with little previous experience with stress and coping responses.

7. Which of the following is not a risk factor for cardiovascular disease?

   a. high blood pressure and high cholesterol
   b. exposure to the cold pressor test
   c. genetic differences in brain chemistry
   d. high emotional reactivity

8. Why did the emotional response of a group of rats to inescapable shock disappear after they learned a coping response?

   a. The pain was diminished.
   b. The number of shocks was reduced.
   c. Their stomach ulcers healed.
   d. They were permitted some control over the situation.

9. The neural mechanisms responsible for coping responses may involve the secretion of

   a. endogenous opioids.
   b. glucocorticoids.
   c. endogenous benzodiazepines.
   d. GABA.

10. The immune system develops _____ through exposure to _____.

    a. antibodies; antigens
    b. interferon; antibodies
    c. antigens; antibodies
    d. antibodies; B-lymphocytes

11. Cytokines

    a. are the body's first defense against malignant tumors.
    b. stimulate cell division.
    c. develop in the bone marrow.
    d. are unique proteins on the surface of infectious microorganisms

12. Which of the following is true of the immunoglobulin, IgA?

    a. High levels of IgA are associated with an unhappy mood in the subject.
    b. IgA blood levels are elevated in people with autoimmune diseases.
    c. IgA is secreted in the nose, mouth, throat, and lungs, and acts as a defense against infection.
    d. Stress stimulates the production of IgA.

Answers for Self Tests

Lesson I

1.	d	Obj. 18-1
2.	c	Obj. 18-1
3.	b	Obj. 18-1
4.	a	Obj. 18-1
5.	c	Obj. 18-2
6.	b	Obj. 18-2

7.	d	Obj. 18-2
8.	d	Obj. 18-2
9.	c	Obj. 18-3
10.	b	Obj. 18-3
11.	b	Obj. 18-3
12.	a	Obj. 18-3

Lesson II

1. c Obj. 18-4
2. c Obj. 18-4
3. a Obj. 18-4
4. c Obj. 18-4
5. d Obj. 18-4
6. b Obj. 18-5

7. b Obj. 18-5
8. d Obj. 18-5
9. c Obj. 18-5
10. a Obj. 18-6
11. b Obj. 18-6
12. c Obj. 18-6

CHAPTER 19
Drug Abuse

Lesson I: Common Features of Addiction

Read the interim summary on page 590 in your text to re-acquaint yourself with the material in this section.

Learning Objective 19-1   Examine the role of physical and psychological factors in drug addiction.

Read pages 583-584 and answer the following questions.

1. Describe some of the adverse effects of the following addictive substances:

   a. alcohol

   b. smoking

   c. cocaine

   d. designer drugs

2. Briefly review the history of addictive drugs.

3. How do Eddy et al. (1965) define the following terms?

   a. physical dependence

   b. psychic dependence

4. Once again, define

   a. tolerance.

   b. withdrawal symptoms.

5. Carefully explain how the body's compensatory mechanisms to re-establish homeostasis may account for both tolerance and the accompanying withdrawal symptoms.

6. a. Explain why withdrawal symptoms are not the reason why someone becomes a drug addict or remains addicted.

    b   What is the reason people take drugs?

    c. Why did many experts at first neglect the addictive properties of cocaine? Which is more addictive: cocaine or heroin?

    d. Explain why we must consider both physiological or psychological factors if we are to understand addiction.

Learning Objective 19-2 Describe two common features of addiction: positive and negative reinforcement.

Read pages 584-587 and answer the following questions.

1. Drugs that lead to dependency must first reinforce _____ _____.

2. a. If, in a particular situation, the behavior of an animal or a person is regularly followed by an appetitive stimulus, how is their behavior subsequently affected?

    b. How are appetitive stimuli thought to affect the brain?

    c. When is the effectiveness of reinforcing stimuli the greatest?

3. To better understand drug addiction, let's look more closely at the role of immediate reinforcement.

    a. Why did hungry rats prefer the corridor in the maze that delivered less food to the corridor that delivered more food? (Logan, 1965)

    b. How do these results explain why some drugs are more addictive than others?

    c. Explain why someone willingly takes an addictive drug with powerful, long-term, aversive effects.

    d. Why are nonhuman animals unlikely to become addicted to drugs administered in the form of a pill?

4. Once again, what physiological effect is common to all natural reinforcers? (White, 1996)

5. List two ways in which drugs can trigger the release of dopamine.

    1.   2.

6. What other chemical may be involved in reinforcement?

7. a. Define *negative reinforcement* in your own words.

b. How does it differ from punishment?

8. Indicate whether the situations is an example of negative reinforcement or punishment by writing NR or P in the space.

   a _____After burning her hand on the hot exhaust manifold, Haley avoided touching it when she checked the oil level in her car's engine.

   b. _____In order to avoid getting trapped in conversation with another resident in his apartment complex nearly every time he comes in, Marco has decided to park behind the building and use the back entrance.

9. Carefully explain how an addictive drug provides both positive and negative reinforcement.

Learning Objective 19-3 Describe the neural mechanisms responsible for tolerance and withdrawal and craving and relapse.

Read pages 587-590 and answer the following questions.

1. Explain how long-term drug use affects opiate receptors. (Trujillo and Akil, 1991; Zukin et al., 1993)

2. a. Martin et al. (1999) electrically stimulated slices of rats brains that included the nucleus accumbens. Compare the size of the EPSPs of normal tissue and tissue that had been chronically treated with morphine.

   b. What is the presumed explanation for the results?

3. Compare the amount of dopamine release in subjects who were cocaine abusers and had been given a drug that blocks dopamine reuptake with that of control subjects. (Volkow et al., 1997; Volkow et al., 1999)

4. When Robinson and Kolb (1999) examined the brains of morphine dependent rats, what kind of structural changes did they observe?

5. Explain how a compensatory reaction to an injection of a chemical such as insulin can be classically conditioned. (See Figure 19.1 in your text.)

   a. When the rat is first injected with insulin, what is the

      1. neutral stimulus?

      2. unconditioned stimulus (US)?

      3. unconditioned response (UR)?

   b. If the rat is now injected with a placebo, what happens to the blood sugar level?

6. Discuss why a heroin addict experiences withdrawal symptoms when stimuli associated with drug use are encountered by referring to the effects of classical conditioning. (See Figure 19.2 in your text.)

7. a. Rats were given daily injections of heroin in the same cage until tolerance was established. Some of the rats were then given a large dose of heroin in the familiar chamber and others were given the same dose in an unfamiliar chamber. What happened to each group? (Siegel et al., 1982

    b. Explain why some of the rats died and what the implications of this research are for human subjects. Be sure to mention the importance of the environment.

8. Review explanations for craving from

    a. Robinson and Berridge (1993).

    b. Hyman (1996b).

9. People with and without a history of drug abuse were shown neutral stimuli and stimuli associated with drug use. Describe the neural changes, as recorded by PET scans, that occurred when both groups of subjects saw the drug-related stimuli. (Grant et al., 1996)

10. How does long-term cocaine abuse appear to affect brain regions implicated in reinforcement? (Levesque et al., 1992)

11. Only squirrel monkey with a long history of intravenous self-administration would press a lever for an injection of a direct agonist of D_3 dopamine receptors. Why? (Nader and Mach, 1996)

12. Study Figure 19.3 in your text and describe the changes that Staley and Mash (1996) found in the brains of people who had died of cocaine overdoses.

13. Explain how BP897, the recently discovered drug with promise in treating cocaine addiction, affects D_3 receptors. (Pilla et al., 1999)

14. Discuss research on stimuli that trigger drug-seeking behavior.

    a. What change in the brain may produce the priming effect of a small amount of a drug? (Self et al., 1996)

    b. Why do stressful situations often provoke a return to drug use among former drug users?

    c. Explain how researchers eliminated the priming effect of stress in cocaine addicted rats. (Erb et al., 1998)

Lesson I Self Test

1. Which statement about drug addiction is *incorrect?*

   a. Psychic dependence may be just as important as physical dependence is maintaining drug addiction.
   b. Withdrawal symptoms and tolerance are the result of compensatory mechanisms.
   c. All addictive drugs produce physical dependency.
   d. Withdrawal symptoms are primarily the opposite of the effects of the drug itself.

2. Drug tolerance is the _____ that comes from its continued use.

   a. ability to delay a drug dose
   b. decreased sensitivity to a drug
   c. ability to accept the unpleasant side effects when a drug dose is not available
   d. increased sensitivity to a drug after a period of abstinence

3. Compensatory mechanisms

   a. that mimic the effects of a drug begin when a user tries to withdraw from drug use.
   b. do not occur if the drug does not produce physical addiction.
   c. cease once drug use ceases.
   d. explain why a user must take increasing amounts of a drug to achieve the same effect.

4. Appetitive stimuli that activate reinforcement mechanisms in the brain

   a. increase the likelihood that the most recent response will be repeated.
   b. work better for humans than for laboratory animals.
   c. are less effective than negative stimuli that activate reinforcement mechanisms in the brain.
   d. diminish in strength over time.

5. When rats were given the choice between a small amount of food delivered immediately and a larger amount of food delivered after a delay,

   a. they eventually learned to wait for the larger amount of food.
   b. they showed signs of stress from the approach-avoidance conflict.
   c. they preferred the immediate reward to the greater reward.

   d. they chose the small amount of food when they were sated and the larger amount of food when they were hungry.

6. Addictive drugs can trigger the release of dopamine in the nucleus accumbens by

   a. stimulating the reuptake of dopamine by terminal buttons.
   b. blocking the secretion of endogenous opioids.
   c. increasing the activity of dopaminergic neurons of the mesolimbic system.
   d. inhibiting the postsynaptic effects of dopamine.

7. Dopamine release in the nucleus accumbens

   a. can be triggered by both reinforcing and aversive stimuli.
   b. is necessary and sufficient for addiction to occur.
   c. occurs only if a drug produces immediate reinforcement.
   d. can increase the addictive effects of many drugs.

8. Drug users can make unpleasant feelings disappear by taking a drug. The drug-taking behavior is an example of

   a. positive reinforcement.
   b. negative reinforcement.
   c. punishment.
   d. psychological dependence.

9. All of the following are compensatory mechanisms that have been proposed to explain the phenomena of tolerance to and withdrawal from drugs *except*

   a. downregulation of opiate receptors.
   b. reduced effects of opioid receptors on physiological processes within cells on which they are found.
   c. classical conditioning of homeostatic response to environmental stimuli.
   d. dopamine receptors in the nucleus accumbens becoming supersensitive.

10. The brains of people who died of cocaine overdoses had _____ dopamine D_2 receptors.

    a. an increased density of
    b. atrophied dendritic branching on
    c. abnormalities in the ion channels of

d. a decreased density of

11. When long-term drug users were shown drug-related stimuli, which brain regions became active?

a. dorsolateral prefrontal cortex, amygdala, and cerebellum
b. amygdala and periaqueductal gray matter
c. cerebellum, nucleus accumbens, and reticular formation

d. nucleus accumbens, preoptic area, and hippocampus

12. Which event will probably *not* induce drug-seeking behavior?

a. the priming effect of a small dose
b. stressful situations
c. fatigue
d. the sight of drug-related paraphernalia

Lesson II: Commonly Abused Drugs, Heredity and Drug Abuse, and Therapy for Drug Abuse

Read the interim summary on pages 602-603 in your text to re-acquaint yourself with the material in this section.

Learning Objective 19-4 Review the neural basis of the reinforcing effects and withdrawal effects of opiates.

Read pages 590-594 and answer the following questions.

1. Briefly discuss some of the serious personal and social costs of opiate addiction.

2. To review: Why are endogenous opioids important for the survival of species?

3. When opiate receptors are stimulated by an injection of an opiate, they produce different effects in the body. List four locations of opiate receptors and the effects they are responsible for.

   1.   3.

   2.   4.

4. a. List the three major types of opiate receptors and the effects they produce when stimulated.

   1.

   2.

   3.

   b. How did animals without mu opiate receptors respond to morphine? (Study Figure 19.4 in your text. Matthes et al., 1996)

   c. How do kappa receptor agonists affect the nucleus accumbens? (Devine et al., 1993)

   d. What other condition produces the same response?

5. a. What is the general behavioral effect of injections of opiates into both ends of the mesolimbic dopaminergic system? (Wise et al., 1995; Devine and Wise, 1994; Goeders et al., 1984)

    b. Why may this effect occur? (Johnson and North, 1992)

6. How did destruction of dopaminergic axons and terminals in the nucleus accumbens affect lever pressing by rats for intravenous cocaine? intravenous heroin? (Gerrits and Vanree, 1996)

7. a. Draw or describe the apparatus shown in Figure 19.5 in your text. Go on to explain how it is used in a conditioned place preference task.

    b. What testing procedures will cause an animal to develop a conditioned place preference? a conditioned place aversion?

    c. How did destruction of the nucleus accumbens affect the development of a conditioned place preference to amphetamine? to morphine? (Olmstead and Franklin, 1996)

    d. What do these results suggest about the way opiates and amphetamine reinforce behavior?

8. a. Using the conditioned place preference procedure, what did Agmo et al., (1993) find about the physiology of reinforcement produced by natural reinforcers?

    b. What evidence suggests that endogenous opioids may also play a role in the reinforcing effects of addictive drugs?

9. List three regions of the brain which may be involved in the withdrawal effects of opiates and a function of each.

    1.

    2.

    3.

10. a. Define *antagonist-precipitated withdrawal* in your own words.

    b. Summarize results from research using this and a similar technique to study brain locations involved in withdrawal symptoms.
        1. (Maldonado et al., 1992)

        2. (Bozarth, 1994)

11. a. Let's look more closely at the role of the neurons in the locus coeruleus. How is the firing rate of these neurons affected by

    1. a single dose of an opiate?

    2. chronically administered opiate?

    3. administration of an opiate antagonist after addiction has been established? What chemical is released? (Hyman, 1996b; Koob, 1996; Hestler, 1996)

    b. How do lesions of the locus coeruleus affect the severity of withdrawal symptoms? (Maldonado and Koob, 1993)

    c. How does withdrawal affect the level of excitatory neurotransmitters in the locus coeruleus? (Aghajanian et al., 1994)

12 a. Explain why drug tolerance must be the result of intracellular change. Be sure to refer to downregulation in your answer. (Hyman, 1996a)

    b. Identify the protein that appears to be involved in this process and explain its probable role. (Study Figure 19.6 in your text. Maldonado et al., 1996)

    c. Which neuropeptide may also be involved in withdrawal?

Learning Objective 19-5 Describe the behavioral and physical effects of cocaine, amphetamine, and nicotine.

Read pages 594-598 and answer the following questions.

1. Complete these sentences.

    a. Cocaine and amphetamine have similar behavioral effects because

    b. Cocaine binds with

    c. In addition to inhibiting the re-uptake of dopamine, amphetamine directly stimulates

    d. Of all available drugs, probably the most effective reinforcer is

2. a. How do people and laboratory animals behave after they have taken cocaine? (Geary, 1987)

    b. If rats are given continuous access to self-administered cocaine, what often happens? (Study Figure 19.7 in your text. Bozarth and Wise, 1985)

3. Describe the psychotic behavior that usually results from the regular abuse of cocaine and amphetamine.

4. Let's examine some of the physical and behavioral effects of the use of cocaine and amphetamine.

    a. Almost three years after drug abuse ceased, what change was observed in the caudate nucleus and putamen of users? (Study Figure 19.8 in your text. McCann et al., 1998)

b. What possible long-term health risk do these people face?

c. How do injections of both drugs affect the nucleus accumbens? (Study Figure 19.9 in your text. Petit and Justice, 1989; Di Ciano et al, 1995; Wise et al., 1995)

d. How are the reinforcing effects of cocaine and amphetamine altered if

   1. drugs that block dopamine receptors are injected into the nucleus accumbens? (McGregor and Roberts, 1993; Caine et al., 1995)

   2. lesions are produced in the nucleus accumbens or dopaminergic terminals are destroyed?

   3. 6-HD is injected into the nucleus accumbens? (Study Figure 19.10 in your text. Caine and Koob, 1994)

5. Summarize how groups of neurons in the nucleus accumbens respond in anticipation of, in the reinforcing effects of, and in the craving for cocaine. (Koob et al., 1998)

6. a. What are some of the behavioral effects of withdrawal from long-term use of cocaine?

   b. Carefully explain how withdrawal also affects the interaction between dopamine, dynorphin, and kappa receptors in the nucleus accumbens. (Rossetti et al., 1992; Engber et al., 1992; Xu et al., 1994; Steiner and Gerfen, 1995)

   c. How may long-term use of cocaine or amphetamine affect dynorphin-secreting neurons in the nucleus accumbens? (See Figure 19.11 in your text. Hyman, 1996a)

7. Summarize some of the health risks and explain the addictive potential of nicotine. (Stolerman and Jarvis, 1995)

8. How does nicotine affect

   a. acetylcholine receptors?

   b. dopaminergic neurons of the mesolimbic system? (Mereu et al., 1987)

   c. the nucleus accumbens? (Study Figure 19.12 in your text. Damsma et al., 1989)

9. a. Where do the reinforcing effects of nicotine appear to occur? Cite research to support your answer. (For example, study Figure 19.13 in your text. Nisell et al., 1994)

   b. What additional site plays a role in the reinforcing effects of tobacco smoke? Cite evidence. (Rose et al., 1998)

10. What are some of the symptoms of nicotine withdrawal? Explain why they contribute to a resumption of smoking, but not to beginning to smoke. (Hughes et al., 1989; Fung et al., 1996)

11. Why may smoking and drinking alcohol make it more difficult to withdraw from cocaine or heroin use? Be sure to refer to the role of dopamine in reinforcement in your answer. (Reid et al., 1999)

Learning Objective 19-6 Describe the behavioral and physical effects of alcohol, barbiturates, and cannabis.

Read pages 598-602 and answer the following questions.

1. To establish the importance of understanding the behavioral and physiological effects of this drug, summarize some of the social costs of alcohol use, especially its effect on brain development. (Be sure to look at Figure 19.14 in your text. Abel and Sokol, 1986)

2. Define *anxiolytic* in your own words.

3. Explain how the anxiolytic effects of alcohol

   a. influence the behavior of both laboratory animals and people? (Koob et al., 1984)

   b. produce negative reinforcement.

4. Explain why the negative reinforcement provided by alcohol alone does not explain its addictive potential.

5. Explain how sweetening with saccharine and the reinforcing effects of alcohol combine to induce dependency in laboratory animals? (Reid, 1996)

6. a. How does alcohol affect the mesolimbic system? the nucleus accumbens? (Gessa et al., 1985; Imperato and Di Chiara, 1986)

   b. How can alcohol intake be decreased? (Samson et al., 1993; Hodge et al., 1993)

7. List the sites of action of alcohol in low to moderate doses.

   1.   2.

8. a. Describe the drug discrimination procedure.

   b. Using this procedure, what did Shelton and Balster (1994) conclude about the similarity of the perceptual effects of alcohol with other classes of other drugs?

9. a. Compare the effects of alcohol with those of other NMDA antagonists. (Tabakoff and Hoffman, 1996; Imperato et al., 1990; Loscher et al., 1991)

    b. How may alcohol affect NMDA receptors to affect cognitive function? (Givens and McMahon et al., 1995; Matthews et al., 1996)

10. a. Carefully explain what happens to NMDA receptors when an alcoholic suddenly stops drinking.

    b. How is this medical emergency treated? Why?

11. a. Two strains of mice have been used to study sudden alcohol withdrawal. How did the brains of withdrawal-seizure prone mice differ from those of resistant mice? (Valverius et al., 1990)

    b. What treatment prevented seizures, and what does its effectiveness suggest about the role of NMDA receptors in producing seizures? (Liljequist, 1991)

12. a. When alcohol binds with the $GABA_A$ receptor, how is the function of the receptor altered? (Proctor et al., 1992)

    b. What behavioral effects of alcohol appear to result from this interaction?

    c. How can the sedative effects of alcohol be blocked? What would be the tragic consequences of the use of this drug? (See Figure 19.15 in your text. Suzdak et al., 1986)

13. The effects of alcohol and barbiturates are _____ and the combined use of both drugs can be _____. Why?

14. a. Name the active ingredient in marijuana and describe where and how it affects dopamine levels. (See Figure 19.16 in your text. Chen et al., 1990; Chen et al., 1993)

    b. How may the drug produce memory deficits?

15. List some of the damaging effects of long-term marijuana use. (See Figure 19.17 in your text. Fletcher et al., 1996; Hall and Solowij, 1998)

Read the interim summary on page 606 in your text to re-acquaint yourself with the material in this section.

Learning Objective 19-7 Describe research on the role that heredity plays in addiction.

Read pages 603-606 and answer the following questions.

1. _____ and _____ are the only two possible sources of individual differences in any characteristic.

2. Explain why most research on the effects of hereditary on addiction has focused on alcoholism.

3. Briefly describe some personal characteristics linked to nicotine addiction. (Gilbert and Gilbert, 1995; Heath et al., 1995)

4. Summarize the findings of research on twins (True et al., 1999) and siblings (Bierut et al., 1998) to determine the influence of genetics on alcohol and nicotine addiction.

5. a. Why are adoption studies particularly useful in the study of the role of heredity in susceptibility to alcoholism?

   b. Circle the factor—heredity or environment—which is much more important in the development of alcoholism. (Cloninger et al., 1981; 1985; Sigvardsson et al., 1996)

6. Describe the two principal types of alcoholics—binge drinkers and steady drinkers. (See Table 19.1 in your text. Cloninger, 1987)

7. Steady drinking is strongly influenced by _____, and binge drinking is influenced by both _____ and _____.

8. How did having a steady drinking biological father affect the sons? the daughters? Be sure to use the term *somatization disorder* in your answer.

9. a. Briefly describe some of the personality characteristics and social behavior of steady and binge drinkers. (Cloninger, 1987)

   b. Describe the EEGs of binge drinkers. (Propping et al., 1981)

   c. How do binge drinkers report they feel after taking alcohol? (Propping et al., 1980)

10. Explain how particular punishment or reinforcement systems may contribute to both forms of alcoholism. (Heath et al., 1999)

11. Describe the discrepancy in recent research on differences in dopaminergic mechanisms and susceptibility to addiction. (Blum et al., 1990; Endenberg et al., 1998)

12. a. Describe how the use of animal models has contributed to the understanding of alcohol addiction by comparing the behavior of alcohol-preferring rats and alcohol-nonpreferring rats when given

    1. the choice of drinking or not drinking alcohol. (Li et al., 1993. See Figure 19.18 in your text.)

    2. small doses and high doses of alcohol. (Gongwer et al., 1989; McBride et al., 1991)

  b. What are some possible explanations for these behaviors? (Li et al., 1993; Stewart et al., 1994)

13. What physical differences have been documented in the brains of alcohol-preferring rats? (Murphy et al., 1987; Zhou et al., 1995; McBride et al., 1995)

14. What evidence suggests a link between opioid mechanisms and alcohol preference? (Li et al., 1998; Myers and Robinson, 1999)

15. What hereditary factor may contribute to alcoholic intake by rhesus monkeys? environmental factor? (Higley et al., 1996)

Read the interim summary on page 609 in your text to re-acquaint yourself with the material in this section.

> *Learning Objective 19-8* Discuss different methods of therapy for drug abuse.

Read pages 606-609 and answer the following questions.

1. Describe the most common treatment for opiate addiction.

2. a. Emergency rooms treat patients who have taken an overdose of heroin with drugs that act as

    _____ _____ _____.

  b. Why are drugs that either block or stimulate dopamine receptors not used to treat addiction?

  c. Which drugs may someday be useful in treating cocaine dependency?

3. Describe how Carrera et al. (1996) managed to "immunize" rats to cocaine.

4. a. Now describe how Dewey et al., (1997) reduced the reinforcing effects of cocaine in baboons. Be sure to mention GVG in your answer.

   b. What other addictive drug is affected by GVG? (Dewey et al., 1999)

5. Describe nicotine maintenance as a treatment for withdrawal from cigarette smoking. (See Figure 19.19 in your text.)

6. How do serotonin agonists help treat addiction to alcohol? (Naranjo et al., 1992)

7. College students who participated in research on social drinking took either naltrexone or a placebo. How did these drugs affect their behavior when they were given alcoholic beverages during test sessions? (Davidson et al., 1996)

8. Describe the effectiveness of programs using naltrexone to treat alcohol abuse. (See Figure 19.20 in your text. O'Brien et al., 1996)

9. What other drug appears to be a promising treatment for alcoholism? What may be its site of action? (Wickelgren, 1998)

Lesson II Self Test

1. Opiate receptors in the _____ play a role in the reinforcing effects of opiates.

   a. periaqueductal gray matter and locus coeruleus
   b. ventral tegmental area and the nucleus accumbens
   c. preoptic area.
   d. reticular formation

2. The reinforcing effects of opiates

   a. involve the μ opiate receptor.
   b. involve the κ opiate receptor.
   c. are abolished by lesions of the nucleus accumbens.
   d. prevent the occurrence of a conditioned place preference.

3. Which substance is involved in the development of withdrawal symptoms?

   a. CREB
   b. substance P
   c. enkephalin
   d. κ receptor antagonists

4. Cocaine _____ and amphetamine _____.

   a. stimulates the reuptake of dopamine; inhibits the reuptake of dopamine
   b. stimulates dopamine synthesis; does too, but for a shorter duration.
   c. stimulates the release of dopamine before synaptic vesicles reach the presynaptic membrane; blocks the postsynaptic membrane

d. deactivates dopamine transporter molecules; stimulates dopamine release at terminal buttons.

5. Withdrawal from long-term cocaine use

   a. is more difficult than withdrawal from alcohol.
   b. is facilitated by drugs that decrease the production of dynorphin.
   c. produces a drastic reduction in the level of dopamine in the nucleus accumbens.
   d. is facilitated if the user also smokes cigarettes.

6. The reinforcing effects of nicotine appear to occur in the

   a. locus coeruleus.
   b. striate nucleus.
   c. ventral tegmental area.
   d. periaqueductal gray matter.

7. The anxiolytic effect of alcohol

   a. reduces the discomfort of anxiety.
   b. forces the drinker to consume more and more to feel the same effects.
   c. reinforces social controls on behavior.
   d. provides positive reinforcement.

8. If an animal is given electric shocks whenever it make a particular response, it will stop doing so. If it is then given alcohol, it will

   a. avoid making that response.
   b. begin making the response again.
   c. show signs of extinction.
   d. exhibit a conditioned place preference.

9. Marijuana may affect short-term memory by disrupting the normal function of the

   a. acetylcholine receptors.
   b. GABA receptors.
   c. the nucleus accumbens.
   d. the hippocampus.

10. Steady drinkers are most likely to

    a. be male; have a biological parent who is a steady drinker; begin drinking late in life.
    b. be male; have a father who is a steady drinker; begin drinking early in life.
    c. be female; have two biological parents who are alcoholic; drink secretly.
    d. be either male or female; be exposed to a family environment of heavy drinking; begin drinking early in life.

11. Monkeys with the lowest levels of _____ had the highest levels of alcohol intake.

    a. dopamine
    b. 5-HIAA
    c. acetylcholine
    d. dynorphin

12. The most common treatment for opiate addiction is

    a. naltrexone treatment.
    b. treatment with drugs that block dopamine receptors.
    c. treatment with serotonin agonists.
    d. methadone maintenance.

Answers for Self Tests

Lesson I			Lesson II		
1.	c	Obj. 19-1	1.	b	Obj. 19-4
2.	b	Obj. 19-1	2.	a	Obj. 19-4
3.	d	Obj. 19-1	3.	a	Obj. 19-4
4.	a	Obj. 19-2	4.	d	Obj. 19-5
5.	c	Obj. 19-2	5.	c	Obj. 19-5
6.	c	Obj. 19-2	6.	c	Obj. 19-5
7.	a	Obj. 19-2	7.	a	Obj. 19-6
8.	b	Obj. 19-2	8.	b	Obj. 19-6
9.	d	Obj. 19-3	9.	d	Obj. 19-6
10.	a	Obj. 19-3	10.	b	Obj. 19-7
11.	a	Obj. 19-3	11.	b	Obj. 19-7
12.	c	Obj. 19-3	12.	d	Obj. 19-8

1.1 dualism	1.10 model
1.2 monism	1.11 doctrine of specific nerve energies
1.3 blindsight	1.12 experimental ablation
1.4 corpus callosum	1.13 functionalism
1.5 split-brain operation	1.14 natural selection
1.6 cerebral hemispheres	1.15 mutation
1.7 generalization	1.16 selective advantage
1.8 reduction	1.17 evolution
1.9 reflex	1.18 neoteny

1.10 A mathematical or physical analogy for a physiological process; for example, computers have been used as models for various functions of the brain.	1.1 The belief that the body is physical but the mind (or soul) is not.
1.11 Müller's conclusion that because all nerve fibers carry the same type of message, sensory information must be specified by the particular nerve fibers that are active.	1.2 The belief that the world consists only of matter and energy and the mind is part of it.
1.12 The research method in which the function of a part of the brain is inferred by observing the behaviors an animal can no longer perform after that part is damaged.	1.3 The ability of a person who cannot see objects in his or her blind field to accurately reach for them while remaining unconscious of perceiving them; caused by damage to the "mammalian" visual system of the brain.
1.13 The principle that the best way to understand a biological phenomenon (a behavior or a physiological structure) is to try to understand its useful functions for the organism.	1.4 The largest commissure of the brain, interconnecting the areas of neocortex on each side of the brain.
1.14 The process by which inherited traits that confer a selective advantage (increase an animal's likelihood to live and reproduce) become more prevalent in a population.	1.5 Brain surgery that is occasionally performed to treat a form of epilepsy; the surgeon cuts the corpus callosum, which connects the two hemispheres of the brain.
1.15 A change in the genetic information contained in the chromosomes of sperms or eggs, which can be passed on to an organism's offspring; provides genetic variability.	1.6 The two symmetrical halves of the brain; constitute the major part of the brain.
1.16 A characteristic of an organism that permits it to produce more than the average number of offspring of its species.	1.7 A type of scientific explanation; a general conclusion based on many observations of similar phenomena.
1.17 A gradual change in the structure and physiology of plant and animal species generally producing more complex organisms as a result of natural selection.	1.8 A type of scientific explanation; a phenomenon is described in terms of the more elementary processes that underlie it.
1.18 A slowing of the process of maturation, allowing more time for growth; an important factor in the development of large brains.	1.9 An automatic, stereotyped movement produced as the direct result of a stimulus.

1.19 physiological psychologist	2.9 axon
2.1 sensory neuron	2.10 multipolar neuron
2.2 motor neuron	2.11 bipolar neuron
2.3 interneuron	2.12 unipolar neuron
2.4 central nervous system (CNS)	2.13 terminal button
2.5 peripheral nervous system (PNS)	2.14 transmitter substance/neurotransmitter
2.6 soma	2.15 membrane
2.7 dendrite	2.16 nucleus
2.8 synapse	2.17 nucleolus (*new* **clee** *o lus*)

2.9 The long, thin, cylindrical structure that conveys information from the soma of a neuron to its terminal buttons.	1.19 A scientist who studies the physiology of behavior, primarily by performing physiological and behavioral experiments with laboratory animals.
2.10 A neuron with one axon and many dendrites attached to its soma.	2.1 A neuron that detects changes in the external or internal environment and sends information about these changes to the central nervous system.
2.11 A neuron with one axon and one dendrite attached to its soma.	2.2 A neuron located within the central nervous system that controls the contraction of a muscle or the secretion of a gland.
2.12 A neuron with one axon attached to its soma; the axon divides, with one branch receiving sensory information and the other sending the information into the central nervous system.	2.3 A neuron located entirely within the central nervous system.
2.13 The bud at the end of a branch of an axon; forms synapses with another neuron; sends information to that neuron.	2.4 The brain and spinal cord.
2.14 A chemical that is released by a terminal button; has an excitatory or inhibitory effect on another neuron.	2.5 That part of the nervous system outside the brain and spinal cord, including the nerves attached to the brain and spinal cord.
2.15 A structure consisting principally of lipid molecules that defines the outer boundaries of a cell and also constitutes many of the cell organelles, such as the Golgi apparatus.	2.6 The cell body of a neuron, which contains the nucleus.
2.16 A structure in the central region of a cell, containing the nucleolus and chromosomes.	2.7 A branched, treelike structure attached to the soma of a neuron; receives information from the terminal buttons of other neurons.
2.17 A structure within the nucleus of a cell that produces the ribosomes.	2.8 A junction between the terminal button of an axon and the membrane of another neuron.

2.18 ribosome (*ry bo soam*)	2.27 endoplasmic reticulum
2.19 chromosome	2.28 Golgi apparatus (**goal** *jee*)
2.20 deoxyribonucleic acid (DNA) (*dee ox ee* **ry** *bo new* **clay** *ik*)	2.29 exocytosis (**ex** *o sy* **toe** *sis*)
2.21 gene	2.30 lysosome (**lye** *so soam*)
2.22 messenger ribonucleic acid (mRNA)	2.31 cytoskeleton
2.23 enzyme	2.32 microtubule (*my kro* **too** *bule*)
2.24 cytoplasm	2.33 axoplasmic transport
2.25 mitochondria	2.34 anterograde
2.26 adenosine triphosphate (ATP) (*uh* **den** *o seen*)	2.35 retrograde

2.27 Parallel layers of membrane found within the cytoplasm of a cell. The rough form contains ribosomes; the smooth form is the site of synthesis of lipids and provides channels for the segregation of molecules involved in various cellular processes.	2.18 A cytoplasmic structure, made of protein, that serves as the site of production of proteins translated from mRNA.
2.28 A complex of parallel membranes in the cytoplasm that wraps the products of a secretory cell.	2.19 A strand of DNA, with associated proteins, found in the nucleus; carries genetic information.
2.29 The secretion of a substance by a cell through means of vesicles; the process by which neurotransmitters are secreted.	2.20 A long, complex macromolecule consisting of two interconnected helical strands; along with associated proteins, strands of DNA constitute the chromosomes.
2.30 An organelle surrounded by membrane; contains enzymes that break down waste products.	2.21 The functional unit of the chromosome, which directs synthesis of one or more proteins.
2.31 Formed of microtubules and other protein fibers, linked to each other and forming a cohesive mass that gives a cell its shape.	2.22 A macromolecule that delivers genetic information concerning the synthesis of a protein from a portion of a chromosome to a ribosome.
2.32 A long strand of bundles of protein filaments arranged around a hollow core; part of the cytoskeleton and involved in transporting substances from place to place within the cell.	2.23 A molecule that controls a chemical reaction, combining two substances or breaking a substance into two parts.
2.33 An active process by which substances are propelled along microtubules that run the length of the axon.	2.24 The viscous, semiliquid substance contained in the interior of a cell.
2.34 In a direction along an axon from the cell body toward the terminal buttons.	2.25 An organelle that is responsible for extracting energy from nutrients.
2.35 In a direction along an axon from the terminal buttons toward the cell body.	2.26 A molecule of prime importance to cellular energy metabolism; its breakdown liberates energy.

2.36 glia (*glee* ah)	2.45 area postrema (*poss* **tree** *ma*)
2.37 astrocyte	2.46 electrode
2.38 phagocytosis (**fagg** *o sy* **toe** *sis*)	2.47 microelectrode
2.39 oligodendrocyte (*oh li go* **den** *droh site*)	2.48 membrane potential
2.40 myelin sheath (*my a lin*)	2.49 oscilloscope
2.41 node of Ranvier (**raw** *vee ay*)	2.50 resting potential
2.42 microglia	2.51 depolarization
2.43 Schwann cell	2.52 hyperpolarization
2.44 blood brain barrier	2.53 action potential

2.45 A region of the medulla where the blood brain barrier is weak; poisons can be detected there and can initiate vomiting.	**2.36** The supporting cells of the central nervous system.
2.46 A conductive medium that can be used to apply electrical stimulation or to record electrical potentials.	**2.37** A glial cell that provides support for neurons of the central nervous system, provides nutrients and other substances, and regulates the chemical composition of the extracellular fluid.
2.47 A very fine electrode, generally used to record activity of individual neurons.	**2.38** The process by which cells engulf and digest other cells or debris caused by cellular degeneration.
2.48 The electrical charge across a cell membrane; the difference in electrical potential inside and outside the cell.	**2.39** A type of glial cell in the central nervous system that forms myelin sheaths.
2.49 A laboratory instrument capable of displaying a graph of voltage as a function of time on the face of a cathode ray tube.	**2.40** A sheath that surrounds axons and insulates them, preventing messages from spreading between adjacent axons.
2.50 The membrane potential of a neuron when it is not being altered by excitatory or inhibitory postsynaptic potentials; approximately 70 mV in the giant squid axon.	**2.41** A naked portion of a myelinated axon, between adjacent oligodendroglia or Schwann cells.
2.51 Reduction (toward zero) of the membrane potential of a cell from its normal resting potential.	**2.42** The smallest of glial cells; act as phagocytes and protect the brain from invading microorganisms.
2.52 An increase in the membrane potential of a cell, relative to the normal resting potential.	**2.43** A cell in the peripheral nervous system that is wrapped around a myelinated axon, providing one segment of its myelin sheath.
2.53 The brief electrical impulse that provides the basis for conduction of information along an axon.	**2.44** A semipermeable barrier between the blood and the brain produced by the cells in the walls of the brain's capillaries.

2.54 threshold of excitation	2.63 voltage-dependent ion channel
2.55 diffusion	2.64 all-or-none law
2.56 electrolyte	2.65 rate law
2.57 ion (cation, anion)	2.66 cable properties
2.58 electrostatic pressure	2.67 saltatory conduction
2.59 intracellular fluid	2.68 postsynaptic potential
2.60 extracellular fluid	2.69 neuromodulator
2.61 sodium-potassium transporter	2.70 endocrine gland
2.62 ion channel	2.71 target cell

2.63 An ion channel that opens or closes according to the value of the membrane potential.	**2.54** The value of the membrane potential that must be reached to produce an action potential.
2.64 The principle that once an action potential is triggered in an axon, it is propagated, without decrement, to the end of the fiber.	**2.55** Movement of molecules from regions of high concentration to regions of low concentration.
2.65 The principle that variations in the intensity of a stimulus or other information being transmitted in an axon are represented by variations in the rate at which that axon fires.	**2.56** An aqueous solution of a material that ionizes namely, a soluble acid, base, or salt.
2.66 The passive conduction of electrical current, in a decremental fashion, down the length of an axon.	**2.57** A charged molecule. *Cations* are positively charged, and *anions* are negatively charged.
2.67 Conduction of action potentials by myelinated axons. The action potential "jumps" from one node of Ranvier to the next.	**2.58** The attractive force between atomic particles charged with opposite signs or the repulsive force between atomic particles charged with the same sign.
2.68 Alterations in the membrane potential of a postsynaptic neuron, produced by liberation of neurotransmitter at the synapse.	**2.59** The fluid contained within cells.
2.69 A naturally secreted substance that acts like a neurotransmitter except that it is not restricted to the synaptic cleft but diffuses through the extracellular fluid.	**2.60** Body fluids located outside of cells.
2.70 A gland that liberates its secretions into the extracellular fluid around capillaries and hence into the bloodstream.	**2.61** A protein found in the membrane of all cells that extrudes sodium ions from and transports potassium ions into the cell.
2.71 The type of cell that is directly affected by a hormone or nerve fiber.	**2.62** A specialized protein molecule that permits specific ions to enter or leave cells.

2.72 binding site	2.81 pinocytosis (*pee no sy* **toh** *sis*)
2.73 ligand (**ligh** *gand* or **ligg** *and*)	2.82 postsynaptic receptor
2.74 dendritic spine	2.83 neurotransmitter-dependent ion channel
2.75 presynaptic membrane	2.84 ionotropic receptor (*eye on oh* **trow** *pik*)
2.76 postsynaptic membrane	2.85 metabotropic receptor (*meh tab oh* **trow** *pik*)
2.77 synaptic cleft	2.86 G protein
2.78 synaptic vesicle (**vess** *i kul*)	2.87 excitatory postsynaptic potential (EPSP)
2.79 release zone	2.88 inhibitory postsynaptic potential (IPSP)
2.80 cisterna	2.89 second messenger

2.81 The pinching off of a bud of cell membrane, which travels to the interior of the cell.	2.72 The location on a receptor protein to which a ligand binds.
2.82 A receptor molecule in the postsynaptic membrane of a synapse that contains a binding site for a neurotransmitter.	2.73 A chemical that binds with the binding site of a receptor.
2.83 An ion channel that opens when a molecule of a neurotransmitter binds with a postsynaptic receptor.	2.74 A small bud on the surface of a dendrite, with which a terminal button from another neuron forms a synapse.
2.84 A receptor that contains a binding site for a neurotransmitter and an ion channel that opens when a molecule of the neurotransmitter attaches to the binding site.	2.75 The membrane of a terminal button that lies adjacent to the postsynaptic membrane.
2.85 A receptor that contains a binding site for a neurotransmitter; activates an enzyme that begins a series of events that opens an ion channel elsewhere in the membrane of the cell when a molecule of the neurotransmitter attaches to the binding site.	2.76 The cell membrane opposite the terminal button in a synapse; the membrane of the cell that receives the message.
2.86 A protein coupled to a metabotropic receptor; conveys messages to other molecules when a ligand binds with and activates the receptor.	2.77 The space between the presynaptic membrane and the postsynaptic membrane.
2.87 An excitatory depolarization of the postsynaptic membrane of a synapse caused by the liberation of a neurotransmitter by the terminal button.	2.78 A small, hollow, beadlike structure found in terminal buttons; contains molecules of a neurotransmitter.
2.88 An inhibitory hyperpolarization of the postsynaptic membrane of a synapse caused by the liberation of a neurotransmitter by the terminal button.	2.79 A region of the interior of the presynaptic membrane of a synapse to which synaptic vesicles attach and release their neurotransmitter into the synaptic cleft.
2.89 A chemical produced when a G protein activates an enzyme; carries a signal that results in the opening of the ion channel or causes other events to occur in the cell.	2.80 A part of the Golgi apparatus; through the process of pinocytosis, it receives portions of the presynaptic membrane and recycles them into synaptic vesicles.

2.90 reuptake	2.99 peptide
2.91 enzymatic deactivation	2.100 steroid
2.92 acetylcholine (ACh) (*a see tul* **koh** *leen*)	3.1 neuraxis
2.93 acetylcholinesterase (AChE) (*a see tul koh lin* **ess** *ter ace*)	3.2 anterior
2.94 neural integration	3.3 posterior
2.95 autoreceptor	3.4 rostral
2.96 presynaptic inhibition	3.5 caudal
2.97 presynaptic facilitation	3.6 dorsal
2.98 gap junction	3.7 ventral

2.99 A chain of amino acids joined together by peptide bonds.	**2.90** The reentry of a neurotransmitter just liberated by a terminal button back through its membrane, thus terminating the postsynaptic potential.
2.100 A chemical of low molecular weight, derived from cholesterol. Steroid hormones affect their target cells by attaching to receptors found within the cell.	**2.91** The destruction of a neurotransmitter by an enzyme after its release for example, the destruction of acetylcholine by acetylcholinesterase.
3.1 An imaginary line drawn through the center of the length of the central nervous system, from the bottom of the spinal cord to the front of the forebrain.	**2.92** A neurotransmitter found in the brain, spinal cord, and parts of the peripheral nervous system; responsible for muscular contraction.
3.2 With respect to the central nervous system, located near or toward the head.	**2.93** The enzyme that destroys acetylcholine soon after it is liberated by the terminal buttons, thus terminating the postsynaptic potential.
3.3 With respect to the central nervous system, located near or toward the tail.	**2.94** The process by which inhibitory and excitatory postsynaptic potentials summate and control the rate of firing of a neuron.
3.4 "Toward the beak"; with respect to the central nervous system, in a direction along the neuraxis toward the front of the face.	**2.95** A receptor molecule located on a neuron that responds to the neurotransmitter released by that neuron.
3.5 "Toward the tail"; with respect to the central nervous system, in a direction along the neuraxis away from the front of the face.	**2.96** The action of a presynaptic terminal button in an axoaxonic synapse; reduces the amount of neurotransmitter released by the postsynaptic terminal button.
3.6 "Toward the back"; with respect to the central nervous system, in a direction perpendicular to the neuraxis toward the top of the head or the back.	**2.97** The action of a presynaptic terminal button in an axoaxonic synapse; increases the amount of neurotransmitter released by the postsynaptic terminal button.
3.7 "Toward the belly"; with respect to the central nervous system, in a direction perpendicular to the neuraxis toward the bottom of the skull or the front surface of the body.	**2.98** A special junction between cells that permits direct communication by means of electrical coupling.

3.8 lateral	3.17 vertebral artery (*ver **tee** brul*)
3.9 medial	3.18 internal carotid artery
3.10 ipsilateral	3.19 meninges (singular: **meninx**) (*men **in** jees*)
3.11 contralateral	3.20 dura mater
3.12 cross section	3.21 arachnoid membrane (*a **rak** noyd*)
3.13 frontal section	3.22 pia mater
3.14 horizontal section	3.23 subarachnoid space
3.15 sagittal section (***sadj** i tul*)	3.24 cerebrospinal fluid (**CSF**)
3.16 midsagittal plane	3.25 ventricle (***ven** trik ul*)

3.17 An artery whose branches serve the posterior region of the brain.	3.8 Toward the side of the body, in a direction at right angles with the neuraxis and away from it.
3.18 An artery whose branches serve the rostral and lateral portions of the brain.	3.9 Toward the neuraxis, away from the side of the body.
3.19 The three layers of tissue that encase the central nervous system: the dura mater, arachnoid membrane, and pia mater.	3.10 Located on the same side of the body.
3.20 The outermost of the meninges; tough, flexible, unstretchable.	3.11 Located on the opposite side of the body.
3.21 The middle layer of the meninges, between the outer dura mater and inner pia mater. The subarachnoid space beneath the arachnoid membrane is filled with cerebrospinal fluid, which cushions the brain.	3.12 With respect to the central nervous system, a slice taken at right angles to the neuraxis.
3.22 The layer of the meninges adjacent to the surface of the brain.	3.13 A slice through the brain parallel to the forehead.
3.23 The fluid-filled space between the arachnoid membrane and the pia mater.	3.14 A slice through the brain parallel to the ground.
3.24 A clear fluid, similar to blood plasma, that fills the ventricular system of the brain and the subarachnoid space surrounding the brain and spinal cord.	3.15 A slice through the brain parallel to the neuraxis and perpendicular to the ground.
3.25 One of the hollow spaces within the brain, filled with cerebrospinal fluid.	3.16 The plane through the neuraxis perpendicular to the ground; divides the brain into two symmetrical halves.

3.26 lateral ventricle	3.35 ventricular zone
3.27 third ventricle	3.36 cerebral cortex
3.28 cerebral aqueduct	3.37 radial glia
3.29 fourth ventricle	3.38 founder cells
3.30 choroid plexus	3.39 symmetrical division
3.31 arachnoid granulation	3.40 asymmetrical division
3.32 superior sagittal sinus	3.41 apoptosis (*ay po* **toe** *sis*)
3.33 obstructive hydrocephalus	3.42 forebrain
3.34 neural tube	3.43 cerebral hemisphere (*sa ree brul*)

3.35 A layer of cells that line the inside of the neural tube; contains founder cells that divide and give rise to cells of the central nervous system.	3.26 One of the two ventricles located in the center of the telencephalon.
3.36 The outermost layer of gray matter of the cerebral hemispheres.	3.27 The ventricle located in the center of the diencephalon.
3.37 Special glia with fibers that grow radially outward from the ventricular zone to the surface of the cortex; provide guidance for neurons migrating outward during brain development.	3.28 A narrow tube interconnecting the third and fourth ventricles of the brain, located in the center of the mesencephalon.
3.38 Cells of the ventricular zone that divide and give rise to cells of the central nervous system.	3.29 The ventricle located between the cerebellum and the dorsal pons, in the center of the metencephalon.
3.39 Division of a founder cell that gives rise to two identical founder cells; increases the size of the ventricular zone and hence the brain that develops from it.	3.30 The highly vascular tissue that protrudes into the ventricles and produces cerebrospinal fluid.
3.40 Division of a founder cell that gives rise to another founder cell and a neuron, which migrates away from the ventricular zone toward its final resting place in the brain.	3.31 Small projections of the arachnoid membrane through the dura mater into the superior sagittal sinus; CSF flows through them to be reabsorbed into the blood supply.
3.41 Death of a cell caused by a chemical signal that activates a genetic mechanism inside the cell.	3.32 A venous sinus located in the midline just dorsal to the corpus callosum, between the two cerebral hemispheres.
3.42 The most rostral of the three major divisions of the brain; includes the telencephalon and diencephalon.	3.33 A condition in which all or some of the brain's ventricles are enlarged; caused by an obstruction that impedes the normal flow of CSF.
3.43 One of the two major portions of the forebrain, covered by the cerebral cortex.	3.34 A hollow tube, closed at the rostral end, that forms from ectodermal tissue early in embryonic development; serves as the origin of the central nervous system.

3.44 subcortical region	3.53 central sulcus (*sul kus*)
3.45 sulcus (plural: sulci) (*sul kus, sul sigh*)	3.54 primary motor cortex
3.46 fissure	3.55 frontal lobe
3.47 gyrus (plural: gyri) (*jye russ, jye rye*)	3.56 parietal lobe (*pa rye i tul*)
3.48 primary visual cortex	3.57 temporal lobe (*tem por ul*)
3.49 calcarine fissure (*kal ka rine*)	3.58 occipital lobe (*ok sip i tul*)
3.50 primary auditory cortex	3.59 sensory association cortex
3.51 lateral fissure	3.60 motor association cortex
3.52 primary somatosensory cortex	3.61 prefrontal cortex

3.53 The sulcus that separates the frontal lobe from the parietal lobe.	3.44 The region located within the brain, beneath the cortical surface.
3.54 The region of the cerebral cortex that contains neurons that control movements of skeletal muscles.	3.45 A groove in the surface of the cerebral hemisphere, smaller than a fissure.
3.55 The anterior portion of the cerebral cortex, rostral to the parietal lobe and dorsal to the temporal lobe.	3.46 A major groove in the surface of the brain, larger than a sulcus.
3.56 The region of the cerebral cortex caudal to the frontal lobe and dorsal to the temporal lobe.	3.47 A convolution of the cortex of the cerebral hemispheres, separated by sulci or fissures.
3.57 The region of the cerebral cortex rostral to the occipital lobe and ventral to the parietal and frontal lobes.	3.48 The region of the cerebral cortex whose primary input is from the visual system.
3.58 The region of the cerebral cortex caudal to the parietal and temporal lobes.	3.49 A fissure located in the occipital lobe on the medial surface of the brain; most of the primary visual cortex is located along its upper and lower banks.
3.59 Those regions of the cerebral cortex that receive information from the regions of primary sensory cortex.	3.50 The region of the cerebral cortex whose primary input is from the auditory system.
3.60 The region of the frontal lobe rostral to the primary motor cortex; also known as the premotor cortex.	3.51 The fissure that separates the temporal lobe from the overlying frontal and parietal lobes.
3.61 The region of the frontal lobe rostral to the motor association cortex.	3.52 The region of the cerebral cortex whose primary input is from the somatosensory system.

3.62 corpus callosum (*ka loh sum*)	3.71 mammillary body (***mam*** *i lair ee*)
3.63 neocortex	3.72 basal ganglia
3.64 limbic cortex	3.73 diencephalon (*dy en **seff** a lahn*)
3.65 cingulate gyrus (***sing*** *yew lett*)	3.74 thalamus
3.66 commissure (***kahm*** *i sher*)	3.75 projection fiber
3.67 limbic system	3.76 nucleus (plural: nuclei)
3.68 hippocampus	3.77 lateral geniculate nucleus
3.69 amygdala (*a **mig** da la*)	3.78 medial geniculate nucleus
3.70 fornix	3.79 ventrolateral nucleus

3.71 A protrusion of the bottom of the brain at the posterior end of the hypothalamus, containing some hypothalamic nuclei.	**3.62** The largest commissure of the brain, interconnecting the areas of neocortex on each side of the brain.
3.72 A group of subcortical nuclei in the telencephalon, the caudate nucleus, the globus pallidus, and the putamen; important parts of the motor system.	**3.63** The phylogenetically newest cortex, including the primary sensory cortex, primary motor cortex, and association cortex.
3.73 A region of the forebrain surrounding the third ventricle; includes the thalamus and the hypothalamus.	**3.64** Phylogenetically old cortex, located at the medial edge ("limbus") of the cerebral hemispheres; part of the limbic system.
3.74 The largest portion of the diencephalon, located above the hypothalamus; contains nuclei that project information to specific regions of the cerebral cortex and receive information from it.	**3.65** A strip of limbic cortex lying along the lateral walls of the groove separating the cerebral hemispheres, just above the corpus callosum.
3.75 An axon of a neuron in one region of the brain whose terminals form synapses with neurons in another region.	**3.66** A fiber bundle that interconnects corresponding regions on each side of the brain.
3.76 An identifiable group of neural cell bodies in the central nervous system.	**3.67** A group of brain regions including the anterior thalamic nuclei, amygdala, hippocampus, limbic cortex, and parts of the hypothalamus, as well as their interconnecting fiber bundles.
3.77 A group of cell bodies within the lateral geniculate body of the thalamus that receives fibers from the retina and projects fibers to the primary visual cortex.	**3.68** A forebrain structure of the temporal lobe, constituting an important part of the limbic system; includes the hippocampus proper (Ammon's horn), dentate gyrus, and subiculum.
3.78 A group of cell bodies within the medial geniculate body of the thalamus; receives fibers from the auditory system and projects fibers to the primary auditory cortex.	**3.69** A structure in the interior of the rostral temporal lobe, containing a set of nuclei; part of the limbic system.
3.79 A nucleus of the thalamus that receives inputs from the cerebellum and sends axons to the primary motor cortex.	**3.70** A fiber bundle that connects the hippocampus with other parts of the brain, including the mammillary bodies of the hypothalamus.

3.80 hypothalamus	3.89 inferior colliculi
3.81 optic chiasm (*kye az'm*)	3.90 brain stem
3.82 anterior pituitary gland	3.91 tegmentum
3.83 neurosecretory cell	3.92 reticular formation
3.84 posterior pituitary gland	3.93 periaqueductal gray matter
3.85 midbrain	3.94 red nucleus
3.86 mesencephalon (*mezz en **seff** a lahn*)	3.95 substantia nigra
3.87 tectum	3.96 hindbrain
3.88 superior colliculi (*ka **lik** yew lee*)	3.97 cerebellum (*sair a **bell** um*)

3.89 Protrusions on top of the midbrain; part of the auditory system.	3.80 The group of nuclei of the diencephalon situated beneath the thalamus; involved in regulation of the autonomic nervous system, control of the anterior and posterior pituitary glands, and integration of species-typical behaviors.
3.90 The "stem" of the brain, from the medulla to the diencephalon, excluding the cerebellum.	3.81 An X-shaped connection between the optic nerves, located below the base of the brain, just anterior to the pituitary gland.
3.91 The ventral part of the midbrain; includes the periaqueductal gray matter, reticular formation, red nucleus, and substantia nigra.	3.82 The anterior part of the pituitary gland; an endocrine gland whose secretions are controlled by the hypothalamic hormones.
3.92 A large network of neural tissue located in the central region of the brain stem, from the medulla to the diencephalon.	3.83 A neuron that secretes a hormone or hormonelike substance.
3.93 The region of the midbrain surrounding the cerebral aqueduct; contains neural circuits involved in species-typical behaviors.	3.84 The posterior part of the pituitary gland; an endocrine gland that contains hormone-secreting terminal buttons of axons whose cell bodies lie within the hypothalamus.
3.94 A large nucleus of the midbrain that receives inputs from the cerebellum and motor cortex and sends axons to motor neurons in the spinal cord.	3.85 The mesencephalon; the central of the three major divisions of the brain.
3.95 A darkly stained region of the tegmentum that contains neurons that communicate with the caudate nucleus and putamen in the basal ganglia.	3.86 The midbrain; a region of the brain that surrounds the cerebral aqueduct; includes the tectum and the tegmentum.
3.96 The most caudal of the three major divisions of the brain; includes the metencephalon and myelencephalon.	3.87 The dorsal part of the midbrain; includes the superior and inferior colliculi.
3.97 A major part of the brain located dorsal to the pons, containing the two cerebellar hemispheres, covered with the cerebellar cortex; an important component of the motor system.	3.88 Protrusions on top of the midbrain; part of the visual system.

3.98 cerebellar cortex	3.107 dorsal root
3.99 deep cerebellar nuclei	3.108 ventral root
3.100 cerebellar peduncle (*pee dun kul*)	3.109 spinal nerve
3.101 pons	3.110 afferent axon
3.102 medulla oblongata (*me **doo** la*)	3.111 dorsal root ganglion
3.103 spinal cord	3.112 efferent axon (***eff** ur ent*)
3.104 spinal root	3.113 cranial nerve
3.105 cauda equina (*ee **kwye** na*)	3.114 vagus nerve
3.106 caudal block	3.115 olfactory bulb

3.107 The spinal root that contains incoming (afferent) sensory fibers.	3.98 The cortex that covers the surface of the cerebellum.
3.108 The spinal root that contains outgoing (efferent) motor fibers.	3.99 Nuclei located within the cerebellar hemispheres; receive projections from the cerebellar cortex and send projections out of the cerebellum to other parts of the brain.
3.109 A peripheral nerve attached to the spinal cord.	3.100 One of three bundles of axons that attach each cerebellar hemisphere to the dorsal pons.
3.110 An axon directed toward the central nervous system, conveying sensory information.	3.101 The region of the metencephalon rostral to the medulla, caudal to the midbrain, and ventral to the cerebellum.
3.111 A nodule on a dorsal root that contains cell bodies of afferent spinal nerve neurons.	3.102 The most caudal portion of the brain; located in the myelencephalon, immediately rostral to the spinal cord.
3.112 An axon directed away from the central nervous system, conveying motor commands to muscles and glands.	3.103 The cord of nervous tissue that extends caudally from the medulla.
3.113 A peripheral nerve attached directly to the brain.	3.104 A bundle of axons surrounded by connective tissue that occurs in pairs, which fuse and form a spinal nerve.
3.114 The largest of the cranial nerves, conveying efferent fibers of the parasympathetic division of the autonomic nervous system to organs of the thoracic and abdominal cavities.	3.105 A bundle of spinal roots located caudal to the end of the spinal cord.
3.115 The protrusion at the end of the olfactory nerve; receives input from the olfactory receptors.	3.106 The anesthesia and paralysis of the lower part of the body produced by injection of a local anesthetic into the cerebrospinal fluid surrounding the cauda equina.

3.116 somatic nervous system	4.1 psychopharmacology
3.117 autonomic nervous system (ANS)	4.2 drug effect
3.118 sympathetic division	4.3 sites of action
3.119 sympathetic ganglia	4.4 pharmacokinetics
3.120 sympathetic ganglion chain	4.5 intravenous (IV) injection
3.121 preganglionic neuron	4.6 intraperitoneal (IP) injection (*in tra pair i toe **nee** ul*)
3.122 postganglionic neuron	4.7 intramuscular (IM) injection
3.123 adrenal medulla	4.8 subcutaneous (SC) injection
3.124 parasympathetic division	4.9 oral administration

4.1 The study of the effects of drugs on the nervous system and on behavior.	3.116 The part of the peripheral nervous system that controls the movement of skeletal muscles or transmits somatosensory information to the central nervous system.
4.2 The changes a drug produces in an animal's physiological processes and behavior.	3.117 The portion of the peripheral nervous system that controls the body's vegetative functions.
4.3 The locations at which molecules of drugs interact with molecules located on or in cells of the body, thus affecting some biochemical processes of these cells.	3.118 The portion of the autonomic nervous system that controls functions that accompany arousal and expenditure of energy.
4.4 The process by which drugs are absorbed, distributed within the body, metabolized, and excreted.	3.119 Nodules that contain synapses between preganglionic and postganglionic neurons of the sympathetic nervous system.
4.5 Injection of a substance directly into a vein.	3.120 One of a pair of groups of sympathetic ganglia that lie ventrolateral to the vertebral column.
4.6 Injection of a substance into the *peritoneal cavity* the space that surrounds the stomach, intestines, liver, and other abdominal organs.	3.121 The efferent neuron of the autonomic nervous system whose cell body is located in a cranial nerve nucleus or in the intermediate horn of the spinal gray matter and whose terminal buttons synapse upon postganglionic neurons in the autonomic ganglia.
4.7 Injection of a substance into a muscle.	3.122 Neurons of the autonomic nervous system that form synapses directly with their target organ.
4.8 Injection of a substance into the space beneath the skin.	3.123 The inner portion of the adrenal gland, located atop the kidney, controlled by sympathetic nerve fibers; secretes epinephrine and norepinephrine.
4.9 Administration of a substance into the mouth, so that it is swallowed.	3.124 The portion of the autonomic nervous system that controls functions that occur during a relaxed state.

4.10 sublingual administration (*sub **ling** wul*)	4.19 therapeutic index
4.11 intrarectal administration	4.20 affinity
4.12 inhalation	4.21 tolerance
4.13 topical administration	4.22 sensitization
4.14 intracerebral administration	4.23 withdrawal symptom
4.15 intracerebroventricular (ICV) administration	4.24 placebo (*pla **see** boh*)
4.16 depot binding	4.25 antagonist
4.17 albumin (*al **bew** min*)	4.26 agonist
4.18 dose-response curve	4.27 direct agonist

4.19 The ratio between the dose that produces the desired effect in 50 percent of the animals and the dose that produces toxic effects in 50 percent of the animals.	**4.10** Administration of a substance by placing it beneath the tongue.
4.20 The readiness with which two molecules join together.	**4.11** Administration of a substance into the rectum.
4.21 A decrease in the effectiveness of a drug that is administered repeatedly.	**4.12** Administration of a vaporous substance into the lungs.
4.22 An increase in the effectiveness of a drug that is administered repeatedly.	**4.13** Administration of a substance directly onto the skin or mucous membrane.
4.23 The appearance of symptoms opposite to those produced by a drug when the drug is administered repeatedly and then suddenly no longer taken.	**4.14** Administration of a substance directly into the brain.
4.24 An inert substance given to an organism in lieu of a physiologically active drug; used experimentally to control for the effects of mere administration of a drug.	**4.15** Administration of a substance into one of the cerebral ventricles.
4.25 A drug that opposes or inhibits the effects of a particular neurotransmitter on the postsynaptic cell.	**4.16** Binding of a drug with various tissues of the body or with proteins in the blood.
4.26 A drug that facilitates the effects of a particular neurotransmitter on the postsynaptic cell.	**4.17** A protein found in the blood; serves to transport free fatty acids and can bind with some lipid-soluble drugs.
4.27 A drug that binds with and activates a receptor.	**4.18** A graph of the magnitude of an effect of a drug as a function of the amount of drug administered.

4.28 receptor blocker	4.37 black widow spider venom
4.29 direct antagonist	4.38 neostigmine (*nee o **stig** meen*)
4.30 noncompetitive binding	4.39 hemicholinium (*hem ee koh **lin** um*)
4.31 indirect antagonist	4.40 nicotinic receptor
4.32 indirect agonist	4.41 muscarinic receptor (*muss ka **rin** ic*)
4.33 presynaptic heteroreceptor	4.42 atropine (***a** tro peen*)
4.34 acetyl-CoA (*a **see** tul*)	4.43 curare (*kew **rahr** ee*)
4.35 choline acetyltransferase (ChAT) (***koh** leen a see tul **trans** fer ace*)	4.44 monoamine (***mahn** o a meen*)
4.36 botulinum toxin (*bot you **lin** um*)	4.45 catecholamine (*cat a **kohl** a meen*)

4.37 A poison produced by the black widow spider that triggers the release of acetylcholine.	4.28 A drug that binds with a receptor but does not activate it; prevents the natural ligand from binding with the receptor.
4.38 A drug that inhibits the activity of acetylcholinesterase.	4.29 A synonym for receptor blocker.
4.39 A drug that inhibits the uptake of choline.	4.30 Binding of a drug to a site on a receptor; does not interfere with the binding site for the principal ligand.
4.40 An ionotropic acetylcholine receptor that is stimulated by nicotine and blocked by curare.	4.31 A drug that attaches to a binding site on a receptor and interferes with the action of the receptor; does not interfere with the binding site for the principal ligand.
4.41 A metabotropic acetylcholine receptor that is stimulated by muscarine and blocked by atropine.	4.32 A drug that attaches to a binding site on a receptor and facilitates the action of the receptor; does not interfere with the binding site for the principal ligand.
4.42 A drug that blocks muscarinic acetylcholine receptors.	4.33 A receptor located in the membrane of a terminal button that receives input from another terminal button by means of an axoaxonic synapse; binds with the neurotransmitter released by the presynaptic terminal button.
4.43 A drug that blocks nicotinic acetylcholine receptors.	4.34 A cofactor that supplies acetate for the synthesis of acetylcholine.
4.44 A class of amines that includes indolamines such as serotonin and catecholamines such as dopamine, norepinephrine, and epinephrine.	4.35 The enzyme that transfers the acetate ion from acetyl coenzyme A to choline, producing the neurotransmitter acetylcholine.
4.45 A class of amines that includes the neurotransmitters dopamine, norepinephrine, and epinephrine.	4.36 An acetylcholine antagonist; prevents release by terminal buttons.

4.46 dopamine (DA) (***dope*** *a meen*)	4.55 methylphenidate (*meth ul **fen** i date*)
4.47 L-DOPA (*ell **dope** a*)	4.56 monoamine oxidase (MAO) (***mahn** o a meen*)
4.48 nigrostriatal system (*nigh grow stry **ay** tul*)	4.57 deprenyl (***depp** ra nil*)
4.49 mesolimbic system (*mee zo **lim** bik*)	4.58 chlorpromazine (*klor **proh** ma zeen*)
4.50 mesocortical system (*mee zo **kor** ti kul*)	4.59 clozapine (***kloz** a peen*)
4.51 Parkinson's disease	4.60 norepinephrine (NE) (*nor epp i **neff** rin*)
4.52 AMPT	4.61 epinephrine (*epp i **neff** rin*)
4.53 reserpine (*ree **sur** peen*)	4.62 fusaric acid (*few **sahr** ik*)
4.54 apomorphine (*ap o **more** feen*)	4.63 moclobemide (*mok low **bem** ide*)

4.55 A drug that inhibits the reuptake of dopamine.	**4.46** A neurotransmitter; one of the catecholamines.
4.56 A class of enzymes that destroy the monoamines: dopamine, norepinephrine, and serotonin.	**4.47** The levorotatory form of DOPA; the precursor of the catecholamines; often used to treat Parkinson's disease because of its effect as a dopamine agonist.
4.57 A drug that blocks the activity of MAO-B; acts as a dopamine agonist.	**4.48** A system of neurons originating in the substantia nigra and terminating in the neostriatum (caudate nucleus and putamen).
4.58 A drug that reduces the symptoms of schizophrenia by blocking dopamine D_2 receptors.	**4.49** A system of dopaminergic neurons originating in the ventral tegmental area and terminating in the nucleus accumbens, amygdala, and hippocampus.
4.59 A drug that reduces the symptoms of schizophrenia, apparently by blocking dopamine D_4 receptors.	**4.50** A system of dopaminergic neurons originating in the ventral tegmental area and terminating in the prefrontal cortex.
4.60 One of the catecholamines; a neurotransmitter found in the brain and in the sympathetic division of the autonomic nervous system.	**4.51** A neurological disease characterized by tremors, rigidity of the limbs, poor balance, and difficulty in initiating movements; caused by degeneration of the nigrostriatal system.
4.61 One of the catecholamines; a hormone secreted by the adrenal medulla; serves also as a neurotransmitter in the brain.	**4.52** A drug that blocks the activity of tyrosine hydroxylase and thus interferes with the synthesis of the catecholamines.
4.62 A drug that inhibits the activity of the enzyme dopamine-beta-hydroxylase and thus blocks the production of norepinephrine.	**4.53** A drug that interferes with the storage of monoamines in synaptic vesicles.
4.63 A drug that blocks the activity of MAO-A; acts as a noradrenergic agonist.	**4.54** A drug that blocks dopamine autoreceptors at low doses; at higher doses blocks postsynaptic receptors as well.

4.61 locus coeruleus (*sur oo lee us*)	4.73 glutamate
4.65 axonal varicosity	4.74 NMDA receptor
4.66 serotonin (5-HT) (*sair a toe nin*)	4.75 AMPA receptor
4.67 PCPA	4.76 kainate receptor (*kay in ate*)
4.68 D system	4.77 metabotropic glutamate receptor (*meh tab a troh pik*)
4.69 M system	4.78 PCP
4.70 fluoxetine (*floo ox i teen*)	4.79 GABA
4.71 fenfluramine (*fen fluor i meen*)	4.80 allylglycine
4.72 LSD	4.81 muscimol (*musk i mawl*)

4.73 An amino acid; the most important excitatory neurotransmitter in the brain.	4.64 A dark-colored group of noradrenergic cell bodies located in the pons near the rostral end of the floor of the fourth ventricle.
4.74 A specialized ionotropic glutamate receptor that controls a calcium channel that is normally blocked by Mg^{2+} ions; has several other binding sites.	4.65 An enlarged region along the length of an axon that contains synaptic vesicles and releases a neurotransmitter or neuromodulator.
4.75 An ionotropic glutamate receptor that controls a sodium channel; stimulated by AMPA and blocked by CNQX.	4.66 An indolamine neurotransmitter; also called 5-hydroxytryptamine.
4.76 An ionotropic glutamate receptor that controls a sodium channel; stimulated by kainic acid and blocked by CNQX.	4.67 A drug that inhibits the activity of tryptophan hydroxylase and thus interferes with the synthesis of 5-HT.
4.77 A category of metabotropic receptors sensitive to glutamate.	4.68 A system of serotonergic neurons that originates in the dorsal raphe nucleus; its axonal fibers are thin, with spindle-shaped varicosities that do not appear to form synapses with other neurons.
4.78 Phencyclidine; a drug that binds with the PCP binding site of the NMDA receptor and serves as an indirect antagonist.	4.69 A system of serotonergic neurons that originates in the median raphe nucleus; its axonal fibers are thick and rounded and appear to form conventional synapses with other neurons.
4.79 An amino acid; the most important inhibitory neurotransmitter in the brain.	4.70 A drug that inhibits the reuptake of 5-HT.
4.80 A drug that inhibits the activity of GAD and thus blocks the synthesis of GABA.	4.71 A drug that stimulates the release of 5-HT.
4.81 A direct agonist for the GABA binding site on the $GABA_A$ receptor.	4.72 A drug that stimulates $5-HT_{2A}$ receptors.

4.82 bicuculline (*by* **kew** *kew leen*)	4.91 anandamide (*a* **nan** *da mide*)
4.83 benzodiazepine (*ben zoe dy* **azz** *a peen*)	4.92 adenosine (*a* **den** *oh seen*)
4.84 anxiolytic (*angz ee oh* **lit** *ik*)	4.93 caffeine
4.85 beta-CCM	4.94 nitric oxide (NO)
4.86 glycine (**gly** *seen*)	4.95 nitric oxide synthase
4.87 strychnine (**strik** *neen*)	5.1 experimental ablation
4.88 endogenous opioid (*en* **dodge** *en us* **oh** *pee oyd*)	5.2 lesion study
4.89 enkephalin (*en* **keff** *a lin*)	5.3 excitotoxic lesion (*ek sigh tow* **tok** *sik*)
4.90 naloxone (*na* **lox** *own*)	5.4 6-hydroxydopamine (6-HD)

4.91 A lipid; the endogenous ligand for receptors that bind with THC, the active ingredient of marijuana.	4.82 A direct antagonist for the GABA binding site on the $GABA_A$ receptor.
4.92 A nucleoside; a combination of ribose and adenine; serves as a neuromodulator in the brain.	4.83 A category of anxiolytic drugs; an indirect agonist for the $GABA_A$ receptor.
4.93 A drug that blocks adenosine receptors.	4.84 An anxiety-reducing effect.
4.94 A gas produced by cells in the nervous system; used as a means of communication between cells.	4.85 A direct agonist for the benzodiazepine binding site of the $GABA_A$ receptor.
4.95 The enzyme responsible for the production of nitric oxide.	4.86 An amino acid; an important inhibitory neurotransmitter in the lower brain stem and spinal cord.
5.1 The removal or destruction of a portion of the brain of a laboratory animal; presumably, the functions that can no longer be performed are the ones the region previously controlled.	4.87 A direct antagonist for the glycine receptor.
5.2 A synonym for experimental ablation.	4.88 A class of peptides secreted by the brain that act as opiates.
5.3 A brain lesion produced by intracerebral injection of an excitatory amino acid, such as kainic acid.	4.89 One of the endogenous opioids.
5.4 A chemical that is selectively taken up by axons and terminal buttons of noradrenergic or dopaminergic neurons and acts as a poison, damaging or killing them.	4.90 A drug that blocks opioid receptors.

5.5 sham lesion	5.14 scanning electron microscope
5.6 stereotaxic surgery (*stair ee oh* **tak** *sik*)	5.15 anterograde labeling method (**ann** *ter oh grade*)
5.7 bregma	5.16 PHA-L
5.8 stereotaxic atlas	5.17 immunocytochemical method
5.9 stereotaxic apparatus	5.18 retrograde labeling method
5.10 fixative	5.19 fluorogold (**flew** *roh gold*)
5.11 formalin (**for** *ma lin*)	5.20 computerized tomography (CT)
5.12 perfusion (*per* **few** *zhun*)	5.21 magnetic resonance imaging (MRI)
5.13 microtome (**my** *krow tome*)	5.22 microelectrode

5.14 A microscope that provides three-dimensional information about the shape of the surface of a small object.	5.5 A "placebo" procedure that duplicates all the steps of producing a brain lesion except for the one that actually causes the brain damage.
5.15 A histological method that labels the axons and terminal buttons of neurons whose cell bodies are located in a particular region.	5.6 Brain surgery using a stereotaxic apparatus to position an electrode or cannula in a specified position of the brain.
5.16 Phaseolus vulgaris leukoagglutinin; a protein derived from kidney beans and used as an anterograde tracer; taken up by dendrites and cell bodies and carried to the ends of the axons.	5.7 The junction of the sagittal and coronal sutures of the skull; often used as a reference point for stereotaxic brain surgery.
5.17 A histological method that uses radioactive antibodies or antibodies bound with a dye molecule to indicate the presence of particular proteins of peptides.	5.8 A collection of drawings of sections of the brain of a particular animal with measurements that provide coordinates for stereotaxic surgery.
5.18 A histological method that labels cell bodies that give rise to the terminal buttons that form synapses with cells in a particular region.	5.9 A device that permits a surgeon to position an electrode or cannula into a specific part of the brain.
5.19 A dye that serves as a retrograde label; taken up by terminal buttons and carried back to the cell bodies.	5.10 A chemical such as formalin; used to prepare and preserve body tissue.
5.20 The use of a device that employs a computer to analyze data obtained by a scanning beam of X-rays to produce a two-dimensional picture of a "slice" through the body.	5.11 The aqueous solution of formaldehyde gas; the most commonly used tissue fixative.
5.21 A technique whereby the interior of the body can be accurately imaged; involves the interaction between radio waves and a strong magnetic field.	5.12 The process by which an animal's blood is replaced by a fluid such as a saline solution or a fixative in preparing the brain for histological examination.
5.22 A very fine electrode, generally used to record activity of individual neurons.	5.13 An instrument that produces very thin slices of body tissues.

5.23 single-unit recording	5.32 multi-barreled micropipette
5.24 macroelectrode	5.33 microiontophoresis
5.25 electroencephalogram (EEG)	5.34 in situ hybridization (*in see too*)
5.26 2-deoxyglucose (2-DG) (*dee ox ee **gloo** kohss*)	5.35 double labeling
5.27 autoradiography	5.36 targeted mutation
5.28 Fos (*fahs*)	6.1 sensory receptor
5.29 positron emission tomography (PET)	6.2 sensory transduction
5.30 functional MRI (fMRI)	6.3 receptor potential
5.31 microdialysis	6.4 hue

5.32 A group of micropipettes attached together, used to infuse several different substances by means of iontophoresis while recording from a single neuron.	**5.23** Recording of the electrical activity of a single neuron.
5.33 A procedure that uses electricity to eject a chemical from a micropipette to determine the effects of the chemical on the electrical activity of a cell.	**5.24** An electrode used to record the electrical activity of large numbers of neurons in a particular region of the brain; much larger than a microelectrode.
5.34 The production of DNA complementary to a particular messenger RNA in order to detect the presence of the RNA.	**5.25** An electrical brain potential recorded by placing electrodes on in the scalp.
5.35 Labeling neurons in a particular region by two different means, for example, by using an anterograde tracer and a label for a particular enzyme.	**5.26** A sugar that enters cells along with glucose but is not metabolized.
5.36 A mutated gene (also called a "knockout gene") produced in the laboratory and inserted into the chromosomes of mice; fails to produce a functional protein.	**5.27** A procedure that locates radioactive substances in a slice of tissue; the radiation exposes a photographic emulsion or a piece of film that covers the tissue.
6.1 A specialized neuron that detects a particular category of physical events.	**5.28** A protein produced in the nucleus of a neuron in response to synaptic stimulation.
6.2 The process by which sensory stimuli are transduced into slow, graded receptor potentials.	**5.29** The use of a device that reveals the localization of a radioactive tracer in a living brain.
6.3 A slow, graded electrical potential produced by a receptor cell in response to a physical stimulus.	**5.30** A modification of the MRI procedure that permits the measurement of regional metabolism in the brain.
6.4 One of the perceptual dimensions of color; the dominant wavelength.	**5.31** A procedure for analyzing chemicals present in the interstitial fluid through a small piece of tubing made of a semipermeable membrane that is implanted in the brain.

6.5 brightness	6.14 photoreceptor
6.6 saturation	6.15 fovea (*foe vee a*)
6.7 vergence movement	6.16 optic disk
6.8 saccadic movement (*suh **kad** ik*)	6.17 bipolar cell
6.9 pursuit movement	6.18 ganglion cell
6.10 accommodation	6.19 horizontal cell
6.11 retina	6.20 amacrine cell (***amm** a krin*)
6.12 rod	6.21 lamella
6.13 cone	6.22 photopigment

6.14 One of the receptor cells of the retina; transduces photic energy into electrical potentials.	6.5 One of the perceptual dimensions of color; intensity.
6.15 The region of the retina that mediates the most acute vision of birds and higher mammals. Color-sensitive cones constitute the only type of photoreceptor found in the fovea.	6.6 One of the perceptual dimensions of color; purity.
6.16 The location of the exit point from the retina of the fibers of the ganglion cells that form the optic nerve; responsible for the blind spot.	6.7 The cooperative movement of the eyes, which ensures that the image of an object falls on identical portions of both retinas.
6.17 A bipolar neuron located in the middle layer of the retina, conveying information from the photoreceptors to the ganglion cells.	6.8 The rapid. jerky movement of the eyes used in scanning a visual scene.
6.18 A neuron located in the retina that receives visual information from bipolar cells; its axons give rise to the optic nerve.	6.9 The movement that the eyes make to maintain an image of a moving object on the fovea.
6.19 A neuron in the retina that interconnects adjacent photoreceptors and the outer processes of the bipolar cells.	6.10 Changes in the thickness of the lens of the eye, accomplished by the ciliary muscles, that focus images of near or distant objects on the retina.
6.20 A neuron in the retina that interconnects adjacent ganglion cells and the inner processes of the bipolar cells.	6.11 The neural tissue and photoreceptive cells located on the inner surface of the posterior portion of the eye.
6.21 A layer of membrane containing photopigments; found in rods and cones of the retina.	6.12 One of the receptor cells of the retina; sensitive to light of low intensity.
6.22 A protein dye bonded to retinal, a substance derived from vitamin A; responsible for transduction of visual information.	6.13 One of the receptor cells of the retina; maximally sensitive to one of three different wavelengths of light and hence encodes color vision.

6.23 opsin (*opp* sin)	6.32 striate cortex (**stry** ate)
6.24 retinal (**rett** i nahl)	6.33 optic chiasm
6.25 rhodopsin (roh **dopp** sin)	6.34 receptive field
6.26 transducin	6.35 protanopia (pro tan **owe** pee a)
6.27 dorsal lateral geniculate nucleus	6.36 deuteranopia (dew ter an **owe** pee a)
6.28 magnocellular layer	6.37 tritanopia (try tan **owe** pee a)
6.29 parvocellular layer	6.38 negative afterimage
6.30 koniocellular sublayer (koh nee oh **sell** yew lur)	6.39 complementary colors
6.31 calcarine fissure (**kal** ka rine)	6.40 simple cell

6.32 The primary visual cortex.	6.23 A class of protein that, together with retinal, constitutes the photopigments.
6.33 A cross-shaped connection between the optic nerves, located below the base of the brain, just anterior to the pituitary gland.	6.24 A chemical synthesized from vitamin A; joins with an opsin to form a photopigment.
6.34 That portion of the visual field in which the presentation of visual stimuli will produce an alteration in the firing rate of a particular neuron.	6.25 A particular opsin found in rods.
6.35 An inherited form of defective color vision in which red and green hues are confused; "red" cones are filled with "green" cone opsin.	6.26 A G protein that is activated when a photon strikes a photopigment; activates phosphodiesterase molecules, which destroy cyclic GMP and close cation channels in the photoreceptor.
6.36 An inherited form of defective color vision in which red and green hues are confused; "green" cones are filled with "red" cone opsin.	6.27 A group of cell bodies within the lateral geniculate body of the thalamus; receives inputs from the retina and projects to the primary visual cortex.
6.37 An inherited form of defective color vision in which hues with short wavelengths are confused; "blue" cones are either lacking or faulty.	6.28 One of the inner two layers of neurons in the dorsal lateral geniculate nucleus; transmits information necessary for the perception of form, movement, depth, and small differences in brightness to the primary visual cortex.
6.38 The image seen after a portion of the retina is exposed to an intense visual stimulus; consists of colors complementary to those of the physical stimulus.	6.29 One of the four outer layers of neurons in the dorsal lateral geniculate nucleus; transmits information necessary for perception of color and fine details to the primary visual cortex
6.39 Colors that make white or gray when mixed together.	6.30 One of the sublayers of neurons in the dorsal lateral geniculate nucleus found ventral to each of the magnocellular and parvocellular layers; transmits information from short-wavelength ("blue") cones to the primary visual cortex.
6.40 An orientation-sensitive neuron in the striate cortex whose receptive field is organized in an opponent fashion.	6.31 A horizontal fissure on the inner surface of the posterior cerebral cortex; the location of the primary visual cortex.

6.41	6.50
complex cell	extrastriate cortex
6.42	6.51
hypercomplex cell	color constancy
6.43	6.52
sine-wave grating	achromatopsia (*ay krohm a* **top** *see a*)
6.44	6.53
spatial frequency	inferior temporal cortex
6.45	6.54
retinal disparity	visual agnosia (*ag* **no** *zha*)
6.46	6.55
cytochrome oxidase (CO) blob	apperceptive visual agnosia
6.47	6.56
ocular dominance	prosopagnosia (*prah soh pag* **no** *zha*)
6.48	6.57
cortical blindness	inversion effect
6.49	6.58
blindsight	associative visual agnosia

6.50 A region of visual association cortex; receives fibers from the striate cortex and from the superior colliculi and projects to the inferior temporal cortex.	6.41 A neuron in the visual cortex that responds to the presence of a line segment with a particular orientation located within its receptive field, especially when the line moves perpendicularly to its orientation.
6.51 The relatively constant appearance of the colors of objects viewed under varying lighting conditions.	6.42 A neuron in the visual cortex that responds to the presence of a line segment with a particular orientation that ends at a particular point within the cell's receptive field.
6.52 Inability to discriminate among different hues; caused by damage to the visual association cortex.	6.43 A series of straight parallel bands varying continuously in brightness according to a sine-wave function, along a line perpendicular to their lengths.
6.53 In primates the highest level of the ventral stream of the visual association cortex; located on the inferior portion of the temporal lobe.	6.44 The relative width of the bands in a sine-wave grating, measured in cycles per degree of visual angle.
6.54 Deficits in visual perception in the absence of blindness; caused by brain damage.	6.45 The fact that points on objects located at different distances from the observer will fall on slightly different locations on the two retinas; provides the basis for stereopsis.
6.55 Failure to perceive objects, even though visual acuity is relatively normal.	6.46 The central region of a module of the primary visual cortex, revealed by a stain for cytochrome oxidase; contains wavelength-sensitive neurons; part of the parvocellular system.
6.56 Failure to recognize particular people by the sight of their faces.	6.47 The extent to which a particular neuron receives more input from one eye than from the other.
6.57 The increased difficulty in learning to recognize visual stimuli that are normally seen in a particular orientation when they are inverted turned upside-down.	6.48 Blindness caused by damage to the optic radiations or primary visual cortex.
6.58 Inability to identify objects that are perceived visually, even though the form of the perceived object can be drawn or matched with similar objects.	6.49 The ability of a person to reach for objects located in his or her "blind" field; occurs after damage restricted to the primary visual cortex.

6.59 optic flow	7.5 tympanic membrane
6.60 Balint's syndrome	7.6 ossicle (*ahss i kul*)
6.61 optic ataxia (*ay **tack** see a*)	7.7 malleus
6.62 ocular apraxia (*ay **prak** see a*)	7.8 incus
6.63 simultanagnosia (*sime ul tane ag **no** zha*)	7.9 stapes (***stay** peez*)
7.1 pitch	7.10 cochlea (*cock lee uh*)
7.2 hertz (Hz)	7.11 oval window
7.3 loudness	7.12 organ of Corti
7.4 timbre (***tim** ber or **tamm** ber*)	7.13 hair cell

7.5 The eardrum.	**6.59** The complex motion of points in the visual field caused by relative movement between the observer and environment; provides information about the relative distance of objects from the observer and of the relative direction of movement.
7.6 One of the three bones of the middle ear.	**6.60** A syndrome caused by bilateral damage to the parieto-occipital region; includes optic ataxia, ocular apraxia, and simultanagnosia.
7.7 The "hammer"; the first of the three ossicles.	**6.61** Difficulty in reaching for objects under visual guidance.
7.8 The "anvil"; the second of the three ossicles.	**6.62** Difficulty in visual scanning.
7.9 The "stirrup"; the last of the three ossicles.	**6.63** Difficulty in perceiving more than one object at a time.
7.10 The snail-shaped structure of the inner ear that contains the auditory transducing mechanisms.	**7.1** A perceptual dimension of sound; corresponds to the fundamental frequency.
7.11 An opening in the bone surrounding the cochlea that reveals a membrane, against which the baseplate of the stapes presses, transmitting sound vibrations into the fluid within the cochlea.	**7.2** Cycles per second.
7.12 The sensory organ on the basilar membrane that contains the auditory hair cells.	**7.3** A perceptual dimension of sound; corresponds to intensity.
7.13 The receptive cell of the auditory apparatus.	**7.4** A perceptual dimension of sound; corresponds to complexity.

7.14 Deiters's cell (***dye*** *terz*)	7.23 cochlear nucleus
7.15 basilar membrane (***bazz*** *i ler*)	7.24 superior olivary complex
7.16 tectorial membrane (*tek **torr** ee ul*)	7.25 lateral lemniscus
7.17 round window	7.26 tonotopic representation (*tonn oh **top** ik*)
7.18 cilium	7.27 belt region
7.19 tip link	7.28 parabelt region
7.20 insertional plaque	7.29 place code
7.21 cochlear nerve	7.30 cochlear implant
7.22 olivocochlear bundle	7.31 rate code

7.23 One of a group of nuclei in the medulla that receive auditory information from the cochlea.	**7.14** A supporting cell found in the organ of Corti; sustains the auditory hair cells.
7.24 A group of nuclei in the medulla; involved with auditory functions, including localization of the source of sounds.	**7.15** A membrane in the cochlea of the inner ear; contains the organ of Corti.
7.25 A band of fibers running rostrally through the medulla and pons; carries fibers of the auditory system.	**7.16** A membrane located above the basilar membrane; serves as a shelf against which the cilia of the auditory hair cells move.
7.26 A topographically organized mapping of different frequencies of sound that are represented in a particular region of the brain.	**7.17** An opening in the bone surrounding the cochlea of the inner ear that permits vibrations to be transmitted, via the oval window, into the fluid in the cochlea.
7.27 The first level of auditory association cortex; surrounds the primary auditory cortex.	**7.18** A hairlike appendage of a cell involved in movement or in transducing sensory information; found on the receptors in the auditory and vestibular system.
7.28 The second level of auditory association cortex; surrounds the belt region.	**7.19** An elastic filament that attaches the tip of one cilium to the side of the adjacent cilium.
7.29 The system by which information about different frequencies is coded by different locations on the basilar membrane.	**7.20** The point of attachment of a tip link to a cilium.
7.30 An electronic device surgically implanted in the inner ear that can enable a deaf person to hear.	**7.21** The branch of the auditory nerve that transmits auditory information from the cochlea to the brain.
7.31 The system by which information about different frequencies is coded by the rate of firing of neurons in the auditory system.	**7.22** A bundle of efferent axons that travel from the olivary complex of the medulla to the auditory hair cells on the cochlea.

7.32 fundamental frequency	7.41 cutaneous sense (*kew **tane** ee us*)
7.33 overtone	7.42 kinesthesia
7.34 phase difference	7.43 organic sense
7.35 vestibular sac	7.44 glabrous skin (***glab** russ*)
7.36 semicircular canal	7.45 Ruffini corpuscle
7.37 utricle (***you** trih kul*) and saccule (***sak** yule*)	7.46 Pacinian corpuscle (*pa **chin** ee un*)
7.38 ampulla (*am **pull** uh*)	7.47 Meissner's corpuscle
7.39 cupula (***kew** pew luh*)	7.48 Merkel's disk
7.40 vestibular ganglion	7.49 phantom limb

7.41 One of the somatosenses; includes sensitivity to stimuli that involve the skin.	**7.32** The lowest, and usually most intense, frequency of a complex sound; most often perceived as the sound's basic pitch.
7.42 Perception of the body's own movements.	**7.33** The frequency of complex tones that occurs at multiples of the fundamental frequency.
7.43 A sense modality that arises from receptors located within the inner organs of the body.	**7.34** The difference in arrival times of sound waves at each of the eardrums.
7.44 Skin that does not contain hair; found on the palms and the soles of the feet.	**7.35** One of a set of two receptor organs in each inner ear that detect changes in the tilt of the head.
7.45 A vibration-sensitive organ located in hairy skin.	**7.36** One of the three ringlike structures of the vestibular apparatus that detect changes in head rotation.
7.46 A specialized, encapsulated somatosensory nerve ending that detects mechanical stimuli, especially vibrations.	**7.37** The vestibular sacs.
7.47 The touch-sensitive end organs located in the papillae, small elevations of the dermis that project up into the epidermis.	**7.38** An enlargement in a semicircular canal; contains the cupula and the crista.
7.48 The touch-sensitive end organs found at the base of the epidermis, adjacent to sweat ducts.	**7.39** A gelatinous mass found in the ampulla of the semicircular canals; moves in response to the flow of the fluid in the canals.
7.49 Sensations that appear to originate in a limb that has been amputated.	**7.40** A nodule on the vestibular nerve that contains the cell bodies of the bipolar neurons that convey vestibular information to the brain.

7.50 nucleus raphe magnus	8.1 skeletal muscle
7.51 gustducin (*gust **doo** sin*)	8.2 flexion
7.52 umami (*oo mah mee*)	8.3 extension
7.53 chorda tympani	8.4 extrafusal muscle fiber
7.54 nucleus of the solitary tract	8.5 alpha motor neuron
7.55 olfactory epithelium	8.6 intrafusal muscle fiber
7.56 olfactory bulb	8.7 gamma motor neuron
7.57 mitral cell	8.8 motor unit
7.58 olfactory glomerulus (*glow **mare** you luss*)	8.9 myofibril

8.1 One of the striated muscles attached to bones.	7.50 A nucleus of the raphe that contains serotonin-secreting neurons that project to the dorsal gray matter of the spinal cord and is involved in analgesia produced by opiates.
8.2 A movement of a limb that tends to bend its joints; opposite of extension.	7.51 A G protein that plays a vital role in the transduction of sweetness and bitterness.
8.3 A movement of a limb that tends to straighten its joints; the opposite of flexion.	7.52 The taste sensation produced by glutamate.
8.4 One of the muscle fibers that are responsible for the force exerted by contraction of a skeletal muscle.	7.53 A branch of the facial nerve that passes beneath the eardrum; conveys taste information from the anterior part of the tongue and controls the secretion of some salivary glands.
8.5 A neuron whose axon forms synapses with extrafusal muscle fibers of a skeletal muscle; activation contracts the muscle fibers.	7.54 A nucleus of the medulla that receives information from visceral organs and from the gustatory system.
8.6 A muscle fiber that functions as a stretch receptor, arranged parallel to the extrafusal muscle fibers, thus detecting changes in muscle length.	7.55 The epithelial tissue of the nasal sinus that covers the cribriform plate; contains the cilia of the olfactory receptors.
8.7 A neuron whose axons form synapses with intrafusal muscle fibers.	7.56 The protrusion at the end of the olfactory tract; receives input from the olfactory receptors.
8.8 A motor neuron and its associated muscle fibers.	7.57 A neuron located in the olfactory bulb that receives information from olfactory receptors; axons of mitral cells bring information to the rest of the brain.
8.9 An element of muscle fibers that consists of overlapping strands of actin and myosin; responsible for muscular contractions.	7.58 A bundle of dendrites of mitral cells and the associated terminal buttons of the axons of olfactory receptors.

8.10 actin	8.19 monosynaptic stretch reflex
8.11 myosin	8.20 decerebrate
8.12 striated muscle	8.21 decerebrate rigidity
8.13 neuromuscular junction	8.22 clasp-knife reflex
8.14 motor endplate	8.23 agonist
8.15 endplate potential	8.24 antagonist
8.16 Golgi tendon organ	8.25 somatotopic organization
8.17 smooth muscle	8.26 supplementary motor area
8.18 cardiac muscle	8.27 premotor cortex

8.19 A reflex in which a muscle contracts in response to its being quickly stretched; involves a sensory neuron and a motor neuron, with one synapse between them.	8.10 One of the proteins (with myosin) that provide the physical basis for muscular contraction.
8.20 Describes an animal whose brain stem has been transected.	8.11 One of the proteins (with actin) that provide the physical basis for muscular contraction.
8.21 Simultaneous contraction of agonistic and antagonistic muscles; caused by decerebration or damage to the reticular formation.	8.12 Skeletal muscle; muscle that contains striations.
8.22 A reflex that occurs when force is applied to flex or extend the limb of an animal showing decerebrate rigidity; resistance is replaced by sudden relaxation.	8.13 The synapse between the terminal buttons of an axon and a muscle fiber.
8.23 A muscle whose contraction produces or facilitates a particular movement.	8.14 The postsynaptic membrane of a neuromuscular junction.
8.24 A muscle whose contraction resists or reverses a particular movement.	8.15 The postsynaptic potential that occurs in the motor endplate in response to release of acetylcholine by the terminal button.
8.25 A topographically organized mapping of parts of the body that are represented in a particular region of the brain.	8.16 The receptor organ at the junction of the tendon and muscle that is sensitive to stretch.
8.26 A region of motor association cortex of the dorsal and dorsomedial frontal lobe, rostral to the primary motor cortex.	8.17 Nonstriated muscle innervated by the autonomic nervous system, found in the walls of blood vessels, in the reproductive tracts, in sphincters, within the eye, in the digestive system, and around hair follicles.
8.27 A region of motor association cortex of the lateral frontal lobe, rostral to the primary motor cortex.	8.18 The muscle responsible for the contraction of the heart.

8.28 lateral group	8.37 vestibulospinal tract
8.29 ventromedial group	8.38 tectospinal tract
8.30 corticospinal tract	8.39 reticulospinal tract
8.31 pyramidal tract	8.40 apraxia
8.32 lateral corticospinal tract	8.41 callosal apraxia
8.33 ventral corticospinal tract	8.42 sympathetic apraxia
8.34 corticobulbar pathway	8.43 left parietal apraxia
8.35 rubrospinal tract	8.44 constructional apraxia
8.36 corticorubral tract	8.45 caudate nucleus

8.37 A bundle of axons that travels from the vestibular nuclei to the gray matter of the spinal cord; controls postural movements in response to information from the vestibular system.	8.28 The corticospinal tract, the corticobulbar tract, and the rubrospinal tract.
8.38 A bundle of axons that travels from the tectum to the spinal cord; coordinates head and trunk movements with eye movements.	8.29 The vestibulospinal tract, the tectospinal tract, the reticulospinal tract, and the ventral corticospinal tract.
8.39 A bundle of axons that travels from the reticular formation to the gray matter of the spinal cord; controls the muscles responsible for postural movements.	8.30 The system of axons that originates in the motor cortex and terminates in the ventral gray matter of the spinal cord.
8.40 Difficulty in carrying out purposeful movements, in the absence of paralysis or muscular weakness.	8.31 The portion of the corticospinal tract on the ventral border of the medulla.
8.41 An apraxia of the left hand caused by damage to the anterior corpus callosum.	8.32 The system of axons that originates in the motor cortex and terminates in the contralateral ventral gray matter of the spinal cord; controls movements of the distal limbs.
8.42 A movement disorder of the left hand caused by damage to the left frontal lobe; similar to callosal apraxia.	8.33 The system of axons that originates in the motor cortex and terminates in the ipsilateral ventral gray matter of the spinal cord; controls movements of the upper legs and trunk.
8.43 An apraxia caused by damage to the left parietal lobe; characterized by difficulty in producing sequences of movements by verbal request or in imitation of movements made by someone else.	8.34 A bundle of axons from the motor cortex to the fifth, seventh, ninth, tenth, eleventh, and twelfth cranial nerves; controls movements of the face, neck, tongue, and parts of the extraocular eye muscles.
8.44 Difficulty in drawing pictures or diagrams or in making geometrical constructions of elements such as building blocks or sticks; caused by damage to the right parietal lobe.	8.35 The system of axons that travels from the red nucleus to the spinal cord; controls independent limb movements.
8.45 A telencephalic nucleus, one of the input nuclei of basal ganglia; involved with control of voluntary movement.	8.36 The system of axons that travels from the motor cortex to the red nucleus.

8.46 putamen	8.55 fastigial nucleus
8.47 globus pallidus	8.56 interposed nuclei
8.48 ventral anterior nucleus (of thalamus)	8.57 pontine nucleus
8.49 ventrolateral nucleus (of thalamus)	8.58 dentate nucleus
8.50 direct pathway (in basal ganglia)	8.59 mesencephalic locomotor region
8.51 indirect pathway (in basal ganglia)	9.1 electromyogram (EMG) (*my oh gram*)
8.52 Huntington's disease	9.2 electro-oculogram (EOG) (*ah kew loh gram*)
8.53 flocculonodular lobe	9.3 alpha activity
8.54 vermis	9.4 beta activity

8.55 A deep cerebellar nucleus; involved in the control of movement by the reticulospinal and vestibulospinal tracts.	8.46 A telencephalic nucleus; one of the input nuclei of the basal ganglia; involved with control of voluntary movement.
8.56 A set of deep cerebellar nuclei; involved in the control of the rubrospinal system.	8.47 A telencephalic nucleus; the primary output nucleus of the basal ganglia; involved with control of voluntary movement.
8.57 A large nucleus in the pons that serves as an important source of input to the cerebellum.	8.48 A thalamic nucleus that receives projections from the basal ganglia and sends projections to the motor cortex.
8.58 A deep cerebellar nucleus; involved in the control of rapid, skilled movements by the corticospinal and rubrospinal systems.	8.49 A thalamic nucleus that receives projections from the basal ganglia and sends projections to the motor cortex.
8.59 A region of the reticular formation of the midbrain whose stimulation causes alternating movements of the limbs normally seen during locomotion.	8.50 The pathway that includes the caudate nucleus and putamen, the external division of the globus pallidus, the subthalamic nucleus, the internal division of the globus pallidus, and the ventral anterior/ventrolateral thalamic nuclei; has an inhibitory effect on movement.
9.1 An electrical potential recorded from an electrode placed on or in a muscle.	8.51 The pathway that includes the caudate nucleus and putamen, the internal division of the globus pallidus, and the ventral anterior/ventrolateral thalamic nuclei; has an excitatory effect on movement.
9.2 An electrical potential from the eyes, recorded by means of electrodes placed on the skin around them; detects eye movements.	8.52 A fatal inherited disorder that causes degeneration of the caudate nucleus and putamen; characterized by uncontrollable jerking movements, writhing movements, and dementia.
9.3 Smooth electrical activity of 8-12 Hz recorded from the brain; generally associated with a state of relaxation.	8.53 A region of the cerebellum; involved in control of postural reflexes.
9.4 Irregular electrical activity of 13-30 Hz recorded from the brain; generally associated with a state of arousal.	8.54 The portion of the cerebellum located at the midline; receives somatosensory information and helps to control the vestibulospinal and reticulospinal tracts through its connections with the fastigial nucleus.

9.5 synchrony	9.14 rebound phenomenon
9.6 desynchrony	9.15 locus coeruleus (*sa **roo** lee us*)
9.7 theta activity	9.16 raphe nuclei (*ruh **fay***)
9.8 delta activity	9.17 tuberomammillary nucleus
9.9 REM sleep	9.18 ventrolateral preoptic area (VLPA)
9.10 non-REM sleep	9.19 PGO wave
9.11 slow-wave sleep	9.20 peribrachial area (*pair ee **bray** kee ul*)
9.12 basic rest-activity cycle	9.21 carbachol (***car** ba call*)
9.13 fatal familial insomnia	9.22 medial pontine reticular formation (MPRF)

9.14 The increased frequency or intensity of a phenomenon after it has been temporarily suppressed; for example, the increase in REM sleep seen after a period of REM sleep deprivation.	**9.5** High-voltage, low-frequency EEG activity, characteristic of slow-wave sleep or coma, during which neurons fire together in a regular fashion.
9.15 A dark-colored group of noradrenergic cell bodies located in the pons near the rostral end of the floor of the fourth ventricle; involved in arousal and vigilance.	**9.6** Irregular electrical activity recorded from the brain, generally associated with periods of arousal.
9.16 A group of nuclei located in the reticular formation of the medulla, pons, and midbrain, situated along the midline; contain serotonergic neurons.	**9.7** EEG activity of 3.5-7.5 Hz that occurs intermittently during early stages of slow-wave sleep and REM sleep.
9.17 A nucleus in the ventral posterior hypothalamus, just rostral to the mammillary bodies; contains histaminergic neurons involved in cortical activation and behavioral arousal.	**9.8** Regular, synchronous electrical activity of less than 4 Hz recorded from the brain; occurs during the deepest stages of slow-wave sleep.
9.18 A group of GABAergic neurons in the preoptic area whose activity suppresses alertness and behavioral arousal and promotes sleep.	**9.9** A period of desynchronized EEG activity during sleep, at which time dreaming, rapid eye movements, and muscular paralysis occur; also called *paradoxical sleep*.
9.19 Bursts of phasic electrical activity originating in the pons, followed by activity in the lateral geniculate nucleus and visual cortex; a characteristic of REM sleep.	**9.10** All stages of sleep except REM sleep.
9.20 The region around the brachium conjunctivum, located in the dorsolateral pons; contains acetylcholinergic neurons involved in the initiation of REM sleep.	**9.11** Non-REM sleep, characterized by synchronized EEG activity during its deeper stages.
9.21 A drug that stimulates acetylcholine receptors.	**9.12** A 90-min cycle (in humans) of waxing and waning alertness, controlled by a biological clock in the caudal brain stem; controls cycles of REM sleep and slow-wave sleep.
9.22 A region that contains neurons involved in the initiation of REM sleep; activated by acetylcholinergic neurons of the peribrachial area.	**9.13** A fatal inherited disorder characterized by progressive insomnia.

9.23 magnocellular nucleus	9.32 circadian rhythm (*sur **kay** dee un* or *sur ka **dee** un*)
9.24 drug dependency insomnia	9.33 zeitgeber (***tsite** gay ber*)
9.25 sleep apnea (***app** nee a*)	9.34 suprachiasmatic nucleus (SCN) (*soo pra ky az **mat** ik*)
9.26 narcolepsy (***nahr** ko lep see*)	9.35 intergeniculate leaflet (IGL)
9.27 sleep attack	9.36 neuropeptide Y
9.28 cataplexy (***kat** a plex ee*)	9.37 pineal gland (*py **nee** ul*)
9.29 sleep paralysis	9.38 melatonin (*mell a **tone** in*)
9.30 hypnagogic hallucination (*hip na **gah** jik*)	10.1 sexually dimorphic behavior
9.31 REM without atonia (*ay **tone** ee a*)	10.2 gamete (***gamm** eet*)

9.32 A daily rhythmical change in behavior or physiological process.	9.23 A nucleus in the medulla; involved in the atonia (muscular paralysis) that accompanies REM sleep.
9.33 A stimulus (usually the light of dawn) that resets the biological clock responsible for circadian rhythms.	9.24 An insomnia caused by the side effects of ever-increasing doses of sleeping medications.
9.34 A nucleus situated atop the optic chiasm. It contains a biological clock responsible for organizing many of the body's circadian rhythms.	9.25 Cessation of breathing while sleeping.
9.35 A part of the lateral geniculate nucleus that receives information from the retina and projects to the SCN.	9.26 A sleep disorder characterized by periods of irresistible sleep, attacks of cataplexy, sleep paralysis, and hypnagogic hallucinations.
9.36 A peptide released by the terminals of the neurons that project from the IGL to the SCN.	9.27 A symptom of narcolepsy; an irresistible urge to sleep during the day, after which the person awakes feeling refreshed.
9.37 A gland attached to the dorsal tectum; produces melatonin and plays a role in circadian and seasonal rhythms.	9.28 A symptom of narcolepsy; complete paralysis that occurs during waking.
9.38 A hormone secreted during the night by the pineal body; plays a role in circadian and seasonal rhythms.	9.29 A symptom of narcolepsy; paralysis occurring just before a person falls asleep.
10.1 A behavior that has different forms or that occurs with different probabilities or under different circumstances in males and females.	9.30 A symptom of narcolepsy; vivid dreams that occur just before a person falls asleep; accompanied by sleep paralysis.
10.2 A mature reproductive cell; a sperm or ovum.	9.31 A neurological disorder in which the person does not become paralyzed during REM sleep and thus acts out dreams.

10.3 sex chromosome	10.12 masculinizing effect
10.4 gonad (rhymes with **moan** ad)	10.13 testosterone (*tess **tahss** ter own*)
10.5 organizational effect (of hormone)	10.14 dihydrotestosterone (*dy hy dro tess **tahss** ter own*)
10.6 activational effect (of hormone)	10.15 androgen insensitivity syndrome
10.7 Müllerian system	10.16 persistent Müllerian duct syndrome
10.8 Wolffian system	10.17 Turner's syndrome
10.9 anti-Müllerian hormone	10.18 gonadotropin releasing hormone (*go nad oh **trow** pin*)
10.10 defeminizing effect	10.19 gonadotropic hormone
10.11 androgen (***an** dro jen*)	10.20 follicle-stimulating hormone (FSH)

10.12 An effect of a hormone present early in development that promotes the later development of anatomical or behavioral characteristics typical of males.	10.3 The X and Y chromosomes, which determine an organism's gender. Normally, XX individuals are female, and XY individuals are male.
10.13 The principal androgen found in males.	10.4 An ovary or testis.
10.14 An androgen, produced from testosterone through the action of the enzyme 5Ó reductase.	10.5 The effect of a hormone on tissue differentiation and development.
10.15 A condition caused by a congenital lack of functioning androgen receptors; in a person with XY sex chromosomes, causes the development of a female with testes but no internal sex organs.	10.6 The effect of a hormone that occurs in the fully developed organism; may depend on the organism's prior exposure to the organizational effects of hormones.
10.16 A condition caused by a congenital lack of anti-Müllerian hormone or receptors for this hormone; in a male, causes development of both male and female internal sex organs.	10.7 The embryonic precursors of the female internal sex organs.
10.17 The presence of only one sex chromosome (an X chromosome); characterized by lack of ovaries but otherwise normal female sex organs and genitalia.	10.8 The embryonic precursors of the male internal sex organs.
10.18 A hypothalamic hormone that stimulates the anterior pituitary gland to secrete gonadotropic hormone.	10.9 A peptide secreted by the fetal testes that inhibits the development of the Müllerian system, which would otherwise become the female internal sex organs.
10.19 A hormone of the anterior pituitary gland that has a stimulating effect on cells of the gonads.	10.10 An effect of a hormone present early in development that reduces or prevents the later development of anatomical or behavioral characteristics typical of females.
10.20 The hormone of the anterior pituitary gland that causes development of an ovarian follicle and the maturation of its oocyte into an ovum.	10.11 A male sex steroid hormone. Testosterone is the principal mammalian androgen.

10.21 luteinizing hormone (LH) (*lew tee a nize ing*)	10.30 Coolidge effect
10.22 estradiol (*ess tra dye ahl*)	10.31 aromatization (*air oh mat i zay shun*)
10.23 estrogen (*ess trow jen*)	10.32 oxytocin (*ox ee tow sin*)
10.24 menstrual cycle (*men strew al*)	10.33 prolactin
10.25 estrous cycle	10.34 lordosis
10.26 ovarian follicle	10.35 pheromone (*fair oh moan*)
10.27 corpus luteum (*lew tee um*)	10.36 Lee-Boot effect
10.28 progesterone (*pro jess ter own*)	10.37 Whitten effect
10.29 refractory period (*ree frak to ree*)	10.38 Vandenbergh effect

10.30 The restorative effect of introducing a new female sex partner to a male that has apparently become "exhausted" by sexual activity.	10.21 A hormone of the anterior pituitary gland that causes ovulation and development of the ovarian follicle into a corpus luteum.
10.31 A chemical reaction catalyzed by an aromatase; the process by which testosterone is transformed into estradiol.	10.22 The principal estrogen of many mammals, including humans.
10.32 A hormone secreted by the posterior pituitary gland; causes contraction of the smooth muscle of the milk ducts, the uterus, and the male ejaculatory system; also serves as a neurotransmitter in the brain.	10.23 A class of sex hormones that cause maturation of the female genitalia, growth of breast tissue, and development of other physical features characteristic of females.
10.33 A hormone of the anterior pituitary gland, necessary for production of milk; has an inhibitory effect on male sexual behavior.	10.24 The female reproductive cycle of most primates, including humans; characterized by growth of the lining of the uterus, ovulation, development of a corpus luteum, and (if pregnancy does not occur), menstruation.
10.34 A spinal sexual reflex seen in many four-legged female mammals; arching of the back in response to approach of a male or to touching the flanks, which elevates the hindquarters.	10.25 The female reproductive cycle of mammals other than primates.
10.35 A chemical released by one animal that affects the behavior or physiology of another animal; usually smelled or tasted.	10.26 A cluster of epithelial cells surrounding an oocyte, which develops into an ovum.
10.36 The slowing and eventual cessation of estrous cycles in groups of female animals that are housed together; caused by a pheromone in the animals' urine; first observed in mice.	10.27 A cluster of cells that develops from the ovarian follicle after ovulation; secretes estradiol and progesterone.
10.37 The synchronization of the menstrual or estrous cycles of a group of females, which occurs only in the presence of a pheromone in a male's urine.	10.28 A steroid hormone produced by the ovary that maintains the endometrial lining of the uterus during the later part of the menstrual cycle and during pregnancy; along with estradiol it promotes receptivity in female mammals with estrous cycles.
10.38 The earlier onset of puberty seen in female animals that are housed with males; caused by a pheromone in the male's urine; first observed in mice.	10.29 A period of time after a particular action (for example, an ejaculation by a male) during which that action cannot occur again.

10.39 Bruce effect	10.48 nucleus paragigantocellularis (PGi)
10.40 vomeronasal organ (*voah mer oh **nay** zul*)	10.49 ventromedial nucleus of the hypothalamus (VMH)
10.41 accessory olfactory bulb	10.50 periaqueductal gray matter (PAG)
10.42 medial nucleus of the amygdala (*a **mig** da la*)	10.51 parturition (*par tew **ri** shun*)
10.43 congenital adrenal hyperplasia (CAH) (*hy per **play** zha*)	10.52 stria terminalis (***stree** a ter mi **nal** is*)
10.44 spinal nucleus of the bulbocavernosus (SNB) (*bul bo kav er **no** sis*)	11.1 medial nucleus
10.45 medial preoptic area (MPA)	11.2 lateral/basolateral nuclei
10.46 sexually dimorphic nucleus	11.3 central nucleus
10.47 vasopressin (*vay zo **press** in*)	11.4 basal nucleus

10.48 A nucleus of the medulla that receives input from the medial preoptic area and contains neurons whose axons form synapses with motor neurons in the spinal cord that participate in sexual reflexes in males.	10.39 Termination of pregnancy caused by the odor of a pheromone in the urine of a male other than the one that impregnated the female; first identified in mice.
10.49 A large nucleus of the hypothalamus located near the walls of the third ventricle; plays an essential role in female sexual behavior.	10.40 A sensory organ that detects the presence of certain chemicals, especially when a liquid is actively sniffed; mediates the effects of some pheromones.
10.50 The region of the midbrain that surrounds the cerebral aqueduct; plays an essential role in various species-typical behaviors, including female sexual behavior.	10.41 A neural structure located in the main olfactory bulb that receives information from the vomeronasal organ.
10.51 The act of giving birth.	10.42 A nucleus that receives olfactory information from the olfactory bulb and accessory olfactory bulb; involved in the effects of odors and pheromones on reproductive behavior.
10.52 A long fiber bundle that connects portions of the amygdala with the hypothalamus.	10.43 A condition characterized by hypersecretion of androgens by the adrenal cortex; in females, causes masculinization of the external genitalia.
11.1 A group of subnuclei of the amygdala that receives sensory input, including information about the presence of odors and pheromones, and relays it to the medial basal forebrain and hypothalamus.	10.44 A nucleus located in the lower spinal cord; in some species of rodents, present only in males.
11.2 Nuclei of the amygdala that receive sensory information from the neocortex, thalamus, and hippocampus and send projections to the ventral striatum, the dorsomedial nucleus of the thalamus, and the central nucleus.	10.45 An area of cell bodies just rostral to the hypothalamus; plays an essential role in male sexual behavior.
11.3 The region of the amygdala that receives information from the basolateral division and sends projections to a wide variety of regions in the brain; involved in emotional responses.	10.46 A nucleus in the preoptic area that is much larger in males than in females; first observed in rats; plays a role in male sexual behavior.
11.4 A group of subnuclei of the amygdala that receive sensory input from the lateral and basolateral nuclei and relay information to other amygdaloid nuclei and to the periaqueductal gray matter.	10.47 A hormone secreted by the posterior pituitary gland that controls the secretion of urine by the kidneys; also serves as a neurotransmitter in the brain.

11.5 conditioned emotional response	11.14 threat behavior
11.6 coping response	11.15 defensive behavior
11.7 orbitofrontal cortex	11.16 submissive behavior
11.8 akinetic mutism	11.17 predation
11.9 display rule	12.1 homeostasis (*home ee oh* **stay** *sis*)
11.10 volitional facial paresis	12.2 ingestive behavior (*in* **jess** *tiv*)
11.11 emotional facial paresis	12.3 system variable
11.12 Wada test	12.4 set point
11.13 James-Lange theory	12.5 detector

11.14 A stereotypical species-typical behavior that warns another animal that it may be attacked if it does not flee or show a submissive behavior.	**11.5** A classically conditioned response that occurs when a neutral stimulus is followed by an aversive stimulus; usually includes autonomic, behavioral, and endocrine components such as changes in heart rate, freezing, and secretion of stress-related hormones.
11.15 A species-typical behavior by which an animal defends itself against the threat of another animal.	**11.6** A response through which an organism can avoid, escape from, or minimize an aversive stimulus; reduces the stressful effects of an aversive stimulus.
11.16 A stereotyped behavior shown by an animal in response to threat behavior by another animal; serves to prevent an attack.	**11.7** The region of the prefrontal cortex at the base of the anterior frontal lobes.
11.17 Attack of one animal directed at an individual of another species on which the attacking animal normally preys.	**11.8** A motor disorder characterized by a relative lack of movement and lack of speech; caused by damage to the cingulate gyrus.
12.1 The process by which the body's substances and characteristics (such as temperature and glucose level) are maintained at their optimal level.	**11.9** A culturally determined rule that modifies the expression of emotion in a particular situation.
12.2 Eating or drinking.	**11.10** Difficulty in moving the facial muscles voluntarily; caused by damage to the face region of the primary motor cortex or its subcortical connections.
12.3 A variable that is controlled by a regulatory mechanism, for example, temperature in a heating system.	**11.11** Lack of movement of facial muscles in response to emotions in people who have no difficulty moving these muscles voluntarily; caused by damage to the insular prefrontal cortex, subcortical white matter of the frontal lobe, or parts of the thalamus.
12.4 The optimal value of the system variable in a regulatory mechanism.	**11.12** A test often performed before brain surgery; verifies the functions of one hemisphere by testing patients while the other hemisphere is anesthetized.
12.5 In a regulatory process, a mechanism that signals when the system variable deviates from its set point.	**11.13** A theory of emotion that suggests that behaviors and physiological responses are directly elicited by situations and that feelings of emotions are produced by feedback from these behaviors and responses.

12.6 correctional mechanism	12.15 hypotonic
12.7 negative feedback	12.16 hypovolemia (*hy poh voh **lee** mee a*)
12.8 satiety mechanism	12.17 nephron
12.9 intracellular fluid	12.18 ureter (***your** eh ter*)
12.10 extracellular fluid	12.19 aldosterone (*al **dahs** ter own*)
12.11 intravascular fluid	12.20 vasopressin (*vay zo **press** in*)
12.12 interstitial fluid	12.21 supraoptic nucleus (*sue pra **op** tik*)
12.13 isotonic	12.22 paraventricular nucleus
12.14 hypertonic	12.23 diabetes insipidus (*in **sipp** i duss*)

12.15 The characteristic of a solution that contains so little solute that a cell placed in it will absorb water, through the process of osmosis.	12.6 In a regulatory process, the mechanism that is capable of changing the value of the system variable.
12.16 Reduction in the volume of the intravascular fluid.	12.7 A process whereby the effect produced by an action serves to diminish or terminate that action; a characteristic of regulatory systems.
12.17 A functional unit of the kidney; extracts fluid from the blood and carries the fluid, through collecting ducts, to the ureter.	12.8 A brain mechanism that causes cessation of hunger or thirst, produced by adequate and available supplies of nutrients or water.
12.18 One of two tubes that carries urine from the kidneys to the bladder.	12.9 The fluid contained within cells.
12.19 A hormone of the adrenal cortex that causes the retention of sodium by the kidneys.	12.10 All body fluids outside cells: interstitial fluid, blood plasma, and cerebrospinal fluid.
12.20 A hormone secreted by the posterior pituitary gland that causes the kidneys to excrete a more concentrated urine, thus retaining water in the body.	12.11 The fluid found within the blood vessels.
12.21 A hypothalamic nucleus that contains cell bodies of neurons that produce vasopressin and transport it through their axons to the posterior pituitary gland.	12.12 The fluid that bathes the cells, filling the space between the cells of the body (the interstices).
12.22 A hypothalamic nucleus that contains cell bodies of neurons that produce vasopressin and oxytocin and transport them through their axons to the posterior pituitary gland.	12.13 Equal in osmotic pressure to the contents of a cell. A cell placed in an isotonic solution neither gains nor loses water.
12.23 The loss of excessive amounts of water through the kidneys; caused by lack of secretion of vasopressin.	12.14 The characteristic of a solution that contains enough solute that it will draw water out of a cell placed in it, through the process of osmosis.

12.24 osmometric thirst	12.33 angiotensinogen (*ann gee oh ten* **sin** *oh jen*)
12.25 osmoreceptor	12.34 angiotensin (*ann gee oh* **ten** *sin*)
12.26 OVLT (organum vasculosum of the lamina terminalis)	12.35 saralasin (*sair a* **lay** *sin*)
12.27 duodenum (*doo oh* **dee** *num*)	12.36 losartan (*low* **sar** *tan*)
12.28 hepatic portal vein	12.37 nucleus of the solitary tract
12.29 volumetric thirst	12.38 subfornical organ (SFO)
12.30 colloid (**kalh** *oyd*)	12.39 median preoptic nucleus
12.31 salt appetite	12.40 zona incerta (*in* **sir** *ta*)
12.32 renin (**ree** *nin*)	12.41 furosemide (*few* **row** *se myde*)

12.33 A protein in the blood that can be converted by renin to angiotensin.	12.24 Thirst produced by an increase in the osmotic pressure of the interstitial fluid relative to the intracellular fluid, thus producing cellular dehydration.
12.34 A peptide hormone that constricts blood vessels, causes the secretion of aldosterone, and produces thirst and a salt appetite.	12.25 A neuron that detects changes in the solute concentration of the interstitial fluid that surrounds it.
12.35 A drug that blocks angiotensin receptors.	12.26 A circumventricular organ located anterior to the anteroventral portion of the third ventricle; served by fenestrated capillaries and thus lacks a blood-brain barrier.
12.36 A drug that blocks angiotensin receptors.	12.27 The portion of the small intestine immediately adjacent to the stomach.
12.37 A nucleus of the medulla that receives information from visceral organs and from the gustatory system.	12.28 The vein that receives blood from the digestive system and passes it to the liver.
12.38 A small organ located in the confluence of the lateral ventricles, attached to the underside of the fornix; contains neurons that detect the presence of angiotensin in the blood and excite neural circuits that initiate drinking.	12.29 Thirst produced by hypovolemia.
12.39 A small nucleus situated around the decussation of the anterior commissure; plays a role in thirst stimulated by angiotensin.	12.30 A soluble, gluelike substance made of large molecules that cannot penetrate cell membranes.
12.40 An oblong extension of the midbrain reticular formation, extending from the midbrain to the medial diencephalon.	12.31 A craving for sodium chloride.
12.41 A diuretic; a drug that increases the production of urine.	12.32 A hormone secreted by the kidneys that causes the conversion of angiotensinogen in the blood into angiotensin.

12.42 esophageal fistula (*ee soff a **jee** ul **fiss** tew la*)	13.7 fasting phase
12.43 pylorus (*pie **lorr** us*)	13.8 absorptive phase
12.44 atrial natriuretic peptide (*nay tree ur **ett** ik*)	13.9 glucoprivation
13.1 glycogen (***gly** ko jen*)	13.10 lipoprivation
13.2 insulin	13.11 methyl palmoxirate (MP)
13.3 glucagon (***gloo** ka gahn*)	13.12 mercaptoacetate (MA)
13.4 triglyceride (*try **gliss** er ide*)	13.13 2,5-AM
13.5 glycerol (***gliss** er all*)	13.14 l-ethionine
13.6 fatty acid	13.15 sham feeding

13.7 The phase of metabolism during which nutrients are not available from the digestive system; glucose, amino acids, and fatty acids are derived from glycogen, protein, and adipose tissue during this phase.	12.42 A diversion of the esophagus so that when an animal eats or drinks, the substance does not reach the stomach.
13.8 The phase of metabolism during which nutrients are absorbed from the digestive system; glucose and amino acids constitute the principal source of energy for cells during this phase, and excess nutrients are stored in adipose tissue in the form of triglycerides.	12.43 The ring of smooth muscle at the junction of the stomach and duodenum that controls the release of the stomach contents.
13.9 A dramatic fall in the level of glucose available to cells; can be caused by a fall in the blood level of glucose or by drugs that inhibit glucose metabolism.	12.44 A peptide secreted by the atria of the heart when blood volume is higher than normal; increases water and sodium excretion, inhibits renin, vasopressin, and aldosterone secretion, and inhibits salt appetite.
13.10 A dramatic fall in the level of fatty acids available to cells; usually caused by drugs that inhibit fatty acid metabolism.	13.1 A polysaccharide often referred to as *animal starch;* stored in liver and muscle; constitutes the short-term store of nutrients.
13.11 A drug that inhibits fatty acid metabolism and produces lipoprivic hunger.	13.2 A pancreatic hormone that facilitates entry of glucose and amino acids into the cell, conversion of glucose into glycogen, and transport of fats into adipose tissue.
13.12 A drug that inhibits fatty acid metabolism and produces lipoprivic hunger.	13.3 A pancreatic hormone that promotes the conversion of liver glycogen into glucose.
13.13 A drug that inhibits carbohydrate metabolism in the liver by making phosphate unavailable, thus blocking the production of ATP.	13.4 The form of fat storage in adipose cells; consists of a molecule of glycerol joined with three fatty acids.
13.14 A drug that inhibits carbohydrate metabolism in the liver by making adenosine unavailable, thus blocking the production of ATP.	13.5 A substance (also called glycerine) derived from the breakdown of triglycerides, along with fatty acids; can be converted by the liver into glucose.
13.15 Feeding behavior of an animal with an open gastric or esophageal fistula that prevents food from remaining in the stomach.	13.6 A substance derived from the breakdown of triglycerides, along with glycerol; can be metabolized by most cells of the body except for the brain.

13.16 cholecystokinin (CCK) (*coal i sis toe* **ky** *nin*)	13.25 arcuate nucleus
13.17 ob mouse	13.26 CART
13.18 leptin	13.27 agouti mouse
13.19 decerebration	13.28 melanocortin-4 receptor (MC-4R)
13.20 lateral parabrachial nucleus	13.29 alpha-melanocyte-stimulating hormone (alpha-MSH)
13.21 melanin-concentrating hormone (MCH)	13.30 agouti-related protein (ARP)
13.22 orexin	13.31 uncoupling protein (UCP)
13.23 neuropeptide Y (NPY)	13.32 anorexia nervosa
13.24 paraventricular nucleus	13.33 bulimia nervosa

13.25 A nucleus in the base of the hypothalamus that controls secretions of the anterior pituitary gland; contains NPY-secreting neurons involved in feeding and control of metabolism.	13.16 A hormone secreted by the duodenum that regulates gastric motility and causes the gallbladder (cholecyst) to contract; appears to provide a satiety signal transmitted to the brain through the vagus nerve.
13.26 Cocaine- and amphetamine-regulated transcript; a peptide neurotransmitter found in a system of neurons of the arcuate nucleus that inhibit feeding.	13.17 A strain of mice whose obesity and low metabolic rate is caused by a mutation that prevents the production of leptin.
13.27 A strain of mice whose yellow fur and obesity are caused by a mutation that causes the production of a peptide that blocks MC-4 receptors in the brain.	13.18 A hormone secreted by adipose tissue; decreases food intake and increases metabolic rate, primarily by inhibiting NPY-secreting neurons in the arcuate nucleus.
13.28 A receptor found in the brain that binds with Ó-MSH and agouti-related protein; plays a role in control of appetite.	13.19 A surgical procedure that severs the brain stem, disconnecting the hindbrain from the forebrain.
13.29 A neuropeptide that acts as an agonist at MC-4 receptors and inhibits eating.	13.20 A nucleus in the pons that receives gustatory information and information from the liver and digestive system and relays it to the forebrain.
13.30 A neuropeptide that acts as an antagonist at MC-4 receptors and increases eating.	13.21 A peptide neurotransmitter found in a system of lateral hypothalamic neurons that stimulate appetite and reduce metabolic rate.
13.31 A mitochondrial protein that facilitates the conversion of nutrients into heat.	13.22 A peptide neurotransmitter found in a system of lateral hypothalamic neurons that stimulate appetite and reduce metabolic rate.
13.32 A disorder that most frequently afflicts young women; exaggerated concern with overweight that leads to excessive dieting and often compulsive exercising; can lead to starvation.	13.23 A peptide neurotransmitter found in a system of neurons of the arcuate nucleus that stimulate feeding, insulin and glucocorticoid secretion, decrease the breakdown of triglycerides, and decrease body temperature.
13.33 Bouts of excessive hunger and eating, often followed by forced vomiting or purging with laxatives; sometimes seen in people with anorexia nervosa.	13.24 A nucleus of the hypothalamus located adjacent to the dorsal third ventricle; contains neurons involved in control of the autonomic nervous system and the posterior pituitary gland.

14.1 perceptual learning	14.10 hippocampal formation
14.2 stimulus-response learning	14.11 entorhinal cortex
14.3 classical conditioning	14.12 granule cell
14.4 Hebb rule	14.13 dentate gyrus
14.5 instrumental conditioning	14.14 perforant path
14.6 reinforcing stimulus	14.15 field CA3
14.7 punishing stimulus	14.16 pyramidal cell
14.8 motor learning	14.17 field CA1
14.9 long-term potentiation	14.18 population EPSP

14.10 A forebrain structure of the temporal lobe, constituting an important part of the limbic system; includes the hippocampus proper (Ammon's horn), dentate gyrus, and subiculum.	14.1 Learning to recognize a particular stimulus.
14.11 A region of the limbic cortex that provides the major source of input to the hippocampal formation.	14.2 Learning to automatically make a particular response in the presence of a particular stimulus; includes classical and instrumental conditioning.
14.12 A small, granular cell; those found in the dentate gyrus send axons to the field CA3 of the hippocampus.	14.3 When a neutral stimulus is followed several times by an *unconditional stimulus* that produces a defensive or appetitive response (the *unconditional response*), the first stimulus (now called a *conditional stimulus*) itself evokes the response (now called a *conditional response*).
14.13 Part of the hippocampal formation; receives inputs from the entorhinal cortex and projects to the field CA3 of the hippocampus.	14.4 The hypothesis proposed by Donald Hebb that the cellular basis of learning involves strengthening of a synapse that is repeatedly active when the postsynaptic neuron fires.
14.14 The system of axons that travel from cells in the entorhinal cortex to the dentate gyrus of the hippocampal formation.	14.5 A learning procedure whereby the effects of a particular behavior in a particular situation increase (reinforce) or decrease (punish) the probability of the behavior; also called *operant conditioning*.
14.15 Part of the hippocampus; receives inputs from the dentate gyrus and projects to field CA1.	14.6 An appetitive stimulus that follows a particular behavior and thus makes the behavior become more frequent.
14.16 A category of large neurons with a pyramid shape; found in the cerebral cortex and Ammon's horn of the hippocampal formation.	14.7 An aversive stimulus that follows a particular behavior and thus makes the behavior become less frequent.
14.17 Part of the hippocampus; receives inputs from field CA3 and projects out of the hippocampal formation via the subiculum.	14.8 Learning to make a new response.
14.18 An evoked potential that represents the EPSPs of a population of neurons.	14.9 A long-term increase in the excitability of a neuron to a particular synaptic input caused by repeated high-frequency activity of that input.

14.19 associative long-term potentiation	14.28 short-term memory
14.20 NMDA receptor	14.29 delayed matching-to-sample task
14.21 AP5	14.30 paired-associate task
14.22 AMPA receptor	14.31 nucleus basalis
14.23 dendritic spike	14.32 MGm
14.24 protein kinase	14.33 extinction
14.25 CaM-KII	14.34 self-stimulation
14.26 nitric oxide synthase	14.35 medial forebrain bundle (MFB)
14.27 long-term depression	14.36 mesolimbic system

14.28 Memory for a stimulus that has just been perceived.	14.19 A long-term potentiation in which concurrent stimulation of weak and strong synapses to a given neuron strengthens the weak ones.
14.29 A task that requires the subject to indicate which of several stimuli has just been perceived.	14.20 A specialized ionotropic glutamate receptor that controls a calcium channel that is normally blocked by Mg^{2+} ions; involved in long-term potentiation.
14.30 A task that requires the subject to learn to recognize pairs of stimuli.	14.21 2-Amino-5-phosphonopentanoate; a drug that blocks NMDA receptors.
14.31 A nucleus of the basal forebrain that contains most of the acetylcholine-secreting neurons that send axons to the neocortex; degenerates in patients with Alzheimer's disease.	14.22 An ionotropic glutamate receptor that controls a sodium channel; when open, it produces EPSPs.
14.32 The medial division of the medial geniculate nucleus; transmits auditory and somatosensory information to the lateral nucleus of the amygdala.	14.23 An action potential that occurs in the dendrite of some types of pyramidal cells.
14.33 With respect to classical conditioning, the reduction or elimination of a conditional response by repeatedly presenting the conditional stimulus without the unconditional stimulus.	14.24 An enzyme that attaches a phosphate (PO_4) to a protein and thereby causes it to change its shape.
14.34 Making a response that causes the electrical stimulation of a particular region of the brain through an implanted electrode.	14.25 Type II calcium-calmodulin kinase, an enzyme that must be activated by calcium; may play a role in the establishment of long-term potentiation.
14.35 A fiber bundle that runs in a rostral-caudal direction through the basal forebrain and lateral hypothalamus; electrical stimulation of these axons is reinforcing.	14.26 An enzyme responsible for the production of nitric oxide.
14.36 A system of dopaminergic neurons whose cell bodies are located in the ventral tegmental area and whose terminal buttons are located in the nucleus accumbens, amygdala, lateral septum, hippocampus, and bed nucleus of the stria terminalis.	14.27 A long-term decrease in the excitability of a neuron to a particular synaptic input caused by stimulation of the terminal button while the postsynaptic membrane is hyperpolarized or only slightly depolarized.

14.37 nucleus accumbens	15.6 long-term memory
14.38 mesocortical system	15.7 consolidation
14.39 conditioned reinforcer	15.8 priming
14.40 conditioned punisher	15.9 declarative memory
15.1 anterograde amnesia	15.10 nondeclarative memory
15.2 retrograde amnesia	15.11 perirhinal cortex
15.3 Korsakoff's syndrome	15.12 parahippocampal cortex
15.4 confabulation	15.13 working memory
15.5 short-term memory	15.14 reference memory

15.6 Relatively stable memory of events that occurred in the more distant past, as opposed to short-term memory.	**14.37** A nucleus of the basal forebrain near the septum; receives dopamine-secreting terminal buttons from neurons of the ventral tegmental area and is thought to be involved in reinforcement and attention.
15.7 The process by which short-term memories are converted into long-term memories.	**14.38** A system of dopaminergic neurons whose cell bodies are located in the ventral tegmental area and whose terminal buttons are located in the cerebral cortex and hippocampus.
15.8 A phenomenon in which exposure to a particular stimulus automatically facilitates perception of that stimulus or related stimuli.	**14.39** A previously neutral stimulus that has been paired with an appetitive stimulus, which then itself becomes capable of reinforcing a response.
15.9 Memory that can be verbally expressed, such as memory for events in a person's past.	**14.40** A previously neutral stimulus that has been followed by an aversive stimulus, which then itself becomes capable of punishing a response.
15.10 Memory whose formation does not depend on the hippocampal formation; a collective term for perceptual, stimulus-response, and motor memory.	**15.1** Amnesia for events that occur after some disturbance to the brain, such as head injury or certain degenerative brain diseases.
15.11 A region of limbic cortex adjacent to the hippocampal formation that, along with the parahippocampal cortex, relays information between the entorhinal cortex and other regions of the brain.	**15.2** Amnesia for events that preceded some disturbance to the brain, such as a head injury or electroconvulsive shock.
15.12 A region of limbic cortex adjacent to the hippocampal formation that, along with the perirhinal cortex, relays information between the entorhinal cortex and other regions of the brain.	**15.3** Permanent anterograde amnesia caused by brain damage resulting from chronic alcoholism or malnutrition.
15.13 Memory of what has just been perceived and what is currently being thought about; consists of new information and related information that has recently been "retrieved" from long-term memory.	**15.4** The reporting of memories of events that did not take place without the intention to deceive; seen in people with Korsakoff's syndrome.
15.14 A form of long-term memory of stable conditions and contingencies in the environment; includes perceptual memory and stimulus-response memory.	**15.5** Immediate memory for events, which may or may not be consolidated into long-term memory.

15.15 place cells	16.7 agrammatism
15.16 theta rhythm	16.8 anomia
15.17 recurrent collateral	16.9 apraxia of speech
16.1 cerebrovascular accident	16.10 Wernicke's area
16.2 aphasia	16.11 Wernicke's aphasia
16.3 Broca's aphasia	16.12 pure word deafness
16.4 function word	16.13 transcortical sensory aphasia
16.5 content word	16.14 autotopagnosia
16.6 Broca's area	16.15 arcuate fasciculus

16.7 One of the usual symptoms of Broca's aphasia; a difficulty in comprehending or properly employing grammatical devices, such as verb endings and word order.	**15.15** A neuron of the hippocampus that becomes active when the animal is in a particular location in the environment.
16.8 Difficulty in finding (remembering) the appropriate word to describe an object, action, or attribute; one of the symptoms of aphasia.	**15.16** EEG activity of 5-8 Hz; an important indication of the physiological state of the hippocampus.
16.9 Impairment in the ability to program movements of the tongue, lips, and throat required to produce the proper sequence of speech sounds.	**15.17** A branch of an axon leaving a particular region of the brain that turns back and forms synapses with neurons near the one that gives rise to it.
16.10 A region of auditory association cortex on the left temporal lobe of humans, which is important in the comprehension of words and the production of meaningful speech.	**16.1** A "stroke"; brain damage caused by occlusion or rupture of a blood vessel in the brain.
16.11 A form of aphasia characterized by poor speech comprehension and fluent but meaningless speech.	**16.2** Difficulty in producing or comprehending speech not produced by deafness or a simple motor deficit; caused by brain damage.
16.12 The ability to hear, to speak, and (usually) to read and write without being able to comprehend the meaning of speech; caused by damage to Wernicke's area or disruption of auditory input to this region.	**16.3** A form of aphasia characterized by agrammatism, anomia, and extreme difficulty in speech articulation.
16.13 A speech disorder in which a person has difficulty comprehending speech and producing meaningful spontaneous speech but can repeat speech; caused by damage to the region of the brain posterior to Wernicke's area.	**16.4** A preposition, article, or other word that conveys little of the meaning of a sentence but is important in specifying its grammatical structure.
16.14 Inability to name body parts or to identify body parts that another person names.	**16.5** A noun, verb, adjective, or adverb that conveys meaning.
16.15 A bundle of axons that connects Wernicke's area with Broca's area; damage causes conduction aphasia.	**16.6** A region of frontal cortex, located just rostral to the base of the left primary motor cortex, that is necessary for normal speech production.

16.16 conduction aphasia	16.25 spelling dyslexia
16.17 circumlocution	16.26 direct dyslexia
16.18 prosody	16.27 phonological dysgraphia
16.19 pure alexia	16.28 orthographic dysgraphia
16.20 whole-word reading	16.29 developmental dyslexia
16.21 phonetic reading	17.1 schizophrenia
16.22 surface dyslexia	17.2 positive symptom
16.23 phonological dyslexia	17.3 thought disorder
16.24 word-form dyslexia	17.4 delusion

16.25 An alternative name for word-form dyslexia.	16.16 An aphasia characterized by inability to repeat words that are heard but normal speech and the ability to comprehend the speech of others.
16.26 A language disorder caused by brain damage in which the person can read words aloud without understanding them.	16.17 A strategy by which people with anomia find alternative ways to say something when they are unable to think of the most appropriate word.
16.27 A writing disorder in which the person cannot sound out words and write them phonetically.	16.18 The use of changes in intonation and emphasis to convey meaning in speech besides that specified by the particular words; an important means of communication of emotion.
16.28 A writing disorder in which the person can spell regularly spelled words but not irregularly spelled ones.	16.19 Loss of the ability to read without loss of the ability to write; produced by brain damage.
16.29 A reading difficulty in a person of normal intelligence and perceptual ability; of genetic origin or caused by prenatal or perinatal factors.	16.20 Reading by recognizing a word as a whole; "sight reading."
17.1 A serious mental disorder characterized by disordered thoughts, delusions, hallucinations, and often bizarre behaviors.	16.21 Reading by decoding the phonetic significance of letter strings; "sound reading."
17.2 A symptom of schizophrenia evident by its presence: delusions, hallucinations, or thought disorders.	16.22 A reading disorder in which a person can read words phonetically but has difficulty reading irregularly spelled words by the whole-word method.
17.3 Disorganized, irrational thinking.	16.23 A reading disorder in which a person can read familiar words but has difficulty reading unfamiliar words or pronounceable nonwords.
17.4 A belief that is clearly in contradiction to reality.	16.24 A disorder in which a person can read a word only after spelling out the individual letters.

17.5 hallucination	17.14 hypofrontality
17.6 negative symptom	17.15 major affective disorder
17.7 chlorpromazine	17.16 bipolar disorder
17.8 clozapine	17.17 unipolar depression
17.9 tardive dyskinesia	17.18 tricyclic antidepressant
17.10 supersensitivity	17.19 specific serotonin reuptake inhibitor
17.11 epidemiology	17.20 electroconvulsive therapy (ECT)
17.12 seasonality effect	17.21 lithium
17.13 latitude effect	17.22 carbamazepine

17.14 Decreased activity of the prefrontal cortex; believed to be responsible for the negative symptoms of schizophrenia.	17.5 Perception of a nonexistent object or event.
17.15 A serious mood disorder; includes unipolar depression and bipolar disorder.	17.6 A symptom of schizophrenia characterized by the absence of behaviors that are normally present: social withdrawal, lack of affect, and reduced motivation.
17.16 A serious mood disorder characterized by cyclical periods of mania and depression.	17.7 A dopamine receptor blocker; a commonly prescribed antischizophrenic drug.
17.17 A serious mood disorder that consists of unremitting depression or periods of depression that do not alternate with periods of mania.	17.8 An "atypical" antipsychotic drug; blocks D_4 receptors in the nucleus accumbens.
17.18 A class of drugs used to treat depression; inhibits the reuptake of norepinephrine and serotonin; named for the molecular structure.	17.9 A movement disorder that can occur after prolonged treatment with antipsychotic medication, characterized by involuntary movements of the face and neck.
17.19 A drug that inhibits the reuptake of serotonin without affecting the reuptake of other neurotransmitters.	17.10 The increased sensitivity of neurotransmitter receptors; caused by damage to the afferent axons or long-term blockage of neurotransmitter release.
17.20 A brief electrical shock, applied to the head, that results in an electrical seizure; used therapeutically to alleviate severe depression.	17.11 The study of the distribution and causes of diseases in populations.
17.21 A chemical element; lithium carbonate is used to treat bipolar disorder.	17.12 The increased incidence of schizophrenia in people born during late winter and early spring.
17.22 A drug (trade name: Tegretol) that is used to treat seizures originating from a focus, generally in the medial temporal lobe.	17.13 The increased incidence of schizophrenia in people born far from the equator.

17.23 monoamine hypothesis	18.2 panic disorder
17.24 5-HIAA	18.3 anticipatory anxiety
17.25 tryptophan depletion procedure	18.4 agoraphobia
17.26 substance P	18.5 obsessive-compulsive disorder (OCD)
17.27 silent cerebral infarction (SCI)	18.6 obsession
17.28 seasonal affective disorder	18.7 compulsion
17.29 summer depression	18.8 Tourette's syndrome
17.30 phototherapy	18.9 Sydenham's chorea
18.1 anxiety disorder	18.10 autistic disorder

18.2 A disorder characterized by episodic periods of symptoms such as shortness of breath, irregularities in heartbeat, and other autonomic symptoms, accompanied by intense fear.	**17.23** A hypothesis that states that depression is caused by a low level of activity of one or more monoaminergic synapses.
18.3 A fear of having a panic attack; may lead to the development of agoraphobia.	**17.24** A breakdown product of the neurotransmitter serotonin (5-HT).
18.4 A fear of being away from home or other protected places.	**17.25** A procedure involving a low-tryptophan diet and a tryptophan-free amino acid "cocktail" that lowers brain tryptophan and consequently decreases the synthesis of 5-HT.
18.5 A mental disorder characterized by obsessions and compulsions.	**17.26** A peptide secreted as a neurotransmitter and neuromodulator in several regions of the brain; may be involved in emotional behavior, the response to stress, and the symptoms of depression.
18.6 An unwanted thought or idea with which a person is preoccupied.	**17.27** A small cerebrovascular accident (stroke) that causes minor brain damage without producing obvious neurological symptoms.
18.7 The feeling that one is obliged to perform a behavior, even if one prefers not to do so.	**17.28** A mood disorder characterized by depression, lethargy, sleep disturbances, and craving for carbohydrates during the winter season when days are short.
18.8 A neurological disorder characterized by tics and involuntary vocalizations and sometimes by compulsive uttering of obscenities and repetition of the utterances of others.	**17.29** A mood disorder characterized by depression, sleep disturbances, and loss of appetite.
18.9 An autoimmune disease that attacks parts of the brain including the basal ganglia and produces involuntary movements and often the symptoms of obsessive-compulsive disorder.	**17.30** Treatment of seasonal affective disorder by daily exposure to bright light.
18.10 A chronic disorder whose symptoms include failure to develop normal social relations with other people, impaired development of communicative ability, lack of imaginative ability, and repetitive, stereotyped movements.	**18.1** A psychological disorder characterized by tension, overactivity of the autonomic nervous system, expectation of an impending disaster, and continuous vigilance for danger.

18.11 phenylketonuria	18.20 psychoneuroimmunology
18.12 stress	18.21 natural killer cell
18.13 stressor	18.22 antigen
18.14 stress response	18.23 antibody
18.15 fight-or-flight response	18.24 B-lymphocyte
18.16 glucocorticoid	18.25 immunoglobulin
18.17 corticotropin-releasing factor (CRF)	18.26 T-lymphocyte
18.18 adrenocorticotropic hormone (ACTH)	18.27 cytokine
18.19 posttraumatic stress disorder	19.1 tolerance

18.20 The branch of neuroscience involved with interactions between environmental stimuli, the nervous system, and the immune system.	**18.11** A hereditary disorder caused by the absence of an enzyme that converts the amino acid phenylalanine to tyrosine; causes brain damage unless a special diet is implemented soon after birth.
18.21 A white blood cell that destroys cells infected by viruses.	**18.12** A general, imprecise term that can refer either to a stress response or to a stressor (stressful situation).
18.22 A protein present on a microorganism that permits the immune system to recognize it as an invader.	**18.13** A stimulus (or situation) that produces a stress response.
18.23 A protein produced by a cell of the immune system that recognizes antigens present on invading microorganisms.	**18.14** A physiological reaction caused by the perception of aversive or threatening situations.
18.24 A white blood cell that originates in the bone marrow; part of the immune system.	**18.15** A species-typical response preparatory to fighting or fleeing; thought to be responsible for some of the deleterious effects of stressful situations on health.
18.25 An antibody released by B-lymphocytes that bind with antigens and help to destroy invading microorganisms.	**18.16** One of a group of hormones of the adrenal cortex that are important in protein and carbohydrate metabolism, secreted especially in times of stress.
18.26 A white blood cell that originates in the thymus gland; part of the immune system.	**18.17** A hypothalamic hormone that stimulates the anterior pituitary gland to secrete ACTH (adrenocorticotrophic hormone).
18.27 A category of chemicals released by certain white blood cells when they detect the presence of an invading microorganism; causes other white blood cells to proliferate and mount an attack against the invader.	**18.18** A hormone released by the anterior pituitary gland in response to CRF; stimulates the adrenal cortex to produce glucocorticoids.
19.1 The fact that increasingly large doses of drugs must be taken to achieve a particular effect; caused by compensatory mechanisms that oppose the effect of the drug.	**18.19** A psychological disorder caused by exposure to a situation of extreme danger and stress; symptoms include recurrent dreams or recollections; can interfere with social activities and cause a feeling of hopelessness.

19.2 withdrawal symptoms	
19.3 negative reinforcement	
19.4 dynorphin	
19.5 conditioned place preference	
19.6 naloxone	
19.7 pimozide	
19.8 antagonist-precipitated withdrawal	
19.9 CREB	
19.10 drug discrimination procedure	

	19.2 The appearance of symptoms opposite to those produced by a drug when the drug is suddenly no longer taken; caused by the presence of compensatory mechanisms.
	19.3 The removal or reduction of an aversive stimulus that is contingent on a particular response, with an attendant increase in the frequency of that response.
	19.4 An endogenous opioid; the natural ligand for kappa opiate receptors.
	19.5 The learned preference for a location in which an organism encountered a reinforcing stimulus, such as food or a reinforcing drug.
	19.6 A drug that blocks mu opiate receptors; antagonizes the reinforcing and sedative effects of opiates.
	19.7 A drug that blocks dopamine receptors.
	19.8 Sudden withdrawal from long-term administration of a drug caused by cessation of the drug and administration of an antagonistic drug.
	19.9 Cyclic AMP-responsive element-binding protein; a nuclear protein to which cyclic AMP can bind and affect the activity of a gene or set of genes.
	19.10 An experimental procedure in which an animal shows, through instrumental conditioning, whether the perceived effects of two drugs are similar.

NOTES

NOTES

NOTES

NOTES

NOTES

NOTES

NOTES

NOTES

NOTES

NOTES

NOTES

NOTES